Same-Sex Cultures and Sexualities

Blackwell Readers in Anthropology

1. *Anthropology of Globalization: A Reader*
   Edited by Jonathan Xavier Inda and Renato Rosaldo
2. *The Anthropology of Media: A Reader*
   Edited by Kelly Askew and Richard R. Wilk
3. *Genocide: An Anthropological Reader*
   Edited by Alexander Laban Hinton
4. *The Anthropology of Space and Place: Locating Culture*
   Edited by Setha Low and Denise Lawrence-Zúñiga
5. *Violence in War and Peace: An Anthology*
   Edited by Nancy Scheper-Hughes and Philippe Bourgois
6. *Same-Sex Cultures and Sexualities: An Anthropological Reader*
   Edited by Jennifer Robertson

As anthropology moves beyond the limits of so-called area studies, there is an increasing need for texts that attempt to do the work of both synthesizing the literature and of challenging more traditional or subdisciplinary approaches to anthropology. This is the object of the exciting new series, *Blackwell Readers in Anthropology.*

Each volume in the series offers what have emerged as seminal readings on a chosen theme, and provides the finest, most thought-provoking recent works in the given thematic area. A number of these volumes bring together for the first time a body of literature on a certain topic. Inasmuch, these books are intended to become more than definitive collections; they demonstrate the very ways in which anthropological inquiry has evolved and is evolving.

Same-Sex Cultures and Sexualities

An Anthropological Reader

Edited by

Jennifer Robertson

BLACKWELL PUBLISHING
350 Main Street, Malden, MA 02148–5020, USA
108 Cowley Road, Oxford OX4 1JF, UK
550 Swanston Street, Carlton, Victoria 3053, Australia

First published 2005 by Blackwell Publishing Ltd

Library of Congress Cataloging-in-Publication Data

Same-sex cultures and sexualities : an anthropological reader / edited by Jennifer Ellen Robertson.
p. cm. – (Blackwell readers in anthropology ; 6)
ISBN 0–631–23299–0 (cloth : alk. paper) — ISBN 0–631–23300–8 (pbk. : alk. paper)
1. Homosexuality. 2. Lesbianism. 3. Gay and lesbian studies. 4. Gay men. 5. Lesbians. I. Robertson, Jennifer. II. Series.

GN484.35.S36 2005
306.76′6—dc22

2003026674

A catalogue record for this title is available from the British Library.

Typeset in 10/12pt Sabon
by Kolam Information Services Pvt. Ltd, Pondicherry, India
Printed and bound in the United Kingdom
by MPG Books Ltd, Bodmin, Cornwall

The publisher's policy is to use permanent paper from mills that operate a sustainable forestry policy, and which has been manufactured from pulp processed using acid-free and elementary chlorine-free practices. Furthermore, the publisher ensures that the text paper and cover board used have met acceptable environmental accreditation standards.

For further information on
Blackwell Publishing, visit our website:
http://www.blackwellpublishing.com

Contents

Acknowledgments

I was very pleased when Jane Huber, Blackwell's energetic and enterprising anthropology editor, invited me to edit a reader on same-sex sexualities, and it is to her that I owe the first of many grateful thanks. I also owe thanks to Annie Lenth, an assistant editor at Blackwell, from whose cheerful efficiency I greatly benefited, and to Juanita Bullough, whose attentive and expert copy-editing was greatly appreciated. Celeste Brusati made room in her own busy publication schedule to read over the introduction and I am, as always, grateful for her valuable suggestions. I owe hearty thanks to the fifteen contributors whose rigorous and scrutinizing scholarship made this *Reader* possible in the first place. Thanks also to the journals and presses who granted copyright permission, and to Mary Hancock, Evelyn Blackwood, and the other (anonymous) reviewers of the initial proposal and my introductory essay whose comments helped to further shape this volume.

The editor and publishers wish to thank the following for permission to use copyright material:

1. Carole S. Vance, "Anthropology rediscovers sexuality: A theoretical comment." *Social Science and Medicine* 33(8): 875–84, 1991. Reprinted by permission of Elsevier Science.
2. Bonnie Spanier, "Biological determinism and homosexuality." *NWSA Journal* 7: 54–71, 1995. Reprinted by permission of Indiana University Press.
3. Barbara L. Voss, "Feminisms, queer theories, and the archaeological study of past sexualities." *World Archaeology* 32(2): 180–92, 2000. Reprinted by permission of Taylor & Francis Ltd. http://www.tandf.co.uk/journals
4. Don Kulick, "No." *Language and Communication* 23(2): 139–51, 2003. Reprinted by permission of Elsevier.
5. Alisa Klinger, "Resources for lesbian ethnographic research in the lavender archives." *Journal of Homosexuality* 34(3–4): 205–24, 1998. Reprinted by permission of The Haworth Press.

6. Deborah A. Elliston, "Erotic anthropology: 'Ritualized homosexuality' in Melanesia and beyond." *American Ethnologist* 22(4): 848–67, 1995. Reprinted by permission of the American Anthropological Association and the author. Not for sale or further reproduction.
7. Corinne P. Hayden, "Gender, genetics, and generation: Reformulating biology in lesbian kinship." *Cultural Anthropology* 10: 41–63, 1995. Reprinted by permission of the American Anthropological Association and the author. Not for sale or further reproduction.
8. Judith Shapiro, "Transsexualism: Reflections on the persistence of gender and the mutability of sex." In *Body Guards: The Cultural Politics of Gender Ambiguity*, Julia Epstein and Kristina Straub, eds. Pp. 248–79. New York and London: Routledge, 1991. Reproduced by permission of Routledge, Inc., part of The Taylor & Francis Group.
9. Estelle B. Freedman and John D'Emilio, "Problems encountered in writing the history of sexuality: Sources, theory and interpretation." *Journal of Sex Research* 27(4): 481–95, 1990. Reprinted by permission of the publisher.
10. Edward Stein, "Choosing the sexual orientation of children." *Bioethics* 12(1): 1–24, 1998. Reprinted by permission of the publisher.
11. Jennifer Robertson, "Yoshiya Nobuko: Out and outspoken in practice and prose." In *The Human Tradition in Modern Japan*, Anne Walthall, ed. Pp. 155–74. Copyright 1996 by Scholarly Resources Inc. Reprinted by permission of Scholarly Resources Inc.
12. Matti Bunzl, "Outing as performance/outing as resistance: A queer reading of Austrian (homo)sexualities." *Cultural Anthropology* 12: 129–51, 1997. Reprinted by permission of the American Anthropological Association and the author. Not for sale or further reproduction.
13. Evelyn Blackwood, "*Tombois* in West Sumatra: Constructing masculinity and erotic desire." *Cultural Anthropology* 13(4): 491–521, 1998. Reprinted by permission of the American Anthropological Association and the author. Not for sale or further reproduction.
14. Donald L. Donham, "Freeing South Africa: The 'modernization' of male-male sexuality in Soweto." *Cultural Anthropology* 13(1): 3–21, 1998. Reprinted by permission of the American Anthropological Association and the author. Not for sale or further reproduction.
15. Timothy Wright, "Gay organizations, NGOs, and the globalization of sexual identity: The case of Bolivia." *Journal of Latin American Anthropology* 5(2): 89–111, 2000. Reprinted by permission of the American Anthropological Association and the author. Not for sale or further reproduction.

Every effort has been made to trace copyright holders and to obtain their permission for the use of copyright material. The authors and publishers will gladly receive any information enabling them to rectify any error or omission in subsequent editions.

Introduction: Sexualizing Anthropology's Fields

Jennifer Robertson

Over the past quarter-century, sexuality[1] has moved from the periphery to the center of anthropological research and lesbian and gay studies has followed in its wake. Queer, transgendered, bisexual, transsexual, and intersexed are now familiar (non-slang) terms that, with lesbian and gay, have more or less replaced "homosexual," a wooden, if overdetermined, term coined in the nineteenth century that does not capture the plasticity and malleability of human sexual practices and identities. In the meantime, "heterosexual" is becoming a less self-evident orientation or ideology through its interrogation by scholars and laypersons alike, although it remains the dominant default mode of sexuality in most societies. This is not to claim, however, that these now familiar terms are free from ideological content, or that as categories they are automatically more accommodating and expansive than "homosexual."

The essays comprising this anthropological reader all question and challenge, in different yet related ways, the a priori assumption among many people of a connection between same-sex sexual *desires*, *practices*, and *identifications*, and lesbian, gay, bisexual, transgendered, queer, etc. *identities*. Viewed retrospectively, one might argue that human sexual desires and practices per se have not multiplied, but rather, that since the 1980s, multiple academic, legal, and medical ways have been coined and created in an effort to categorize and contain them. Consequently, multiple "ready-made" identities and their attendant politics have formed around and on the basis of human sexual practices (cf. Robertson 2002). If not themselves understood as relational and their relevance part of a continuous process of sociocultural change, these new categories and identities will become as reified and rendered as inadequate as the terms – like "homosexual" – they initially helped to complicate.

This *Reader* aspires to channel the comparative anthropological and historical study of same-sex cultures and sexualities into a full-spectrum anthropological mainstream. It also aims to demonstrate the centrality of the complicated relationship of sex, gender, and sexuality to the development and refinement of anthropological theories in general. As the constituent essays make absolutely clear, studies of sexuality, in this case same-sex sexualities, are not limited to, and are much more than, studies *by and for* self-identified lesbian, gay, bisexual, transgendered, or transsexual scholars. Similarly, by titling this volume *Same-Sex Cultures and Sexualities* I am not referring to reified things. Rather, I am advocating a kind of "cultural physics" in which sexuality operates as a vector that occasions multiple interactions among groups of humans, and that transmits through manifold media different kinds of energy among humans. Kinship, for example, is one of the variety of effects and outcomes generated.

That the time is right both for mainstreaming sexuality within anthropology and for publishing this *Reader* is evidenced in part by the appearance of, in the 1993 and 2000 editions of the *Annual Review of Anthropology*, essays surveying a range of anthropological scholarship on same-sex sexualities.[2] Another indicator, based on my own experience, of the timeliness of this *Reader* is the increasingly vocal demand on the part of anthropology students, both graduate and undergraduate, for theoretical and comparative work on the sexualities of actual (as opposed to fictional) human beings, past and present.

A concerted effort is made in this volume to consider the relationship of sex, gender, and sexuality through the lenses of the sociocultural, biological, linguistic, and archaeological sub-fields of anthropology along with historical and applied anthropology. It is surprising that the place of biology and archaeology in the anthropology curriculum continues to be debated by anthropologists. The general public, it seems, holds a different view. Even a quick perusal of a recent year's worth of the Science section of the *New York Times* is telling: the vast majority of articles with anthropological content and implications deal with the human genome and genetics or with skeletal remains and human evolution. It seems to me that anthropologists cannot afford to ignore the enormous popular authority of biology and archaeology. It is imperative that we understand the basis for the allure of science, and to learn how to respond effectively to misappropriations of biology and archaeology, such as the "gay" gene and the "nuclear family" of *Australopithicus africanus*.

I have selected essays that treat (same-sex) sexuality not as an isolable thing, but as a nexus comprised of myriad intersecting fields and forces, sites, and situations. This *Reader* does not pretend to be a comprehensive history of anthropological research on sexualities, much less same-sex sexualities, although several articles provide a historical overview of such. Though it is impossible to do justice to the amazing variety of sexual practices and desires across cultural areas, I did attempt to include essays based on ethnography in specific cultural areas at specific points in history. Collectively, these essays represent epistemological and research topoi that have emerged as especially salient over the past decade to the development of an anthropology of same-sex sexuality. These include biotechnology and bioethics, sexual categories and boundaries, language and terminology, ethnicity and identity politics, kinship and family, citizenship and politics, and policy-making. I have made every effort to avoid redundancies and duplications with other anthologies on same-sex sexualities that either focus on anthropology or include the work of anthropologists.[3]

Given the centrality of sex in the lives of humans individually and collectively, one would think that anthropologists, whose intellectual and pedagogical mission is to explore and represent the colorful and complex varieties of human cultures and experiences, were at the forefront of the investigation of human sexualities. On the contrary, as Carole Vance has argued (in this volume), they have been "far from courageous or even adequate," especially in regard to same-sex practices.[4] A point I made in *Takarazuka: Sexual Politics and Popular Culture in Modern Japan* [(Robertson 2001 [1998]) pertains equally to the discipline of anthropology and its practitioners. Contrary to the opinion of majority of my colleagues in Japanese Studies, I realized that the all-female Takarazuka Revue was an ideal site for an exploration of the contested discourse of sexuality in modern Japan.[5] That such a connection had either been overlooked or dismissed was one manifestation of the relative lack of serious attention that scholars of Japan had paid to ideas about gender and sexuality beyond the completely normative. Some shortsightedly eschewed the subject itself as unscholarly and/or motivated by a radical (i.e., feminist or lesbian) agenda; others apparently were afraid of being stigmatized and ostracized for undertaking research on the subject of sex and gender – and, in particular, on the subject of same-sex sexualities. Apparently the threat encoded in the insidious expression "It takes one to know one" overpowered the fear of incomplete or even bad scholarship. Unfortunately, it still is too often the case that indifference, ignorance, and prejudice prevent researchers from considering the historical and cultural significance of gender attribution and sexual practices even when these have been and remain part of a very *public* discourse. Imagine scholars fifty or one hundred years from now writing about marriage in the late twentieth-century United States without mentioning the enormous amount of attention, popular and legal alike, paid to the issue of same-sex marriage (Robertson 2001 [1998]: 45).

It is thus no wonder, as Vance keenly observed over a decade ago, that "the recent development of a more cultural and non-essentialist discourse about sexuality has sprung not from the centre of anthropology but from its periphery, from other disciplines (especially history), and from theorizing done by marginal groups." The role of historians has been especially important in laying a foundation for the rigorous study of sexuality, beginning with the crucial point that the "very term 'sexuality' is a modern construct which originated in the nineteenth century," as Freedman and D'Emilio point out (in this volume).[6] Historian Robert Padgug usefully distinguishes between sexuality as ideology and sexuality as praxis; that is, sexuality as an essence or group of essences, and sexuality as an ensemble of active social relations (Padgug 1989: 22). He notes that "the most commonly held twentieth-century assumptions about sexuality imply that it is a separate category of existence (like "the economy," or "the state," other supposedly independent spheres of reality), almost identical with the sphere of private life" (ibid.: 18–19).

Predicated on a classic division of individual and society, these assumptions fuel various psychological and biological determinisms about sexuality (ibid.: 19), determinisms that some researchers – and some ideologues – seek to attribute to brain morphology as well as to genetics. Invoking the axiom, "good politics, like good intentions, are not sufficient to produce valid science," Bonnie Spanier (in this volume) analyzes and deconstructs scientific claims about biological bases for differences in sexuality. She focuses on the widely publicized research of Simon LeVay, a self-identified gay neurobiologist who "found," in the structure of the hypothalamus, a difference between ostensibly heterosexual and homosexual males. For LeVay, a biological determinant of homosexuality served as evidence against the belief that it was a mental illness, or criminal, or immoral. Edward Stein (in this volume) confronts the ethical implications of such scientific studies of sexual orientation in conjunction with the popular belief – despite serious flaws in those studies – that a person's sexuality is genetically determined. Will prospective parents advocate for and apply biotechnologies to select the sexual orientation of their children and/or to prevent the birth of children who will not be heterosexual? In answering this troubling question, Stein attempts to reconcile the tension between, on the one hand, the application of biotechnologies in the name of reproductive liberty and, on the other hand, the legal protection of lesbians, gay men, and bisexuals through the regulation of certain reproductive technologies.

Recent developments in reproductive technologies – alternative (artificial) insemination (AI), in vitro fertilization (IVF), zygote intrafallopian transfer (ZIFT), surrogacy, etc. – have exacerbated (rather than caused) a "crisis of kinship." However, human beings across cultures and over centuries have been far more resilient and innovative about "the structures that connect society to the natural world and generations to each other" (Laqueur 2000: 80) than those (and not just in the United States) who currently advocate so-called traditional marriages and family values. Female–female marriages in parts of Africa are a case in point. Kath Weston, in *Families We Choose* (1991), explicitly challenged the dominant model of American kinship and its foundation in procreation and biological ties, and Corinne Hayden (in this volume) demonstrates that whereas "chosen families may *decentralize* biology, lesbian families' explicit mobilization of biological ties challenges the notion of biology as a *singular* category through which kin ties are reckoned." How the so-called core symbols of American kinship are reworked and recontextualized by both lesbian mothers and the new reproductive and genetic biotechnologies is the main focus of Hayden's essay.

In addition to procreation and biological ties, the dominant model of American kinship is understood to be premised on a strict, naturalized alignment of sex, gender, and sexuality: males are bodies with penises, are masculine men, and are heterosexual; females are bodies with vaginas, are feminine women, and are heterosexual. The phenomenon of transsexualism, writes Judith Shapiro (in this volume), paradoxically both "raises questions about what it means to consider external genitals as the 'basis' for systems of gender difference," and reinforces the dominant, conservative assumption that there are only two sexes and two genders, that genitals are essential signs of gender, and that one's gender is "invariant and permanent." Sex-change surgery, she argues, is in the domain of "heroic medicine." A biotechnological tour de force, the transsexed body[7] calls attention both to competing ideologies of essential ("natural") and socially constructed gender, and to the naturalization of "nature" by biomedical specialists. Similarly, in *Lessons from the Intersexed* (1990), Suzanne Kessler explores how infants born having physical gender markers (genitals, gonads, or chromosomes) that are neither clearly "female" nor "male" compel a rethinking of the relationship of sex (*qua* genitals), gender, and sexuality.

Shapiro also draws from others' ethnographic research in order to compare Euro-American transsexualism with forms of what she calls "institutionalized gender crossing" in cultures where dominant Euro-American notions about sexuality have little or no cachet: the Native American *berdache*, the Omani *xanith*, and female–female marriage in Africa. In this volume, articles by Deborah Elliston, Evelyn Blackwood, Donald Donham, Timothy Wright, and myself deal with same-sex practices, desires, and erotics in Melanesia, West Sumatra, South Africa, Bolivia, and Japan, respectively.

Elliston critiques the concept of "institutionalized" or "ritualized" homosexuality, arguing that although it helped to destigmatize anthropological research on same-sex sexualities, the concept is fundamentally problematic in that it promotes a certain "erotic ethnocentrism" which may exist only in the mind's eye of the beholding ethnographer. Focusing on semen practices in Melanesian societies, she makes the case that erotics and sexuality (as under stood in a Euro-American context) are neither central nor relevant to the local meanings of these practices. Rather, age and gender hierarchies, and local models of (male/masculine) identity development – in other words, the stuff of everyday life – provide a more accurate theoretical framework for understanding boys' initiation into manhood.

Most anthropologists tend to pay close attention to how people make sense of their world, seeking out local "voices," and engaging in transparent interactions over the course of their fieldwork. But those of us working on sexualities often encounter silences and opaque references and transactions. Alisa Klinger (in this volume) discusses how lesbian lives have been "disappeared" from the historical record, and elaborates on the ways in which those lives can be retrieved from seemingly insignificant ephemera. She urges scholars to complement text-based scholarship with fieldwork and archival research in order to resist and counter the "historic tendency to silence lesbians" as well as to forge a strong(er) relationship between the academy and local communities.[8]

Timothy Wright's essay on Bolivia (in this volume) reminds us that silence is an equally "valuable and malleable resource," and that just because (male) homosexuality and silence have been inseparable partners, this does not mean that homosexuality is never mentioned. Wright explains that male homosexuality is a "safe" topic provided references to it are made in "tones of indignation, repulsion, anger, or pity" or in the form of degrading jokes and tabloid articles about immorality and crime. However, the more personal the connection to homosexuality, the more often the subject is shrouded in silence.

Wright's work as a regional gay men's outreach coordinator for HIV/AIDS prevention provided him with direct insights into contradictions between local understandings of same-sex practices and the "gay" identity fostered by, in this case, USAID-funded public health programs. He, and the other contributors to this volume who work in Indonesia, Japan, and South Africa, found that transnational encounters introduced changes in local cultural attitudes toward, definitions of, and identifications with various sexualities, just as local sexual practices confound theories of sexuality premised on reified norms, whatever their provenance.

Blackwood writes about the Minangkabau *tomboi*, understood as "a female acting in the manner of men," and the "normative" (that is, unmarked) womanly females who choose a *tomboi* partner. She argues that two forms of gender transgression among females are collectively produced by the "hegemonic heterosexuality" of the Indonesian state, the Minangkabau kinship system, and the opportunities for self-sufficiency provided by the capitalist economy. These forms are the *tomboi* and the womanly female who participates in "compulsory heterosexuality" by marrying and bearing children, who then, her obligations fulfilled, pursues erotic relationships with *tombois*.

This situation is very similar to the predominant ideology in Japan regarding marriage, which is recognized less as a product of romantic love – which is not to imply that Japanese married couples do not love each other – and more as a means to achieve social adulthood and normality, to ensure genealogical continuity, and to secure economic security, etc. Consequently, as I have written elsewhere, as long as an individual's sexual practices do not interfere with or challenge the legitimacy of the twinned institutions of marriage and household, Japanese society accommodates – and in the case of males, even indulges – a diversity of sexual behaviors. One of the most tenacious of mistaken assumptions that anthropologists need to dismantle if any progress is to be made in understanding sexuality and its theories is the easy equation of marriage with sexuality, and heterosexuality in particular (Robertson 2001 [1998]: 145). I explore a case in point (in this volume) in contextualizing the life and (female) loves of Yoshiya Nobuko (1896–1973), one of Japan's most popular novelists and, most unusually in the early twentieth century, an economically self-sufficient woman thanks to her literary successes. When she realized that, like its predecessor, the post-World War II constitution would not recognize same-sex marriage, Yoshiya made radical use of the flexible Japanese kinship system by adopting her life partner, Monma Chiyo, in 1957, thus ensuring that Monma would be legally recognized as her successor.

For Yoshiya and other Japanese women writers of modern Japan, traveling throughout Europe and the United States was considered *de rigueur*, and their experiences abroad directly informed their literary efforts. Yoshiya, who claimed to be "impressed by the liberated women of America," vowed "never again to write about female characters who cried a lot and simply endured their miserable lot in life." Similarly, the worldwide transmission of a lesbian and gay discourse, circulated through "rainbow" NGOS and their media, the internet, and AIDS-related outreach programs, has influenced the formation of a supra-local lesbian and gay identity politics in countries and regions across the globe. In this connection, it is crucial to realize that transcultural encounters, while not strictly dialectical, and however uneven or unequal in power or degree, are "shifting processes": they do not constitute unidirectional teleologies. All parties involved in the encounter are affected and modified by it, albeit with different consequences (Taylor 1991: 63; Robertson 2001 [1998]: 219, n. 23).

In Indonesia, for example, *tomboi* identity has been incorporated into the formation of a national lesbian and gay "community" and movement. And in Soweto, South Africa, as Donald Donham (in this volume) writes, the end of apartheid occasioned the creation, for some black men, of an identity based on sexuality, that is, a *gay* identity. In apartheid-era urban black culture, gender apparently overrode biological sex. Males who cross-dressed or who expressed a sexual interest in other males were identified, and identified themselves, as "women." However, Donham elaborates, this new way of looking at the sexual world was not taken up consistently, evenly, or completely. He reiterates emphatically the crucial importance of ethnography both in challenging theories, however useful, now taken as self-evident and universally relevant, and in analyzing the interreferential relationship between the local and the global.

The clarion call of the anthropologists represented in this volume is for more ethnography–empirical and historical information – about *actual* human sexual desires and practices, and less abstract and "presentist" philosophy. Problems of accurate interpretation and representation arise when local, everyday sexual practices are diluted and distorted by an ethnographer's fealties to a particular theory or theoretical matrix. In anthropology, at least, theories are congealed from the living flux, or the animated archive, of quotidian, patterned experience. If theories are not to become frozen as formulaic explanation, and consequently rendered atheoretical, they must be challenged, modified, and refined by empirical, everyday "stuff." Thus, for example, although Michel Foucault's work on sexuality has been foundational to the anthropology of sexuality, Donham points out that it also presents serious limitations. He explains that Foucault overstressed a unidirectional narrative of supersession, when, in fact, cultural change tends to be more various, more fractured, more incomplete. A second limitation of Foucault's work on sexuality, Donham notes, stems from his over-reliance on the texts of medical specialists to infer the categories and commitments of ordinary people.

Matti Bunzl (in this volume) makes an analogous argument in his critical analysis of the politics of outing in Austria. His essay also effectively makes problematic any notion of "Europe" or "the West" as an internally coherent culture in its own right. Taking as his subject the 1995 *Outing-Aktion* of a leading activist in Austria's oldest lesbian and gay organization, Homosexuellen-Initiative, Bunzl aims to show the perilous contingencies of lesbian/gay political work. The targets of the outing were Catholic bishops and their "clandestine homosexuality," and the objective was to draw attention to the ongoing legal discrimination that continues to denigrate lesbians and gay men in Austria. Through a close, analytical reading of the various texts generated in preparation for and by this event, Bunzl determines that while outing closeted homophobes exposes their hypocrisy, it also turns these closeted persons into "Others," thereby, ironically, reinforcing the normativity and dominance of heterosexuality.

Whereas anthropologists studying sexuality need to work at generating new theoretical insights from inter- and intra-cultural encounters, archaeologists need to do just the opposite. Working with "broken pots, faunal remains, collapsed structures, burials, soil residues, and other evidentiary sources," archaeologists need to, in Barbara Voss's words (in this volume), stretch "theories of sexuality in new chronological and cultural directions." This is more easily said than done. Feminist archaeology was formally – and *finally* – introduced in the United States in the early 1980s by pioneers like Margaret Conkey, Joan Gero, and Janet Spector, among others. Judging from citational practices, there exists a "degree of theoretical conservatism in feminist archaeology with regard to conceptions of sexuality and its relationship to gender." Voss further elaborates that it is difficult for those feminist archaeologists who are occupied with legitimizing and developing gender studies simultaneously to embrace queer theories that deconstruct gender and sexuality. Deconstructions of sex and gender destabilize precisely those categories (e.g., male, female, woman, man) that are necessarily invoked to model engendered social worlds of the past. In other words, Voss argues, the fear of compromising "gender" as a category of archaeological analysis may account for the apparent reluctance of many archaeological researchers consistently and critically to engage with queer theory.

Two decades ago, one of the key accomplishments of feminist archaeologists was to encourage their colleagues to become more self-conscious about assumptions they held about sex and gender (which more often than not were conflated), femaleness and maleness, together with notions of "family" and "kinship." These assumptions tended to be premised uncritically on their own culture's present-day dominant constructions of sex, gender, and sexuality. Non-feminist archaeologists tended to read into the fossil record those naturalized and unquestioned – those taken-for-granted and "self-evident" – ideas about human social behavior which, consequently, compromised the accuracy of their interpretations of the material data.

A somewhat similar situation characterizes much of the research on "gay and lesbian language," which, as Don Kulick noted in his review on the subject in the *Annual Review of Anthropology*, is plagued by serious conceptual difficulties (Kulick 2000: 247). One problem is the belief that gay and lesbian language is somehow grounded in gay and lesbian identities and instantiated in the speech of people who self-identify as gay and lesbian. Kulick maintains that this assumption not only confuses symbolic and empirical categories and reduces sexuality to sexual identity, it also steers research away from examining the ways in which the characteristics seen as queer are linguistic resources available to everybody to use, regardless of their sexual orientation (ibid.).

Not content merely to point out the problems confronting research on the lavender lexicon, Kulick proposes a solution to them that shifts the focus of research on the dubious concept of lesbian and gay language away from a preoccupation with identities and toward an inquiry based on culturally grounded semiotic practices. In other words, he shifts the focus to an exploration of the relationship between language and sexuality (and "desire") (ibid.: 273). His essay in this volume explores how saying "no" in particular social situations effectively sexualizes those situations, and turns particular subjects into sexual subjects. Drawing a distinction between performance and performativity, identity and identification, Kulick explores the semiotics of the word "no" in three different empirical contexts: rape, "Homosexual Panic Defense," and sadomasochistic scenes. He asks not who says "no," but rather what does saying or not saying "no" produce, a question that leads to imagining what he terms a sociolinguistics of identification.

The basic pedagogical mission of this volume is twofold: to augment, thicken, and extend the anthropological information available on same-sex sexuality, and to debunk and demystify various presumptions and preconceptions that have muddled the scientific study and popular understanding of human sexualities. To facilitate this mission, I elected to group the fifteen essays into three interrelated parts, each of which addresses issues central to at least three or more of the fields within anthropology.[9] The essays in Part I, Anthropology's Sexual Fields, provide a general introduction to the place and treatment of (same-sex) sexuality within both the four fields of anthropology (sociocultural, linguistic, biological, archaeology) and historical and archival anthropological research. The various theoretical and methodological problems both faced by anthropologists working within and outside the United States on the subject of same-sex sexualities, and evident in the anthropological literature on such, are identified and addressed in the essays comprising Part II, Problems and Propositions. Part III, Ethics, Erotics, and Exercises, is made up of essays that introduce definitions and expressions of same-sex sexualities and erotic behaviors, and same-sex practices (or "exercises," in the sense of actions manifested as practices) in various cultural and historical settings. Some of the essays also consider the "real-world" applications of anthropological insights into sexual activities, together with the global circulation and local modifications and ramifications of sexual identity politics of Euro-American provenance. Finally, the fifteen essays collectively present and represent anthropological approaches to the subject of same-sex sexuality, as well as contribute to the recasting of concepts both central to the discipline and hotly debated today in public forums.

NOTES

1 I alternate between using this term in its singular and plural forms to remind readers of the manifold varieties of sexual behaviors and practices compressed into the term "sexuality."
2 Weston (1993) and Kulick (2000).
3 Among those anthologies – and this is but a small number of relevant publications – are Henry Abelove, Michele Aina Barale, and David Halperin, eds., *The Lesbian and Gay Studies Reader* (New York: Routledge, 1993); Richard Parker and Peter Aggleton, eds., *Culture, Society and Sexuality: A Reader* (London: UCL Press, 1999); Timothy Murphy, ed., *Reader's Guide to Lesbian and Gay Studies* (Chicago: Fitzroy Dearborn Publishers, 2000); Anna Livia and Kira Hall, eds., *Queerly Phrased: Language, Gender, and Sexuality* (New York: Oxford University Press, 1997; John Corvino, ed., *Same Sex: Debating the Ethics, Science, and Culture of Homosexuality* (Lanham, MD: Rowman & Littlefield, 1997); Leslie Moran, Daniel Monk, and Sarah Beresford, eds., *Legal Queeries: Lesbian, Gay, and Transgender Legal Studies* (New York: Cassell, 1998); Joan Nestle, ed., *The Persistent Desire: A Femme-Butch Reader* (Boston: Alyson Publications, 1992); Carol Vance, ed., *Pleasure and Danger: Exploring Female Sexuality* (New York: Routledge and Kegan Paul, 1985 [1984]); Cindy Patton and Benigno Sanchez-Eppler, eds., *Queer Diasporas* (Durham, NC: Duke University Press, 2000); Evelyn Blackwood, ed., *The Many Faces of Homosexuality: Anthropological Approaches to Homosexual Behavior* (New York: Harrington Park, 1986); Gilbert Herdt, ed., *Third Sex, Third Gender: Beyond Sexual Dimorphism in Culture and History* (New York: Zone, 1994); Wayne R. Dynes and Stephen Donaldson, eds., *Ethnographic Studies of Homosexuality* (New York: Garland, 1992); and Ellen Lewin and William Leap, eds., *Out in the Field: Reflections of Lesbian and Gay Anthropologists* (Urbana: University of Illinois Press, 1996). An excellent cross-cultural bibliography of texts dealing with same-sex sexualities and desires can be accessed on line at http://www.lib.uchicago. edu/e/su/gaylesb/. Finally, although I do not address the anthropologically relevant subject of a lesbian and gay filmography, I would like to reference here a recently edited volume, Chris Holmlund and Cynthia Fuchs, eds., *Between the Sheets, In the Streets: Queer, Lesbian, Gay Documentary* (Minneapolis: University of Minnesota Press, 1997).
4 This introduction by no means is intended to represent a comprehensive investigation of the study of same-same sexualities within the discipline of anthropology. In addition to Vance (in this volume), scholars who do present an overview of anthropological discourses on same-sex sexualities include Blackwood (1986) and Weston (1993), two of the few

anthropologists who actually address female–female sexual relations; the vast majority of anthropological studies of sexuality focus almost exclusively on male–male relations.

5 The all-female Takarazuka Revue was founded in 1913 and continues to enjoy enormous popularity today. From the outset, the Revue has been the focus of heated debates in the mass media on the relationship of sex, gender, and sexuality.

6 This point also pertains to societies outside of Western Europe and the United States. See Sabine Fruhstuck's *Colonizing Sex: Sexology and Social Control in Modern Japan* (Berkeley: University of California Press, 2003) for a stimulating account of the history and ramifications of sexology in Japan.

7 Juxtaposing Klein and Shapiro, one could conjure, cynically, the following Orwellian scenario: parents would have to choose whether to induce the abortion of a baby whose genes indicate that it will be gay, or to subject the infant to transsexual surgery and hormone "therapy" to ensure that its anatomy fits its (genetic) sexuality!

8 For a recent book that embodies Klinger's message, see James Vinson Carmichael, Jr., *Daring to Find Our Names: The Search for Lesbigay Library History* (Westport, CT: Greenwood Press, 1998).

9 As one reviewer, Evelyn Blackwood, noted, there are various ways in which I could have grouped the fifteen essays. She saw affinities between Spanier and Stein (challenges to biology), Hayden and Robertson ("queering" kinship"), Blackwood, Donham, and Wright (transnational encounters), Klinger and Freedman and D'Emilio (history), and Kulick, Elliston, Shapiro, Bunzl, and Voss (contesting dominant models).

REFERENCES

Blackwood, Evelyn, ed.
1986 The Many Faces of Homosexuality: Anthropological Approaches to Homosexual Behavior. New York: Harrington Park.

Kessler, Suzanne
1990 Lessons from the Intersexed. New Brunswick: Rutgers University Press.

Kulick, Don
2000 Lesbian and Gay Language. Annual Review of Anthropology 29: 243–85.

Lacqueur, Thomas
2000 "From Generation to Generation": Imagining Connectedness in the Age of Reproductive Technologies. *In* Biotechnology and Culture: Bodies, Anxieties, Ethics. Paul E. Brodwin, ed. Pp. 75–98. Bloomington: University of Indiana Press.

Padgug, Robert
1989 Sexual Matters: On Conceptualizing Sexuality in History. *In* Passion and Power: Sexuality in History. Kathy Peiss and Christina Simmons, eds. Pp. 14–31 Philadelphia: Temple University Press.

Robertson, Jennifer
2002 Reflexivity Redux: A Pithy Polemic on "Positionality." Anthropological Quarterly 75 (4):755–62.

Robertson Jennifer
2001 [1998] Takarazuka: Sexual Politics and Popular Culture in Modern Japan. Berkeley: University of California Press.

Taylor, Diane
1991 Transculturating Transculturation. *In* Interculturalism and Performance. Bonnie Marranca and Gautam Dasgupta, eds. Pp. 60–74. New York: PAJ Publications.

Weston, Kath
1991 Families We Choose: Lesbians, Gays, Kinship. New York: Columbia University Press.
Weston, Kath
1993 Lesbian/Gay Studies in the House of Anthropology. Annual Review of Anthropology 22: 339–67.

Part I

Anthropology's Sexual Fields

1

Anthropology Rediscovers Sexuality: A Theoretical Comment

Carole S. Vance

> 'In the Beginning was sex and sex will be in the end... I maintain – and this is my thesis – that sex as a feature of man and society was always central and remains such...'[1]
>
> Alexander Goldenweiser (1929)

This opening sentence from Alexander Goldenweiser's essay, "Sex and Primitive Society", suggests that sexuality has been an important focus for anthropological investigation. Indeed, such is the reputation anthropologists have bestowed upon themselves: fearless investigators of sexual customs and mores throughout the world, breaking through the erotophobic intellectual taboos common in other, more timid disciplines.

In reality, anthropology's relationship to the study of sexuality is more complex and contradictory. Anthropology as a field has been far from courageous or even adequate in its investigation of sexuality[2,3]. Rather, the discipline often appears to share the prevailing cultural view that sexuality is not an entirely legitimate area of study, and that such study necessarily casts doubt not only on the research but on the motives and character of the researcher. In this, we have been no worse but also no better than other social science disciplines.

Manifestations of this attitude abound in graduate training and in the reward structure of the profession. Few graduate departments provide training in the study of human sexuality. As a result, there are no structured channels to transmit anthropological knowledge concerning sexuality to the next generation of students. The absence of a scholarly community engaged with issues of sexuality effectively prevents the field from advancing; students interested in the topic perceive that they must rediscover past generations' work on their own. Most advisors actively discourage graduate students from fieldwork or dissertations on sexuality for fear that the topic will prove a career liability. At best, students are advised to complete their doctoral degrees, build up reputations and credentials, and even obtain tenure, all of which are said to put one in a better position to embark on the study of sexuality. Rather than the collective effort needed to remedy a serious structural limitation in our discipline, this advice conveys the clear message that sexuality is so dangerous an intellectual terrain it can ruin the careers of otherwise competent graduate students and academics.

Nor is there any career track after graduate school for professional anthropologists interested in sexuality. Never attaining the status of an appropriate specialization, sexuality remains marginal. Funding is difficult, as agencies continue to be fearful of the subject's potential for public controversy. Colleagues often remain suspicious and hypercritical, as discomfort with the very subject of sexuality is cast instead in terms of scholarly adequacy or legitimacy[4]. Field projects rarely, if ever, focus fully or directly on sexuality; rather, field workers collect data as they can, some of which are never published for fear of harm to one's professional reputation. Some anthropologists retreat into sexology, more hospitable perhaps, yet seriously limited itself as an intellectual ghetto of disciplinary refugees[5,6].

In light of these disincentives, it is perhaps not surprising that the recent development of a more cultural and non-essentialist discourse about sexuality has sprung not from the center of anthropology but from its periphery, from other disciplines (especially history), and from theorizing done by marginal groups. The explosion of exciting and challenging work in what has come to be called social construction theory during the past 15 years has yet to be felt fully in mainstream anthropology.

The intellectual history of social construction theory is complex, and the moments offered here are for purposes of illustration, not comprehensive review (for basic texts, see Refs[7–18]). Social construction theory drew on developments in several disciplines: social interactionism, labeling theory, and deviance in sociology[19,20]; social history, labor studies, women's history, and Marxist history[21]; and symbolic anthropology, cross-cultural work on sexuality, and gender studies in anthropology, to name only the most significant streams. In addition, theorists in many disciplines responded to new questions raised by feminist and lesbian/gay scholarship concerning gender and identity.

Sexuality and Gender

Feminist scholarship and activism undertook the project of rethinking gender, which had a revolutionary impact on notions of what is natural. Feminist efforts focused on a critical review of theories which used reproduction to link gender with sexuality, thereby explaining the inevitability and naturalness of women's subordination (for anthropology, see Refs[22–27]).

This theoretical re-examination led to a general critique of biological determinism, in particular of received knowledge about the biology of sex differences[28–33]. Historical and cross-cultural evidence undermined the notion that women's roles, which varied so widely, could be caused by a seemingly uniform human reproduction and sexuality. In light of the diversity of gender roles in human society, it seemed unlikely that they were inevitable or caused by sexuality. The ease with which such theories had become accepted suggested that science was conducted within and mediated by powerful beliefs about gender and in turn provided ideological support for current social relations. Moreover, this increased sensitivity to the ideological aspects of science led to a wide-ranging inquiry into the historical connection between male dominance, scientific ideology, and the development of Western science and biomedicine[34–41].

Feminist practice in grass-roots activism also fostered analyses which separated sexuality and gender. Popular struggles to advance women's access to abortion and birth control represented an attempt to separate sexuality from reproduction and women's gendered role as wives and mothers. Discussions in consciousness-raising groups made clear that what seemed to be a naturally gendered body was in fact a highly socially mediated product: femininity and sexual attractiveness were achieved through persistent socialization regarding standards of beauty, makeup, and body language. Finally, discussions between different generations of women made clear how variable their allegedly natural sexuality was, moving within our own century from marital duty to multiple orgasm, vaginal to clitoral eroticism, and Victorian passionlessness to a fittingly feminine enthusiasm. Sexuality and gender went together, it seemed, but in ways that were subject to change.

In 1975, anthropologist Gayle Rubin's influential essay, "The Traffic in Women", made a compelling argument against essentialist explanations that sexuality and reproduction caused gender difference in any simple or inevitable way[42]. Instead, she explored the shape of "a systematic social apparatus which takes up females as raw materials and fashions domesticated women as products"[42], p. 158. She proposed the term "sex/gender system" to describe "the set of arrangements by which society transforms biological sexuality into products of human activity, and in which these transformed sexual needs are satisfied"[42], p. 159.

In 1984, Rubin suggested a further deconstruction of the sex/gender system into two separate domains in which sexuality and gender were recognized as distinct systems[43]. Most prior feminist analyses considered sexuality a totally derivative category whose organization was determined by the structure of gender inequality. According to Rubin's formulation, sexuality and gender were analytically distinct phenomena which required separate explanatory frames, even though they were interrelated in specific historical circumstances. Theories of sexuality could not explain gender, and taking the argument to a new level, theories of gender could not explain sexuality.

This perspective suggested a novel framework: sexuality and gender are separate systems which are interwoven at many points. Although members of a culture experience this interweaving as natural, seamless, and organic, the points of connection vary historically and cross-culturally. For researchers in sexuality, the task is not only to study changes in the expression of sexual behavior and attitudes, but to examine the relationship of these changes to more deeply-based shifts in how gender and sexuality were organized and interrelated within larger social relations.

Sexuality and Identity

A second impetus for the development of social construction theory arose from issues that emerged in the examination of male homosexuality in nineteenth-century

Europe and America[7,8,10,12]. It is interesting to note that a significant portion of this early research was conducted by independent scholars, non-academics, and maverick academics usually working without funding or university support, since at this time the history of sexuality (particularly that of marginal groups) was scarcely a legitimate topic. As this research has recently achieved the barest modicum of academic acceptance, it is commonplace for properly-employed academics to gloss these developments by a reference to Foucault and *The History of Sexuality*[44]. Without denying his contribution, such a singular genealogy obscures an important origin of social construction theory, and inadvertently credits the university and scholarly disciplines with a development they never supported.

The first attempt to grapple with questions of sexual identity in a way now recognizable as social construction appears in Mary McIntosh's 1968 essay on the homosexual role in England[45]. A landmark article offering many suggestive insights about the historical construction of sexuality in England, her observations initially vanished like pebbles in a pond until the mid-1970s, when they were again taken up by writers involved in the questions of feminism and gay liberation. It is at this time that an identifiably constructionist approach first appears.

The earliest scholarship in lesbian and gay history attempted to retrieve and revive documents, narratives, and biographies which had been lost or made invisible due to historical neglect as well as active efforts to suppress the material by archivists, historians, and estates. These documents and the lives represented therein were first conceived of as "lesbian" or "gay", and the enterprise as a search for historical roots. To their credit, researchers who started this enterprise sharing the implicit cultural ideology of fixed sexual categories then began to consider other ways of looking at their material and to ask more expansive questions.

Jeffrey Weeks, English historian of sexuality, first articulated this theoretical transition[8]. Drawing on McIntosh's concept of the homosexual role, he distinguished between homosexual behavior, which he considered universal, and homosexual identity, which he viewed as historically and culturally specific and, in Britain, a comparatively recent development. His rich and provocative analysis of changing attitudes and identities also contextualized sexuality, examing its relationship to the reorganization of family, gender, and household in nineteenth century Britain.

Jonathan Katz's work also demonstrates this process. His first book, *Gay American History*, is in the tradition of a search for gay ancestors[7]. In the course of researching his second book, however, he began to consider that the acts of sodomy reported in American colonial documents from the 17th century might not be equivalent to contemporary homosexuality[12]. Colonial society did not seem to conceive of a unique type of person – a homosexual – who engaged in these acts. Nor was there any evidence of a homosexual subculture or individuals whose subjective sense of identity was organized around what we understand as sexual preference or identity. Katz's second book marks a sharp departure from the first, in that records or accounts that document same-sex emotional or sexual relations are not taken as evidence of "gay" or "lesbian" identity, but are treated as jumping off points for a whole series of questions about the meanings of these acts to the people who engaged in them and to the culture and time in which they lived.

These intellectual developments are also evident in early work on the formation of lesbian identity[46–49] and work considering the question of sexual behavior and identity in non-Western cultures, for example, Gilbert Herdt's work in New Guinea[50–52]. From this expanding body of work[18,53–59] came an impressive willingness to imagine: had the categories "homosexual" and "lesbian" always existed? and if not, what were their points of origin and conditions for development? If identical physical acts had different subjective meanings, how was sexual meaning constructed? If sexual subcultures come into being, what leads to their formation? And although these questions were initially phrased in terms of homosexual identity and history, it is clear that they are equally applicable to heterosexual identity and history, implications just now being explored[60–64].

Sexuality as a Contested Domain

Continuing work on the history of the construction of sexuality in modern, state-level society shows that sexuality is an actively contested political and symbolic terrain in which groups struggle to implement sexual programs and alter sexual arrangements and ideologies. The growth of state interest in regulating sexuality (and the related decline of religious control) made legislative and public policy domains particularly attractive fields for political and intellectual struggles around sexuality in the nineteenth and twentieth centuries. Mass movements mobilized around venereal disease, prostitution, masturbation, social purity, and the double standard, employing grass-roots political organizing, legislative lobbying, mass demonstrations, and cultural interventions utilizing complex symbols, rhetoric, and representations[10,15,65–70]. Because state intervention was increasingly formulated in a language of health, physicians and scientists became important participants in the newly developing regulatory discourses. They also actively participated in elaborating these discourses as a way to legitimize their newly professionalizing specialities.

Although socially powerful groups exercised more discursive power, they were not the only participants in sexual struggles. Minority reformers, progressives, suffragists, and sex radicals also put forward programs for change and introduced new ways of thinking about and organizing sexuality. The sexual subcultures that had grown up in urban areas were an especially fertile field for these experiments. Constructionist work shows how their attempt to carve out partially protected public spaces in which to elaborate and express new sexual forms, behaviors, and sensibilities is also part of a larger political struggle to define sexuality. Subcultures give rise not only to new ways of organizing behavior and identity but to new ways of symbolically resisting and engaging with the dominant order, some of which grow to have a profound impact beyond the small groups in which they are pioneered. In this respect, social construction work has been valuable in exploring human agency and creativity in sexuality, moving away from uni-directional models of social change to describe complex and dynamic relationships among the state, professional experts, and sexual subcultures. This attempt to historicize sexuality has produced an innovative body of work to which historians, anthropologists, sociologists, and others have contributed in an unusual interdisciplinary conversation.

The Development of Social Construction Models, 1975–1990

The increasing popularity of the term "social construction" obscures the fact that constuctionist writers have used this term in diverse ways. It is true that all reject transhistorical and transcultural definitions of sexuality and suggest instead that sexuality is mediated by historical and cultural factors. But a close reading of constructionist texts shows that social constructionists differ in their views of what might be constructed, variously including sexual acts, sexual identities, sexual communities, the direction of erotic interest (object choice), and sexual desire itself. Despite these differences, all share the urge to problematize the terms and field of study.

At minimum, all social construction approaches adopt the view that physically identical sexual acts may have varying social significance and subjective meaning depending on how they are defined and understood in different cultures and historical periods. Because a sexual act does not carry with it a universal social meaning, it follows that the relationship between sexual acts and sexual meanings is not fixed, and it is projected from the observer's time and place at great peril. Cultures provide widely different categories, schema, and labels for framing sexual and affective experiences. These constructions not only influence individual subjectivity and behavior, but they also organize and give meaning to collective sexual experience through, for example, the impact of sexual identities, definitions, ideologies, and regulations. The relationship of sexual acts and identities to organized sexual communities is equally variable and complex. These distinctions, then, between sexual acts, identities, and communities are widely employed by constructionist writers.

A further step in social construction theory posits that even the direction of erotic interest itself, for example, object choice (heterosexuality, homosexuality, and bisexuality, as contemporary sexology would conceptualize it) is not intrinsic or inherent in the individual, but is constructed from more polymorphous possibilities. Not all constructionists take this step; and for those who do not, the direction of desire and erotic interest may be thought of as fixed, although the behavioral form this interest takes will be constructed by prevailing cultural frames, as will the subjective experience of individuals and the social significance attached to it by others.

The most radical form of constructionist theory[71] is willing to entertain the idea that there is no essential, undifferentiated sexual "impulse," "sex drive," or "lust," which resides in the body due to physiological functioning and sensation. Sexual desire, then, is itself constructed by culture and history from the energies and capacities of the body. In this case, an important constructionist question concerns the origin of these impulses, since they are no longer assumed to be intrinsic or perhaps even necessary. This position, of course, contrasts sharply with more middle-ground constructionist theory which implicitly accepts an inherent desire which is then constructed in terms of acts, identity, community, and object choice. The contrast between middle-ground and radical positions makes it evident that constructionists may well have arguments with each other, as well as with those working in essentialist and cultural influence traditions. Nevertheless, social construction literature, making its first appearance in the mid-1970s, demonstrates a gradual development of the ability to imagine that sexuality is constructed.

Cultural Influence Models of Sexuality, 1920–1990

By contrast, conventional anthropological approaches to sexuality from 1920–1990 remained remarkably consistent. Just as sexuality itself remained an unexamined construct, the theoretical foundations remained unexamined, unnamed, and implicit, as if they were so inevitable and natural that there could be little dispute or choice about this standard, almost generic, approach. For that reason I want to suggest the name "cultural influence model," to call attention to its distinctive features and promote greater recognition of this paradigm. In this model, sexuality is seen as the basic material – a kind of universal Play Doh – on which culture works, a naturalized category which remains closed to investigation and analysis.

On the one hand, the cultural influence model emphasizes the role of culture and learning in shaping sexual behavior and attitudes. In this respect, it rejects obvious forms of essentialism and universalizing. Variation was a key finding in many studies, in cross-cultural surveys[72–76], in ethnographic accounts ofsingle societies whose sexual customs stood in sharp contrast to those of the Euro-American reader[77–89], and in theoretical overviews[1,90–93]. Culture is viewed as encouraging or discouraging the expression of generic sexual acts, attitudes, and relationships. Oral – genital contact, for example, might be a part of normal heterosexual expression in one group but taboo in another; male homosexuality might be severely punished in one tribe yet tolerated in another. Anthropological work from this period was characterized by a persistent emphasis on variability.

On the other hand, although culture is thought to shape sexual expression and customs, the bedrock of sexuality is assumed – and often quite explicitly stated – to be universal and biologically determined; in the literature, it appears as "sex drive" or "impulse"[94]. Although capable of being shaped, the drive is conceived of as powerful, moving toward expression after its awakening in puberty, sometimes exceeding social regulation, and taking a distinctively different form in men and women.

The core of sexuality is reproduction. Although most anthropological accounts by no means restrict themselves to analyzing reproductive behavior alone, reproductive sexuality (glossed as heterosexual intercourse) appears as the meat and potatoes in the sexual menu, with other forms, both heterosexual and homosexual, arranged as appetizers, vegetables, and desserts. (These metaphors are not unknown in anthropological narratives.) Ethnographic and survey accounts almost always follow a reporting format that deals first with "real sex" and then moves on to the "variations." Some accounts supposedly about sexuality are noticeably short on details about non-reproductive behavior; Margaret Mead's article about the cultural determinants of sexual behaviors (in a wonderfully titled volume called *Sex and Internal Secretions*)[95] travels a dizzying trail which includes pregnancy, menstruation, menopause, and lactation but very little about non-reproductive sexuality or eroticism. Similarly, a more recent book, expansively titled *Varieties of Sexual Experience* (1985), devotes virtually all but a few pages to reproduction, marriage, and family organization[76].

Within the cultural influence model, the term "sexuality" covers a broad range of topics. Its meaning is often taken for granted, left implicit as a shared understanding between the reader and author. Tracking its use through various articles and books shows that sexuality includes many wildly different things: intercourse, orgasm, foreplay; erotic fantasies, stories, humor; sex differences and the organization of masculinity and femininity; and gender relations (often called sex roles in the earlier literature).

In this model, sexuality is not only related to gender but blends easily, and is often conflated, with it. Sexuality, gender arrangements, masculinity and femininity are assumed to be connected, even interchangeable. This assumption, however, never illuminates their culturally and historically-specific connections; it obscures them. The confusion springs from our own folk beliefs that (1) sex causes gender, that is, male–female reproductive differences and the process of reproduction (framed as and equated with "sexuality") give rise to gender differentiation, and (2) gender causes sex, that is, women as a marked gender group constitute the locus of sexuality, sexual desire, and motivation. Reproduction and its organization become the prime movers in all other male/female differentiation and in the flowering of the gender system. Gender and sexuality are seamlessly knit together.

Finally, the cultural influence model assumes that sexual acts carry stable and universal significance in terms of identity and subjective meaning. The literature routinely regards opposite gender sexual contact as "heterosexuality" and same gender contact as "homosexuality," as if the same phenomena were being observed in all societies in which these acts occurred. With hindsight, these assumptions are curiously ethnocentric, since the meanings attached to these sexual behaviors are those of the observers and 20th century complex, industrial society. Cross-cultural surveys could fairly chart the distribution of same or opposite gender sexual contact or the frequency of sexual contact before marriage. But when investigators report instead on the presence or absence of "homosexuality" or "sexual permissiveness," they engage in a spurious translation from sexual act or behavior to sexual meaning and identity, something later theoretical developments would come to reject.

To summarize, the cultural influence model recognizes variations in the occurrence of sexual behavior and in cultural attitudes which encourage or restrict behavior, but not in the meaning of the behavior itself. In addition, anthropologists working within this framework accept without question the existence of universal categories like heterosexual and homosexual, male and female sexuality, and sex drive.

Despite these many deficiencies, it is important to recognize the strengths of this approach, particularly in its intellectual, historical, and political context. Anthropology's commitment to cross-cultural comparison made it the most relativistic of social science disciplines in regard to the study of sexuality. Its finding of variation called into question prevailing notions about the inevitability or naturalness of sexual norms and behavior common in America and Europe, and the connection between sexual regulation and social or familial stability. The variability it reported suggested that human sexuality was malleable and capable of assuming different forms. Work in the cultural influence tradition undercut more mechanistic theories of sexual behavior, still common in medicine and psychiatry, that suggested sexuality was largely a function of physiological functioning or instinctual drives. It began to develop social and intellectual space in which it was possible to regard sexuality as something other than a simple function of biology.

Although work in the cultural influence model contributed to the development of social construction theory, there is a sharp break between them in many respects. This difference has not been recognized by many anthropologists still working within the cultural influence tradition. Indeed, many mistakenly seem to regard these new developments as theoretically compatible, even continuous with earlier work. Some have assimilated terms or phrases (like "social construction" or "cultural construction") in their work, yet their analytic frames still contain many unexamined essentialist elements[96]. It is not the case that the cultural influence model, because it recognizes cultural variation, is the same as social construction theory. The cultural influence model, then, no longer remains the only anthropological paradigm, although it still dominates contemporary work[76,97].

It would seem that the development of anthropology in this century – a general movement away from biologized frameworks toward perspectives that are denaturalizing and anti-essentialist – would foster the application of social construction theory to the study of sexuality. Despite its challenge to the natural and universalized status of many domains, however, anthropology has largely excluded sexuality from this endeavor of suggesting that human actions have been and continue to be subject to historical and cultural forces and, thus, to change.

A social construction approach to sexuality would examine the range of behavior, ideology, and subjective meaning among and within human groups, and would view the body, its functions, and sensations as potentials (and limits) which are incorporated and mediated by culture. The physiology of orgasm and penile erection no more explains a culture's sexual schema than the auditory range of the human ear explains its music. Biology and physiological functioning are determinative only at the most extreme limits, and there to set the boundary of what is physically possible. The more interesting question for anthropological research on sexuality is to chart what is culturally possible – a far more expansive domain. Ecological adaptation and reproductive demands similarly explain only a small portion of sexual organization, since fertility adequate for replacement and even growth is relatively easy for most groups to achieve. More important, sexuality is not coterminous with or equivalent to reproduction: reproductive sexuality constitutes a small portion of the larger sexual universe.

In addition, a social construction approach to sexuality must also problematize and question Euro-American folk and scientific beliefs about sexuality, rather than project them onto other groups in a manner which would be most unacceptably ethnocentric in any other subject area. Thus, statements about the universally compelling force of sexual impulse, the importance of sexuality in human life, the universally private status of sexual behavior, or its quintessentially reproductive nature need to be presented as hypotheses, not *a priori* assumptions. Anthropology seems especially well suited to problematize these most naturalized categories, yet sexuality has been the last domain (trailing even gender) to have its natural, biologized status called into question. For many of us, essentialism was our first way of thinking about sexuality and still remains hegemonic.

Social construction theory offers a radically different perspective in the study of sexuality, encouraging novel and fruitful research questions. Its influence has been increasing in anthropology[98–106], although cultural influence models still dominate[76, 107–111]. One might have predicted a gradually intensifying competition between paradigms, possibly even a paradigm shift. The appearance of AIDS, however, has altered this dynamic.

AIDS and Research on Sexuality

The great concern about AIDS has dramatically increased the interest in conducting and funding sex research. Early in the epidemic, epidemiologists routinely began to include batteries of questions concerning the frequency and nature of their subjects' sexual behavior. Their problems in measurement and conceptualization, as well as their futile search for baseline data, highlighted the scientific neglect of sex research. Indeed, the fact that no large-scale study on American sexual habits has been conducted since the Kinsey volumes[112, 113] now stands as a major embarrassment, resulting in our inability to answer even the most basic questions. As scientific groups and policy makers recognized the need for this information, they strongly recommended drastic increases in funding and research efforts in affected countries[114–116]. Although in many ways a positive and necessary step, the rush to funding nevertheless raises the possibility that the inadequate essentialist and cultural influence models of sexuality will be revived and strengthened.

AIDS encourages the resurgence of biomedical approaches to sexuality through the repeated association of sexuality with disease. The medicalization of sexuality is intensifying, as the public turns to medical authorities for sexual information and advice. In addition, biomedical investigators in medical schools and schools of public health are conducting a significant portion of AIDS-related research in sexuality[117]. This signals a shift from a general trend developing after World War II, when research on sexuality increasingly moved out of medical arenas. Thus, medicine's interest in sexuality is expanding to new areas beyond the specialties to which it was traditionally confined; sexually transmitted diseases, obstetrics and gynecology, and psychiatry.

This development poses several dangers. Biomedical approaches to sexuality often regard sexuality as derivative from physiology and a supposedly universal functioning of the body. Biomedical models tend to be the most unreflective about the influence of science and medical practice in constructing categories like "the body" and "health." Social construction approaches are virtually unknown, and the concept that sexuality varies with culture and history is expressed at best via primitive cultural influence models. There is limited recognition that sexuality has a history and that its definitions and meanings change over time and within populations. The reliance on survey instruments and easily quantified data in biomedically-based research increases the tendency to count acts rather than explore meaning. Such surveys have frequently equated sexual identities with sexual acts, for example, and treated "gay men" and "heterosexuals" as unproblematic categories. In addition, the high status of medical practitioners in the twentieth century and their recruitment from privileged class, gender, and racial groups has resulted historically in their close alliances with dominant ideologies, including the sexual. Should this pattern persist, they are as unlikely to be aware of marginal sexual subcultures and sensibilities as they are to be sensitive to them.

Framing sexual research within a biomedical model and the perspective of disease also threatens to re-pathologize sexuality. This promises to return sexuality to the position it occupied in the late 19th and early 20th centuries, where its public discussion was largely motivated and circumscribed by the discourses of venereal disease, prostitution, and masturbation. These public discussions framed by medical experts, ostensibly about health and disease, were implicitly discussions about morality, gender, and social order. This danger is heightened by the respect accorded medicine and science and the widespread public belief that science contains no values. The expansion of a supposedly objective and value-free discourse about sexuality organized under the guise of health opens the door to vastly increased governmental and professional intervention.

The emphasis placed on gay men and their sexual behavior in the early stages of the epidemic constitutes a sharp departure from previous inattention to subordinate sexual groups. This attention, however, highlights their "otherness" in a manner reminiscent of 19th-century pathology models of homosexuality,[118] emphasizing the naturalness of identity and reinforcing the sharp dichotomy between heterosexuality and homosexuality. This otherness is expanding to involve additional stigmatized groups at risk for AIDS, such as IV drug users, their partners, and inner city minority women, drawing on historically and culturally resonant stereotypes[119].

The danger posed by increased funding for research on sexuality connected with AIDS is not restricted to biomedicine. Within anthropology, it is unlikely that essentialist models will make a come back; however, the field may well experience the impact of increasingly biomedical approaches to sexuality in interdisciplinary work conducted in medical settings. More important, increased funding and urgent calls for research are likely to strengthen cultural influence models of sexuality, as more and more anthropologists will be drawn into work on AIDS[120–124].

Most of these are likely to be medical anthropologists or specialists in affected geographic areas without specialized training in sexuality. As anthropologists, they can be relied on to bring with them an expectation of human diversity, sensitivity to ethnocentrism, and a respect for the role of culture in shaping behavior, sexuality included. But this is precisely the problem, as these perspectives will reinvent the cultural influence model as the common-sense, anthropological approach to sexuality. Anthropologists new to sex research may easily think that, because it allows for cultural variation, their own cultural influence approach is identical to social construction theory. Their own comparisons with work done from more biologized, biomedical approaches, particularly in non-Western cultures, will make cultural influence models seem advanced, even cause for self-congratulation.

In all fields, the belated recognition of serious gaps in knowledge about sexual behavior may emphasize the importance of behavioral data, which appear more easily measured than fantasy, identity, and subjective meaning. Behavioral data lend themselves to easy quantification, fitting into the methodological biases of positivist social science. Amid an epidemic, researchers press for rapid results and reject the time, patience, and tolerance for uncertainty that ethnographic and deconstructive techniques seem to require.

Despite these tendencies which reinforce cultural influence and biologized approaches, the picture remains complex and contradictory. AIDS-inspired investigations into the realities of peoples' sexual worlds have already disclosed discrepancies between ideologies about sexuality and lived experience. Contradictions increase exponentially in other cultural contexts. These gaps exist in many areas, but are particularly insistent in regard to classificatory systems, identity, congruence between behavior and self-definition, the meaning of sexual acts, and the stability of sexual preference. These inconsistencies point to the usefulness of social construction theory and have spurred new work in anthropology[125–131]. Much as was the case with early gay history, researchers in sexuality and AIDS may confront the limitations of their models, generating provocative and imaginative work.

Moreover, the entire phenomenon of "safer sex" has emphasized the culturally malleable aspects of sexual behavior. The safer sex campaign mounted by the gay community, surely one of the most dramatic and effective public health campaign on record, made clear that sexual acts can only be understood within a cultural and subcultural context and that careful attention to meaning and symbolism allows the possibility of change, even for adults[132–135]. The self-conscious leadership and participation of gay men, as opposed to biomedical experts, in this endeavor suggests that individuals actively participate in creating and changing cultural and erotic meanings, particularly when they have a stake in doing so. Safer sex campaigns reveal active sexual agents with an awareness of their symbolic universe and an ability to manipulate and re-create it, rather than passively receive a static sexual enculturation.

The political and symbolic mobilizations around the sexual dimensions and meanings of AIDS on the part of many different constituencies also belie the notion that sexuality and its meaning are derived simply from the body, unchanging or easily read. Yet various groups proffer their interpretations of AIDS and its sexual significance as lessons to be read from nature and the body[132,133,135–142]. The multiplicity of competing lessons and the ferocious struggle for whose interpretation will prevail suggest that sexual meaning is a hotly contested, even political terrain. That dominant sectors, particularly the state, religion, and the professional groups exercise a disproportionate influence on the sexual discourse does not mean that their views are hegemonic or unchallenged by other groups. Nor does it mean that marginal groups only respond reactively and do not create their own subcultures and worlds of meaning.

In the midst of the creation of new discourses about sexuality, it is crucial that we become conscious of how these discourses are created and our own role in creating them. Anthropologists have a great deal to contribute to research in sexuality. The new situation brought about by AIDS in regard to sex research is filled with possibilities: to build on the challenging questions social construction theory has raised, or to fall back onto cultural influence and essentialist models. The stakes are not low – for research in sexuality, for applied work in AIDS education and prevention, for sexual politics, for human lives. If this is a moment in which anthropology "rediscovers" sex, we need to consider two questions: who will do the looking? and more to the point, what will we be able to see? We need to be explicit about our theoretical models, mindful of their history, and self-conscious about our practice.

REFERENCES

1 Goldenweiser A. Sex and primitive society. In *Sex in Civilization* (Edited by Calverton V. F. and Schmalhausen S. D.), p. 53. Macaulay Company, New York, 1929.
2 Fisher L. Relationships and sexuality in contexts and culture. In *Handbook of Sexuality* (Edited by Wolman B. B. and Money J.), p. 164. Prentice Hall, Englewood Cliffs, 1980.
3 Davis D. L. and Whitten R. G. The cross-cultural study of human sexuality. *Ann. Rev. Anthropol.* 16, 69, 1987.
4 This resistance can have paradoxical effects, to judge from personal experience. My own grant application in 1977 to complete a conventional annotated anthropological bibliography on biocultural influences on sexuality was rejected on the grounds that the investigator "was too young to engage in research on this topic" and, being unable to read Japanese, "could not read the important new literature on Japanese macaques in the original." Far from being discouraging, these comments piqued my interest all the more, since it appeared that anthropologists' volatile reactions deserved scrutiny at least as much as the cross-cultural material.
5 Vance C. S. Gender systems, ideology and sex research. In *Powers of Desire* (Edited by Snitow A., Stansell C. and Thompson S.), p. 371. Monthly Review Press, New York, 1983.
6 Irvine J. *Disorders of Desire*. Temple University Press, Philadelphia, 1990.
7 Katz J. *Gay American History*. Crowell, New York, 1976.
8 Weeks J. *Coming Out: Homosexual Politics in Britain from the 19th Century to the Present*. Quartet Books, London, 1977.
9 Padgug R. A. Sexual matters: on conceptualizing sexuality in history. *Radical History Review* 20, 3, 1979.
10 Weeks J. *Sex, Politics and Society: The Regulation of Sexuality Since 1800*. Longman, New York, 1981.
11 Snitow A., Stansell C. and Thompson S. (Eds) *Powers of Desire*. Monthly Review Press, New York, 1983.
12 Katz J. *Gay/Lesbian Almanac*. Harper and Row, New York, 1983.
13 Vance C. S. (Ed.) *Pleasure and Danger: Exploring Female Sexuality*. Routledge & Kegan Paul, New York, 1984.
14 Weeks J. *Sexuality*. Tavistock, London, 1986.
15 Peiss C. and Simmons C. (Eds) *Passion and Power: Sexuality in History*. Philadelphia, Temple University Press, 1989.
16 D'Emilio J. and Freedman E. B. *Intimate Matters: A Social History of Sexuality in America*. New York, 1988.
17 Altman D., Vance C., Vicinus M., Weeks J. *et al.* (Eds) *Homosexuality, Which Homosexuality?* An Dekker/Schorer, Amsterdam, 1989.
18 Duberman M. B., Vicinus M. and Chauncey G. (Eds) *Hidden from History: Reclaiming the Gay and Lesbian Past*. New American Library, New York, 1989.
19 Gagnon J. H. and Simon W. *Sexual Conduct: The Social Sources of Human Sexuality*. Aldine, Chicago, 1973.
20 Plummer K. Symbolic interactionism and sexual conduct: an emergent perspective. In *Human Sexual Relations* (Edited by Brake M.), p. 223. Pantheon, New York, 1982.
21 Duggan L. From instincts to politics: writing the history of sexuality in the U.S. *J. Sex Res.* 27, 95, 1990.
22 Reiter R. (Ed.) *Toward an Anthropology of Women*. Monthly Review Press, New York, 1975.

23 Rosaldo M. Z. and Lamphere L. (Eds) *Women, Culture and Society*. Stanford University Press, Stanford, 1974.
24 Lamphere L. Anthropology: a review essay. *Signs* **2**, 612, 1977.
25 Rapp R. Anthropology: a review essay. *Signs* 4, 497, 1979.
26 Atkinson J. M. Anthropology: a review essay. *Signs* 8, 236, 1982.
27 Moore H. L. *Feminism and Anthropology*. University of Minnesota Press, Minneapolis, 1988.
28 Bleier R. *Science and Gender: A Critique of Biology and Its Theories on Women*. Pergamon Press, New York, 1984.
29 Fausto-Sterling A. *Myths of Gender: Biological Theories about Women and Men*. Basic Books, New York, 1985.
30 Sayers J. *Biological Politics: Feminist and Anti-Feminist Perspectives*. Tavistock Publications, New York, 1982.
31 Lowe M. and Hubbard R. *Women's Nature: Rationalizations of Inequality*. Pergamon Press, New York, 1983.
32 Hubbard R., Henifin M. S. and Fried B. (Eds) *Biological Woman: The Convenient Myth*. Schenkman, Cambridge, 1982.
33 Tobach E. and Rosoff B. (Eds) *Genes and Gender* Vols 1–4. Gordian Press, New York, 1978.
34 Harding S. *The Science Question in Feminism*. Cornell University Press, Ithaca, 1986.
35 Schiebinger L. *The Mind Has No Sex: Women in the Origin of Modern Science*. Harvard University Press, Cambridge, 1989.
36 Ehrenreich B. and English D. *For Her Own Good: 150 Years of Experts' Advice to Women*. Doubleday, New York, 1979.
37 Barker-Benfield G. J. *The Horrors of the Half-Known Life*. Harper and Row, New York, 1976.
38 Haraway D. *Primate Visions: Gender, Race and Nature in the World of Modern Science*. Routledge, New York, 1989.
39 Jordanova L. J. *Sexual Visions: Images of Gender in Science and Medicine between the Eighteenth and Twentieth Centuries*. University of Wisconsin Press, Madison, 1989.
40 Keller E. F. *Reflections on Gender and Science*. Yale University Press, New Haven, 1984.
41 Harding S. and Hintikka M. (Eds) *Discovering Reality: Feminist Perspectives on Epistemology, Metaphysics, Methodology and Philosophy of Science*. Reidel, Dordrecht, 1983.
42 Rubin G. The traffic in women: notes on the 'political economy' of sex. In *Toward an Anthropology of Women* (Edited by Reiter R.), p. 157. Monthly Review Press, New York, 1975.
43 Rubin G. Thinking sex. In *Pleasure and Danger: Exploring Female Sexuality*. (Edited by Vance C. S.), p. 267. Routledge & Kegan Paul, New York, 1984.
44 Foucault M. *The History of Sexuality*. Pantheon, New York, 1978.
45 McIntosh M. The homosexual role. *Social Problems* 16, 182, 1968.
46 Sahli N. Smashing: women's relationships before the fall. *Chrysalis* 8, 17, 1979.
47 Rupp L. "Imagine my surprise": women's relationships in mid-twentieth century America. *Frontiers* 5, 1980.
48 Faderman L. *Surpassing the Love of Men*. New York, 1981.
49 Rubin G. Introduction to *A Woman Appeared to Me* by Renee Vivien. Naiad Press, Weatherby Lake, Missouri, 1979.
50 Herdt G. *Guardians of the Flutes*. McGraw Hill, New York, 1981.
51 Herdt G. Semen transaction in Sambia culture. In *Ritualized Homosexuality in Melanesia* (Edited by Herdt G.), p. 167. University of California Press, Berkeley, 1984.
52 Herdt G. *The Sambia: Ritual and Gender in New Guinea*. Holt, Rinehardt, Winston, New York, 1987.

53 Plummer K. (Ed.) *The Making of the Modern Homosexual*. Hutchinson, London, 1981.
54 D'Emilio J. *Sexual Politics, Sexual Communities*. University of Chicago Press, Chicago, 1983.
55 Bray A. *Homosexuality in Renaissance England*. Gay Men's Press, London, 1982.
56 Newton E. The mythic mannish lesbian: Radclyffe Hall and the new woman. *Signs* 9, 567, 1984.
57 Davis M. and Kennedy E. Oral history and the study of sexuality in the lesbian community: Buffalo, New York, 1940–1960. *Feminist Studies* 12, 7, 1986.
58 Vicinus M. "They wonder to which sex I belong": the historical roots of the modern lesbian identity. In *Homosexuality, Which Homosexuality?* [17], p. 171.
59 Gerard K. and Hekma G. (Eds) *The Pursuit of Sodomy: Male Homosexuality in Renaissance and Enlightenment Europe. Journal of Homosexuality* 16, [special issue], 1988.
60 Peiss C. 'Charity girls' and city pleasures: historical notes on working class sexuality. In *Powers of Desire* [11], p. 74.
61 Peiss C. *Cheap Amusements: Working Women and Leisure in Turn-of-the-Century New York*. Temple University Press, Philadelphia, 1986.
62 Stansell C. *City of Women: Sex and Class in New York, 1789–1860*. New York, 1986.
63 Trimberger E. K. Feminism, men and modern love: Greenwich Village, 1900–1925. In *Powers of Desire* [11], p. 131.
64 Katz J. The invention of heterosexuality. *Socialist Review* 20, 7, 1990.
65 Walkowitz J. R. *Prostitution and Victorian Society: Women, Class, and the State*. Cambridge University Press, Cambridge, 1980.
66 Bristow E. J. *Vice and Vigilance: Purity Movements in Britain since 1700*. Rowman and Littlefield, New Jersey, 1977.
67 Pivar D. *Purity Crusade: Sexual Morality and Social Control 1868–1900*. Greenwood Press, Connecticut, 1972.
68 Brandt A. M. *No Magic Bullet: A Social History of Venereal Disease in the United States since 1880*. Oxford University Press, New York, 1985.
69 Kendrick W. *The Secret Museum*. Viking, New York, 1987.
70 Gordon L. *Woman's Body, Woman's Right: A Social History of Birth Control in America*. Penguin, New York, 1974.
71 There is no suggestion here that the most radical forms of social construction theory are necessarily the best, although the exercise of totally deconstructing one of the most essential categories, sexuality, often has an electrifying and energizing effect on one's thinking. Whether this degree of deconstruction can be plausibly maintained is another question.
72 Ford C. S. and Beach F. A. *Patterns of Sexual Behavior*. Harper and Row, New York, 1951.
73 Minturn L., Grosse M. and Haider S. Culture patterning of sexual beliefs and behavior. *Ethnology* 8, 301, 1969.
74 Broude G. J. and Greene S. J. Cross-cultural codes on twenty sexual attitudes and practices. *Ethnology* 15, 409, 1976.
75 Gray J. P. Cross-cultural factors associated with sexual foreplay. *J. soc. Psychol.* 111, 3, 1980.
76 Frayser S. G. *Varieties of Sexual Experience: An Anthropological Perspective on Human Sexuality*. HRAF Press, New Haven, 1985.
77 Mead M. *Coming of Age in Samoa*. Morrow, New York, 1923.
78 Malinowski B. *The Sexual Life of Savages in North-Western Melanesia*. Halcyon House, New York, 1941 (orig. edition 1929).
79 Schapera I. *Married Life in an African Tribe*. Sheridan House, New York, 1941.

80 Goodenough W. H. Premarital freedom on Truk: theory and practice. *Am. Anthrop.* 51, 615, 1949.
81 Berndt R. M. and Berndt C. *Sexual Behavior in Western Arnhem Land.* Viking Fund, New York, 1951.
82 Levine R. A. Gusii sex offenses: a study in social control. *Am. Anthrop.* 61, 965, 1959.
83 Howard A. and Howard I. Premarital sex and social control among the Rotumans. *Am. Anthrop.* 66, 266, 1964.
84 Davenport W. Sexual patterns and their regulation in a society of the South West Pacific. In *Sex and Behavior* (Edited by Beach F.), p. 164. Wiley, New York, 1965.
85 Suggs R. C. *Marquesan Sexual Behavior.* Harcourt, Brace and World, New York, 1966.
86 Lessa W. A. Sexual behavior. In *Ulithi: A Design for Living*, pp. 77–92. Holt, Rinehardt, Winston, New York, 1966.
87 Marshall D. S. and Suggs R. C. (Eds) *Human Sexual Behavior.* Prentice Hall, Englewood Cliffs, New Jersey, 1972.
88 Heider K. G. Dani sexuality: a low-energy system. *Man* 11, 188, 1976.
89 Marshall D. S. Too much in Mangaia. In *Readings in Human Sexuality: Contemporary Perspectives* (Edited by Gordon C. and Johnson G.), p. 217. Holt Rinehardt Winston: New York, 1976.
90 Bateson G. Sex and culture. *Ann. NY Acad. Sci.* XLVII, 647, 1947.
91 Murdock G. P. The social regulation of sexual behavior. In *Psychosexual Development in Health and Disease* (Edited by Hoch P. H. and Zubin J.), p. 256. Grune and Stratton, New York, 1949.
92 Honigman J. J. An anthropological approach to sex. *Social Problems* 2, 7, 1954.
93 Gebhard P. H. Human sexual behavior: a summary statement. In *Readings in Human Sexuality: Contemporary Perspectives* (Edited by Gordon C. and Johnson G.), p. 95. Harper and Row, New York, 1976.
94 Heider's work on the Dani is an exception in regard to conceptualizing variable levels of sexual energy.
95 Mead M. Cultural determinants of sexual behaviors. In *Sex and Internal Secretions* (Edited by Young W. C.), p. 1433. Williams and Wilkins, Philadelphia, 1961.
96 A different attempt at assimilation is found in the assertion that the debate between essentialists and social constructionists in regard to sexuality is a replay of the nature–nurture controversy. This is a profound misunderstanding of social construction theory.

In nature–nurture debates, researchers are proposing alternative biological or cultural mechanisms to explain phenomena they observe. At present, most observers agree that human behavior is produced by a complex interaction of biological and cultural factors; they differ on the relative weight they assign to each.

Although it might be appropriate to find some similarity between essentialists and the nature camp, to equate social construction to the nurture camp is mistaken. Social construction theory is not simply arguing for cultural causation. In addition and more important, it encourages us to deconstruct and examine the behavior or processes which both nature and nurture camps have reified and want to "explain." Social construction suggests that the object of study deserves at least as much analytic attention as the suspected causal mechanism.
97 Mascia-Lees F. E. (Ed.) *Human Sexuality in Biocultural Perspective. Med. Anthrop.* 11, 1989.
98 Newton E. *Mother Camp: Female Impersonators in America.* University of Chicago Press, Chicago, 1979.
99 Caplan P. (Ed.) *The Cultural Construction of Sexuality.* Tavistock, London, 1987.

100 Davis M. and Kennedy E. The reproduction of butchfem roles: a social constructionist approach. In *Passion and Power* [15], p. 241.
101 Whitehead H. The bow and the burden strap: a new look at institutionalized homosexuality in native North America. In *Sexual Meanings* (Edited by Ortner S. B. and Whitehead H.), p. 80. Cambridge University Press, Cambridge, 1981.
102 Blackwood E. (Ed.) *Anthropology and Homosexuality.* The Haworth Press, New York, 1986.
103 Fry P. Male homosexuality and spirit possession in Brazil. *Journal of Homosexuality* 11, 137, 1985.
104 Carrier J. M. Mexican male bisexuality. *Journal of Homosexuality* 11, 75, 1985.
105 Vance C. S. Negotiating sex and gender in the Attorney General's Commission on Pornography. In *Uncertain Terms: Negotiating Gender in American Culture* (Edited by Ginsburg F. and Tsing A. L.), p. 118. Beacon Press, Boston, 1990.
106 Parker R. *Bodies, Pleasures, and Passions: Sexual Culture in Contemporary Brazil.* Beacon Press, Boston, 1991.
107 Gregor T. *Anxious Pleasures: The Sexual Lives of an Amazonian People.* University of Chicago Press, Chicago, 1985.
108 Cohen C. B. and Mascia-Lees F. E. Lasers in the jungle: reconfiguring questions of human and non-human primate sexuality. *Medical Anthropology* 11, 351, 1989.
109 Mascia-Lees F. R., Tierson F. D. and Relethford J. H. Investigating the biocultural dimensions of human sexual behavior. *Medical Anthropology* 11, 367, 1989.
110 Frayser S. G. Sexual and reproductive relationships: cross-cultural evidence and biosocial implications. *Medical Anthropology* 11, 385, 1989.
111 Perper T. Theories and observations on sexual selection and female choice in human beings. *Medical Anthropology* 11, 409, 1989.
112 Kinsey A., Pomeroy W. and Martin C. E. *Sexual Behavior in the Human Male.* Saunders, Philadelphia, 1948.
113 Kinsey A., Pomeroy W., Martin C. E. and Gebhard R. H. *Sexual Behavior in the Human Female.* Saunders, Philadelphia, 1953.
114 Turner C. F., Miller H. G. and Moses L. E. (Eds) Committee on AIDS Research and the Behavioral, Social and Statistical Sciences. National Research Council *AIDS: Sexual Behavior and Intravenous Drug Use*, Ch. 2. National Academy Press, Washington, D.C., 1989.
115 Booth W. Asking America about its sex life. *Science* 242, 304, 20 Jan. 1989.
116 Booth W. WHO seeks global data on sexual practices. *Science* 244, 418, 28 April 1989.
117 This is not to say that research is not also being conducted by social scientists outside of medical institutions or that social scientists do not also contribute to studies based in medical schools, albeit usually in a lesser role. However, the sheer number of biomedically-oriented population surveys coupled with their large sample sizes and budgets threatens to overshadow and displace sexuality research conducted by less-biomedically oriented investigators. In addition, medical doctors are perceived to speak more authoritatively than social scientists about the body. Given this, increasingly essentialist perspectives which frame sexuality in relation to AIDS as a bodily matter will automatically increase the legitimacy of medical speakers and texts.
118 Gever M. Pictures of sickness: Stuart Marshall's *Bright Eyes*. In Crimp D. (Ed.) *AIDS: Cultural Analysis, Cultural Activism.* MIT Press, Cambridge, 1989.
119 Gilman S. L. *Disease and Representation: Images of Illness from Madness to AIDS.* Cornell University Press, Ithaca, 1988.
120 Feldman D. A. and Johnson T. M. *The Social Dimension of AIDS: Method and Theory.* Praeger, New York, 1986.

121 Gorman E. M. The AIDS Epidemic in San Francisco: Epidemiological and Anthropological Perspectives. In *Anthropology and Epidemiology* (Edited by Janes C., Stall R. and Gifford S.), p. 157. Reidel, Dordrecht, 1986.
122 Bateson M. C. and Goldsby R. *Thinking AIDS: The Social Response to Biological Threat.* Addison-Wesley, Reading, Mass., 1988.
123 Bolton R. The AIDS Pandemic: A Global Emergency. *Med. Anthrop.* 10 [special issue], 1989.
124 Marshall P. A. and Bennett L. A. (Eds) *Culture and Behavior in the AIDS Epidemic. Med. Anthrop. Q.* 4 [special issue], 1990.
125 Parker R. Acquired immunodeficiency syndrome in urban Brazil. *Med. Anthrop. Q.* 1, 155, 1987.
126 Murray S. O. and Payne K. The social classification of AIDS in American epidemiology. *Med. Anthrop. Q.* 10, 115, 1989.
127 Carrier J. M. Sexual behavior and the spread of AIDS in Mexico. *Med. Anthrop.* 10, 129, 1989.
128 Singer M., Flores C., Davison L., Burke G., Castillo Z., Scanlon K. and Rivera M. SIDA: the economic, social and cultural context of AIDS among Latinos. *Med. Anthrop. Q.* 4, 72, 1990.
129 Kane S. AIDS, addiction and condom use: sources of sexual risk for heterosexual women. *J. Sex Res.* 27, 427, 1990.
130 Asencio M. Puerto Rican adolescents playing by the rules. Unpublished paper presented at the American Anthropological Association annual meeting, 1990.
131 Hawkeswood W. G. "I'm a Black gay man who just happens to be gay": the sexuality of Black gay men. Unpublished paper presented at the American Anthropological Association annual meeting, 1990.
132 Patton C. *Sex and Germs.* South End Press, Boston, 1985.
133 Altman D. *AIDS in the Mind of America: The Social, Political, and Psychological Impact of a New Epidemic.* Anchor Press/Doubleday, New York, 1986.
134 Crimp D. (Ed.) *AIDS: Cultural Analysis, Cultural Activism.* MIT Press, Cambridge, 1989.
135 Watney S. *Policing Desire: Pornography, AIDS, and the Media.* University of Minnesota Press, Minneapolis, 1987.
136 Grover J. Z. AIDS: keywords. In Crimp D. (Ed.) [134], p. 17.
137 Treichler P. A. AIDS, homophobia and biomedical discourse: an epidemic of signification. In Crimp D. (Ed.) [134], 31, 1987.
138 Gilman S. AIDS and syphilis: the iconography of disease. In Crimp D. (Ed.) [134], p. 87.
139 Watney S. The spectacle of AIDS. In Crimp D. (Ed.) [134], p. 71.
140 Treichler P. A. AIDS, gender, and biomedical discourse: current contests for meaning. In *AIDS: The Burden of History* (Edited by Fee E. and Fox D. M.), p. 190. University of California Press, Berkeley, 1988.
141 Juhasz A. The contained threat: women in mainstream AIDS documentary. *J. Sex Res.* 27, 25, 1990.
142 Williamson J. Every virus tells a story: the meanings of HIV and AIDS. In *Taking Liberties: AIDS and Cultural Politics* (Edited by Carter E. and Watney S.), p. 69. Serpents Tail, London, 1989.

2

Biological Determinism and Homosexuality

Bonnie Spanier

"Why Are Men and Women Different? It isn't just upbringing. New studies show they are born that way."

(Gorman)

"Is Homosexuality Born or Bred? Two new studies seem to find the origins of homosexuality in genetics, not parenting."

(Gelman)

The recent upsurge in scientific claims about biological bases for male-female differences (including assumed characteristics such as "female intuition") and for differences in sexual orientation (cast as either homosexual or heterosexual) comes from some unexpected quarters. Openly gay or pro-gay scientists have joined traditionally conservative biological determinists and are apparently impelled by reasons ranging from simply feeling they were born gay to recognizing the strength of legal arguments that if gayness is inborn rather than a lifestyle choice, people cannot be blamed for something over which they have no control.[1]

Despite its emergence from worthwhile motives promoting gay rights, the optimistic reception of such biological theories downplays two key histories: first, the use of biological determinism to support racism, sexism, class bias, ethnocentrism, and heterosexism – where difference is used to form a hierarchy of superior-inferior values that justify undeserved advantages for some over others; and second, the trail of bad science associated with biological-determinist claims (Gould; Lewontin, Rose, and Kamin among many).

In *Myths of Gender*, feminist scientist and activist Anne Fausto-Sterling offers a detailed analysis of the science behind biological determinist assertions about sex differences in ability and cognition. She shows that such purportedly scientific claims work with predominating theories of the time but *consistently and with few exceptions* are abandoned in the face of conflicting evidence, inadequacies in theory, nonreproducible results, or major sociopolitical events (such as the Nazis' use of biological determinist theories to support mass murder) which discredit assumptions that frame the social and scientific significance of questions. Many of the purported explanations for sex differences have flip-flopped when new data prove the first theory wrong, as occurred regarding theories about the effect differences in lateralization of the brain.[2] How and why does this process continue to repeat itself?

If self-policing and self-correcting norms of traditional science were sufficient to detect — and correct – this kind of "bad science" (science that does not meet the criteria of accepted scientific method), we would not have to confront the long and tragic history of biological determinist claims about differences deemed significant in our society. It is up to feminist educators to provide the tools for analyzing scientists' findings and for understanding the science in its social and political context – no matter what the political stance of the scientists involved.

Corpus-Callosum Sex Differences Research: A Cautionary Tale

On January 20, 1992, the cover of *Time* magazine featured the sensational announcement I quoted to open this essay, proclaiming that scientific studies show men and women are different because they are "born that way." With a disconcerted expression, the girl on the cover watches a boy make a muscle, although it is hardly any different from what hers would be. The magazine's feature article shows a diagram of a human brain with three regions – frontal lobe, corpus callosum, and hypothalamus – pinpointed in relation to sex or sexuality differences. Despite the absurdity of using images of hats and red lips to represent inborn and fixed characteristics of maleness and femaleness respectively, the caption over the brain diagram points to "Differences That Are All in the Head." Scientific studies are summarized: normal girls prefer dolls to trucks and sports cars, while girls with higher levels of prenatal testosterone play with those male trucks, cars, and even Lincoln Logs *just as much as normal boys*! The article asserts that women's "often wider" corpus callosum may even account for "woman's intuition."

It is of particular significance that the issue in this case is sex differences research. Furthermore, a second claim printed in the *Time* article ties sex differences to differences in "sexual behavior" or sexual orientation. A group of nerve cells in the anterior hypothalamus are reported to be twice as large in heterosexual men than in women or homosexual men, supporting "the idea that varying hormone levels before birth may immutably stamp the developing brain in one erotic direction or another" (45). I will return later to the issue of biological determination of sexual orientation/preference, since the trail of sex differences claims about the brain leads to Simon LeVay's research on the hypothalamus.

Time's first claim, that scientific studies ("often") show a size difference between the corpus callosum in men and women, provides an exemplary case that sheds light on the problems endemic in the current process of scientific knowledge production and on what gets to count as scientific truth (and for whom). We can ask if this is simply a case of bad science reporting by the popular media – or is it bad science? Only going back to the original scientific articles and understanding them in their social and scientific contexts will provide answers on which we can make our own judgments.

In 1982, C. DeLacoste-Utamsing and R. L. Holloway published an article in *Science* magazine, a major multidisciplinary science journal and the publication of the largest US organization of scientists, the American Association for the Advancement of Science. The article reported a significant sex difference (sexual dimorphism) in the size of the corpus callosum, a sheet of nerves linking the right and left halves of the brain. The number of subjects (fourteen) was small, and the authors did not provide sufficient information to show whether the selection was random and took into account factors known to affect the corpus callosum, such as handedness and age. This means that the research was inadequate to be considered scientifically valid. Holloway himself admitted to a newspaper reporter that his small sample size bothered him, but that the results were too "intriguing" to wait for more reliable data (Bleier, "Decade," 192–3).

Individual scientists are not the only ones to be blamed in these instances. The trusted checks and balances of peer review and editorial boards (in this case, the board and the editor of *Science*) sometimes fail to rule out what should be recognized as bad science. Here, cultural values and beliefs that shape the predominating explanatory frameworks in science hold sway over scientific evidence.

The inadequacies of the DeLacoste-Holloway paper *and* the long tradition of invalid and contradictory science in the field of brain and behavior prompted the (now deceased) neurophysiologist Ruth Bleier to write a review essay for *Science* that critiqued not only DeLacoste-Holloway but whole areas of research on sex differences and the brain (Bleier, "Decade"). One *Science* reviewer supported publication of the essay, while the other simply rejected Bleier's argument, which emphasized the importance of environmental factors in shaping observed sex differences in behavior without denying the possibility of biological influences. What sounds like a balanced and open-minded perspective on the basis of evidence Bleier cited in her review was instead taken as bias against the prevailing paradigm in brain and behavior research.

Given the split opinion of the peer reviewers, the decision to reject the review essay had to be made at the level of the editor and/or editorial board of *Science* magazine. Bleier's analysis of her experience as a feminist scientist foregrounds the relationships among individual scientists, their peers, the gateways to publication, the hierarchies of journals, and predominant and alternative explanatory frameworks and values. Bleier helps us understand how the current science system tends to support even scientifically inadequate research within prevailing paradigms.

Equally disturbing is *Science*'s rejection of original research by Bleier and her colleagues on the corpus callosum and gender. In contrast to DeLacoste and Holloway, Bleier and her colleagues studied thirty-nine subjects (instead of fourteen) and controlled for age and left- or right-handedness, factors known to influence the size of the corpus callosum. Their study – like three others – failed to find sex-related differences in that part of the brain (Bleier, Houston, and Byrne; Demeter, Ringo, and Doty; Weber and Weis; Witelson).[3] Despite the the better construction of these studies, DeLacoste and Holloway's incorrect conclusion that the corpus callosum is larger in women than in men is widely cited, as in the *Time* issue quoted in the epigraph. The field of sex differences research is framed as an interest in *differences*. Studies with "null findings," results showing no effect or no difference, are inherently of less interest, while even questionable studies showing difference are accorded a place of scientific respect.

Furthermore, the paradigm that frames most research on sex differences in the field of brain and behavior is inherently distorted, as it is based on the belief that hormones labeled male and female determine male-specific and female-specific behaviors in humans (and assumes those behaviors are different). Calling hormones "male" and "female" is inaccurate and misleading, since both types are found in human males and females and since the hormones affect many things beside the development of secondary sexual characteristics (Spanier, chap. 5; Bleier). The current theory assumes that male hormones in the fetus create a male brain, while the absence of male hormones creates a female brain (Bleier; Burr). The maleness of the male brain then determines male-typical behaviors.

That is why feminist education must include training in how to evaluate original scientific research and the paradigms on which they are based. Close critical readings of papers published in the field of brain and behavior can identify studies whose conclusions are invalid. In addition, beyond obviously bad science, apparently sound studies of the brain and behavior often contradict each other. Contradictory findings often signal problems in the conceptualization of the studies involved (faulty questions; inadequately controlled design) and should prompt researchers to be cautious about drawing conclusions. When we find scientists failing to be cautious, we are documenting how the norms of the scientific community, including the values shaping decisions about when to give more leeway on what is labeled valid science, play a significant role in perpetuating bad science as well as Social Darwinism in its new incarnation.

The second epigraph brings us to another biological determinist claim about the brain and sex and requires a close critique of recent scientific research.

Simon LeVay's Research

Simon LeVay's research is another useful example of the dynamic of science and politics, in this case, politics supporting gay rights.[4] LeVay was a neurobiologist at the Salk Institute in California (a highly reputable research institute) when he published an article in *Science* that put another twist on the "nature vs. nurture" debate. For at least a hundred years, claims have been made that homosexuals are biologically different from heterosexuals, so the claim is not new. What is new is the context in which the claim is made, a context in which a combination of gay and lesbian liberation movements and the AIDS crisis have forced greater acceptance of homosexual activity to a limited but nonetheless considerable degree. Of great significance here is the fact that LeVay is an openly gay scientist, and that this information was revealed in an issue of *Science* subsequent to the article's publication. (LeVay may well be the first scientist to be identified as gay in *Science* (Barinaga).) Along with many other supporters of gay rights, he sees the "scientific" evidence of a biological determinant of gayness as a crucial factor in preventing psychiatrists, lawmakers, and citizens in general from slipping back into believing that homosexuality is a mental illness – or that it is criminal or immoral.[5]

In August of 1991 *Science* magazine published an article by LeVay entitled "A Difference in Hypothalamic Structure between Heterosexual and Homosexual Men." The article claims that one of four particular groups of cells (called INAH 1, 2, 3, and 4 for the interstitial nuclei of the anterior hypothalamus) of the brain was twice as large in heterosexual men as in homosexual men or in women (no sexual orientation specified). From that observation, LeVay concludes in the highlighted abstract that precedes the paper: "This finding indicates that INAH [3] is dimorphic with sexual orientation, at least in men, and suggests that sexual orientation has a biological substrate" (1034). LeVay chose this area of the brain by (questionably) correlating sexual activity and brain studies on monkeys ("the medial zone of the anterior hypothalamus has been implicated in the generation of male-typical sexual behavior" [1034]) with studies comparing the size of INAH groups 1–4 in human males and females. Working with human brains, Laura Allen, a postdoctoral researcher in Roger Gorski's laboratory (known for work on sex differences in the human brain), had compared four groups of cells (INAH 1–4) in the anterior part of the hypothalamus and had found that two of them, INAH 2 and INAH 3, were larger in men than in women (Allen et al.).

LeVay's originality lies in proposing that the larger size of INAH 2 and INAH 3 correlates with sexual orientation – "desire for women" – rather than with gender – maleness – as the previous studies had done. He summarizes and postulates at the same time, "Thus, these two nuclei could be involved in the generation of male-typical sexual behavior" (1035), asserting that brain structures may cause certain behaviors. He explains his hypothesis:

> I tested the idea that one or both of these nuclei exhibit a size dimorphism, not with sex, but with sexual orientation. Specifically, I hypothesized that INAH 2 or INAH 3 is large in individuals sexually oriented toward women (heterosexual men and homosexual women) and small in individuals sexually oriented toward men (heterosexual women and homosexual men) (1035).

Not only does LeVay's thesis propose that the difference in size is due not to gender difference as previously claimed but to sexual orientation difference, but he also asserts that the size difference proves a biological basis for sexual orientation. The qualification, "at least in men" (1034), immediately pinpoints a primary problem with LeVay's study as he conceives it. To test his theory, he should be comparing large enough numbers in (at least) *four* categories: heterosexual men, homosexual men, heterosexual women, and homosexual women. Note, too, that while Laura Allen's work found sexual dimorphism for *both* INAH 2 and 3, LeVay points only to INAH 3 in his conclusion. What do we make of this? A close analysis and critique reveals even more serious problems with the construction of the study leading to LeVay's claims.

Close Analysis and Critique of Scientific Research

To analyze validity, we can examine and critique a number of points in the construction of any scientific claim: the *explanatory framework and premises* on which it is based, the *methods and design* of the study, the *presentation and manipulation of data and conclusions* drawn, and the *interpretations of the data and conclusions.*

When the *premises* on which a study is based are faulty or highly questionable, the question being asked in the study is flawed. This occurs, more broadly, when the paradigm within which the study is conducted – the *explanatory framework* that guides the original question and the approach taken to answer it – is defective or questionable (Longino). In this case, measurements may be correct but whole conclusions may be questioned or deemed invalid. The framework or paradigm of an area of science can also influence the results obtained, as Stephen Jay Gould has shown in remeasuring the size of skulls studied by an eminent scientist in the nineteenth century.

Research results can be similarly faulty when a study is poorly set up, with improper or too few controls, with an inadequate sample size, with a nonrepresentative or nonrandom sample. In this case, the *methods and experimental design* are often inadequate for scientific validity.

Data can also be manipulated improperly and misrepresented. For example, the effects of increasing dosages of a drug may be presented numerically but not displayed on a graph, when graphing would show a dose-response curve inconsistent with a study's conclusions. In this and other ways, the *conclusions stated about the data* can be wrong or limited in ways not addressed by the author. Often the conclusions summarized in the abstract are simplified or overstated and are not supported by data buried in tables and diagrams.

The interpretations *drawn from research conclusions* can also be highly suspect. Here the premises on which the study is based, including previous research cited and the explanatory framework, play a big role.

By analyzing any study we can locate where and how the authors make judgments affected by biases, and then we can draw our own conclusions about the limitations of the study as well as the ways that scientists incorporate their biases into their work – and how that affects what we can learn from scientific research.

Deconstructing LeVay's Claims

Several premises are embedded in LeVay's introduction, in addition to the jump from studies of monkeys to humans. (1) The anterior hypothalamus in the brain exerts some control over sexual orientation in humans. (2) Size differences in one or more clusters of cells recognizable within the anterior hypothalamus of humans reflect differences in influence over sexual orientation, that is, cell cluster size somehow determines sexual behavior. This premise assumes that variations in INAH 2 and 3 are due to the difference that matters to LeVay – sexual orientation in men – rather than to other factors affecting the size of those cell clusters. (3) There exists such a thing as "male-typical sexual behavior" in humans, it differs from some other unnamed behavior, and it is *the same thing* as "sexual orientation, . . . the direction of sexual feelings or behavior toward members of one's own or the opposite sex" (1034). As we critique this premise, we reveal LeVay's assumption *conflating sexual orientation with gender* through the concept of "male-typical sexual behavior," that is, unspecified behavior based on the *gender* of the persons toward whom an individual is oriented ("sexually oriented toward women" or toward men). (4) Sexual orientation is based on biological influences that are specific to male and female identities.

Other premises or assumptions built into LeVay's explanatory framework include a dichotomy of "typical sexual behavior," oriented either to women (male-typical) or to men (unspecified). The author sidesteps the relationship of those concepts to actual sexual behavior, although he refers in his later discussion to insertive and receptive roles among gay men While LeVay seems to be challenging the significance of *gender* (he uses "sex") in brain differences, his framework and premises strongly depend on bipolar gender categories.

LeVay's introduction setting the framework for his approach moves quickly through traditional explanations of sexual behavior (from the fields of psychology, anthropology, and religion/ethics) to "the biological basis of sexual orientation," citing the failures of methods involving studies of chromosomes, hormones, and brain structures to "establish any consistent differences between homosexual and heterosexual individuals" (1034).

He has chosen the anterior hypothalamus as the "likely biological substrate for sexual orientation" because in nonhuman primates, damaging that part of the brain "impair[s] heterosexual behavior without eliminating sexual drive" (1034). The studies he cites assume that the "heterosexual behavior" of monkeys is the same thing as "male-typical" sexual behavior, that is, mounting of females by male monkeys. Uncited is the evidence that mounting or presenting, whether in monkeys or mice, is not sex-specific. Females mount males and other females, as males also mount other males (Bleier 87, 174). The edges of "male" and "female" categories of behavior are blurred in monkeys and mice, as they also are in humans. "Sexual drive" in the studies LeVay cites means masturbation, a conclusion that is already somewhat questionable given the constructed and ambiguous nature of the terms "male-typical sexual behavior" and "sex drive."

What is this distinctively male-typical sexual behavior that distinguishes heterosexual men from heterosexual women such that the larger size of a region of the brain "could be involved in *the generation of* male-typical sexual behavior" (1035; my emphasis)? What does "typical male sex behavior, such as attraction to females" (Nimmons 66, quoting LeVay) mean? Does the person – male or female – desiring women exhibit some male-typical sexual behavior by wanting to insert a penis into a vagina? Where does that leave lesbians? Is desiring to insert a penis into an anus very different from wishing to insert one into a vagina? Similar or different for whom? In an interview in *Discover* LeVay states:

> I am saying that gay men have a woman's INAH 3 – they've got a woman's brain in that particular part. In a brain region regulating sexual attraction, it would make sense that what you see in gay men is like what you see in heterosexual women. But people get nervous, as if I'm painting gay men as women in disguise. (Nimmons 66)

LeVay's scientific article and comments made in interviews make it very clear that the *framework* within which LeVay conceptualizes the causes of sexual orientation derives from a belief that specific parts of our brains control our behaviors, including those related to sex. The reification of complex, dynamic processes (such as intelligence) and the imputation of causality to physical parts of the body (such as the cerebral cortex or sets of genes) are common errors in the long history of biological determinist claims (Hubbard; Lewontin, Rose, and Kamin). To support such claims, much evidence is ignored, such as a functioning medical student who has only 10% of his cerebral cortex (Fausto-Sterling, chap. 2).

The deterministic view of the brain's relation to behavior also often assumes that brain structures influence behavior in a one-way, cause-and-effect direction, an assumption utilized throughout LeVay's article until the author discusses some of the limitations of his study. At that point he notes that his results *do not* determine whether different cell cluster sizes are the *cause or the consequence* of certain sexual behavior ("the results do not allow one to decide if the size of INAH 3 in an individual is the cause or the consequence of that individual's sexual orientation, or if the size of INAH 3 and sexual orientation co-vary under the influence of some third, unidentified variable" [1036]). Nonetheless, LeVay offers evidence from studies of rats and a "comparable hypothalamic nucleus, the sexually dimorphic nucleus of the preoptic area" (comparable because it is supposedly sexually dimorphic!) to support the theory that hypothalamic size (in rats, correlated with *sex*) is fixed by prenatal hormones and does not change with experimental changes in hormone levels (1036).

In the same breath LeVay cites another study of rats: "even among normal male rats there is a variability in the size of [the region in the preoptic area] that is strongly correlated with the amount of male-typical sexual behavior shown by the animals" (1036) – suggesting that nerve clusters may change size as a consequence of behavior. Nonetheless, based on these rat studies, LeVay asserts: "Although the validity of the comparison between species is *uncertain*, it seems *more likely* that in humans, too, the size of INAH 3 is established early in life and later influences sexual behavior than that the reverse is true" (1036; my emphasis). Why does it seem more likely than not? LeVay does not provide sufficient evidence to support that judgment. Indeed, he ignores the implication of the study he himself cites, that the size of the cluster of brain cells of interest to him in rats varies perhaps as a result (not cause) of sexual behavior. LeVay also neglects to cite studies showing that behavior *can* affect the size of brain cells. For example, the hypothalamus cells in male African cichlid fish change size significantly when their mating behavior changes (Angier), results that challenge a one-way cause-and-effect relationship between brain structure and behavior. LeVay's *interpretation* of the difference he claims to have found is highly questionable. Despite studies showing the influences of behavior on brain structures, LeVay's approach is the predominant one in the field of brain and behavior. In that context, it is apparent that the shortcomings of his study and his arguments were not deemed important enough to stand in the way of the article's publication.

How comparable are the parts of the rats' and the humans' brains in relation to behaviors? Then again, how comparable is the male-typical sexual behavior (mounting) of rats to the homosexual and heterosexual behaviors of humans? The jump from one species to another, arguing for comparable behaviors and comparable biological bases, is a common sleight of hand in comparative behavior claims, but the latter do not hold up to close examination. Humans in particular, although not exclusively, exhibit dramatic changes in behavior across different cultures and times, and within the same lifetime as well. Gender-specific behavior and sexual behavior are particularly elastic, as many women's lives spanning the women's movement attest.

What are typical homosexual and heterosexual behaviors in humans? Is masturbation a homosexual act since it is same-sex behavior? If masturbation is considered a basic manifestation of our sex drive, as the studies of monkeys cited by LeVay assume, then homosexual activity would seem to be a basic or natural aspect of human sexuality, making heterosexual activity a variant thereof.

LeVay assumes the validity of two categories of biological difference based on sexual orientation, categories based on the gender of the desired person, acknowledging and at the same time sidestepping the issue of differences for same-sex attraction of different genders as well as the issue of combined same- and different-sex attraction (simplified into the term "bisexual"). His assertion that simplification is sometimes needed to make scientific progress is one of the key value judgments he makes that affect his willingness to stretch the boundaries of valid science.

Assumptions built into the categories (heterosexual men, homosexual men, presumably heterosexual women) LeVay chose for comparison raise fundamental problems with respect to the *experimental design* of this research. LeVay obtained brain tissue from forty-one individuals who had died in hospitals in two states. Nineteen were self-identified homosexual men (and a self-identified bisexual LeVay decided to include); sixteen were men labeled heterosexual because they did not self-identify as gay, and six women were presumed to be heterosexual simply because their sexual orientation was not known.[6] The number of women in the study is simply too small to be valid, while the sample numbers as a whole are so small that any change one way or the other would be statistically significant. Equally problematic is LeVay's temerity in classifying both men and women as heterosexual simply because they were not otherwise identified. Indeed, to support his classifying all unknowns as heterosexual, LeVay uses the 1948 Kinsey report (!) showing "the numerical preponderance of heterosexual men in the population" (1036 n. 7). This in itself should have disqualified the article from publication, since the study purports to compare three categories, assignment to which was suspect for the majority of subjects.

Even if we had records of every subject's self-identified sexual orientation, however, the designations must be suspect, at least for purportedly heterosexual individuals. Many studies, both anecdotal and quantitative, show that many heterosexual men and women are actively engaged in homosexual activities (Miller; Fay et al.). And there is no reason to exclude the possibility that some who self-identify as homosexual hide their heterosexual activities from their peers.

Indeed, the categories of "homosexual" and "heterosexual" are ambiguous and often arbitrary. LeVay does not clearly distinguish between identity and behavior. For example, why did he include the identified bisexual in the homosexual male category, if at all? The paper acknowledges only that insufficient "information about the sexuality of the subjects . . . limits the ability to make correlations between brain structure and the diversity of sexual behavior that undoubtedly exists within the homosexual and the heterosexual populations" (1036).

This attempt to classify sexual orientation into two categories, sometimes with a nod toward another "type" – the bisexual – is common in the scientific literature, as is the absence of attention to variations in sexual activity throughout a lifetime (Spanier, chap. 5). Cultural influences, such as compulsory heterosexuality, on sexual behavior – or, more often, on acceptable sexual behavior – are generally ignored in biological studies of sexuality. Historical contexts, too, such as changes in the meaning of homosexual and heterosexual activities and identities (cf. "a homosexual" to "a person engaging in homosexual activities"), are passed over in silence. Are Plato and his privileged and married male peers of ancient Greece (see Foucault) the same "homosexuals" in scientific terms as LeVay or the married male scientist whose strongest sexual feelings are for men? And what of gender, race, class, ethnicity, age in influencing the construction and meaning of sexual experience? According to LeVay's definitions, heterosexual women and homosexual men share the same sexual orientation because they desire men. It is unclear whether the corollary is that heterosexual men and homosexual women share the same sexual desire for women. In this schema, what does the brain look like in the man who desires young children, male or female, or the individual who desires shoes? The more we try to take many real individuals across histories and across cultures into account in this scientific theory, the more oversimplification becomes a major conceptual error.

The LeVay study's experimental design displays a number of important flaws, such as that revealed in the author's own comments about the "difficulty in precisely defining the neurons belonging to INAH 3 [with the result that] no attempt [was] made to measure cell number or density" (1036). Some variables are addressed, but the study simply did not have sufficient numbers in it (1037, n. 12). In a subsequent issue of *Science* a letter was published that criticized the magazine itself for publishing "such preliminary results" from a study of "questionable design with subjects drawn from a small, highly selected, and nonrepresentative sample" (Carrier and Gellert 630). LeVay's response sidesteps this valid criticism and addresses another issue raised, that of "misclassification bias" and ambiguity: "I may well have over simplified the problem in my study, but sometimes such oversimplification is necessary, to make progress in a novel field" (LeVay, Letter 63). Anyone looking up LeVay's paper will not be directed to the critical letters published months later.

Then, too, few science writers bother to read and analyze the original science papers they refer to in popular media articles. To his credit, Chandler Burr's "Homosexuality and Biology" in *Atlantic Monthly* does quote from LeVay's article and does note some inconsistencies in brain research. But Burr does not catch, for example, a major inconsistency between LeVay's data on INAH2 and that of Allen et al., the major study on which LeVay builds his case for the significance of INAH 3 (Burr 55). Recall that LeVay looked at the four INAH cell groups studied by Allen et al., conjecturing that the sex differences they reported for INAH 2 and 3 might be due not to gender but to sexual orientation. LeVay found a size difference only for INAH 3, and he briefly discusses the contradiction between his results and those of Allen et al. for INAH 2 (1035). Calling it a "failure to replicate" the finding of sexual dimorphism in INAH2, LeVay argues that this failure may be due to the "relatively young age" of his subjects, a suggestion supported by Allen et al.'s report that no sex difference was found "when women of reproductive age were compared with men of similar ages" (1035). At the very least, age may be a significant variable in the relative size of INAH 2, but why not for INAH 3? How can LeVay's explanatory framework account for the fact that sex/uality dimorphism is present in one group of cells at one time in the life cycle and at another time in another cell group? Such variations and inconsistent results are simply swept aside with assertions unsupported by data.

Another example of LeVay's selectivity in choosing similar studies is found buried in note 10: "INAH 1 is the same as the nucleus named the 'sexually dimorphic nucleus' and reported to be larger in men than in women [D. F. Swaab and E. Fiers, *Science* 228, 1112 (1985)]. My results support the contention by Allen et al. (6) that this nucleus is not dimorphic" (1037). Obviously, the result of Swaab and Fliers's study conflicted with those of Allen's et al. on INAH 1. LeVay simply notes that his study agrees with the latter; his data on INAH 2, in contrast, does not (which is explained away by age). While this may seem like a travesty to those unfamiliar with how science is actually done, it is not unusual at all to have seriously conflicting results in certain areas of research, brain and behavior for one (Fausto-Sterling, *Myths*). For some scientists such contradictory results signal poor researchers, a poorly conceptualized research design, or a deeply flawed explanatory framework. For others, particularly those who accept the explanatory framework of a whole field, the uncertainties are the price paid for investigating complex or ill-understood phenomena. Clearly the peer reviewers and *Science*'s editorial board allowed LeVay considerable leeway in his research design, explanatory framework, interpretations, and conclusions.

Science and Politics: What Do Feminists Need to Know?

LeVay's research is touted on the cover of the March 1994 issue of *Discover*, a popular science magazine, and he has been cast into the public eye as a gay hero in science: "Sex and the Brain: One Brave Scientist Is Exposing the Link." I do not fault Simon LeVay for trying to make a contribution to understanding sexuality and for changing his life dramatically from quiet scientist to public activist, revealing his long relationship with a doctor who died in 1990 from AIDS. LeVay has co-founded the West Hollywood Institute of Gay and Lesbian Education and has been attending many of the classes. I welcome other scientists who, like myself, have changed their lives to join science and politics to make a better world. But LeVay's work is scientifically inadequate, and he has not researched or taken seriously the problems rife in the field of brain and behavior, particularly in gender and sexuality studies. Nor has he paid sufficient attention to feminist theorizing about societal influences on sexuality. His view, "I happen to think gay people quite likely *are* born gay" (Nimmons 68), is not sufficiently warranted scientifically or politically to be applicable to all people who engage in same-sex sexual activities or have same-sex desire.

All science, all endeavors, are shaped to varying degrees by the politics of the culture at large, the controlling interests, and the particular, sometimes counterculture interests of the people and institutions involved. Instead of rejecting all of science because of this reality, as a feminist scientist I urge that we do everything we can to hold science and scientists accountable to the standards of equity politics and the standards of valid science. Organizations like the Women's Community Cancer Project, CINBIOSE, and the Center for Science in the Public

Interest[7] focus on this effort, and women's studies programs are working on their role in education. The power of the information that can be gained by the correct application of scientific methods guided by feminist values is great. Properly controlled experiments can help us choose therapies that are effective for certain conditions. But we must engage in the struggle over scientific objectivity and overcome the common belief that politics only contaminates science (and the corollary belief that conservative politics are absent when they are simply hidden) (Spanier, chap. 8).

Unfortunately, *Science* magazine singled out Simon LeVay as one of three examples of a scientist's passions causing conflict of interest and biasing research (Marshall). The sensationally titled portion, "Sex on the Brain," presents some criticisms of LeVay's research, but none that deeply questions either the brain-causes-behaviors version of biological determinist explanations or sex differences theories. On the positive side, the issues of personal bias and the role of scientists as advocates of social change are introduced. LeVay's comment concludes the section: "Everyone...has some place they're coming from; every scientist is a human being" (621).

While I have pointed to the ways that LeVay's article incorporates judgments biased toward a biological-determinist interpretation of sexual orientation and skewing his interpretations of his data, I must emphasize that *Science* has never similarly suggested that a researcher's heterosexuality or heterosexism might bias his or her research. Such a double standard often places feminists and gay rights advocates in the difficult position of defending questionable science on the basis of progressive politics alone.

LeVay simply joined other scientists in the not uncommon error of overlooking the limitations of his research to push for an unjustified conclusion. This case is a classic example of the search for some kind of physical difference to account biologically for phenomena that result from complex, multilayered sets of processes clearly influenced if not structured by macro- and microculture. Some scientists will continue to seek out a physical difference to correlate with the behavioral difference at issue. The tendency is to put aside null results and simply look to other regions of the brain, other cell clusters, other genetic markers, until some differences are found.

LeVay is apparently one of these overzealous scientists. I read that he was considering a study of live people's brains, using MRI measurements (magnetic resonance imaging, a noninvasive technique), but I was dismayed when he said that since the hypothalamus was too small, he was interested in looking at the corpus callosum in relation to sexuality.[8] His reported comments suggest that his scientific plans have not been affected by serious critiques of research into brain and sex differences and behavior. I hope he proves me wrong, especially since he may be involved in such media projects as a *Nova* series on sexuality.

Good politics, like good intentions, are not sufficient to produce valid science. The successor science envisioned by Sandra Harding, and increasingly by more scientists, must be sound in more than its politics, and this requires more collaboration and mutual education between feminists and scientists. I believe that the rules guiding Western science can be useful to feminist thinking, if applied with an understanding of their limitations.

Feminists must be able to evaluate the original scientific claims in areas of importance to us. Feminist scientists have called for feminist nonscientists, especially those in a position to reach many people through college women's studies courses, to meet us halfway by overriding the often justified mistrust of science itself and the externally socialized ignorance and fear of science (Fausto-Sterling, "Building"). Judging from the level of interest in the science panels at NWSA over the years, but especially recently,[9] many feminists are doing just that – and encouraging some of us to share our analyses with a wider feminist audience. Thus one of the things feminists need to know to survive is not just that science can be dangerous to our health (indeed, what area of traditional masculinist knowledge isn't?) but how to make sense, feminist sense, of scientific claims that affect our lives and the lives of all oppressed peoples. Whether or not we value masculinist notions of "reason" and "scientific evidence," feminists must understand scientific evidence within the norms of traditional science in order to critique it – speaking the language and using the methods of traditional science while transforming it at the same time. If we are successful in changing science sufficiently as a consequence of liberatory transformations, one day "traditional science" may well include – no, require – the tools and insights of feminist critique and experience. What do feminists need to know about science and technology? As much as possible and always within their social contexts.

NOTES

1 Right-wing fundamentalists who present homosexuality as a sinful choice often provoke the reaction that gays cannot be blamed for the way they were born, a position that assumes that sexual preference is innate and unchanging. Analogies to people with disabilities, women, blacks, and older people are more or less useful in legal arguments.
2 The accepted theory has gone from claiming that men's brains were more lateralized than women's to the opposite. The new theory had to change the meaning of greater or lesser lateralization in relation to greater or lesser math ability, logical reasoning, and intuition. See Fausto-Sterling's *Myths of Gender* and Bleier's *Science and Gender.*
3 The concept of taking into account as many influences or factors as possible (controlling for known variables) is fundamental to standard scientific methods, but complex systems such as brains and behavior are particularly difficult to study, since so many variables exist and many are simply unknown. Because of this, measured differences between two groups or samples may appear to be statistically significant and valid but result from nonrandom sampling and, hence, other factors. When the question is framed as, Are there sex-correlated differences in the size of something? and gender is the only comparison made without controls, spurious and misleading findings result. See Gould for examples of actual mismeasurement – some purposeful, some apparently subconscious – and outright fraud.
4 Let me be clear that politics informs *all* scientific work, just as it informs all other forms of work and knowledge production. I focus on Simon LeVay's research because, contrary to some other researchers in the field of brain and behavior, his motives are pro-gay rights. That does not necessarily mean he is pro-feminist. My point is that while someone may have good political goals, the science s/he produces may not be valid and that feminists must therefore have the tools to analyze scientific research.
5 For example, one of the justices concurring with the Hawaii Supreme Court in support of marriage licenses for gay couples referred to research on the biological determination of homosexuality (Nimmons 71). The argument that "biology is an element the courts have

traditionally used as a marker for the immutability of a characteristic, such as race, gender, or – now – sexual orientation" (Nimmons 71) is a two-edged sword, however, useful because of the legal tradition but blunted by inaccuracy. Historical and scientific evidence demonstrates that race and gender and sexual orientation are socially constructed, highly mutable categories, not biologically fixed characteristics. For an excellent critique of the limitations of immutability as a legal basis for gay rights, see Halley.

6 All of the homosexual men, six of the sixteen presumed heterosexual men, and one of the six women had died of complications of AIDS. LeVay proposes that death from AIDS is not a significant variable because he found no effect when he compared the (nineteen) homosexual men with AIDS to the (six) heterosexual men with AIDS (although the data showing a difference here are less significant statistically) or the (nineteen) homosexual men with AIDS to the women (five of whom died from other causes) or the (six) heterosexual men with AIDS to the (ten) heterosexual men who died from other causes.

7 Women's Community Cancer Project, 46 Pleasant Street, Cambridge, MA 02139. Center for Science in the Public Interest, Suite 300, 1875 Connecticut Avenue, N.W., Washington, DC 20009-5728. See *The Women's Review of Books*, July 1994.

8 This was reported in *Ten Percent* (Winter 1993): 38, but I found several inaccuracies in the article, so I take his interview there with a grain of salt.

9 The Science, Technology, and Gender Symposium hosted by Iowa State and NWSA as part of the 1994 NWSA Conference was the culmination of many efforts in NWSA over the years to bring science and feminist issues together. In particular, Carole Heath and Kris Anderson are to be congratulated.

REFERENCES

Allen, Laura S., M. Hines, J. E. Shryne, and R. A. Gorski. "Two Sexually Dimorphic Cell Groups in the Human Brain." *Journal of Neuroscience* 9 (1989): 497–506.

Angier, Natalie. "In Fish, Social Status Goes Right to the Brain." *New York Times* 12 Nov. 1991: C1, C12.

Barinaga, Marcia. "Is Homosexuality Biological?" *Science* 253 (30 Aug. 1991): 956.

Bleier, Ruth. "A Decade of Feminist Critiques in the Natural Sciences." *Signs* 14 (Autumn 1988): 182–5.

——. *Science and Gender.* New York: Pergamon, 1984.

Bleier, Ruth, L. Houston, and W. Byrne. "Can the Corpus Callosum Predict Gender, Age, Handedness, or Cognitive Differences?" *Trends in Neurosciences* 8 (1986): 391–4.

Burr, Chandler. "Homosexuality and Biology." *Atlantic Monthly* Mar. 1993: 47–65.

Carrier, J. M., and G. Gellert. Letter. *Science* 254 (1 Nov. 1991): 630.

Delacoste-Utamsing, C., and R. L. Holloway. "Sexual Dimorphism in the Human Corpus Callosum." *Science* 216 (1982): 1431–2.

Demeter, S., J. Ringo, and R. W. Doty. "Sexual Dimorphisms in the Human Corpus Callosum." *Abstracts of the Society for Neuroscience* 11 (1985): 868.

Fausto-Sterling, Anne. "Building Two-Way Streets: The Case of Feminism and Science." *NWSA Journal* 4.3 (Fall 1992): 336–49; responses *NWSA Journal* 5.1 (Spring 1993): 45–8 and 5.3 (Fall 1993): 389–91.

——. *Myths of Gender: Biological Theories about Women and Men.* New York: Basic Books, 1985.

Fay, Robert, Charles F. Turner, Albert D. Klassen, and John H. Gagnon. "Prevalence and Patterns of Same-Gender Sexual Contact among Men." *Science* 243 (20 Jan. 1989): 338–48.
Foucault, Michel. *The History of Sexuality*. New York: Pantheon Books, 1978.
Gelman, David, with Donna Foote, Todd Barrett, and Mary Talbot. "Is Homosexuality Born or Bred?" *Newsweek* 24 Feb. 1992: 46–53.
Gorman, Christian. "Sizing Up the Sexes." *Time* 20 Jan. 1992: 42–51.
Gould, Stephen Jay. *The Mismeasure of Man*. New York: Norton, 1981.
Halley, Janet. "Sexual Orientation and the Politics of Biology: A Critique of the Argument from Immutability." *Stanford Law Review* 46 (Feb. 1994): 503–68.
Hubbard, Ruth. *The Politics of Women's Biology*. New Brunswick, NJ: Rutgers UP, 1990.
LeVay, Simon. "A Differences in Hypothalamic Structure between Heterosexual and Homosexual Men." *Science* 253 (30 Aug. 1991): 1034–7.
——. Letter. *Science* 254 (1 Nov. 1991): 630.
Lewontin, Richard, Steven Rose, and Leon Kamin. *Not in Our Genes: Biology, Ideology, and Human Nature*. New York: Pantheon, 1984.
Longino, Helen. *Science as Social Knowledge: Values and Objectivity in Scientific Inquiry*. Princeton: Princeton UP, 1990.
Marshall, Eliot. "When Does Intellectual Passion Become Conflict of Interest?" *Science* 257 (31 July 1992): 620–4.
Miller, Neil. *In Search of Gay America*. New York: Atlantic Monthly, 1989.
Nimmons, David. "Sex and the Brain." *Discover* March 1994: 64–71.
Spanier, Bonnie. *Impartial Science? Gender and Ideology in Molecular Biology*. Bloomington: Indiana UP, forthcoming.
Weber, G., and S. Weis. "Morphometric Analysis of the Human Corpus Callosum Fails to Reveal Sex-Related Differences." *Journal Hirnforschungen* 27 (1986): 237–40.
Witelson, S. "The Brain Connection: The Corpus Callosum Is Larger in Left-Handers." *Science* 229 (1985): 665–8.

3

Feminisms, Queer Theories, and the Archaeological Study of Past Sexualities

Barbara L. Voss

> There is another social function of gender to be considered and that is the social marking of sexually appropriate partners. . . . If the reader accepts this social function of gender, then an archaeology of gender is an archaeology of *sexuality*.
>
> (Classen 1992b)
>
> Gender is out – sex is in.
>
> (dig house graffiti, Çatalhöyük, Turkey, 1998)

It has been eight years since Claasen observed that sexuality is intrinsically linked to the archaeological study of gender in the past, but until recently only a few archaeologists have seriously considered how the archaeological record can be used to produce knowledge about past sexualities. Fortunately, in the last three years this situation has significantly changed. There is now emerging a significant corpus of discourse about sexuality and the archaeological record, a constellation of recent publications and theses that demonstrate that an ever-increasing range of sexual topics can be investigated and interrogated through archaeological research.

A review of archaeological studies of sexuality is in some ways premature, for (despite an anonymous archaeologist's glib assertion that 'sex is in') the undertaking is still controversial and contested. Yet even at this early date it is clear that archaeological investigations of sexuality are being informed and influenced by several distinct – and at times competing – intellectual traditions. In this essay, I particularly consider how feminist archaeology and queer theory articulate with archaeological investigations of sexuality. To do so I step back in time, as archaeologists are wont to do, and discuss the genesis of both feminist archaeology and queer theory in the 1980s and 1990s, examining their relationship to each other through an analysis of citational practices in archaeology. This discussion not only contributes to a review of archaeological research on sexuality but also towards discussions on the sociology of knowledge in archaeology.

Feminist Archaeologies: Gender, Status, and the Division of Labour

The emergence of feminist archaeology is generally attributed to the 1984 publication 'Archaeology and the study of gender' (Conkey and Spector 1984). By the late 1980s, symposia, workshops, and dedicated conferences brought together researchers interested in integrating archaeology, feminist theory, women's studies, and the interpretation of a gendered past. A bloom of publications followed, including the edited volume *Engendering Archaeology* (Gero and Conkey 1991), five conference proceedings (Balme and Beck 1995; Claassen 1992a; du Cros and Smith 1993; Miller 1988; Walde and Willows 1991), a special issue of *Historical Archaeology* (Seifert 1991), and several topical monographs (e.g. Ehrenberg 1989; Gilchrist 1994; Spector 1993; Wall 1994). Not all the researchers involved in these projects necessarily identified themselves or their work as 'feminist' (Wylie 1997b). Recent commentaries have thus referred to this body of literature as 'womanist' or 'gender' archaeology (e.g., Joyce and Claassen 1997; Gilchrist 1999; Nelson 1997; Wright 2000). These commentators and others are correct in emphasizing that research on women or gender is not automatically 'feminist'. Nonetheless, I believe that most of the works listed above can be accurately described as 'feminist-inspired', informed by popular, political, and/or academic feminist thought. Additionally, feminist practice in archaeology certainly has not been limited to research on women or gender (Conkey and Wylie 1999; Wylie in press). Because of this, for the purposes of this essay I have chosen to refer to this body of work as 'feminist archaeology'.

The development of this diverse body of 'feminist' and 'feminist-inspired' archaeologies occurred at a time when feminist theory and politics in the United States and elsewhere were at a crossroads. In the late 1970s and early 1980s, when Conkey and Spector were authoring their 1984 manifesto, North American feminist politics were focused on what then appeared to be the universal oppression of women by patriarchy. Although the exact nature and mechanisms of patriarchal oppression were debated, this focus was generally (but of course not completely) shared by Marxist, socialist, radical, liberal, and cultural feminisms of the time (Jagger 1983: 5–8). In both the humanities and sciences, the omission of women's experiences and accomplishments in academic and popular discourse was identified as one mechanism by which patriarchal ideology replicated itself by privileging male experience. Feminist scholars in anthropology and other disciplines thus prioritized research that documented women's experiences cross-culturally, especially regarding gender roles and the ways that patriarchy acted on women's lives (Rosaldo and Lamphere 1974; Rubin 1975; Reiter 1975).

Informed by this political and academic climate. Conkey and Spector's 1984 article presented a substantial critique of androcentrism in archaeology. They called for new approaches to archaeological interpretation that would promote gender-inclusive models of the past, question the universality of a rigid sexual division of labour, and challenge the ways that men's purported activities are valued more than those believed to be performed by women. In this way feminist theory would be used in archaeology to combat the effects of present-day sexism on archaeological interpretations. Simultaneously, the critical study of gender in the past would provide new information about the long-term history of gender relations. This core agenda was later reiterated by Conkey and Gero in their 1991 edited volume *Engendering Archaeology* with the added aim of problematizing 'underlying assumptions about gender and difference' (Conkey and Gero 1991: 5). Throughout the late 1980s and early 1990s, these goals were largely adopted by most researchers who identified their research as feminist archaeology, gender archaeology, or the archaeology of women. It is perhaps worth noting that these general aims of feminist archaeology are broadly congruent with feminist interventions into the social sciences in general (Harding 1986, 1987; Wylie 1992, 1997a).

Because Conkey and Spector's 1984 article was widely adopted as a central agenda for feminist archaeological studies for the decade to come, the political and intellectual climate within which they wrote significantly affected the way that sexuality has been addressed within archaeological interpretations. Most of the early studies in archaeology that consciously adopted a feminist approach emphasized the sexual (or gendered) division of labour and indices of gender status, an emphasis typified by Spector's task differentiation framework (Conkey and Spector 1984; Spector 1991). There was a particular emphasis on 'finding' women in the archaeological record by debunking anrdocentric methods and interpretations, and on highlighting the contributions of women to the past (e.g. Brumfiel 1991; Gero 1991; Wright 1991). At the same time many studies used a materialist approach that viewed women as a gender class, trying to understand how archaeologically identified conditions such as environmental change, state formation, or the introduction of agriculture intensified or changed women's status (e.g. Claassen 1991; Hastorf 1991; Watson and Kennedy 1991). The prominence of materialist and empiricist research in North American feminist archaeology has been discussed elsewhere (e.g. Gilchrist 1999; ch. 3; Nelson 1997: ch. 5; Wylie 1996: 320–5) and is attributable to both the then-dominant 'New Archaeology' paradigm and also the emphasis on socialist political theory in North American feminism in the 1970s and early 1980s.

These shared emphases in early feminist archaeological studies had significant implications for the ways that issues of sexuality began to be discussed in archaeological interpretation. Feminist archaeologists usually adopted the sex/gender system model, in which gender is taken to be the cultural expression of biological sex (Rubin 1975). Within this framework, sexuality is generally seen as derivative of gender, one of many aspects of social life that is structured by sex/gender systems. As a result, to paraphrase Brumfiel (1992), during the first decade of feminist archaeological practice, 'Gender... [stole] the show'. Feminist archaeological research rarely addressed the topic of sexuality, instead treating sexuality predominantly as a function of gender rather than as a distinct aspect of social relations (see Rubin 1984: 309 for a general discussion of this point). For example, heterosexual marriage has been examined by many feminist archaeologists as a locus for the gendered organization of labour (which, of course, it often is) but only rarely with a consideration of how marriage relates to the regulation and expression of sexuality (e.g. Deagan 1983; Gibb and King 1991; Jackson 1991; Wall 1994; Wright 1991).

In noting these trends. I am not suggesting that the initial goals of feminist-inspired archaeological projects negatively affected archaeological interpretations of sexuality. On the contrary, by highlighting gender as a subject of archaeological research, and by foregrounding interpersonal relationships as an arena of social action, feminist interventions in archaeology created an intellectual climate within which research on sexuality became increasingly viable. Exactly how the priorities and conventions of feminist archaeological practices came to influence archaeological investigations of sexuality is, however, of great interest, and is a topic that I return to later in this essay.

The Sex Wars, AIDS, and Queer Theory: Sexuality Moves Front and Centre

During the emergence of feminist archaeologies in the 1980s and early 1990s. North American feminist politics negotiated a series of epistemological crises that shifted feminist attention towards an examination of differences between women. Among other issues such as race and class, feminist scholars and activists undertook projects that theorized sexuality in ways markedly different from previous treatments of sexuality as some sort of an extension of gender. In the late 1970s works by lesbian and gay scholars (e.g. Katz 1976; Rowbotham and Weeks 1977; Smith-Rosenberg 1979; Weeks 1977), the English translation of Foucault's *History of Sexuality* (1978), and, in anthropology, Ortner and Whitehead's *Sexual Meanings* (1981) challenged conventional feminist wisdom about the primacy of gender as a vector of oppression. By the early 1980s sexuality had become a flashpoint of feminist debate (the so-called 'Sex Wars'), and the relationship of sexuality to patriarchy and liberation was hotly contested (Rubin 1984; Vance 1984; Duggan and Hunter 1995). Homosexuality, pornography, sadomasochism, prostitution, monogamy, rape, promiscuity, butch – femme relationships, interracial and intergenerational sex – these and other sexual practices became prominent topics of often acrimonious public forums and written discourse. Concurrently, the emerging AIDS pandemic propelled male same-sex sexual practices and commercial sex into explicit public discussion through medical, public health, and activist movements, bringing coverage of condom distribution, prostitution, anal and oral sex, and public sex into mainstream print and television media.[1]

Discussions about the politics of sexuality during the early and mid-1980s were at times bitter (see, for example, Vance's discussion of the 1982 Barnard College conference (Vance 1984) or Crimp and Roston's pictorial history of ACT UP (Crimp and Rolston 1990)), but it would be a mistake to characterize this period solely as an era of contentious debate. As Rubin urged, 'The time has come to think about sex' (1984: 267) and thinking about sex was precisely what many feminist, lesbian, and gay researchers, writers, and activists did. What emerged was a sense that theories of gender were not fully adequate to address sexuality, either as a social practice or as a vector of oppression (Vance 1984: 10): that 'it is essential to separate gender and sexuality analytically to more accurately reflect their separate social existence' (Rubin 1984: 308). By the late 1980s and early 1990s, the call to develop theories of sexuality was being answered by an expanding body of literature that addressed the political and cultural positions of gays, lesbians, bisexuals, transsexuals, sex workers, sadomasochists, and others – a diverse conglomeration of sexual 'minorities' who were increasingly identified as 'queer' (de Lauretis 1991: v). Sedgwick's *Epistemology of the Closet* (1990), Butler's *Gender Trouble* (1990) and *Bodies that Matter* (1993a). Warner's *Fear of a Queer Planet* (1993) and two special issues of *differences* (Vol. 5 No. 2 and Vol. 6 Nos. 2 + 3) all signalled the consolidation of an approach to theorizing sexuality that crossed gender lines, integrating (but not collapsing) sexual theories related to masculinity and femininity and to heterosexuality and homosexuality.

Most importantly, the emergence of queer theory within academia marked a radical shift towards positioning abject and stigmatized sexual identities as important entry points to the production of knowledge (Butler 1993b). A move to destabilize sexual and gender categories was and still is an integral part of this process. The adoption of the inclusive moniker 'queer' reflected the rejection of taxonomic sexual categories (e.g. homosexual, heterosexual, fetishist, pederast) that initially had been established through sexological discourse in the late 1800s and early 1900s (see Bland and Doan (1998) for a discussion of sexology and sexual taxonomies). Instead, the term 'queer' reflects an inclusive stand-point based on difference from or opposition to the ideology of heteronormativity (Warner 1993: xxiii). Thus queer theory and queer politics represent a critical moment in the history of Western sexuality in which sexual minorities and deviants who were previously defined by legal statutes and medical/psychological diagnoses are instead creating an always-contested and re-negotiated group identity based on difference from the norm – in other words, a postmodern version of identity politics (see Butler 1993a: 21). Essential to this post-structuralist deployment of opposition is the tenet that what is 'normative' is actually constructed through reference to deviance. Thus it is 'deviance' that is foundational and the 'normative' that is unstable (Butler 1993b).

This emphasis on 'opposition to the normative' (a position repeated in the call for papers for this volume) and on the simultaneous destabilization of the normative are aspects of queer theory that allow great interdisciplinary mobility, as they permit theoretical concepts initially applied to issues of sexual identity and the oppression of sexual minorities to be deployed in studies of other social subgroups as well as in studies of the written and spoken word, the built environment, material objects, and other products of culture. It is, I argue below, precisely this emphasis on normativity and opposition that poses both opportunities and challenges for archaeologists engaging in studies of past sexualities.

Intersections: Connections between Archaeology and Feminist Theories of Sexuality

These brief histories reveal that feminist archaeology and queer theory share certain temporal markers: both were founded on the political and academic feminisms of the late 1970s and early 1980s, emerged in opposition to the dominant political and academic climate of the early and mid-1980s, and, after a period of uncertain exploration, achieved a degree of academic legitimacy and popularity in the early 1990s. Of course this historical narrative may be unduly influenced by the archaeological tendency to interpret cultural developments through the 'formative/pre-classic/classic/post-classic' model. Nonetheless, I suggest that queer theory and feminist archaeology shared somewhat parallel chronological developments.

Despite their parallel trajectories, queer theory and feminist archaeology were rarely in dialogue with each other. Queer theory, grounded in grass-roots political activist movements such as Queer Nation (Berlant and Freeman 1993), arose to meet the particular challenges of sexual politics during the neo-conservative 1980s, while feminist archaeology emerged primarily within academia as a critique of androcentric archaeological practices and interpretations. However, many of the archaeologists involved in the genesis of feminist archaeology were (and still are) themselves feminist activists, concerned not only with representations of gender in the past but also with the politics of gender and sexuality in the present (Hanen and Kelley 1992; Wylie 1991). What, then, were the intersections between the growing feminist theorization of sexuality in the 1980s and the emergence of feminist archaeology? To what extent has queer theory informed feminist archaeologies in recent years?[2]

To consider these questions, I reviewed bibliographies of feminist archaeological studies published throughout the 1980s and 1990s. Citational practices are one way in which scholars acknowledge their intellectual influences and position themselves within the larger field of academia, and thus bibliographies provide one imperfect measure of the extent to which particular schools of thought are being consulted and invoked by scholars in different subfields. My review focused primarily on nine edited volumes and proceedings which had been generated through conferences, conference symposia, and lecture series (Balme and Beck 1995; Claassen 1992a; Claassen and Joyce 1997; du Cros and Smith 1993; Gero and Conkey 1991; Miller 1988; Moore and Scott 1997; Walde and Willows 1991; Wright 1996). Because several of these volumes were limited to studies of prehistory, I also reviewed the 'gender' issue of *Historical Archaeology* (vol. 25 no. 4) and two monographs (Spector 1993; Wall 1994) to increase the representation of historical archaeology within the sample. Finally, I included Conkey and Spector's 1984 article as well as three recently published syntheses of feminist archaeology (Conkey and Gero 1997; Gilchrist 1999; Nelson 1997). Together these sources represent 220 papers, articles, or monographs by authors who identify their work as feminist and/or gender archaeology. Although such a sample is not meant to be exhaustive or even statistically representative (for example, few journal articles are included), it does include papers from a broad geographic and temporal distribution, spanning 1984 to 1999 and including authors from the United States, Australia, Canada, and Great Britain. In reviewing these works I noted citations belonging to three categories: first, early works about sexuality by feminist and gay and lesbian scholars dating to the 1970s and early 1980s; second, the literature surrounding the 'Sex Wars' of the mid-1980s; and, third, the emergent queer theory canon whose benchmarks include publications such as Sedgwick's *Epistemology of the Closet* (1990) and Butler's *Gender Trouble* (1990).[3]

Before beginning this exercise I expected to identify two trends: first, that feminist archaeologists have rarely, if at all, engaged with non-archaeological works on sexuality, and second, that it is only in the last few years that queer theory has entered feminist archaeological discourse at all. My suppositions were wrong on both counts. I found that 18 per cent of the 220 works reviewed cited one or more works that fall into one of the three categories described above. This percentage did not increase or decrease markedly with time, but vacillated within a fairly stable range of 10 per cent to 35 per cent from year to year. This suggests that, while sexuality has not been a central topic of archaeological interpretation (Voss and Schmidt 2000), archaeologists have, over the last fifteen years, consistently considered sexuality to be one important aspect of gender-focused research.

Second, I found that the relationship between queer theory and feminist archaeology is, while uneven, by no means absent. Although almost none of the works I reviewed referenced publications generated during the 'Sex Wars' of the mid-1980s. 'queer theory' publications by Foucault (especially *History of Sexuality* [1978]), Butler (both *Gender Trouble* [1990] and *Bodies that Matter* [1993a]) and Grosz (*Sexual Subversions* [1989] and *Sexy Bodies* [1995, with Probyn]) were cited with regularity. Queer theory citations were especially common in introductions to edited volumes and conference proceedings and rare in archaeological case studies, suggesting that queer theory has been used predominantly to theorize the feminist archaeological project as a whole rather than to interpret archaeological evidence.

Finally, the papers and monographs that I reviewed relied overwhelmingly on one source, Ortner and Whitehead's *Sexual Meanings* (1981), which accounted for over 30 per cent of all noted citations about sexuality. An edited volume of anthropological case studies generated in the mid-1970s, most (but not all) contributed papers in *Sexual Meanings* are focused on band, tribe, or chiefdom societies (1981: x), interpret gender and sexuality through a focus on symbolic constructs and the sex/gender system model (1981: 1–9), and emphasize 'considerations of hierarchical power and differential prestige between men and women' (Gilchrist 1999: 8). The prominence of *Sexual Meanings* as a source about sexuality for feminist-inspired archaeological research has not diminished with time, but appears to be as strong in the late 1990s as it was in the first decade of feminist archaeological inquiry. The persistent citations of *Sexual Meanings* may indicate a degree of theoretical conservatism in feminist archaeology with regard to conceptions of sexuality and its relationship to gender. As Roberts has noted, 'The paradox is that those interested in an archaeology of gender cannot afford to challenge the framework assumptions and paradigms of research practice' (1993: 18). In other words, it is difficult for those feminist archaeologists who are occupied with legitimizing and developing gender studies simultaneously to embrace queer theories that deconstruct gender and sexuality. For example, Butler's position that 'biological sex' is a discursive regulatory practice (Butler 1993a: 1) could be seen to challenge archaeological studies of gender that use physical indices to assign a 'sex' to human skeletal remains. Deconstructions of sex and gender destabilize precisely those categories (e.g. male, female, woman, man) that are necessarily invoked to model engendered social worlds of the past.[4] The fear of erasing or compromising 'gender' as a category of archaeological analysis may account for the apparent reluctance of many archaeological researchers consistently and critically to engage with queer theory.

At the same time, there are also aspects of queer theory that resist its wholesale importation into archaeology. The feminist theories of sexuality that emerged during the particular sexual politics of the 1980s and 1990s addressed the conditions of modern. Western, and predominantly urban sexual subcultures. Rubin particularly notes that the organization of gender and sexuality 'as two distinct arenas of social practice' (1984: 308) may be specific to Western industrial societies. The enduring appeal of the sex/gender system model within feminist archaeology may be because it is sometimes a more appropriate, if imperfect, approach to considering sexuality and gender in pre-industrial and kinship-based cultures (Rubin 1975). Likewise, queer theorists tend to emphasize analyses of fictional texts, cinema, and other representations at the expense of historical or social science research (Rubin 1994: 93) – what historian Duggan has termed 'the discipline problem' (1995).[5] Broken pots, faunal remains, collapsed structures, burials, soil residues, and other evidentiary sources in archaeology rarely resemble the literary works or films that often form the basis of queer theory analyses (e.g. Butler 1993a). It is not always immediately apparent how to apply reading methodologies developed for modern cultural texts to the archaeological record.

Because of the temporal and geographic specificity of queer theory, archaeologists have important contributions to make in developing theories of gender and sexuality that can be applied to material evidence and that are appropriate for analysis of non-'Western' and non-'modern' cultures. Archaeology faces the unique challenge of stretching theories of sexuality in new chronological and cultural directions and in probing the cultural and representational limits of distinctions between gender and sexuality. While neither feminist nor queer theories should be applied unquestioningly to the past, together they provide powerful tools that can broaden archaeological interpretations of past sexualities.

NOTES

1 These debates are perhaps best exemplified by two contradictory publications on lesbian sadomasochism, *Coming to Power* (SAMOIS 1982) and *Against Sadomasochism* (Linden et al. 1982), and by the controversies over the role of gay male bath-houses in safer sex campaigns and AIDS transmission (e.g. Bayer 1989: ch. 2; Berube 1996; Dangerous Bedfellows 1996). Excellent resources on this period include *Pleasure and Danger: Exploring Female Sexuality* (Vance 1984), *Powers of Desire: The Politics of Sexuality* (Snitow et al. 1983), and *Sex Wars: Sexual Dissent and Political Culture* (Duggan and Hunter 1995).

2 One could also, of course, ask the extent to which feminist archaeology affected the growing feminist theorizations of sexuality. However, my readings suggest that feminist scholars outside archaeology are not familiar with feminist archaeological projects, a point also noted by Conkey and Gero (1997: 424–5 – but see Rubin [2000] for a rare exception). In part this is because it is only recently that feminist archaeological work is becoming visible to cross-disciplinary audiences through topical monographs (e.g. Gilchrist 1994; Spector 1993; Wall 1994) and the appearance of archaeological case studies and reviews in multi-disciplinary edited volumes and journals (e.g. Bahn 1992; Conkey and Tringham 1995; Conkey with Williams 1991; Gero 1988; Wright 2000).

3 Data and tabulations from this bibliographic review are on file with the author.

4 Note, however, that some feminist archaeologists (e.g. Joyce 1996, 2000) have found that models of gender performativity and other deconstructive approaches to gender actually enhance the archaeological 'visibility' of prehistoric gendered identities and practices.

5 With this in mind it is not surprising that one of the most prominent uses of queer theory in archaeology at present is found in the interpretation of archaeologically recovered representational imagery, as in the works of Joyce (1996, 2000), Meskell (1996, 1998, 2000), and Vasey (1998) on imagery of the body in prehistoric Mesoamerica, Egypt and Europe, respectively.

REFERENCES

Bahn, P. G. 1992. Review of engendering archaeology. *Journal of Gender Studies*, 1: 338–44.

Balme, J. and Beck, W. (eds) 1995. *Gendered Archaeology: The Second Australian Women in Archaeology Conference*. Canberra: Australian National University Publications.

Bayer, R. 1989. *Private Acts, Social Consequences: AIDS and the Politics of Public Health*. New York: The Free Press.

Berlant, L. and Freeman, E. 1993. Queer nationality. In *Fear of a Queer Planet: Queer Politics and Social Theory* (ed. M. Warner). Minneapolis: University of Minnesota Press, pp. 193–229.

Berube, A. 1996. The history of gay bathhouses. In *Policing Public Sex* (ed. D. Bedfellows). Boston, MA: South End Press, pp. 187–221.

Bland, L. and Doan, L. (eds) 1998. *Sexology in Culture: Labeling Bodies and Desires*. Chicago: University of Chicago Press.

Brumfiel, E. 1992. Distinguished lecture in archaeology: breaking and entering the ecosystem – gender, class, and faction steal the show. *American Anthropologist*, 91: 551–67.

Brumfiel, E. M. 1991. Weaving and cooking: women's production in Aztec Mexico. In *Engendering Archaeology: Women and Prehistory* (eds J. M. Gero and M. W. Conkey). Cambridge, MA: Blackwell, pp. 224–54.

Butler, J. 1990. *Gender Trouble: Feminism and the Subversion of Identity*. New York: Routledge.

Butler, J. 1993a. *Bodies that Matter: On the Discursive Limits of 'Sex'*. London: Routledge.

Butler, J. 1993b. Imitation and gender insubordination. In *The Lesbian and Gay Studies Reader* (eds H. Abelove, M. A. Barale and D. Halperin). New York: Routledge, pp. 307–20.

Claassen, C. (ed.) 1992a. *Exploring Gender through Archaeology: Selected Papers from the 1991 Boone Conference*. Madison, WI: Prehistory Press.

Claassen, C. 1992b. Questioning gender: an introduction. In *Exploring Gender through Archaeology: Selected Papers from the 1991 Boone Conference* (ed. C. Claassen). Madison, WI: Prehistory Press, pp. 1–10.

Claassen, C. and Joyce, R. A. (eds) 1997. *Women in Prehistory: North America and Mesoamerica*. Philadelphia: University of Pennsylvania Press.

Claassen, C. P. 1991. Gender, shellfishing, and the shell mound archaic. In *Engendering Archaeology: Women and Prehistory* (eds J. M. Gero and M. W. Conkey). Cambridge, MA: Blackwell, pp. 276–300.

Conkey, M. W. and Gero, J. 1991. Tensions, pluralities, and engendering archaeology: an introduction to women and prehistory. In *Engendering Archaeology: Women and Prehistory* (eds J. M. Gero and M. W. Conkey). Cambridge, MA: Blackwell, pp. 3–30.

Conkey, M. W. and Gero, J. 1997. From programme to practice: gender and feminism in archaeology. *Annual Review of Anthropology*, 26: 411–37.

Conkey, M. W. and Spector, J. D. 1984. Archaeology and the study of gender. *Advances in Archaeological Method and Theory*, 7: 1–32.

Conkey, M. W. and Tringham, R. E. 1995. Archaeology and the goddess: exploring the contours of feminist archaeology. In *Feminisms in the Academy* (eds D. C. Stanton and A. J. Stewart). Ann Arbor: University of Michigan Press, pp. 199–247.

Conkey, M. W. with Williams, S. H. 1991. Original narratives: the political economy of gender in archaeology. In *Gender at the Crossroads of Knowledge: Feminist Anthropology in the Postmodern Era* (ed. M. d. Leonardo). Berkeley: University of California Press, pp. 102–39.

Conkey, M. W. and Wylie, A. 1999. Summary of 'Doing archaeology as a feminist: moving from theory to practice'. *Newsletter of the Women in Archaeology Interest Group, Society for American Archaeology*, 1(2): 3–4.

Crimp, D. and Rolston, A. 1990. *AIDS Demo Graphics*. Seattle: Bay Press.

Dangerous Bedfellows (eds) 1996. *Policing Public Sex: Queer Politics and the Future of AIDS Activism*. Boston, MA: South End Press.

de Lauretis, T. 1991. Queer theory: lesbian and gay sexualities: an introduction. *Differences*, 3(2): iii–xviii.

Deagan, K. (ed.) 1983. *Spanish St. Augustine: The Archaeology of a Colonial Creole Community.* New York: Academic Press.

du Cros, H. and Smith, L. (eds) 1993. *Women in Archaeology: A Feminist Critique*. Canberra: Department of Prehistory, The Australian National University.

Duggan, L. and Hunter, N. D. (eds) 1995. *Sex Wars: Sexual Dissent and Political Culture.* New York: Routledge.

Ehrenberg, M. 1989. *Women in Prehistory.* London: British Museum Publications.

Foucault, M. 1978. *The History of Sexuality, Vol. I: An Introduction* (trans. Robert Hurley). New York: Pantheon.

Gero, J. 1991. Genderlithics: women's roles in stone tool production. In *Engendering Archaeology: Women and Prehistory* (eds J. M. Gero and M. W. Conkey). Cambridge, MA: Blackwell, pp. 163–93.

Gero, J. M. 1988. Gender bias in archaeology: here, then, and now. In *Feminism within the Science and Health Care Professions: Overcoming Resistance* (ed. S. V. Rosser). New York: Pergamon Press, pp. 33–43.

Gero, J. M. and Conkey, M. W. (eds) 1991. *Engendering Archaeology: Women and Prehistory.* Cambridge, MA: Blackwell.

Gibb, J. G. and King, J. A. 1991. Gender, activity areas, and homelots in the 17th century Chesapeake region. *Historical Archaeology*, 25(4): 109–31.

Gilchrist, R. 1994. *Gender and Material Culture: The Archaeology of Religious Women.* New York: Routledge.

Gilchrist, R. 1999. *Gender and Archaeology: Contesting the Past.* London: Routledge.

Grosz, E. A. 1989. *Sexual Subversions: Three French Feminists.* Sydney: Allen & Unwin.

Grosz, E. A. and Probyn, E. (eds) 1995. *Sexy Bodies: The Strange Carnalities of Feminism.* London: Routledge.

Hanen, M. P. and J. Kelley 1992. Gender and archaeological knowledge. In *Metaarchaeology* (ed. L. Embree). Boston, MA: Reidel, pp. 195–227.

Harding, S. 1986. *The Science Question in Feminism.* Ithaca, NY: Cornell University Press.

Harding, S. 1987. Introduction: is there a feminist method? In *Feminism and Methodology: Social Science Issues* (ed. S. Harding). Bloomington: Indiana University Press, pp. 1–14.

Hastorf, C. A. 1991. Gender, space, and food in prehistory. In *Engendering Archaeology: Women and Prehistory* (eds J. M. Gero and M. W. Conkey). Cambridge, MA: Blackwell, pp. 132–62.

Jackson, T. L. 1991. Pounding acorn: women's production as social and economic focus. In *Engendering Archaeology: Women and Prehistory* (eds J. M. Gero and M. W. Conkey). Cambridge, MA: Blackwell, pp. 301–28.

Jagger, A. M. 1983. *Feminist Politics and Human Nature.* Sussex: Rowman & Allanheld.

Joyce, R. 2000. A Precolumbian gaze: male sexuality among the Ancient Maya. In *Archaeologies of Sexuality* (eds R. A. Schmidt and B. L. Voss). London: Routledge, in press.

Joyce, R. A. 1996. The construction of gender in classic Maya monuments. In *Gender and Archaeology* (ed. R. P. Wright). Philadelphia: University of Pennsylvania Press, pp. 167–98.

Joyce, R. A. and Claassen, C. 1997. Women in the ancient Americas: archaeologists, gender, and the making of prehistory. In *Women in Prehistory: North America and Mesoamerica* (eds C. Claassen and R. A. Joyce). Philadelphia: University of Pennsylvania Press, pp. 1–14.

Katz, J. 1976. *Gay American History: Lesbians and Gay Men in the U.S.A.* New York: Thomas Crowell.

Linden, R. R., Pagano, D. R., Russell, D. E. H. and Star, S. L. (eds) 1982. *Against Sadomasochism: A Radical Feminist Analysis.* East Palo Alto, CA: Frog In The Well Press.

Meskell, L. 1996. The somatization of archaeology: institutions, discourses, corporeality. *Norwegian Archaeological Review*, 29(1): 2–16.

Meskell, L. 1998. An archaeology of social relations in an Egyptian village. *Journal of Archaeological Method and Theory*, 5(3): 209–43.

Meskell, L. 2000. Re-em(bed)ing sex: domesticity, sexuality, and ritual in New Kingdom Egypt. In *Archaeologies of Sexuality* (eds R. A. Schmidt and B. L. Voss). London: Routledge, in press.

Miller, V. E. (ed.) 1988. *The Role of Gender in Precolumbian Art and Architecture.* Washington, DC: University Press of America.

Moore, J. and Scott, E. (eds) 1997. *Invisible People and Processes: Writing Gender and Childhood into European Archaeology.* London: Leicester University Press.

Nelson, S. M. 1997. *Gender In Archaeology: Analyzing Power and Prestige.* Walnut Creek, CA: Altamira Press.

Ortner, S. B. and Whitehead, H. (eds) 1981. *Sexual Meanings: The Cultural Construction of Gender and Sexuality.* Cambridge: Cambridge University Press.

Reiter, R. R. (ed.) 1975. *Toward an Anthropology of Women.* New York: Monthly Review Press.

Roberts, C. 1993. A critical approach to gender as a category of analysis in archaeology. In *Women in Archaeology: A Feminist Critique* (eds H. du Cros and L. Smith). Canberra: Department of Prehistory, The Australian National University, pp. 16–21.

Rosaldo, M. Z. and Lamphere, L. (eds) 1974. *Women, Culture, and Society.* Stanford, CA: Stanford University Press.

Rowbotham, S. and Weeks, J. 1977. *Socialism and the New Life: The Personal and Sexual Politics of Edward Carpenter and Havelock Ellis.* London: Pluto Press.

Rubin, G. 1975. The traffic in women: notes on the 'Political Economy' of sex. In *Toward an Anthropology of Women* (ed. R. R. Reiter). New York: Monthly Review Press, pp. 157–210.

Rubin, G. 1984. Thinking sex: notes for a radical theory of the politics of sexuality. In *Pleasure and Danger: Exploring Female Sexuality* (ed. C. S. Vance). London: Pandora, pp. 267–319.

Rubin, G. 1994. Sexual traffic: an interview with Judith Butler. *differences: A Journal of Feminist Cultural Studies*, 6(2 + 3): 62–99.

Rubin, G. 2000. Sites, settlements, and urban sex: archaeology and the study of gay leathermen in San Francisco, 1955–1995. In *Archaeologies of Sexuality* (eds R. A. Schmidt and B. L. Voss). London: Routledge, in press.

SAMOIS (ed.) 1982. *Coming to Power: Writings and Graphics on Lesbian S/M.* Boston, MA: Alyson Publications.

Sedgwick, E. K. 1990. *Epistemology of the Closet.* Berkeley: University of California Press.

Seifert, D. J. (ed.) 1991. *Historical Archaeology: Gender in Historical Archaeology*, 25(4).

Smith-Rosenberg, C. 1979. The female world of love and ritual: relations between women in nineteenth-century America. In *A Heritage of Her Own* (eds N. F. Cott and E. H. Pleck). New York: Simon & Schuster, Touchstone, pp. 311–42.

Snitow, A., Stansell, C. and Thompson, S. (eds) 1983. *Powers of Desire: The Politics of Sexuality.* New York: Monthly Review Press.

Spector, J. D. 1991. What this awl means: toward a feminist archaeology. In *Engendering Archaeology: Women and Prehistory* (eds J. M. Gero and M. W. Conkey). Cambridge, MA: Blackwell, pp. 388–406.

Spector, J. D. 1993. *What This Awl Means: Feminist Archaeology at a Wahpeton Dakota Village*. St. Paul, Minnesota: Minnesota Historical Society Press.

Vance, C. S. (ed.) 1984. *Pleasure and Danger: Exploring Female Sexuality.* New York: Routledge & Kegan Paul.

Vasey, P. L. 1998. Intimate sexual relations in prehistory: lessons from the Japanese Macaques. *World Archaeology*, 29(3): 407–25.

Voss, B. L. and Schmidt, R. A. 2000. Archaeologies of sexuality: an introduction. In *Archaeologies of Sexuality* (eds R. A. Schmidt and B. L. Voss). London: Routledge, in press.

Walde, D. and Willows, N. D. (eds) 1991. *The Archaeology of Gender: Proceedings of the Twenty-Second Annual Conference of the Archaeological Association of the University of Calgary.* Calgary: Archaeological Association of the University of Calgary.

Wall, D. de 1994. *The Archaeology of Gender: Separating the Spheres in Urban America.* New York: Plenum Press.

Warner, M. (ed.) 1993. *Fear of a Queer Planet: Queer Politics and Social Theory.* Minneapolis: University of Minnesota Press.

Watson, P. J. and Kennedy, M. C. 1991. The development of horticulture in the eastern woodlands: women's role. In *Engendering Archaeology: Women and Prehistory* (eds J. M. Gero and M. W. Conkey). Cambridge, MA: Blackwell, pp. 255–75.

Weeks, J. 1977. *Coming Out: Homosexual Politics in Britain from the Nineteenth Century to the Present*. London: Quartet.

Wright, R. P. 1991. Women's labor and pottery production in prehistory. In *Engendering Archaeology: Women and Prehistory* (eds J. M. Gero and M. W. Conkey). Cambridge, MA: Blackwell, pp. 194–223.

Wright, R. P. (ed.) 1996. *Gender and Archaeology.* Philadelphia: University of Pennsylvania Press.

Wright, R. P. 2000. Digging women: feminism comes to archaeology. *The Women's Review of Books*, 17(5): 18–19.

Wylie, A. 1991. Feminist critiques and archaeological challenges. In *The Archaeology of Gender: Proceedings of the Twenty-Second Annual Conference of the Archaeological Association of the University of Calgary* (eds D. Walde and N. D. Willows). Calgary: Archaeological Association of the University of Calgary, pp. 17–23.

Wylie, A. 1992. Reasoning about ourselves: feminist methodology in the social sciences. In *Women and Reason* (eds E. Harvey and K. Okruhlik). Ann Arbor: University of Michigan Press, pp. 225–44.

Wylie, A. 1996. The constitution of archaeological evidence: gender politics and science. In *The Disunity of Science: Boundaries, Contexts, Power* (eds P. Galison and D. J. Stump). Stanford, CA: Stanford University Press, pp. 311–43.

Wylie, A. 1997a. Good science, bad science, or science as usual? Feminist critiques of science. In *Women and Human Evolution* (ed. L. D. Hager). London: Routledge, pp. 29–55.

Wylie, A. 1997b. The engendering of archaeology: refiguring feminist science studies. *Osiris*, 12: 80–99.

Wylie, A. 2001. Doing social science as a feminist: the engendering of archaeology. In *Feminism in Twentieth-Century Science, Technology, and Medicine* (eds A. N. H. Creager, E. Lunbeck, and L. Schiebinger). Chicago: University of Chicago Press, pp.

4

No

Don Kulick

Performativity as a theory is most closely associated with the American philosopher Judith Butler, who in a number of well-known books has developed what she calls a performative approach to language and culture. The cornerstone of this approach is of course J. L. Austin's concept of the performative, which is concerned with language as action, language that in its enunciation changes the world – it brings about a new social state. The archetypal performatives with which Austin begins his discussion are utterances like 'I bet' or 'I promise'. However, by the conclusion of *How to do things with words*, Austin has collapsed the distinction between performatives and constatives that he established at the beginning, and he declares that even constative utterances are in fact performatives: 'there can hardly be any longer a possibility of not seeing that stating is performing an act', he wrote (Austin 1997: 139).

This collapse of the distinction between performative and constative was the dimension of Austin's theory that Butler developed in her work. Focusing on gender, Butler claimed that utterances like the 'It's a girl' delivered by a doctor to a mother who has just given birth are not merely descriptive. Like the priest's 'I now pronounce you man and wife', an utterance like 'It's a girl' performs an act. It *does something* in Butler's analysis. That act of naming 'initiates the process by which a certain girling is compelled', she wrote (Butler 1993: 232). It requires that the referent so designated act in accordance with particular norms and create, in doing so, the appropriate gender in every culturally legible act that the person so designated performs, from sitting in a chair, to expressing her desire, to deciding what she ought to eat for dinner.

The relevant part of this story for the argument I will develop here is what happened next. After the publication of Butler's 1990 book *Gender Trouble*, performativity suddenly became all the rage. It entered the lexicon of literary studies, history, sociology and anthropology, and it even merits a separate entry in Alessandro Duranti's recent collection *Key Terms in Language and Culture* (Hall 2001).

Now for sociolinguists and linguistic anthropologists, this might appear somewhat odd, because while 'performativity' was busy hypercirculating in other disciplines, another, older, term that seemingly referred to precisely the same thing – or at least it sounded pretty similar – already existed. That term was 'performance'.

But performance is not the same as performativity. The difference is this: performance is something a subject does. But performativity is the process through which the subject emerges (Butler 1993: 2, 7, 95). This is a crucial distinction that was completely missed by many critics of Butler's work. Early rejections of her framework were based on a reading of performativity as performance; on the idea of an entirely self-aware and volitional actor who could choose to put on or take off genders the way people put on or take off clothes (see e.g. Weston 1993). This is wrong. Performance is one dimension of performativity. But performativity theory insists that what is expressed or performed in any social context is importantly linked to that which is not expressed or cannot be performed. Hence, analysis of action and identity must take into account what is not or cannot be enacted. Furthermore, a performative approach to language interrogates the circulation of language in society – not so much who is authorized to use language (which was Austin's concern, as it was a major concern of Pierre Bourdieu, e.g. Bourdieu 1991), as how particular uses of language, be they authorized or not, produce particular effects and particular kinds of subjects in fields or matrices of power.

Performativity is not a linguistic concept – Austin was not a linguist, he was a philosopher, as is Butler – and this may be one reason why there are really very few linguistic studies that might be said to be performative.[1] There are lots of studies of performance, but few of performativity. The difference between the two perspectives is something I hope to illustrate in this paper. I propose to do this through and examination of the linguistic token of rejection or refusal, the word 'no'. My interest is in how the enunciation (or not) of 'no' in particular social situations works to produce those situations as sexual, even as it materializes particular subjects as sexual subjects. I am also interested in how the enunciation of 'no' is structured by certain absences, certain other enunciations that cannot or must not be expressed. I will illustrate my arguments by discussing the occurrence of 'no' in three seemingly very different contexts, which I will link. The three situations I will discuss are situations of (1) sexual harassment and rape, (2) instances where the so-called Homosexual Panic Defense, which I will explain shortly, is invoked, and, finally, (3) sadomasochistic sex.

Sexual Harassment and Rape

The foremost context for the analysis of 'no' in sexual situations is research that examines the language of sexual harassment and rape. This important research focuses on the fact that a woman's 'no' is constrained by cultural expectations and demands of femininity (Ehrlich 1998, 2001; Kitzinger & Frith 1999; Lees 1996; Matoesian 1993; McConnell-Ginet 1989). The strongest articulation of this position is the assertion that a woman's refusal of sex simply cannot be heard in patriarchal culture (MacKinnon 1993). In a culture that relentlessly objectifies and sexualizes women, the illocutionary force of a woman's 'no' to sex is consistently thwarted and distorted to mean 'keep trying', or even its inversion, 'yes'. Hence, men can claim that they misunderstood women's refusal, and women who are raped can be blamed for not having conveyed their refusal clearly enough. This is particularly the case when there is no physical evidence, such as bruises or broken bones, that the woman refused the man's advances.

Phrased in terms of performativity theory, what linguistic analyses of sexual harassment and rape trials demonstrate is that the subject position 'woman' is produced in part by the normatively exhorted utterance 'no' when encountering male desire for sex. This differs from the subject 'man', who, in contrast, is normatively exhorted to *never* say 'no' when confronted with female desire. Indeed, for a male to say 'no' to female desire for sex would threaten to signify him as a homosexual. In order to block this signification, extenuating circumstances need to be asserted, such as extreme physical unattractiveness in the female. All of this configures a cultural grammar in which saying 'no' is part of what produces a female sexual subject, and *not* saying 'no' produces a male sexual subject.[2] 'No' in both its present and absent manifestations facilitates the production of heterosexual subjectivities and heterosexual sexuality. Its utterance invokes a domain in which one interactant can performatively produce himself as a man by responding to it by prolonging the encounter and ideally finally transforming it into a 'yes', and the other interactant can performatively produce herself as female by facilitating – willingly or not – that extension and prolongation of the sexual scene.

Any performative approach to language will ask: where does a particular signifying system run up against its own limits? One place 'no' meets its limits is when a woman does not utter it, and says 'yes' without persuasion. Now, while Conversation Analysts have shown us that a 'yes' is an interactionally preferred response,[3] as a woman's response to a sexual advance, it is culturally a *dispreferred* one. Accordingly, the sexual subjects produced through 'yes' are *marked* in the linguistic, Jakobsonian sense; they are not just women; there are many other names for them, most of them pejorative. A 'yes' to sex can also produce female subjects as being outside heteronormativity, when that 'yes' occurs as a response to the advances of a woman (who, of course, is also marked in this discursive system). As an aside, I can also note that women who say 'yes' to sex are also marked in our academic texts, in this case through their virtual absence – we have several excellent studies on how women say 'no' to sex, but little information on how they say 'yes'. One paper we do have, interestingly enough, indicates that many women say 'yes' to (hetero) sex precisely by saying 'no'. (This was a questionnaire study done in the late 1980s, which asked 610 female undergraduate students if they had ever said 'no' to sex, even though they 'had every intention of and were willing to engage in sexual intercourse'. It turns out that 68.5% of these women reported saying 'no' when they meant 'maybe', and 39.3% reported saying 'no' when they meant 'yes'. When asked why they said 'no' when they meant 'yes', women answered either that they were afraid of appearing promiscuous, or they felt inhibited about sex, or they wanted to manipulate the male – they were angry with him, they wanted to make him more aroused, or more physically aggressive; see Muehlenhard & Hollabaugh 1988).

The field of sexuality produced by 'no' also runs up against its limits when a man says 'no' to a woman. As I already mentioned, this appearance of 'no' threatens to signify the subject as marked 'gay'. But interestingly, this 'no', rather than quelching sexuality, also invites its prolongation. Movies like the 1998 *The Opposite of Sex* (in which the main female character plots to seduce her brother's boyfriend, who says 'no' to her advances, telling her he is gay) make explicit and exploit this domain of possibility raised by a man's 'no' to female desire.

The most striking place where this system of sexual positionings runs up against its own limits is in instances when a man is solicited by another man. The marked subjectivity here is not so much the man doing the pursuing – men are subjects who pursue others sexually, and cultural stereotypes insist that men who pursue other men are the most fully sexed subjects of all (hence the most repellent heterosexual men in the world feel no embarrassment announcing that homosexuality is 'OK' with them, as long as the homosexuals don't try to seduce them...). In this particular erotic choreography, the marked subjectivity is the man who says 'no'. Precisely by saying 'no', this speaker performatively materializes the position reserved in heteronormative praxis for women. By having to utter 'no', the speaker produces a feminine subject; one that importantly does not reject sex so much as facilitate it, by invoking a matrix of persuasion. In other words, the 'no' here ensnares and constrains the male speaker in the same bind that it raises for female speakers who produce it. The fact that 'no' ensnares both women and men in this way is one reason why analysis should not concentrate, I think, on the *performance* of 'no'. What is important to interrogate is the way particular iterations of language *performatively* produce particular subject positions; positions which may in fact undermine the performance of a coherent gender identity.

Homosexual Panic Defense

That 'no' is precisely *not* just 'no', and that the performative force of 'no' facilitates, rather than ends, a sexual scene, is explicitly highlighted in the form of a phenomenon popularly known as the Homosexual Panic Defense. The Homosexual Panic Defense is the name of a legal defense invoked on behalf of men who have murdered other men who they claim made sexual advances towards them. In effect, the Homosexual Panic Defense argues that a sexual advance is in itself an act of aggression, and that the defendant was justified in responding to it with violence.

The Homosexual Panic Defense is based on something called 'acute homosexual panic'. This is a psychiatric condition that was first proposed in 1920. In its original formulation, 'homosexual panic' did not refer to a fear due to advances by other men. Instead, it referred to cases where men who had been in intensively same sex environments became aware of homosexual desires that they felt unable to control, and unable to act on. The original formulation of the disorder was based on diagnosis a small number of soldiers and sailors in a US government mental hospital after World War I (Kempf 1920). These men were not violent – they were, on the contrary, passive. The disorder was characterized by periods of introspective brooding, self-punishment, suicidal assaults, withdrawal, and helplessness. So 'homosexual panic' was generally understood not as a temporary, violent episode, but, rather as an on-going illness that comprised severe bouts of depression. Patients suffering from it were catatonic, not violent. Basically, 'homosexual panic' was the diagnosis given to men who we today would try to get to come out and accept their homosexuality. In fact, some early psychiatrists recognized that the best treatment for the disorder was for the patient to accept his homosexual desires and act on them.

What happened during the course of the 1900s is that the original understanding of this condition shifted, and it came to be applied even to men who reacted violently in situations where homosexual desire was made explicit. In other words, it became used to explain situations where a man allowed himself to be solicited or seduced by another man, but then suddenly turned on that man and beat or even murdered him. In the psychiatric literature, there is no consensus that 'homosexual panic' should or can be used to explain sudden violent outbursts like these. But to the extent that the fury is identified as 'homosexual panic', the violence is explained by latent homosexual cravings and a challenge or collapse of a heterosexual self-image.[4]

The Homosexual Panic Defense builds loosely on this later understanding of homosexual panic. It argues that there is a scientific and medical reason for, and, hence, a justification of, the behavior of defendants who murder gay men. The literary scholar Eve Sedgwick (1990: 19) has noted that the very existence of such a category rests on an assumption that hatred of homosexuals is a private and atypical phenomenon. But think about it, she says. To what extent would anyone accept 'race panic' as an accountability-reducing illness for a German skinhead who bludgeoned a Turk to death? Or 'gender panic' for a woman who shot a man who made an unwanted advance to her? (Consider how many bodies would be swept out of bars and clubs every morning). The fact that the Homosexual Panic Defense exists at all indicates that far from being an individual pathology, hatred of homosexuals is actually more public and more typical than hatred of any other disadvantaged group.

The defense is applied in English speaking countries like the US, Australia and Canada in two ways. One is as an insanity defense – that is, a defense that argues that the accused is in a condition or state where they cannot tell right from wrong or not understand the character of their actions. Legal scholars have argued that in pure legal terms, the Homosexual Panic Defense should not qualify as an insanity defense at all, first of all because to the extent that individuals can be said to panic at homosexuality, they do so precisely because they believe that homosexuality is 'wrong'. Second, cases that invoke the Panic Defense do not assert that defendants do not realize that shooting their victims in the heart, hacking them with meat cleavers, jumping on their heads or beating them with clubs – to take some more charming examples of the cases where the defense has been invoked – it is never asserted that defendants who do this do not realize that these actions might kill the victim.

The second way the defense is applied is as a response to provocation. This defense relies on and promotes a view that there is no difference between a sexual advance and a sexual attack. In fact, the Homosexual Panic Defense argues that a sexual advance from a homosexual male is definitionally a sexual attack, and that the accused is justified in responding violently to such an act of aggression.

In practice, the Homosexual Panic Defense is used in ways that often bear almost no resemblance to any version of the psychiatric disorder. For example, the psychiatric criterion that homosexual panic is related to latent homosexuality in the accused is often disregarded. The most famous case of the Homosexual Panic Defense in recent years was a man named Jonathan Schmitz. Twenty-six-year-old

Schmitz was brought onto an American television program called the *Jenny Jones* show, which is a kind of *Ricki Lake* or *Jerry Springer* show where people surprise their friends, family and lovers by revealing unexpected and often scandalous secrets about themselves on national television. Jonathan Schmitz had been told by the *Jenny Jones's* show's producers that someone he knew was secretly in love with him, and would reveal this crush on the air. It turned out that the person who was secretly in love with Schmitz was a 32-year-old gay man named Scott Amedure. Amedure greeted Schmitz when he appeared on the television stage and professed his attraction. Three days after the taping of the show, Schmitz bought a shotgun, drove to Amedure's home and shot him twice through the heart.

In the subsequent trial, Schmitz blamed the murdered Amedure for his actions – and this is how the Homosexual Panic Defense is increasingly being used. In other words, Schmitz's lawyers did not claim that Schmitz is a latent homosexual who panicked at the collapse of his heterosexual self image. Instead, they claimed that Scott Amedure's public revelation of his desire in itself constituted an 'ambush'.[5] Schmitz's lawyers argued that Amedure's public revelation of an infatuation with Schmitz was, in and of itself, an act of aggression that excused a violent retaliation. The jury agreed with this line of reasoning and found Schmitz guilty not of first-degree premeditated murder, but of the lesser charge of second-degree (i.e. not premeditated) murder.[6]

Now let's look for a moment at the Homosexual Panic Defense in relation to what I have already argued about 'no' in cases of sexual harassment and rape. At first glance, the two kinds of cases seem very different, which may be one reason why I have not seen them discussed together in any detail. In the case of rape, the victim of violence is the woman who rejects the sexual advance of a man. In the case of Homosexual Panic, the victim of violence is the man who (is reported to have) made the sexual advance.

What links the two cases, I am arguing, is 'no'. In both cases, a sexual advance acts as an interpellation, a calling into being of a sexual subject. Like Louis Althusser's famous example of the policeman's call 'Hey, you there!' that produces a subject in the person who turns around (Althusser 1971: 174) – a subject who did not pre-exist the call, but who becomes constituted as a subject upon responding to it – a sexual advance calls into being a sexual subject. And in the case of both rape and Homosexual Panic, from the perspective of performativity theory, a 'no' is not just a refusal of that subjection. It is also an acknowledgement of it; a response to the interpellative call that even in disputing it affirms it. It is a 'no' that says 'I refuse to acknowledge that I am being called into being as a sexual subject'. But a refusal to acknowledge something is already a form of acknowledgment. In structural terms, therefore, a 'no' to a sexual advance is – must be – both a 'no' and a 'yes' at the same time.

This dual indexicality[7] of 'no' is what allows men to claim that they misunderstood a woman's 'no', even as it also facilitates their assertion that sexual solicitation by another man in itself was an act of violence that justified a violent response. Remember that part of what produces the masculine sexual subject is the 'no' of the other. To have to utter that 'no' oneself is to be forced to produce oneself as a non-masculine subject. I think that it is for this reason that in cases in which the Homosexual Panic Defense is invoked, there is often no evidence that any verbal refusal ever even occurred. The word 'no' is not – in a sense, cannot – be uttered.

Instead, the sexual interpellation is acknowledged non-verbally, with vicious physical violence.

I hope it is becoming clear where this argument is leading. My point is that 'no' is essential not so much for the production of a sexual scenario (after all, a 'yes' can produce that), but for the materialization of *a particular kind of sexual scenario* in which the sexual subjects so produced are differentially empowered and differentially gendered. In other words, 'no' produces a sexualized gendered field of power. As a final empirical example, I offer a situation that crystallizes all this, namely sadomasochistic sex.

Sadomasochistic Sex

Sadomasochistic sex is an extremely straightforward example of a case where 'no' is self-consciously used to constitute a sexualized, gendered field of power. To see this, it is important to understand that any description or analysis of S/M discusses what is called a 'safeword'. This is a word or phrase that is negotiated in advance of the sexual scene and used by either the submissive bottom or the dominant top whenever either of them wants to stop some activity. The most important dimension of this for us is the fact that one of the very few words which cannot function as a safeword is, precisely, 'no'.

'Consider... this dialogue', readers are instructed by one S/M manual, in a section on safewords:

> Top: 'Seems to me you deserve a good spanking with this hairbrush, my little slut.' Bottom (in role as obedient slave): 'If it pleases you, sir or madam' – or bottom (in role as reluctant victim): 'No! Please! Not the hairbrush!'[8]

'In either case', the manual explains, 'the top has no guide to the bottom's real feelings' (Easton & Hardy 2001: 39). Why is this? The same authors go on to explain:

> The reason we need [a safeword] is that lots of us like to pretend we don't want to have all these amazing things done to us, and we may pretend by joyously shrieking 'No-nonononono', so we need another word to mean that (Easton & Hardy 2001: 44).

Another S/M manual (Henkin & Holiday 1996: 89) puts it like this:

> Words other than No, Stop, or Slow Down are usually designated [as a safeword] because SM is a *consensual* eroticism in the realm of *erotic theatre*. If a bottom could just say 'Stop' to end a [sexual] scene, the illusion that the Top has total control might be threatened. Besides, many bottoms enjoy the fantasy of nonconsenuality and scream 'No, no, please stop!' – or words to that effect – when the scene is going very well; they would be upset, confused, and even angry if a Top actually did stop in response to their outbursts.

Another S/M manual explains that 'A plea to 'Stop beating me' may well mean 'I love it. Keep going'' (Lee 1983: 186).

It is clear that 'no' in these situations means its inversion, 'yes'. For that reason, manuals explain that safewords should be anything other than words like 'no', 'stop', or 'don't' – that is to say, any words other than negations or expressions of pain. Most manuals recommend either contextually jarring words like 'PICKLE!' or 'RADISH!', or words that invoke associations to traffic lights: 'YELLOW', meaning 'lighter or slower', and 'RED' meaning 'stop'.

In any case, my point is that S/M sex self-consciously exploits the performative potential of 'no' to facilitate and extend sexual scenes. It recognizes the dual indexicality of 'no' and deploys it to produce a domain of sexuality; a domain of sexuality that is, moreover, saturated with power. Because whatever else it may be about, all practitioners and observers of S/M are agreed that it is an eroticization and staging of power. S/M manuals all discuss power. The title of one of the first and most famous S/M manuals ever published, by the lesbian-feminist S/M support group, Samois, was *Coming to Power.*[9] A common definition of S/M is 'consensual exchanges of erotic power' (e.g. Henkin & Holiday 1996: 72). One manual elaborates a distinction between 'power-over', which is power obtained at the expense of others, and 'power-with', which is 'the idea that we can all become more powerful by supporting each other in being more powerful' (Easton & Hardy 2001: 24–5). S/M, this manual explains, is a play with power for the fun of it; hence, a 'power-with' in which erotic pleasure is produced by skillful manipulations of forms of power that are invested with new content. This same manual proposes that all bottoms ought to see themselves as what it calls 'full-power bottoms'.

We can debate the extent to which concepts like 'full-power bottoms' are reasonable ones. But even those who reject them – for example radical feminists who insist that S/M practitioners merely reinscribe the very structures of power they claim to transcend – do not contest that what happens in sado-masochistic sex is an erotic staging of power.

The central role that 'no' plays in this staging is not fortuitous or arbitrary. On the contrary, the structuring role of 'no' in the production of a sadomasochistic sex scene is a distillation and elaboration of 'no's role in wider arenas of social life. And that role, as I have been arguing, is not so much about performance as it is production. 'No' performatively materializes specific kinds of erotic domains, ones in which power is channeled through and constitutive of specific social positions. Those positions are gendered in the sense that they are differently positioned in relation to 'no' – as I mentioned earlier, the subject position 'woman' is produced in part by the normatively exhorted utterance 'no' when encountering a sexual interpellation. This contrasts with the subject 'man', who is normatively exhorted to *never* say 'no' to sex, and whose position as masculine is produced in part through the 'no' of the other. S/M sex invokes this plane in order to exploit the disruptive potential of the erotic to manipulate and invert these positionings. Hence, it provides a space for the male body to temporarily (and socially inconsequentially) inhabit the 'no' that is otherwise disallowed it; just as it provides a space for the female body to inhabit the position that is materialized through the enunciation of the 'no' of the other (It is no secret to anyone that the overwhelming majority of submissive bottoms are males – frequently the same males who exercise a great deal of social power outside the dungeon. Nor is it a secret that the tops that these men pay a lot of money to dominate them are female dominatrixes – how's that for a linguistically *marked* category?). The erotic plane that S/M sex constructs for itself also recognizes the violence that inheres in sexual domains invoked by 'no', and it produces that violence. But it produces it not as realism or tragedy, but, rather, as *melodrama*, a genre that is characterized by the exteriorization of conflict and psychic structures in dramatic excess (see Gledhill 1987: 31; also Nowell-Smith 1987, Williams 1987).

Conclusion

The main point of this essay has been to suggest what I see as a difference between performance and performativity, and the relationship of those two perspectives to language. At several junctures, I noted where a performance perspective differs from a performativity perspective. But there is a particular difference, a crucial one in my view, with which I would like to end. This difference has to do with the concept of identity.

I raise the issue of identity at the end of this paper because of the central role it has come to play in scholarly work on language and sexuality. Sexuality, like gender before it, has come to be conceptualized in sociolinguistic and anthropological linguistic research as primarily a matter of identity. And as such, researchers use linguistic data to discuss how people *perform* different sexual identities, particularly lesbian or gay identities (for extensive summaries and critiques of this work see Kulick 2000, 2002, 2003; Cameron and Kulick 2003a, 2003b).

But perhaps the single most crucial difference between a performance perspective on language, and a performativity perspective is this: whereas studies conceived of in a performance framework will tend to see language in relation to *identity*, research framed as performative will concentrate more on *identification*. The difference is between "identity", which in sociolinguistic and linguistic anthropological work is conventionally presented as a more or less conscious claim-staking of a particular sociological position, and "identification", which is a psychoanalytic concept concerned with the operations through which the subject is constituted. Identifications are processes through which individuals assimilate an aspect or property of an other, and are, in that process, transformed (for a concise summary, see Laplanche and Pontalis 1973: 205–8). A crucial difference between "identity" and "identification" is that identifications are not entirely conscious. On the contrary, identifications are just as much structured by rejections, refusals and disavowals as they are structured by affirmations. In addition, identifications are not imagined to constitute a coherent relational system. In other words, the processes that constitute an individual as a certain kind of subject are not harmonious. Rather, they are conflicting and contradictory, undermining conscious attempts to produce and maintain subjective coherence and consistency.

Because they are not the same thing, it is important to not collapse identification into identity. A performative approach to linguistic phenomena would not start or end with identity. Instead, a performative approach would examine the processes through which some kinds of identifications are facilitated and some are blocked, some are legitimate and others are illegitimate, some are unmarked, and others are marked. I have tried to illustrate this approach by focusing on 'no', examining it not by asking: who says it? but, rather: what does saying it – or not saying it – produce?

That question leads me to another, more consequential one, namely: instead of a sociolinguistics of identity, what would happen if we began imagining a sociolinguistics of identification?

NOTES

1 Earlier work on language and political economy (e.g. Myers and Brenneis 1984), discursive regimes of speaking (e.g. Lindstrom 1990), Bakhtinian dialogism (e.g. Hill and Hill 1986; Tedlock and Mannheim 1995), and, most recently, 'language ideology' (e.g. Schieffelin, Woolard and Kroskrity 1998) shares many concerns with performativity theory in that it examines who is authorized or enabled to say what, and who is silenced. Where this work arguably differs from performativity theory is, first of all, in its inattention to issues of sexuality; secondly, in its relative lack of concern with the processes through which subjects and subjectivities are produced; and thirdly, in its lack of awareness of the complex role that *identifications* (refusals as well as affirmations) play in linguistic practice. There are of course exceptions to this generalization, such as Hill 1995a, which examines the production of a specific moral subject without using the metalanguage of performativity theory. Valentine's paper in this volume is a good example of an empirically-grounded performative study of language (that does reference performativity theory), because it interrogates how particular kinds of language enable or block particular kinds of identifications and subjectivities (2003).

2 Please note the 'part of what...'. I am not claiming that 'no' is the only linguistic iteration that produces sexualized, gendered subjects. But I am claiming that 'no' works as a performative to produce situations as sexual, and it simultaneously materializes sexualized, gendered subjects that are positioned in a specific relation of power.

3 See Kitzinger & Frith 1999 for a discussion of this in the context of sexual harassment and rape.

4 See the following sources on homosexual panic and the Homosexual Panic Defense: Bagnall, Gallagher & Goldstein 1984; Comstock 1989; Freiberg 1988; Glick 1959; New South Wales Government 1998; Suffrendi 2001; Hart 1958.

5 *Michigan Court of Appeals* 1998. 586 N.W. 2d 766, 768.

6 For details about the Schmitz case, see http://www.courttv.com/trials/jennyjones/background.html

7 I am indebted to Jane Hill (1995b: 13) for this term, but I adopt it here to mean something different than what she proposes.

8 For the uninitiated, I should note that the terms 'top' and 'bottom' in SM culture denotes, respectively, the dominant and submissive partner in a sexual scene.

9 'The name Samois was chosen because it evokes several lesbian episodes and the figure of a lesbian dominatrix in *Story of* O, probably the most famous S/M literary classic' (Samois 1979: 4). For a history of the group, see Califia & Sweeney 1996.

10 See Cameron and Kulick 2003, chapter 6, for a more detailed exposition of this assertion.

REFERENCES

Althusser, L., 1971. Ideology and ideological state apparatuses (notes towards an investigation). In Althusser, L., Lenin and Philosophy and Other Essays. London: Monthly Review Press, pp. 127–88.

Astuto, C. & Califia, P., 1988. So you wanna be a sadist? How to make it hurt so good in one easy lesson. In: Califia, P. (Ed.), The Lesbian S/M Manual. Boston: Lace publications, pp. 45–65.

Austin, J. L. 1997 [1962] How to Do Things with Words, 2nd edition. Cambridge, Mass.: Harvard University Press.

Bagnall, R. G., Gallagher, P. C., & Goldstein, J. L., 1984. Burdens on gay litigants and the bias in the court system: Homosexual panic, child custody and anonymous parties. *Harvard Civil Rights-Civil Liberties Law Review* 19(2): 487–559.

Bourdieu, P., 1991. Authorized language. In Bourdieu, P., Language and Symbolic Power. Cambridge, Mass.: Harvard University Press, pp. 107–16.

Butler, J., 1990. Gender Trouble: Feminism and the Subversion of Identity. New York: Routledge.

1993. Bodies that Matter: On the Discursive Limits of 'Sex'. New York: Routledge.

Califia, P. (Ed.), 1988. The Lesbian S/M Safety Manual. Boston, Mass.: Lace Publications.

1996. A house divided: Violence in the lesbian S/M community. In: Califia P., Sweeny, R. (Eds.), The Second Coming: a Leatherdyke Reader. Los Angeles: Alyson Publications, pp. 264–77.

Califia, P. & Sweeney, R., 1996. Come soon, come in, and come as you are: An introduction. In: Califia P., Sweeny, R. (Eds.), The Second Coming: A Leatherdyke Reader. Los Angeles: Alyson Publications, xi–xvii.

Cameron, D. & Kulick, D., 2003a. Language and Sexuality. Cambridge: Cambridge University Press.

2003b. Introduction: Language and desire in theory and practice. *Language and Communication* 23(2): 93–105.

Comstock, G. D., 1989. Developments: Sexual orientation and the law. *Harvard Law Review* 102: 1508–51.

Easton, D. & Hardy, J. W., 2001. The New Bottoming Book. Emeryville, CA.: Greenery Press.

Erlich, S., 1998. The discursive reconstruction of sexual consent. *Discourse & Society* 9(2): 149–71.

2001. Representing Rape: Language and Sexual Consent. New York: Routledge.

Freiberg, P., 1988. Blaming the victim: New life for the 'gay panic' defense. *The Advocate*, May 24, 1988: 10–13.

Gledhill, C., 1987. The melodramatic field: An investigation. In: Gledhill, C. (Ed.), Home is Where the Heart is: Studies in Melodrama and the Woman's Film. London: British Film Institute, pp. 5–42.

Glick, B. S., 1959. Homosexual Panic: Clinical and theoretical considerations. *The Journal of Nervous and Mental Disease* 129: 20–8.

Hall, K., 2001. Performativity. In: Duranti, A. (Ed.), Key Terms in Language and Culture, Oxford: Blackwell, pp. 180–3.

Hart, H. H., 1958. Fear of homosexuality among college students. In Wedge, B. M. (Ed.), Psychosocial Problems of College Men. New Haven: Yale University Press, pp. 200–13.

Henkin, W. A. & Holiday, S., 1996. Consensual Sadomasochism: How to Talk About It and Do It Safely. Los Angeles: Daedalus.

Hill, J. 1995a. The voices of Don Gabriel. In: Tedlock, D., Mannheim, B. (Eds.), The Dialogic Emergence of Culture. Urbana and Chicago: University of Illinois Press, pp. 97–147.
1995b. Mock Spanish: A site for the indexical reproduction of racism in American English. (http://www.language-culture.org/colloquia/ symposia/hill-jane).
Hill, J. & Hill, K., 1986. Speaking Mexicano: Dynamics of a Syncretic Language in Central Mexico. Tucson: University of Arizona Press.
Kamel, G. W. L., 1983. Leathersex: Meaningful aspects of gay sadomasochism. In: Weinberg, T., Kamel, G. W. L. (Eds.), S and M: Studies in Sadomasochism. New York: Prometheus Books, pp. 162–74.
Kempf, E. J., 1920. Psychopathology. St. Louis: C. V. Mosby Company.
Kitzinger, C. & Frith, H., 1999. Just say no? The use of conversation analysis in developing a feminist perspective on sexual refusal. *Discourse & Society* 10 (3): 293–316.
Kulick, D., 2003. Language and desire. In: Holms, J., Myerhoff, M. (Eds.), The Handbook of Language and Gender. Oxford: Blackwell, pp. 119–41.
2002. Queer linguistics? In: Campbell-Kibler, K., Podesva, R. J., Roberts, S. J., Wong, A. (Eds.), Language and Sexuality: Contesting Meaning in Theory and Practice, Stanford, CA: CSLI Publications, pp. 65–8.
2000. Gay & lesbian language. *Annual Review of Anthropology* 29: 243–85.
Laplanche, J. & Pontalis, J.-B., 1973. The Language of Psychoanalysis. London: Karnac Books.
Lee, J. A., 1983. The social organization of sexual risk. In Weinberg, T., Kamel, G. W. L. (Eds.), S and M: Studies in Sadomasochism. New York: Prometheus Books, pp. 175–93.
Lees, S., 1996. Carnal Knowledge: Rape on Trial. London: Hamish Hamilton.
Lindstrom, L., 1990. Knowledge and Power in a South Pacific Society. Washington & London: Smithsonian Institution Press.
MacKinnon, C. A., 1993. Only Words. Cambridge, Mass.: Harvard University Press.
Matoesian, G. M., 1993. Reproducing Rape: Domination Through Talk in the Courtroom. Chicago: University of Chicago Press.
McConnell-Ginet, S., 1989. The (re)production of sexual meaning: A discourse based theory. In: Frank, F., Treichler, P. (Eds.), Language, Gender and Professional Writing, New York: Modern Language Association, pp. 111–34.
Muehlenhard, C. L. & Hollabaugh, L. C., 1988. Do women sometimes say no when they mean yes? The prevalence and correlates to women's token resistance to sex. *Journal of Personality and Social Psychology* 54 (5): 872–9.
Michigan Court of Appeals 1998. 586 N.W. 2d 766, 768.
Myers, F. R. & Brenneis, D. L., 1984. Introduction: Language and politics in the Pacific. In: Brenneis, D. L., Myers, F. R. (Eds.), Dangerous Words: Language and Politics in the Pacific. New York: New York University Press, pp. 1–29.
New South Wales Government 1998. Homosexual Advance Defence: Final report of the working party. http://lawlink.nsw.gov.au/clrd1.nsf/pages/had
Nowell-Smith, G., 1987. Minelli and melodrama. In: Gledhill, C. (Ed.), Home is Where the Heart is: Studies in Melodrama and the Woman's Film. London: British Film Institute, pp. 70–4.
Samois (Eds.), 1979. What Color is Your Handkerchief: A Lesbian S/M Sexuality Reader. Berkeley: Samois.
1981. Coming to Power: Writings and Graphics on Lesbian S/M. Boston: Alyson Publications.
Schieffelin, B. B., Woolard, K. A., & Kroskrity, P. V. (Eds.), 1998. Language Ideologies: Practice and Theory. Oxford & New York: Oxford University Press.

Sedgwick, E. K., 1990. Epistemology of the Closet. Berkeley & Los Angeles: University of California Press.

Suffrendi, K. S., 2001 Pride and prejudice: The homosexual panic defense. *Boston College Third World Law Journal* 21 (2): 279–314.

Tedlock, D. & Mannheim, B. (Eds.), 1995. The Dialogic Emergence of Culture. Urbana and Chicago: University of Illinois Press.

The Opposite of Sex, 1998, Roos, D. (Director), Kirkpatrick, D., Besman, M. (Producers), SONY Pictures Classic Release.

Valentine, D., 2003. 'I went to bed with my own kind once': The erasure of desire in the name of identity. *Language and Communication* 23(2): 123–38.

Weston, K., 1993. Do clothes make the woman? Gender, performance theory, and lesbian eroticism. *Genders* 17: 1–21.

Williams, L., 1987. 'Something else besides a mother': *Stella Dallas* and the maternal dilemma. In: Gledhill, C. (Ed.), Home is Where the Heart is: Studies in Melodrama and the Woman's Film. London: British Film Institute, pp. 299–325.

5

Resources for Lesbian Ethnographic Research in the Lavender Archives

Alisa Klinger

As you open this book and begin to read, I would like you to hold an image in your mind.... millions of letters and diaries of women, famous or obscure, going up in flames, sifting to ash; library stacks of biographies which do not tell the truths we most need to know; hundreds of the private papers of women acclaimed for their public contributions, sealed and placed under lock and key, or doled out by literary executors to those scholars who will accept censorship; dissertations, the work of years, which are forbidden to be published, read or quoted. As you read the stories in this book I would like you to think of those piles of ash, those cages behind which women's words, lesbian words, lie imprisoned, those shelves of life-histories gutted of their central and informing theme.

Adrienne Rich[1]

If all your time and energy has to go into defending yourself, into surviving oppression, there's not going to be much left over for building libraries.

Noretta Koertge[2]

Paper is perishable. It is easily mislaid, forgotten, shredded, burned. It fades with wear; it disintegrates over time. Paper, despite its debility, has been the primary currency of North American lesbian cultural exchange throughout most of the twentieth century. As electronic technology is swiftly rearranging our relationship to print, it seems particularly apropos to ask: what happens to the reams of paper – the novels, the newspapers, the notebooks, the order books, the letters – that have circulated lesbian culture from person to person, town to town, generation to generation? In this discussion, I follow the trail of paper created by lesbians to account for the proliferation of lesbian community archives alongside lesbian-feminist alternative publishing ventures and literary projects. Additionally, I suggest how students, community researchers, and scholars can access, respect, and preserve the traces of lesbian life that contain our individual and collective histories.

If lesbians have historically been "hidden from history," then their books, papers, and artwork – the records of their existence and resistance – have been no more secure.[3] Books with lesbian content are regularly left off reading lists, banned from school libraries, and turned back at borders. While these routine kinds of censorship are detrimental, the availability and safety of lesbian materials is even at risk in research libraries. Take for instance the recent, egregious example of censorious vandalism at the Zimmerman Library at the University of New Mexico. In November 1994, it was discovered that a shelf of bound periodicals, comprising thirty gay literature and women's studies journals valued at over $25,000, had been defaced with swastikas and obscenities. In addition, the complete run of the *Journal of Homosexuality* and several women's studies titles (classed in the HQ1101-HQ1236 section) were reported missing, and books on the Nazi party were found misshelved in the women's studies subject section of the library.[4] Although an extensive search of the library – a 300,000 square foot facility with over 900,000 volumes – did not recover the missing materials, they were later found concealed atop the highest shelves, behind other volumes, in a remote part of the library where discontinued volumes are stored. Such acts of vandalism particularly and the threat of textual terrorism generally make the lavender stacks an endangered community resource.

While the vulnerability of lesbian materials to bias crimes accounts in part for the creation of lesbian community-based archives, mainstream institutional disinterest, neglect, and dissimulation have contributed significantly to lesbian endeavors to conserve their history in community archives of their own making and under their own control. When *The Radcliffe Quarterly*, for example, included an extensive feature commemorating the Schlesinger Library's fiftieth birthday, "demonstrating that women have a history" and that women can no longer be treated as an undifferentiated group, it was regrettable but not surprising that no reference to lesbianism was made (Press 1). Although photographs of both Gertrude Stein and Adrienne Rich appear on one page, the conspicuous omission of specific references to the Schlesinger Library's resources for lesbian studies effectively constitutes a roadblock for students and scholars attempting to reclaim lesbian history.

Whether they choose to publicize their collections or not, university and public libraries are increasingly developing their lesbian holdings by lining their shelves in the first instance with the books and periodicals published by and readily available from academic and mainstream presses. Because lesbian materials historically have been independently rather than mass produced, the college-affiliated scholar or community researcher seeking the more ephemeral yet still consequential traces of lesbian history and culture than scholarly holdings include will more readily find them at a variety of community archives.[5] According to the Gay and Lesbian Task Force Clearinghouse of the American Library Association (ALA), there were in fact more than 110 such collections by 1993 (Owens 86).[6] Brooklyn's Lesbian Herstory Archives, the June L. Mazer Lesbian Collection in West Hollywood, and a host of other lesbian-specific and co-gender gay archives across North America (including the ONE Institute/International Gay and Lesbian Archives in Los Angeles with its new "ONE Lesbian Collection," the Gay and Lesbian Historical Society of Northern

California Archives, the Archives gaies du Québec, and the Canadian Lesbian and Gay Archives in Toronto) are devoted to the collection, preservation, and dissemination of an enormous range of resources essential for undertaking lesbian historical and ethnographic study.[7] As the academic institutionalization of lesbian studies becomes more secure, the value of community-based archives like these and the preservation work that they perform will become more obvious to the scholars who rely on them to provide the raw materials that their studies require. At the same time, these community-based outposts of lesbian print activism will be required to meet new demands and challenges as they renegotiate their relationship to academic institutions.

The archives' collections of community-based publications, providing the most consistent coverage of lesbian personalities, establishments, and accomplishments, are indispensable for chronicling lesbian book history and cultural formation. The minutiae of lesbian existence are recorded in manuscripts, books, periodicals, essays, speeches, pamphlets, leaflets, brochures, letters, unpublished papers, visual and audio works, newspaper clippings, memorabilia (including matchbook covers, lapel buttons, bumper stickers, posters, flyers, and costumes), and ephemera. The Mazer Collection even sports retired softball and baseball uniforms from the 1940s, 1950s, and 1960s, donated by former professional softball player Mary Rudd (Wolt 1). In addition to their special holdings, the lesbian archives own complete sets or substantial runs of both their organizational newsletters and the fleeting and more established lesbian and/or feminist and gay newsletters, periodicals, and newspapers that are often omitted from academic library collections.[8] Germane resources, particularly for a study of lesbian discursive production, include *Black/Out* (the magazine of the National Coalition of Black Lesbians and Gays), *Common Lives/Lesbian Lives, Feminary* (one of the only publications devoted specifically to Southern literary concerns), *Feminist Bookstore News, Gay Community News* (a Boston-based weekly), *Lambda Book Report: A Review of Contemporary Gay and Lesbian Literature, Lesbian Connection, Lesbians of Color Caucus* newsletter, *Matrices: Lesbian Feminist Resource Network, Motheroot Journal: A Women's Review of Small Presses, New Directions for Women, off our backs, Out/Look, Publishing Triangle News*, and *Sojourner, A Third World Women's Research Newsletter.*[9] Given North American lesbians' tremendous penchant for paper, however, it is ironic that there are not more traces of print, other than the published materials themselves, to testify to the reams of paper produced by the women in print movement.[10] In her history of *Lavender Women*, Michal Brody notes that "[i]t seems we couldn't take ourselves seriously as a business, but we understood the seriousness of being a printed medium" (171). Her pithy observation about how the cultural devaluation of women's work has been internalized by lesbians perhaps best explains why there are so few extant organizational records either for the Chicago lesbian newspaper collective that published 26 issues of the paper from 1971 to 1976 or for the Women in Print movement generally.

Despite the overall paucity of records that have survived from now defunct lesbian-feminist print shops, publishing collectives, and book-stores, several regional archival collections house crucial materials for piecing together the history of American lesbian cultural investments and enterprises. For instance, numerous filing cabinet drawers at the Mazer Collection are teeming with Diana Press's production lists, job files, and meeting minutes. The Mazer Collection also has more than 1,000 periodical titles and about 3,000 books, including Barbara Grier's forty-year collection of lesbian periodicals and the papers of the Daughters of Bilitis, in its modest rent-free space in the City of West Hollywood.[11] The operational records of the Women's Press Collective, a conglomerate of three women-owned printing companies (Up Press, the Women's Press Project, and Women's Press) in the San Francisco Bay Area during the 1970s and 1980s, are preserved at the Gay and Lesbian Historical Society of Northern California Archives ("Women's Press Records Preserved" 14). In addition, the GLHS has acquired the records from A Women's Place Bookstore (Glass 12) and Oracle Books, a feminist bookstore operated by lesbians from 1973 to 1980 (Chandler 6). The letters, photographs, and papers belonging to influential Bay Area poet Elsa Gidlow and her lover Isabel Quallo, and such African-American lesbian newspapers, magazines, and journals as *Azalea, Aché*, and *Black Lesbian Newsletter*, are also part of the GLHS collection.[12] Audre Lorde, cofounder of Kitchen Table Women of Color Press, donated a portion of her personal papers and manuscripts to the Lesbian Herstory Archives. Moreover, Barbara Grier and Donna McBride, cofounders in 1973 of the first and largest lesbian publishing house in the world, have made a gift of their extensive collection of books and periodicals, formerly the Lesbian and Gay Archives of Naiad Press in Tallahassee, Florida, to the San Francisco Main Public Library for their Gay and Lesbian Center.[13] The nine-thousand-volume collection, amassed by Grier and McBride since 1950 – well before the first lesbian or women's presses made their mark on the publishing world – is "the most complete personal library of lesbian and gay books in the English Language."[14] The pulp novels and Daughters of Bilitis and Mattachine Society publications that make up the Grier-McBride Collection will be the cornerstone of the new Gay and Lesbian Center, the first such center to be made part of a public library, sharing quarters with the archives of filmmakers Peter Adair (*World Is Out* and *Absolutely Positive*) and Rob Epstein (*Common Threads: Stories from the Quilt* and *The Times of Harvey Milk*), and journalist and author Randy Shilts (*And the Band Played On* and *The Mayor of Castro Street: The Life and Times of Harvey Milk*).

Many community archivists, scholars, and activists contend that the control of lesbian and gay archives must reside with lesbian and gay people themselves rather than with governmental, civic, or academic institutions. The community-based, perhaps separatist, rationale for such libraries as the Gay and Lesbian Historical Society of Northern California Archives, the Lesbian Herstory Archives, and the June Mazer Lesbian Collection was devised precisely to create a "safe-space" for lesbians and gay men and to prevent their culture from being submerged through bureaucratic (fiscal or philosophical) fiat, proxy, or neglect. By and large, the lesbians archival collections subscribe to the feminist principles and goals expressed in the Mazer Collection's mission statement:

> we are committed to seeking out and including materials by or about lesbians of all backgrounds and experiences, especially those who are not usually seen or heard. We are committed to keeping the Collection open and available to every woman, without examination, credential, or fee. ("Our Commitment" 8)

Prioritizing issues of security and accessibility, Bill Walker of the Gay and Lesbian Historical Society of Northern California Archives argues that

> [t]he experience of the lesbian and gay movement has repeatedly shown that we can never rely on simple promises to preserve our rights or serve our interests. Homophobia and bigotry are deep and hardy forces, and rhetoric and good intentions are not effective instruments against them. ("Historical Society News" 5)

Despite the indisputable technological advantages, the Lesbian Herstory Archives in New York, like the Mazer Collection and the Gay and Lesbian Historical Society, is extremely wary about ensconcing its history in public or academic institutions. The Lesbian Herstory Archives was conceived in 1973 by a group seeking to represent lesbian and gay students and instructors at the City University of New York. Some of the lesbians who had been out before the second wave of the women's movement were alarmed that their prefeminist lesbian culture had suffered erasure. Their fear that the historical suppression of lesbians might repeat itself, despite the strides made in lesbian liberation during the 1970s, motivated twenty-five women to initiate the Archives project.[15] While the founding group members eventually dispersed, Deborah Edel and Joan Nestle, lovers at the time, took on the enormous commitment of creating and housing the Lesbian Herstory Archives in their apartment. From 1974 until 1992, the "community's memory" resided in Joan Nestle's West Side apartment and storage facilities (Brandt 43). In an interview with Beth Hodges, Deborah Edel and Joan Nestle defend their decision to keep the Archives a lesbian grassroots and unaffiliated organization, unencumbered by the protocols that invariably accompany government funding or academic support:

> *Deborah:* It's been important that we take our time to build up trust, knowing that the money will come when we need it and when we can handle it, and that we spend our time now building a base that isn't dependent on governmental funds, but is built on what women can give of their own lives. We always need money, but we want it to come from women who believe in our work.
> *Joan:* Something we need to free for ourselves – and this is a controversial issue – is the hold of academic institutions over cultural collections. We must not be tempted to take money from them, not be tempted to install the collection in a university, even if it's a woman's university. We must not be fooled into forgetting that these institutions, which seem to be devoted to learning, are part of the military industrial complex that makes the world impossible for most people, as well as for lesbians. (qtd. in Hodges 101–2)

With the 1992 relocation to its permanent home in Brooklyn's Park Slope district, the Lesbian Herstory Archives (registered as the Lesbian Herstory Educational Foundation, Inc.) attained its greatest measure of independence. The three-story townhouse housing the Archives cost $600,000, purchased with a $300,000 down payment amassed entirely from individual donations. Joan Nestle maintains that the property acquisition, the culmination of a twenty-year dream, creates a unique "place where women from all over c[an] come and be in a place that is just about our history as lesbians. Not a revisionist version, but the history of lesbians as they experienced it, wrote it, lived it" (qtd. in Brownworth 73).[16]

Ironically, some of the greatest research challenges facing patrons of the Lesbian Herstory Archives stem from its radical feminist political commitment to accessibility and collectivity. One of the Archives' first principles, for instance, is "'giving access without judgement (sic)....No woman is refused and no woman's work is refused'" (Nestle qtd. in Hodges 102). Consequently, the collection presently comprises more than "10,000 books, 12,000 photographs, 200 special collections, 1,400 periodical titles, 1,000 organizational and subject files," as well as a plethora of nonprinted matter (Brownworth 73). The Archives' refusal to implement a selection policy ensures an incredible diversity of cherished, provocative, and revealing materials, yet the lack of comprehensive cataloguing or trained librarians forestalls the unearthing of many buried treasures. The "How To Use The Lesbian Herstory Archives: A Pathfinder for Research" (1993), an introductory informational sheet distributed to patrons, recognizes the challenges facing researchers when it warns that conducting searches at the Archives is a labor-intensive and largely self-reliant task: "Our volunteers here at the Archives can assist you by pointing you in the right direction, but it is up to you to dig into the files, periodicals, newsletters, and books to uncover those little gems you are seeking."

It is undeniable and understandable that the grassroots lesbian archives, dependent entirely upon community donations for their financial solvency, do not provide the hours of operation, the regularity of services, the level of organization, or the technological resources consistent with public or academic library practices. The impediments to research notwithstanding, the independent lesbian organizations maintain the autonomy to perform the exceedingly crucial social function of community cohesion in addition to the historical enterprise of document collection. That the photocopier at the Lesbian Herstory Archives sits alongside the kitchen sink and that organizational meetings are held at the kitchen and dining-room tables, best illustrate how lesbian archives attempt to perform simultaneously the multiple functions of a library, a community center, a museum, and a household. It is a sobering reality that, in the wake of the Reagan/Bush/Mulroney era, the Mazer Collection – an archive – remains the only "Lesbian-only-identified resource" in the entire city of Los Angeles ("Mazer to Host Community Meeting" 7). The dire shortage of space and funds that threatens the survival of even this small facility is perhaps best symbolized by the bathtubful of posters, paintings, and signs that are stored in the Collection's bathroom.

The issue of whether to struggle to subsist as an endangered community repository or to be integrated in a more financially secure general library collection is particularly acute for the Gay and Lesbian Historical Society of Northern California. With the creation of the celebrated James C. Hormel Gay and Lesbian Center of the San Francisco Main Public Library, the Society had to reconsider its own goals and determine its future direction. Questions about the "control of the collections and the Center over time" were of greatest concern to the Society during negotiations between the two facilities ("Historical Society News" 5).[17] After three years of discussions, the community-based organization and the public institution signed their 1996 agreement that

> while the material will be housed in state-of-the-art archival vaults in the new main library, accessed through the library's catalogues and other finding aids, available to the

> public whenever the library is open, and cared for by a professional staff, the material nevertheless belongs to the GLHS and is merely on deposit with the library. ("GLHS & The SFPL Sign Historic Agreement" 11)

Similarly, McBride and Grier decided that it is under the stately protection of the San Francisco Public Library that their collection can best endure, achieving the greatest accessibility at no charge to the widest range of individuals. The bequeathing of materials from the private domain to the public (civic) sphere makes the collection available to patrons using wheelchairs and public transit. (The Lesbian Herstory Archives, located on bus and subway lines, is also wheelchair accessible.)[18] From an archivist's or a researcher's perspective, the greatest benefit of housing a lesbian and gay collection in a public library facility is that there are the technological and financial resources for acquisitions, preservation (especially deacidification), cataloguing, electronic communications, and photocopying.[19] The San Francisco Public Library, according to Sherry Thomas, will first treat the paper of 2,000 lesbian pulp paperbacks. The preservation and restoration of these paperbacks, some dating back to the 1940s, is expected to cost $17,000. Subsequently, "the library will copy all of the books, letters, and periodicals onto CD-ROM (compact disk, read-only memory) so that they can be accessed by all library users in San Francisco and from other remote libraries via computer transmission" (Thomas qtd. in Brown 25). The decision to stack materials belonging to the Gay and Lesbian Center with other collections on shelves throughout the library rather than to isolate them in the Gay and Lesbian reading room strategically ensures that the materials will be visible even to patrons who do not specifically choose to visit the Gay and Lesbian Center. This organizational strategy designates lesbian and gay materials as a legitimate branch of knowledge and experience at the same time that their relevance to other subject fields is recognized. The San Francisco Public Library has thus attempted to negotiate between community demands for exclusive lesbian and gay collections and equally persuasive arguments for incorporating lesbian and gay sections in general libraries.[20]

The dichotomous logic of exclusivity versus integration that often justifies whether a library's or a bookstore's lesbian collection remains autonomous or affiliated – a version of the "same versus different" and "single-issue or coalition" debates that tend to pervade virtually all areas of queer thinking and organizing[21] – perhaps best indicates that lesbians should not view the aggregation of their history as an either/or proposition. Rather, we must recognize that there is a dire need for a range of places committed to the preservation of lesbian history, from the drawer in someone's office, to the vertical files in the school library, to community facilities, to national and academic research libraries. As Degania Golove, coordinator of the Mazer Collection, remarked to a news reporter after visiting the new home of the Lesbian Herstory Archives:

> none of the archives are in competition with each other. Not everyone lives on the East Coast, and it's safer to have several collections. We need to have lesbian archives in as many places as we can. ("Mazer Collection Seeks to Buy Building" 73)

One of the most pressing concerns for community and professional librarians, archivists, and historians should be developing racially diverse collections in whatever venues, public or private, that are available outside the urban centers of the Atlantic Northeast, San Francisco, and Los Angeles. The hinterlands, where geographic isolation and limited demographics are acute factors, have a compelling need for the collected remnants that stitch together lesbian history. Bloomington, Indiana's The Shango Project: National Archives for Black Lesbians and Gay Men, a recent arrival in the world of lesbian and gay archiving, is a particularly promising and necessary initiative in the effort to record queer history. The Shango Project and newsletter, *Purple Drum*, is a "newly conceived effort to collect, preserve and maintain materials of historical interest which document aspects of African-American Lesbian and Gay existence in contemporary and historical society."[22] Lesbians, moreover, need to appreciate the legitimate archival value of the odds and ends of their daily lives. Since retrievable aspects of our histories, especially our literary and print histories, are encoded on even the most seemingly insignificant dust jacket, bookmark, and handbill, we must safeguard our legacy and resist the forces that seek to render us invisible by donating our published and unpublished papers, photographs, videos, and memorabilia to libraries and resource centers.

Lacking the sexuality-specific focus of lesbian and gay community archives and such public library collections as those found at the New York Public Library's Gay Information Center Archives and the Eureka Valley Harvey Milk Memorial Branch Library in San Francisco, institutional collections in academic and corporate libraries (including the Kinsey Institute), are nonetheless fertile and largely unexamined repositories for lesbian print materials. Yale University's Beinecke Rare Book and Manuscript Library, the Human Sexuality Collection at California State University, Northridge, and Cornell University's Human Sexuality Collection, as well as academic libraries at Boston University, Rutgers, the University of California, at Los Angeles and at Berkeley, Columbia, Tulane, Michigan State, and the University of Texas at Austin, are establishing and expanding important research, historical, literary, and archival collections "documenting the social prominence of gay and lesbian issues" (Owens 86). With increasing frequency, lesbian and gay organizations are securing the value of their organizational papers, correspondence files, memoranda, publications, galleys, and promotional materials for posterity by making donors' arrangements. For example, in 1994 the Duke University Special Collections Library became the repository for the records of *LGSN: The Lesbian and Gay Studies Newsletter*, a publication of the Gay and Lesbian Caucus for the Modern Languages. During the previous year, the National Gay and Lesbian Task Force decided to donate its project files, reports, publications, and correspondence from its first twenty years of existence to Cornell University's Human Sexuality Collection.[23] The Collection, established in 1989 with financial backing from *The Advocate* publisher David B. Goodstein, is considered to be the "most established and well supported archival program" in the United States.[24] Although academic collections are typically better furnished with gay male rather than lesbian materials, Duke University's collection is particularly strong in lesbiana, as is the Schlesinger Library at Radcliffe College that holds the papers of such eminent lesbians as pacifist feminist leader Barbara Deming and poet Adrienne Rich.

Yet, to continue to expand our vision of how lesbian life has been differently composed and framed at a variety of historical moments, by little-known as well as celebrated individuals, in a range of geographic and social locations, we must comb more thoroughly through the nondiscursive and printed artifacts housed in our community archival collections. The community-based archival work undertaken by Esther Newton for *Cherry Grove, Fire Island: Sixty Years in America's First Gay and Lesbian Town* is an impressive model of how social constructionist logic can best be grounded in the specifics of a particular time and place.[25] Similarly, Elizabeth Lapovsky Kennedy and Madeline D. Davis provide a compelling example of historically specific and community-based research in *Boots of Leather, Slippers of Gold: The History of a Lesbian Community.* Such scrupulously researched projects as Kennedy and Davis's thirteen-year compilation of materials and oral histories for their study are unquestionably time consuming and expensive (*Boots of Leather, Slippers of Gold* xii). When such research is conducted on women's lives, particularly if they are lesbians and/or women of color, it is also subject to the abiding, prohibitive cultural logic that devalues and underfunds women's work.

The global economic recession and the drastic fiscal consequences for higher education spending, at the same moment that the fledgling field of lesbian and gay studies is itself emerging, have no doubt discouraged some scholars from undertaking ethnographic research and contributed to the proliferation of theoretical treatments of sexuality in recent years. Scholars from such traditional humanities disciplines as literature, history, and philosophy, who have had an undeniably formidable role in the development of lesbian, gay, bisexual, and transgender studies and queer theory, are rarely party to the scale of research funding more customarily available to scholars in the social sciences. When compared to the major funding required to do ethnographic or historical field work, the more economical price tag on the production of queer theories, work that typically requires the consideration of printed and visual texts rather than relies extensively on travel, archival searches, and subject interviews, perhaps suggests why queer theoretical discourse, at least at this historical moment, seems to be growing exponentially. For innumerable graduate students, community researchers, and senior scholars, text-based scholarship rather than the study of human subjects has in fact become an economic necessity. In making such an observation, I am not assuming an antitheoretical position or disparaging the growing and important body of theoretical work to emerge in recent years. Rather, I am registering a disciplinary concern that the present, partially market-driven predilection for theory threatens to eclipse some of the still much needed investigation of the traces of lesbians' lived experiences that line the shelves and fill the drawers of our community archives.

If scholarly neglect of community archival resources is detrimental to the disciplinary development of lesbian studies, it also threatens the survival of lesbian archives themselves. Lesbian community archives, like women's bookstores and feminist publishing houses, are entirely dependent upon user support to remain operational in adverse political and economic climates. That support, although essential to the endurance of lesbian community archives, is only the first step lesbian studies scholars must take to protect our cultural resources and to pursue an ethical research methodology.[26] The very conditions that have made it necessary for lesbians to collect and conserve their own history outside of mainstream institutions pose special considerations for researchers. For instance, how can scholars abide by the lesbian community's unwritten rules of discretion when the academy insists that they identify the sources of their information? Scholars who utilize the lavender archives must be especially attentive to issues of discretion since much of the material they find there is personal in nature, relating to lesbians' coming out, intimate relationships, and sexual practices. It is therefore particularly important that scholars demonstrate their respect for the privacy of women who are mentioned in private documents (unpublished journals, letters, and diaries) or who appear in photographs by gaining permission from the appropriate sources for the materials they wish to use.

My own desire to treat equitably and responsibly the materials I discovered in community archives, has made me consider ways to scale the wall of authority – of discourse itself – that separates the academy from the communities that surround it and from which the lesbian "paper uprisings" I study emerged. Lesbian studies scholars might resist the historic tendency to silence lesbians by encouraging their research subjects, when possible, to speak for themselves. The increasing number of interviews and oral histories being collected by independent researchers and community organizations, such as the ongoing oral history project of the Gay and Lesbian Historical Society of Northern California, also offer scholars a wealth of firsthand materials to cite in their work. Lesbian studies scholars, moreover, might contemplate seriously how to make their research readily available to the communities that engender it. The lesbian community archives encourage researchers to donate copies of their published and unpublished materials to the collections, ensuring that interested community members can access them free of charge.

The vulnerability of lesbian cultural institutions to insolvency, censorship, and vandalism, however, argues for extending the reach of reciprocity beyond the printed page. Scholars can strengthen the relationship between the academy and the community not only by financially contributing to nonprofit community research facilities, but by sharing their time and skills with the volunteer labor force that maintains community collections. Scholars can also encourage further lesbian ethnographic research by introducing students to the alternative resources for scholarship available outside the academy. Hence, the survival of the lavender archive can best be safeguarded by patrons who invest their own resources in as well as entrust their words to lesbian community institutions.

NOTES

1 Foreword, *The Coming Out Stories*, xi–xii.
2 *Who Was That Masked Woman?* 179.
3 I borrow the term from the title of Martin Duberman, Martha Vicinus, and George Chauncey's collection of essays, *Hidden from History: Reclaiming the Gay and Lesbian Past*. The editors' introduction to the work provides a concise treatment of the relationship between historical research and lesbian and gay studies (1–13).
4 Jane Hood, one of the speakers at a rally held at the University of New Mexico, Albuquerque, condemning what has been designated "a hate crime against gender studies," claims that the periodicals included *Signs, Gender and Society, The Women's Review of Books*, and *Lesbian Ethics*. In her Internet report, she notes that "[o]n the empty shelf was a note that said, 'Where is your bitch propaganda?' Some books were left around with swastikas scrawled on them, and over the contents page of a journal on lesbian ethics was scrawled, 'God made women for men' (WMST-L, 28 November 1994)." Stephen Rollins, Associate

Dean, General Library, University of New Mexico, reports that *Feminist Studies, Frontiers, Gender and Society, New Directions for Women, Signs* (current 10 years only), *Women, Women's Studies, Psychology of Women Quarterly*, and *Women and Politics* were also targeted (QSTUDY-L, 10 December 1994). The sheer number and weight of volumes involved, and their discovery within the library facility itself, suggests not only that numerous people were involved in moving and hiding the books, but also that the "theft" was an inside job performed when library patrons were not around to witness the perpetrators.

5 In 1979, Stuart Miller of the Social Responsibilities Round Table of the Gay Task Force of the American Library Association issued *Censored, Ignored, Overlooked, Too Expensive? How to Get Gay Materials into Libraries: A Guide to Library Selection Policies for the Non-Librarian*. Although the modest document is now dated, it provides historic insight into the issues at stake for lesbian and gay library patrons and administrators and a good deal of rudimentary information about library book selection procedures that is still relevant. See also Joan Ariel's "The Library As A Feminist Resource," for a pragmatic discussion of how users can best access the materials available from public, school, and academic libraries. Ellen Broidy's "Cyberdykes, or Lesbian Studies in the Information Age" provides an interesting discussion of the ramifications of technology and poststructuralism for library science, offering strategies for identifying relevant lesbian resources in technologically advanced libraries. She argues that

> [t]he central questions for today's librarians and researchers have ceased to revolve around the ability or desirability of isolating a single inoffensive yet definite word or term [for Library of Congress subject heading status]; critical theory and information technology (the ideal postmodern marriage) have combined (or conspired) to create the need first to conceptualize and then to describe bibliographically increasingly complex social and sexual constructs. (203–4).

6 For comprehensive address lists of national and international lesbian, gay, and bisexual archives and a reference guide to relevant periodicals, see Linda Garber, Alan V. Miller, and Stuart Miller. Stan Leventhal's "Starting A Gay Library" includes a list, organized by region, of gay and lesbian archives and libraries throughout the United States, Canada, and Mexico, as well as a brief history of New York's Pat Parker/Vito Russo Center Library (14–15). Useful information about using and starting lesbian and gay library collections is contained as well in the encyclopedic *Gay and Lesbian Library Service*. The edited reference volume treats pragmatically issues from library techniques to censorship. James A. Fraser's and Harold A. Averill's *Organizing an Archives: The Canadian Gay Archives Experience*, although dated particularly with regard to advancements in information and preservation technologies, is also a concise and comprehensive guide to operating a multimedia lesbian and gay archives. The work discusses the intricacies of choosing a name, developing a statement of purpose, designing organizational and administrative structures, handling acquisitions, organizing and indexing materials, maintaining records, and promoting an archieve.

7 Founded in 1973 as the Canadian Gay Liberation Movement Archives before changing its name to the Canadian Gay Archives, the Canadian Lesbian and Gay Archives (CLGA) underwent its most recent name change in March 1994. The new name more accurately reflects the nature of the growing accessions, as well as the communities of patrons who utilize the collection. The Archives gaies du Québec (AGQ), a charitable organization, also underwent considerable changes in recent years. Ten years after its founding in 1983, the AGQ moved into its first office facility. The organizational papers of Labrys and Montréal Gay Women, of particular interest to lesbian researchers, are part of the collection. For a brief update on the holdings and operational interests of CLGA and AGQ, see "More Out and About" (6–7).

8 In addition to the newsletters I refer to in this discussion, it is worth consulting the irregularly published, but tremendously informative, *Gay Archivist: Newsletter of the Canadian Gay Archives*. Issue Number 10 (November 1992) is a particularly useful reference, containing an extensive list of Canadian feminist, lesbian, and gay newspapers and periodicals in the microfiche collection of the national, co-gender Canadian Lesbian and Gay Archives.

9 Clare Potter's *Lesbian Periodicals Index* provides reliable citations for over forty lesbian periodicals in circulation during the 1970s. Linda Garber's *Lesbian Sources*, with 162 subject headings, is a more recent source covering materials not included in Potter's work.

10 The Women In Print movement, or WIP, gets its name from lesbian publisher June Arnold of Daughters, Inc. who called the First Women in Print Conference in 1976. About 130 women came from all over the United States to attend the first event of its kind–an event that heralded the beginning of the North American lesbian publishing and bookselling boom. Participants included such writers, publishers, and booksellers as Dorothy Allison, Barbara Grier, Carol Seajay (who launched *Feminist Bookstore News* following the first WIP Conference), Parke Bowman, Bertha Harris, and Harriet Desmoines and Catherine Nicholson (founders of *Sinister Wisdom*).

11 One of the Mazer Collection's primary goals is to raise funds to purchase a permanent home. See "Mazer Moves Forward," "Mazer to Host Community Meeting," and "Mazer Collection Seeks to Buy Building." The latter article sketches briefly the history of the Collection, from its founding as the West Coast Lesbian Collections in Oakland in 1981, to its 1987 relocation to Connexxus (a lesbian social services agency in West Hollywood), to its move to a private residence before arriving at its present West Hollywood location in 1989.

12 See Eric Garber's "A Different Kind of Roots: African-American Resources in the Archives," for a description of the GLHS lesbian and gay holdings.

13 According to Patricia Holt, "[t]he price tag for the Gay and Lesbian Center is $1.6 million, $1 million of which has already been raised" (59). The construction of the Center is funded by a $109.5 million bond issue approved by San Francisco voters in 1988. The additional $23 million required for equipment, interior furnishings, and books and periodicals is being raised through private donations from lesbian and gay community sources and gay positive national foundations (59). It is a sobering exercise in economies of scale to compare, for example, the budget of the publicly housed collection to the community-based Mazer Collection. The entire annual operational budget for the Mazer Collection amounts to ten to twelve thousand dollars. While the facility is rent-free and the labor is volunteer, the Collection must nonetheless cover its substantial and costly insurance bills as well as equipment and utility expenses (Cotter 35). What it is unable to pay for regrettably is the very level of community outreach and document preservation that is crucial to the expansion and continuance of the Collection.

14 San Francisco City Librarian Ken Dowlin's comment was included in "The Main Campaign: The Campaign for the New Main of the San Francisco Public Library" publicity statement, "Library Gay and Lesbian Center Accepts Major Gifts," for release following the April 23, 1992, groundbreaking ceremonies for the New Main Library (the first national archive of lesbian and gay books, magazines, films, and videos in a public library in America). For information about the Gay and Lesbian Center at the San Francisco Main Public Library, which opened in 1996 with a research center for lesbian and gay culture, contact Curator Jim Van Buskirk, San Francisco Public library, 100 Larkin Steet, San Francisco, CA 94102; (415) 437–4853.

15 For discussions of the Lesbian Herstory Archives see Deborah Edel's "The Lesbian Herstory Archives: A Statement of Cultural Self-Definition"; Beth Hodges's "An Inter-

view with Joan [Nestle] and Deb [Edel] of the Lesbian Herstory Archieves" and "Preserving Our Words and Pictures"; and Joan Nestle's "The Will to Remember: The Lesbian Herstory Archives of New York" (a revised, updated version published in this volume).

16 The top floor of the building has been made into a private residence as a security measure to ensure that the collection is not left unattended.

17 The pressure experienced by archives with substantial lesbian and gay holdings to relinquish their independence is not uncommon. In July 1992, the Canadian Women's Movement Archives/Archives canadiennes du mouvement des femmes (CWMA/ACMF) joined the Archives/Special Collections department of the Morriset Library, University of Ottawa. After operating as "independent, non-profit, community-based, and collectively run archives," for a decade, "[l]evels of funding and staffing required for the operation of the Archives had grown precipitously" ("More Out and About" 6).

18 For a treatment of the zoning complexities involved with installing the $35,000 wheelchair elevator outside of the Archives building, see Brownworth (73).

19 There are numerous Internet newsgroups and discussion lists related to various aspects of lesbian research; one of the most active is the Queer Studies List at the University of Buffalo (Ellen Greenblatt, Listowner, QSTUDY-L, listserv@ubvm.cc.buffalo.edu). In "A Quick Tour of Major Lesbian and Queer Resources on the World Wide Web," Ellen Greenblatt provides an excellent survey of lesbian and queer Web sites. The June L. Mazer Lesbian Collection recently launched its home page on the World Wide Web (Wolt "Mazer Merges Onto The Information Superhighway!"): http://home.earthlink.net/~labonsai; or http://www.lesbian.org/mazer

20 A related, but perhaps more pressing concern for archivists, librarians, and activists is how to make the co-gender collections, in both general and specialized libraries, equally responsive to and representative of the experiences of lesbians and gay men. Sherry Thomas, the director of development for special gifts for the Gay and Lesbian Center and publisher of the former Spinsters Press in San Francisco, notes that it was critical that lesbian materials be integral to the new center from its inception:

> We were particularly concerned about this since the majority of money would come from gay men. I'd known of Barbara Grier's work for years and years. It seemed to me necessary to have a stellar collection that had lesbian books at its core, and start with a center that was so strong in its lesbian representation so that there would never be a question as to what would be available to us. (qtd. in Brown 23)

21 Cruikshank discusses this phenomenon in *The Gay and Lesbian Liberation Movement* (67, 174–175).

22 According to The Shango Project's mission statement,

> [a] long-range goal of the project is to develop a resource center serving not only as archive but maintaining a database of all research and historical materials pertaining to Black Lesbian and Gay men in the African Diaspora. Such a central database will allow the use of a much-needed resource tool in exploring aspects of Lesbian and Gay male life and to further much-needed work on the multidimensional issues and problems faced by Lesbians and Gay men of African descent in society across the world. (WMST-L 25 June 1994)

The Shango Project also announces awards for work enhancing knowledge about Black lesbian and gay male culture and history. Two issues of *Purple Drum* are published annually. For information contact the project director or *Purple Drum* newsletter editor: The Shango Project: National Archives for Black Lesbians and Gay Men, P.O. Box 2341, Bloomington, IN 47402-2341; (812) 334–8860.

23 *LGSN* 21:1 (March) 1994: 12, citing *Chronicle of Higher Education*, 25 August 1993. See also announcement in *Chronicle of Higher Education*, 9 June 1993, A6.
24 See Brenda J. Marston's letter to the editor in *Out* 9 (Dec./Jan.) 1994: 14–15.
25 Esther Newton spells out some of the difficulties involved with undertaking the scale of community-based research she conducted for *Cherry Grove, Fire Island: Sixty Years in America's First Gay and Lesbian Town*:

> Most researchers in gay and lesbian studies are either independent scholars or carry big teaching loads at small colleges. As a result, we lack what scholars at big research universities take for granted: graduate student help, time off to do research, and financial support. Up to the present, few government or private foundations will fund intellectual projects concerning gays and lesbians. Very often I felt frustrated by how long the project was taking in between the demands of my full-time job, and by how much more research and interviewing I could have done with more resources. (xii–xiii)

26 Approximately five hundred people annually visit the June L. Mazer Lesbian Collection in West Hollywood, representing a very small fraction of the number of lesbians living in relative proximity to or traveling in the vicinity of the facility (Cotter 34). That the Collection is underused is especially unfortunate given the high density of colleges and universities in southern California. The Collection's future in fact depends on greater user involvement, particularly to assist with the listing and arranging of its holdings (Cotter 55).

REFERENCES

Ariel, Joan. "The Library As A Feminist Resource." *Words In Our Pockets: The Feminist Writers Guild Handbook on How To Gain Power: Get Published & Get Paid*. Paradise, CA: Dustbooks, 1985. 286–95.

Brandt, Kate. *Happy Endings: Lesbian Writers Talk About Their Lives and Work*. Tallahassee, FL: Naiad, 1993.

Brody, Michal, ed. *Are We There Yet? A Continuing History of* Lavender Women: *A Chicago Lesbian Newspaper: 1971–1976*. Iowa City: Aunt Lute, 1985.

Broidy, Ellen. "Cyberdykes, or Lesbian Studies in the Information Age." *Lesbian Studies: Toward the Twenty-First Century*. Ed. Bonnie Zimmerman and Toni McNaron. New York: The Feminist Press, 1996. 203–7.

Brown, Katie. "Preserving Lesbian Literature." *Deneuve* 2.4 (July/August 1992): 23–5.

Brownworth, Victoria A. "Archives Gets a Home of Her Own." *Lesbian News* (March 1994): 73–4.

Chandler, Robin. "Archives Report." *OurStories: Newsletter of the Gay and Lesbian Historical Society of Northern California* 10.1 (winter 1995): 6.

Cotter, Katie. "The Future of Our Herstory." *Lesbian News* (September 1994): 34+.

Cruikshank, Margaret. *The Gay and Lesbian Liberation Movement*. New York: Routledge, 1992.

Duberman, Martin, Martha Vicinus, and George Chauncey, Jr., eds. *Hidden From History: Reclaiming the Gay and Lesbian Past*. New York: New American Library, 1989.

Edel, Deborah. "The Lesbian Herstory Archives: A Statement of Cultural Self-Definition." *Woman of Power*: "Revisioning History" 16 (spring 1990): 22–3.

Fraser, James, A., and Harold A. Averill. *Organizing an Archives: The Canadian Gay Archives Experience*. Toronto: Canadian Gay Archives Publication, 1983; fourth printing 1989.

Garber, Eric. "A Different Kind of Roots: African-American Resources in the Archives." *OurStories: Newsletter of the Gay and Lesbian Historical Society of Northern California* 10.1 (winter 1995): 4–5.

Garber, Linda. *Lesbian Sources: A Bibliography of Periodical Articles. 1970–1990.* New York: Garland, 1993.

Glass, Christian. "Archives News." *OurStories: Newsletter of the Gay and Lesbian Historical Society of Northern California* 9.1 (spring 1994): 12.

"GLHS & The SFPL Sign Historic Agreement." *OurStories: Newsletter of the Gay and Lesbian Historical Society of Northern California* 11.1 (summer 1996): 11.

Gough, Cal, and R. Ellen Greenblatt, eds. *Gay and Lesbian Library Service.* Jefferson, NC: McFarland, 1990.

Greenblatt, Ellen. "A Quick Tour of Major Lesbian and Queer Resources on the World Wide Web." *Matrices: A Lesbian and Lesbian Feminist Research and Network Newsletter* 11.2 (winter 1996): 8–9.

"Historical Society News: Lesbian and Gay Center of the San Francisco Public Library." *OurStories: Newsletter of the Gay and Lesbian Historical Society of Northern California* 7.3/4 (spring/summer 1992): 5.

Hodges, Beth. "An Interview with Joan [Nestle] and Deb [Edel] of the Lesbian Herstory Archives. (Part 1)." *Sinister Wisdom* 11 (fall 1979): 3–13.

——. "Preserving Our Words and Pictures. Part Two of Interview with Joan Nestle and Deb Edel." *Sinister Wisdom* "Lesbian Writing and Publishing" 13 (summer 1980): 101–5.

Holt, Patricia. "A Room of One's Own." *10 Percent* (fall 1993): 58–9.

Hood, Jane. "Hate Crimes Against Gender Studies." *WMST-L* (28 Nov. 1994): n. p. Online. Internet. 28 Nov. 1994. Available FTP: wmst-l@umdd.umd.edu

Kennedy, Elizabeth Lapovsky, and Madeline D. Davis. *Boots of Leather; Slippers of Gold: The History of a Lesbian Community.* New York: Routledge, 1993.

Koertge, Noretta. *Who Was That Masked Woman?* New York: St. Martin's, 1981.

Leventhal, Stan. "Starting A Gay Library." *Lambda Book Report* 3.3 (March/April 1992): 14–15.

Marston, Brenda J. Letter. *Out* 9 (Dec./Jan. 1994): 14–15.

"Mazer Collection Seeks to Buy Building." *Lesbian News* 19.8 (March 1994): 73.

"Mazer Moves Forward." *In the Life: Newsletter of the June L. Mazer Lesbian Collection* 11 (summer 1996): 3.

"Mazer to Host Community Meeting." *In the Life: Newsletter of the June L. Mazer Lesbian Collection* 7 (summer 1994): 7.

Miller, Alan V., compiler. *Directory of the International Association of Lesbian and Gay Archives and Libraries.* Toronto: IALGAL, 1987.

Miller, Stuart. *Censored, Ignored, Overlooked, Too Expensive? How to Get Gay Materials into Libraries: A Guide to Library Selection Policies for the Non-Librarian.* Philadelphia, PA: Gay Task Force of the American Library Association, 1979.

"More Out and About." *CENTRE/FOLD: Newsletter of the Toronto Centre for Lesbian and Gay Studies* 4 (spring 1993): 6.

"More Out and About." *CENTRE/FOLD: Newsletter of the Toronto Centre for Lesbian and Gay Studies* 6 (spring 1994): 6–7.

Nestle, Joan. "The Will to Remember: The Lesbian Herstory Archives of New York." *Feminist Review.* "Perverse Politics: Lesbian Issues." 34 (spring 1990): 86–99.

Newton, Esther. *Cherry Grove, Fire Island: Sixty Years in America's First Gay and Lesbian Town.* Boston: Beacon, 1993.

"Our Commitment." *In the Life: Newsletter of the June L. Mazer Lesbian Collection* 5 (summer 1993): 8.

Owens, Mitchell. "Pump Up the Volumes." *Out* 7 (September 1993): 85–7.

Potter, Clare. *Lesbian Periodicals Index*. Tallahassee, FL: Naiad, 1986.
Press, Aida K., ed. "Page One." *Radcliffe Quarterly* 79.4 (December 1993): 1.
Rich, Adrienne. "Foreword." *The Coming Out Stories*. Ed. Julia Penelope Stanley and Susan J. Wolfe. Watertown, MA: Persephone, 1980.
Rollins, Stephen. "Censorship of Library Materials–journals were defaced and removed from the shelves. . . . , *QSTUDY-L* (10 Dec. 1994): n. p. Online. Internet. 10 Dec. 1994. Available FTP: qstudy-1@ubvm.cc.buffalo.edu.
Shango Project. "Mission Statement." *WMST-L* (25 June 1994): n. p. Online. Internet. 25 June 1994. Available FTP: wmst-1@umdd.umd.edu.
Wolt, Irene. "Take Me *Out* to the Ballgame." *In the Life: Newsletter of the June L. Mazer Lesbian Collection* 5 (summer 1993): 1+.
——, and Kati Newman. "Mazer Merges Onto The Information Superhigh-way!" *In the Life: Newsletter of the June L. Mazer Lesbian Collection* 11 (summer 1996): 1–2.
"Women's Press Records Preserved." *OurStories: Newsletter of the Gay and Lesbian Historical Society of Northern California* 7.1/2 (fall 1991/winter 1992): 14.

Part II

Problems and Propositions

6

Erotic Anthropology: "Ritualized Homosexuality" in Melanesia and Beyond

Deborah A. Elliston

Gilbert Herdt's monograph on the Sambia, *Guardians of the Flutes* (1981), and his edited collections, *Rituals of Manhood* (Herdt, ed. 1982) and *Ritualized Homosexuality in Melanesia* (Herdt, ed. 1984, 1993), have effectively charted the terrain and terms of the study of "ritualized homosexuality" for Melanesian societies. In practice Herdt's monograph and edited collections have also established a framework for the study of homosexualities cross-culturally, that is, well beyond Papua New Guinea or Melanesia (see Davis and Whitten 1987; Weston 1993). Herdt's works have been used, for example, to sustain and develop the concepts of "institutionalized homosexuality" and age-structured homosexuality, playing a key evidentiary role in bids to legitimize particular typologies for the study of homosexualities cross-culturally.[1] Although, when first published, Herdt's work was groundbreaking and was significantly responsible for legitimizing anthropological investigations of homosexualities, now, as I assert in this article, his writings on "ritualized homosexuality" require sustained critique. In light of developments in lesbian and gay theory, feminist social theory, and questions of ethnographic representation, the assumptions and claims that organize the literature on "ritualized homosexuality" require critique both to counter the authority they have been given in determining the cross-cultural project of understanding homosexualities and to revamp their suggestions for understanding boys' initiations in Melanesia.

In search of more accurate understandings of the indigenous meanings of the boy-man "homosexual practices" that occur under the guise of "growing" boys into men in certain Melanesian societies, I examine the parallels and continuities between Melanesian societies that do and do not use such practices to help install culturally specific ideals of masculinity in their boys.[2] I contend that the "homosexual practices" of boys' initiatory rituals comprise one way of expressing and instantiating a constellation of beliefs about gender and age hierarchies and the efficacy of substances for constituting social identities that are found both in Melanesian societies that do and those that do not have "homosexual" practices. I suggest that the focus on "homosexual" practices in the ethnographic literature of a culture area defined by reference to those practices, and especially when the practices are cast as "ritualized homosexuality," more indexes the aberrant status of homosexuality in Western societies rather than its centrality in the subject Melanesian societies.[3] To identify the man-boy "homosexual" practices as "ritualized homosexuality" imputes a Western model of sexuality to these Melanesian practices, one that relies on Western ideas about gender, erotics, and personhood, and that ultimately obscures the meanings that hold for these practices in Melanesia. While it is not within the scope of this article to detail "Western sexuality," my arguments are organized to reveal the assumptions drawn from Western sexuality that inform the discursive constitution and elaboration of "ritualized homosexuality" as an anthropological genre and category. My aim, then, is to attempt to resituate the study of "ritualized homosexuality" in Melanesia as well as to elucidate contemporary theoretical conundrums in the study of sexuality, erotics, and homosexualities cross-culturally.

Sexual Identities and Sexual Practices

Anthropologists studying homosexualities frequently make a distinction between sexual activities or practices on the one hand and sexual identities on the other. In her recent ethnography of lesbian and gay kinship in the United States, Weston has written that in the United States "at this historical moment, homosexuality is organized in terms of identity rather than acts" (1991:65). The notion that "gay," "lesbian," or "homosexual" can be something one "is," as opposed to tendencies one has or behaviors in which one engages, is a recent historical development in Euro-American societies (see Foucault 1990a [1978]; Katz 1990). The distinction between acts and identities has, however, also become fundamental to the ways in which Western scholars investigate and theorize homosexualities cross-culturally. Many anthropologists writing about homosexualities cross-culturally have tended to delimit "homosexuality" to the level of sexual practices, to avoid weighting the concept with Western cultural specificities: if a sexual practice takes place between two members of the same sex (defined in a Western biological paradigm), labeling the practices and sometimes the participants "homosexual" has been acceptable anthropological practice (see Davis and Whitten 1987).[4]

This distinction between sexual practices and sexual identities is, however, a fundamentally troubling one. While it appears to separate the ostensibly material from the ideological aspects of sexuality, this material/ideological division proves impossible to sustain: ideological distinctions reappear in the implicit criteria of what will count as "sexual." Separating sexual practices from sexual identities leaves unexamined the core problem of what will constitute "sex" or "the sexual" in either category. References to "sexual" practices, however, as an unproblematized domain, are recurrent throughout the key writings on "ritualized homosexuality" (e.g., Herdt 1981, 1984b, 1987, 1993; Herdt, ed. 1984; Herdt and Stoller 1990). It is precisely the composition of the category "the sexual" that I suggest is submerged and in need of fathoming in the writings on "ritualized homosexuality."

The *Oxford English Dictionary's* definitions of sex invoke male/female differences, reproduction, and intercourse motivated by male/female differences. The salient heterosexism of the definition makes its applicability to same-sexed bodies virtually incoherent. Euro-American folk definitions of sex, however, and certainly of sexual practices, tend not to be as rigid, generally allowing for non-reproduction-focused sexual practices and occasionally allowing for same-sex "sex" (but see Frye 1990).[5] The procreative aspects, however, remain problematic. One could take the position that "sex" is an appropriate descriptive term for "ritualized homosexuality" because the practices involve a kind of social reproduction of masculinity, that is, of gender: the symbolism of death and rebirth evident in many boys' initiatory rituals lends itself to a label of reproduction at the symbolic level. But this is not how most anthropologists have deployed the term. Moreover, at the level of practice and discourse, what is being effected through the boys' initiations, and what is of central concern to the participants, is growth – both in the sense of physical growth and in the sense of teaching boys how to become culturally masculine.

In order to avoid the sexual practices/sexual identity problem and also to keep attention focused on what I believe the participants view as central in boys' initiations that include "ritualized homosexuality" in Melanesia, I use the term "semen practices" throughout this article to refer to practices involving the exchange of semen. Here, because my focus is on those practices deemed "homosexual" in the anthropological literature on Melanesia and because I primarily discuss semen practices between males in the subject Melanesian societies, the term semen practices will usually not be qualified by such terms as "boy-man" or "male-male." Semen practices clearly could, however, be used as a de-eroticized label for any practices involving semen, including "heterosexual" exchanges (such as those Knauft has termed "ritualized heterosexuality" [1993:51]), and may prove useful in such contexts precisely because the term can hold in abeyance the erotic and sexual overtones so consistently overlaid by Western anthropologists on practices involving semen. My goal in using the term is to beg the question of homoerotic versus heteroerotic motivation altogether (since I argue that neither is a satisfactory analytic category for understanding semen practices) and thereby to leave open for consideration the meanings of practices involving semen. At base, then, the term "semen practices" is designed to minimize the assumptions that can be imputed to the semen-focused techniques and ordeals through which boys are "made into men" in some Melanesian societies, primarily that they are of a piece with what Euro-Americans hold to be "sexual."[6]

Sexual Geography and Originary Hypotheses

The semen practices occurring in Melanesian societies generally take place between age-specified categories of males during boys' initiations. In his introduction to *Ritualized Homosexuality in Melanesia*, Herdt (1984b) describes the geographical distribution of semen practices in Melanesia. He writes that although there are some cultural groups in the Eastern Highlands of Papua New Guinea having – or known to have had – semen practices, the geographical distribution of cultural groups affiliated with semen practices is concentrated in Southwest Papua New Guinea, extending into Southeast Irian Jaya. In the Eastern Highlands he identifies the Sambia, Baruya, Jeghuje, and other Highlands (Anga) groups and, south of them, one Lowlands Anga group as all having had semen practices. Moving south and westward, Herdt also identifies the Bedamini, Etoro, Kaluli, Onabasalu, and Gebusi as a cluster of societies that have semen practices. In the Trans-Fly area further west, Herdt writes that the Keraki, Suki, and Boadzi have had semen practices. Last, in Southeast Irian Jaya, Herdt writes that anthropologists have identified semen practices among the Kanum, Yei-anim, Marind-anim, Kimam, Jaqai, Casuarina Coastal peoples, and the Asmat.[7]

Anthropologists writing about "ritualized homosexuality," have proposed a variety of originary theories in trying to account for the presence of semen practices in specific areas. Lindenbaum, for example, correlates a purported higher incidence of male pseudohermaphroditism with societies having ritualized semen practices (1987:224), identifying a "theme of cultural hermaphroditism" among these groups (1984:353). She writes that genitally ambiguous persons are often dealt with by infanticide among Western Highlands groups and argues that groups with ritualized semen practices are significantly more tolerant of pseudohermaphroditism and gender ambiguity (1987:225; see also 1984:352–4). The implication of such tolerance is that more tolerant societies will have greater difficulty growing their boys into men than less tolerant societies; the correlation between tolerance of pseudohermaphroditism and ritualized semen practices thus points to the use of various forms of semen-ingestion to assist with this especially difficult growing. Such biological explanations of semen practices and "homosexuality" cross-culturally are common in the anthropological discourse on homosexuality.[8] Such explanations, however, do not attempt to further our understandings of the culturally specific meanings of semen practices and may be most interesting for what they reveal about Western models of biology and homosexuality.

Herdt proposes an ancient diffusionist theory (1984b) that Keesing (1982: 14–15) echoes (with social-structural intonations) to account for the presence and distribution of semen practices in Melanesia. Drawing on linguistic similarities Herdt suggests that there exist "prehistoric connections between (RH) [ritualized homosexuality] groups" (1984b:51), and argues that "ritualized homosexuality... [is]... an ancient ritual complex that diffused through a vast area of lowland and fringe-area Melanesia, perhaps 10,000 years ago or less" (1984b:48). He identifies "various social structural and cultural underpinnings or concomitants of (RH) [ritualized homosexuality] in different social units and subregional traditions... [as] *proximate* transformational causes" creating the variety of ritualized semen practices forms currently found in Papua New Guinea (1984b:54, emphasis in original).

The evidence to which Herdt points is unconvincing. First, the linguistic situation in Papua New Guinea is extremely complex, given that the region has more than 700 separate languages, many of which have shifted through time. Any attempts to demonstrate 10,000-year-old linguistic connections between specific social groups are therefore open to multiple interpretations and challenges. Second, Herdt argues for ancient common links between Melanesian societies with ritualized semen practices on the basis of "various social structural and cultural underpinnings" (1984b:54).[9] These social structural and cultural commonalities, however, can be shown equally to underpin, for example, purging or ingestive practices among boys and men – if, however, attention is directed away from the practices themselves and toward the symbolic work effected by a variety of ritualized practices. Ultimately it is likely that originary and biological hypotheses such as these are responsive to a specifically Euro-American discomfort with what at first glance appear to be "homosexual practices." In such a context, holding that "ritualized homosexuality" is an ancient cultural form is more of a legitimizing tactic than a potent explanatory device.[10]

The apparent need among anthropologists writing on the subject of "ritualized homosexuality" to account for the presence of semen practices – be it historically or contemporarily – has implicitly, if not explicitly, assumed that such practices are aberrant and thus in need of explanation. This pronounced anthropological puzzling over the presence of semen practices is, in part, probably a product of the psychodynamic framework adopted by many of its theorizers.[11] Among the Dema, for example, Van Baal finds both castration anxiety and anal fixations (1984:146, 152). Michael Allen reiterates and supports Layard's Oedipal complex for the Big Nambas, which posits that a man's desire to sleep with his sister cannot be fulfilled so he sleeps, instead, with his sister's husband (1984:90–1). In his analysis of Orokaiva male couples Eric Schwimmer identifies a "close-binding intimate (CBI) mother syndrome" (1984:255) among them and suggests that the closeness between Orokaiva mothers and sons leads "one [to] expect mothers... to impart a negative and repressive view of heterosexuality to their sons" (1984:270). Herdt has written that male transsexualism is a "basic male gender disorder" resulting from a boy's failure to transfer his identification from his mother to male role models (1982:82–3). Finally, at the core of Herdt's argument in support of sorting societies by "homosexuality" lies his privileging of "the youth's fantasy, his erotic desires that create an erection before the pleasurable sex whose fetishized focus is fellatio with a boy" (1981:319). By taking an untheorized "erotics" as the ground on which semen practices occur, and by identifying semen practices as erotic through the invocation of Freudian psychology, Herdt ultimately places the Sambia (on the basis of their "institutionalized fellatio practices") in a category incomparable with – because radically different from – such societies as the Gahuku-Gama, for example. Arguing from these semen erotics, Herdt writes that "Sambia ritual development belongs to its own place and time" (1981:318).

Framing ritualized semen practices as "homosexual" and puzzling over what may most accurately be described as the "etiology" of these ostensibly "homosexual" practices constitutes a theoretical move that not only exoticizes the Melanesian societies so grouped, but also further exoticizes homosexualities. In this article I seek to demonstrate that ritualized semen practices comprise one practice among a range of substance-focused practices that are better understood when analyzed in terms of an ideologically and symbolically based regional pattern, not in terms of a regional complex focused solely on semen practices.[12]

Homosexuality and Ritualized Homosexuality

Herdt uses the term *homosexuality* throughout his writings on the Sambia and, as he does so, admonishes readers that in Melanesia "males who engage in ritual homosexual activities are not 'homosexuals'" (1984a:x). He goes to great lengths in his published materials on "ritualized homosexuality" to "make it explicitly clear that I am *not* asserting (or even hinting)" that the Sambia or other Melanesian peoples who engage in ritualized homosexuality are "homosexuals" (1984b:8; see also 1981:3–4; 1984a:x; 1984b:65, 82–3). At one point he qualifies this claim in a footnote explaining that although 95 percent of Sambia (men) experience fellatio as institutionalized and transitional, "there are a very small number of deviants [*sic*]" (1981:4). Herdt elaborates on the import of using the term "*ritualized* homosexuality" as distinct from "homosexuality":

> *Ritualized* as a modifier [to homosexuality] applies best to the Melanesian situation because: (1) homosexual practices are implemented usually through male initiation rites, having (2) religious overtones, as well as being (3) constrained by broader cultural rules and social roles, for which the full moral and jural force of a society, or a secret men's society, not only condones but often prescribes sexual intercourse among certain categories of males; and (4) various age-related and kinship taboos define and restrict the nature of this male/male sexual behavior. [1984b:6]

Elsewhere he has written:

> In spite of universal [*sic*] involvement in homosexual [*sic*] activities, however, no data indicate that these [Melanesian] males become habitually motivated to same-sex contact later in life, or that the incidence of aberrant [*sic*] lifelong homosexuality, as an identity state, is greater in (RH) [ritualized homosexuality] groups than elsewhere in the world. [1984b:65]

The preceding quotations embed understandings of homosexuality that merit detailed mapping because they illuminate some of the ways in which a Western model of sexuality has informed and undergirded the descriptive analysis of "ritualized homosexuality" in Melanesia. In Herdt's writings, "homosexuality," is defined as "same-sex contact" (1984b:65); "same-sex contact" is only further specified in terms of physical acts – fellatio and anal intercourse, for example – acts whose meanings are presumed to be self-evidently "sexual" and "homosexual."

In the foregoing quotations, "homosexuality" is also marked by the following characteristics: (1) it is a lifelong practice; (2) it is an "identity state"; (3) this precise configuration of homosexuality is "world"-wide. Each of these assertions, I suggest, is problematic. First, the notion of "lifelong homosexuality" reflects neither Euro-American homosexualities nor non-Western homosexualities. Even in Western societies, the basis for Herdt's comparative model, there is considerable evidence that homosexuality is not a lifelong practice: individuals identified as homosexual "come out" at different times in their lives, frequently after heterosexual relationships; they may "return" to heterosexual relationships periodically; and they come out to varying degrees – with many having both homosexual and heterosexual relationships (Weston 1991; see also Greenberg 1988). Cross-culturally the evidence is even more pronounced that engagement in homosexual practices does not exclude heterosexual practices and does not constitute "lifelong" commitments (see Blackwood, ed. 1986).

Perhaps more important, the notion of a lifelong commitment to a sexual orientation and the concept of an "identity state" are both clearly contingent on culturally specific ideas about personhood – not surprisingly, Western ones. In Melanesia, however, personhood is, arguably, far more flexibly constructed than in Western societies. The Western "identity" construct requires radical qualification for Melanesian societies, as durable for a time period much shorter than a lifetime, and as meaningful in relation to the exchange of substances, not in relation to an essentialized and internally consistent, individuated core persona. The legacy of Western intellectual thought, including Western philosophy, is also at issue here: the Western identity construct may require an internalized gaze that is itself contingent on an exteriorized or alienated world. Such an identity construct, although coherent in a society where dualisms such as interior/exterior and mind/body are basic organizing themes, makes little or no sense in Melanesian societies.

Finally, that this particular construction of homosexuality should be worldwide is most clearly contingent on a biologically reductionist view of homosexualities that refuses to encompass the variety of cultural specifics that structure sexual behaviors cross-culturally. Lesbians and gay men in the West draw on biological explanations as a culturally authorized and politically potent justification for homosexuality, one that can be understood as authenticating a "right" to be lesbian or gay in a cultural context that treats such behaviors as aberrant and thus in clear need of some externally authorized justification.[13] Anthropologists, however, should not take such claims and folk models of homosexuality as anything other than Euro-American folk exegeses on the meanings of homosexuality, exegeses that speak to, and through, Western cultural contexts and political dynamics.

To the extent that Euro-American ideas about sexuality, and, hence, the meanings attached to homosexuality, are culturally specific to the West, the concept of "ritualized homosexuality" is intrinsically troubled by Euro-American cultural specificities. These cultural specificities can easily become distorting when Western ideas about homosexuality are deployed to non-Western societies like those of Melanesia.

The Sambia: "Ritualized Homosexuality" Template

Among the Sambia (a cultural group pseudonym) boys' initiations are organized at the phratry or "confederacy" level every 4 to 6 years (Herdt 1981:54), and last from 10 to 15 years between the first initiation status and marriage (1981:174). Sambia boys' initiation consists of six initiation statuses, and a strong emphasis on age-mate solidarities creates bonds among boys of the same initiation status at the phratry level as "regional cohorts" (Herdt 1984c:172). Herdt writes that Sambia believe girls mature and become women "naturally" (that is, with limited cultural assistance) whereas boys do not, in part because being raised by women "hold[s] them back" (1984c:171–2). The point of the initiations, according to Herdt, is to make men out of boys by separating them from all women, especially their mothers, by giving boys oral inseminations of semen (men's "strength") as well as magical ritual treatments, and by instilling in them men's corporate values and interests, which are constructed largely in opposition to women's interests. The masculinist ideal inculcated in initiations is "strength," formerly articulated through a warriorhood ideal of "toughness on arduous, danger-filled guerrilla raids to distant enemy lands," but which now "is virtually synonymous with idealized conformity to ritual routine" (Herdt 1981:51).

Erotics: Whose Erotics?

The central symbol of Sambia boys' initiation is the bamboo flutes that, in Herdt's analysis, stand as multivocal symbols whose meanings reverberate with masculinist power and men's corporate interests. Herdt describes the flutes as a political weapon of boys' and women's oppression; the secret of the flutes revealed to initiates concerns the origins and divergences of masculinity and femininity; and the flute teachings prescribe man-boy semen practices. Through these teachings about semen practices, the flutes embody "a fantasy system concerning the flutes and their sounds" such that the flutes signify both "erotic arousal" and its repression (Herdt 1982:50). The flutes are used as penis substitutes to teach the initiates how to fellate the older bachelors, teachings that Herdt claims highlight "erotic components" of genital stimulation and that fetishize the penis and mouth as erotic (1982:60–8, 78).

It is during the first and second stages of initiation that boys are supposed to fellate older bachelors (third-stage and older initiates) in order to get the semen they need to grow into men (Herdt 1984c:173). Herdt writes that the boys "engage in these practices on a daily basis, first as fellator, and then as fellated" for a period of 10 to 15 years (1981:2). The motivation to fellate stems manifestly from the teaching that the bachelors have what the boys need: biological masculinity in the form of semen (1982:61–3). Yet most boys Herdt interviewed also recounted experiencing both revulsion and significant fear when first told that in order to become men they needed to fellate older boys (1982:70–1). Not all boys submit to the "threats and seductive pleading" of elder men when they present the initiatory secret to the boys, but Herdt does not explore what happens to the boys who consistently refuse (1982:66, 76).

Herdt's claim that semen practices are fundamentally erotic is perhaps his central and most important contribution to analyses of semen practices and comprises the groundwork for his claims that the practices are "sexual" and ultimately meaningful as "ritualized homosexuality." Under the rubric of a seemingly transcultural "erotics," Herdt focuses on the fantasy lives of youths engaging in semen practices and invokes the Freudian concept of the fetish to analyze the experience of fellatio for Sambia youth. The presence of eroticism in semen practices is, however, at best highly variable and certainly not automatic. Hage, for example, has argued that "libidinal satisfaction [is] irrelevant" to semen practices because these practices are based on and heavily invested ideologically in an analogy to – not envy of – women's procreative abilities (1981:272–3). Yet Herdt makes the claim that "sexual acts, ritualized or not, always entail erotic arousal, at least for the inserter" (1984b:7). He thus uses the term "arousal" instead of the more accurate "erection" to shift attention away from physical causes and into the grayer area of erotics.[14] Herdt posits a tautologous ordering of eroticism that makes penile erection contingent on a kind of arousal that is by definition erotic, as opposed to rendering erection the result of arousal that can be caused by a variety of factors, from physical manipulation to emotional desire to physical exertion to intellectual fantasy. Rape, for example, usually involves penile erection, but it would be difficult to show that the impetus for the arousal is fundamentally or necessarily erotic. While this article is not committed to the claim that semen practices must be utterly nonsexual and non-erotic, it is committed to illuminating and questioning the assumptions that have made semen practices appear fundamentally and unquestioningly sexual and erotic. Toward that end my goal here is to install some critical distance between Herdt's analysis and the assumptions embedded within it.[15]

Violence and Fear in Boys' Initiations

While Herdt goes to great lengths to instill in readers the belief that the fellator/fellated relationship is erotic, he does little to analyze the import of the potential for violence embedded in that relationship. The extent to which violence and fear operate at the experiential level of initiates undergoing boys' initiation in societies with boy-man semen practices is striking:

> The bachelors get soundly thrashed and nose-bled, and they otherwise suffer much. This is how it should be, the elders assert, for the youths must become 'strong' and 'angry' because of what has been done to them. But they can 'pay back' that anger by doing to younger initiates what was done to them: beating and otherwise traumatizing them. In addition, they can do something equally laden with power: they are urged to channel that anger and relax their tight penises, by serving as dominant fellateds. [Herdt 1981:56]

This passage is a rare instance in which the potential for violence is made visible, where Herdt identifies "anger" as a key motivator for the fellated bachelor. The coercive nature of oral insemination when it is first introduced to the initiates, the way in which fellator/fellated relationships are structured as submissive/dominant and never reversible relationships, and the intimation that bachelors "pay back" their own suffering by venting their anger on the bodies of younger initiates all introduce a central motif of age-graded hierarchy consolidated through violence and fear. Complicity with the violence of initiatory rites effectively serves as credit against the time when the boys become young men and can themselves subject a new group of initiates to such violence. Such violence and fear, however, are not exclusive to Melanesian societies with semen practices, but also characterize Melanesian societies such as the Gahuku-Gama, which utilize purging practices to inscribe substantially similar ideologies through boys' initiations.

In *The High Valley* (1965) Kenneth Read recounts a pivotal ceremony in the Gahuku-Gama boys' initiation, when he followed a crowd of several hundred, including the initiates and older men, to a local river. There he saw a dozen or so of the older men masturbating into the stream. Following the collective masturbation, the initiates watched and were then forced to emulate nosebleeding, using "two cigar-shaped objects fashioned from the razor-sharp leaves of green pit-pit" that produced, by Read's account, a profuse amount of blood (1965:165). After the nosebleeding, initiates watched and were then forced to emulate an older man who pushed a U-shaped and lengthy piece of cane down his own throat and then down theirs and into their stomachs, sawing it back and forth before withdrawing it to induce vomiting (1965:168–9). Throughout their ordeals each initiate had his upper arms tightly held by two older men – whether to restrain the youths from leaving, to support them, or both, was unclear (1965:163). Read describes panic and fear on the initiates' faces before their nosebleedings, and writes that by the time the boys underwent the cane swallowing "they were already too exhausted, too shocked and weak to resist" (1965:169).

With the violence of the initiatory purification rites as a backdrop, Read details how the older bachelors are scrutinized and criticized by their elders, frequently about marriage, and how the bachelors are expected to turn around and vent their animosities against younger boys, "returning in kind the carping appraisals to which they had recently listened" (1965:187). Both the Sambia and Gahuku-Gama initiations, then, are traumatic lessons in social hierarchy for the initiates (Read 1952, 1965, 1984). For both, ritual teachings about men's and women's differences inculcate among men a generalized suspicion and fear of women while simultaneously exalting men's abilities and supremacy; together these teachings instantiate a gender hierarchy (Herdt 1981; Read 1952, 1982). Simultaneously, the abuse and fear inculcated in both the Sambia and Gahuku-Gama initiates through beatings and hazings and, for the Sambia, adoption of the passive role in fellatio for the initiates, provide clear lessons in the age-graded hierarchy operative among men for the duration of boys' initiation.

Gender and Age Hierarchies

In her recent feminist philosophical works on gender and identity, Butler (1990, 1993) has argued that theorists should not be concerned with origins or with determining essentialized or "authentic" categories of identity. To take her suggestion seriously shifts attention from the "reality" of men and women as categories of actors in Papua New Guinea to the ways the categories of gender are produced through and enmeshed in the operations of power. I take boys' initiations as contexts in and through which gender categories are constructed. Boys' initiations are certainly not the only contexts in which gender is explicitly at issue, but the ideologies and discourses that partially constitute these initiatory contexts (e.g., ritual teachings) provide an illuminating indigenous exegesis on gender ideology that anthropologists can usefully analyze. Locally, boys' initiations comprise condensed contexts for the creation, maintenance, and deployment of power in the form of social hierarchies.

Among the Sambia, Herdt describes the flute ideology and symbolism as hostile to women (1982:88). The ritual teachings of boys' initiation inscribe the supremacy of masculinity over femininity, defining men as superior to women in "physique, personality, and social position" (1982:53). Women are cast as sexually licentious and irresponsible, poised to siphon off men's strength. Herdt writes:

> Women are pictured as relentlessly dangerous to masculine health. Their bodies . . . are polluting; so all heterosexual contact, even touching, is deemed harmful. . . . For all males, this danger is always present; but for youths, who lack defensive ritual knowledge of sexual purification procedures, succumbing to a woman's charms would be fatal, since unlike men they do not understand how to cleanse themselves afterwards of a woman's contamination. [1981:174]

The parallels between the teachings about gender hierarchy explicit in boys' initiations, and the age hierarchy that structures the initiatory practices suggest a broader cultural theme of hierarchy underlying Sambia boys' initiations. At least one anthropologist has argued that although semen practices cement culturally appropriate masculine gender identity, their broader function is as "a mechanism of control that operates to perpetuate a system of inequality based on sex and age" (Creed 1984:165). Arguing that "homosexuality [*sic*] affirms masculine supremacy in the face of female [reproductive] power," thereby ideologically reproducing men's superiority over women, Creed calls for investigating "the possibility that it operates in the parallel contradiction between the ideal of adult supremacy and the reality of youthful vitality" (1984:166). The linchpin of Creed's analysis is that as boys learn the initiatory secrets of manhood they are also forced to accept, embedded in the ideology of manhood, the terms of elder men's new form of control over them: boys' dependence on adult men for semen. Thus the ideology perpetuates their subordination in an age-graded hierarchy, rendering each age-grade subordinate to all age-grades above it.

Complex constructions of gender enter into the fellator/fellated relationships among the Sambia: the boys are positioned as feminized and wifelike in their roles as fellators even while such feminization is deemed necessary for their eventual growth into men (Herdt 1982:70). In the context of boys' initiations, a hierarchical gender ideology models and underpins the age hierarchy instantiated between boys and bachelors of different age grades, as well as between their male elders. It situates the boys in a structurally inferior and subordinate status relative to older men, while still holding that in the larger social context all males, as a category, are hierarchically superior to all females. One could even argue that the experience of initiation serves to solidify the gender hierarchy by subjecting boys to the traumas of initiation while ultimately enabling them to pass through initiatory age grades and, eventually, to become elder high-status holders. That is, the experience of initiation authenticates the rightness of the hierarchical model by requiring the boys to invest in the significance of the age-graded hierarchy from which they will eventually emerge as high-status Sambia men.

The ritual teachings and practices of boys' initiations can usefully be analyzed for their deployment of gender as a conceptual scheme for thinking about relations of difference and, thus, as a model of and justification for the age hierarchy among boys and bachelors of various age grades, and the gender hierarchy. Gender is used in many Melanesian societies as a conceptual schema, an archetypal metaphor for thinking about relations of difference more generally (see Lederman 1990; Strathern 1987, 1988). An impressive amount of cultural work is invested in announcing and maintaining the boundaries between "men" and "women" as individuated indigenous categories of actors. It would, however, be a mistake to construe these conceptual boundaries in Melanesia as similar to the Western boundaries between gender categories. First, in most Melanesian societies kinship is an organizing social motif that results in binary gender categories' being crosscut by kinship designations: different kinship roles designate significantly different patterns of interaction, obligations, and loyalties between "men" and "women." "Women," for example, should be understood as social actors with different patterns of interaction and obligations in their capacities as sisters, daughters, mothers, and/or wives. Second, Western gender ideology fortifies gender distinctions with a biological paradigm, one that is bolstered by the prestige of science, informed by a Western folk model of the concreteness of biological differences, and constructed to render the boundary between "the sexes" absolute.[16] In Melanesia, however, the boundary between "women" and "men" is much more permeable. Social identity – including gender and kinship designations – is frequently constructed through exchange and, more relevant to my purposes here, through the exchange of substances: body fluids and foods, as well as "exchange items" such as *kula* shells (in the Massim) and pigs (in the Highlands).[17]

Meanings and Exchanges of Substances

Gahuku-Gama boys' initiation is organized around men's belief in the need "to rid their bodies of the contaminating influences of women" (Read 1965:166). Although the initiates are first taught the purification rites during their initiations, they are told that grown men practice the rites regularly and that they too need to practice the rites regularly – both as boys in order to grow into men and, once men, to rehabilitate their masculinity from women's "debilitating" influence (Read 1965:166). Herdt similarly writes about the dangers women pose to Sambia masculine health, elaborating on Sambia men's "defensive ritual knowledge of sexual purification procedures" (1981:174). The purification procedures taught to men before they marry include:

> Nose-bleeding, after each of their wives' monthly periods.... Restricting the frequency of sex itself.... Before the act [of heterosexual intercourse], men can also ingest special leaves to strengthen the stomach and skin. They can masticate special substances... to cleanse the mouth. They can (illicitly) place spearmint leaves in the nose to prevent inhalation of women's "vaginal smell." And during actual intercourse they can keep bark or a red seed in their mouths (again, illicitly, as a reminder to themselves not to swallow their [wives'] saliva). [Herdt 1981:248]

In their acts of nosebleeding and ingesting leaves Sambia men are deploying substances for symbolic purification and as symbolic anticontaminants, respectively; mere contact with a woman's skin or body is designated as contaminating, hence the attention to strengthening the man's skin. Mention of inhaling "vaginal smell" and avoiding women's saliva both clearly allude to substances that men interpret as polluting. In addition the Sambia have what Herdt identifies as "insertive rites," a category of rituals that build up masculinity, again through substances: saliva, skin flakes, body hair, sweat, snot, and urine are all deposited on or attached to, in specific order, certain trees or plants in conjunction with rites thought both to stimulate masculine development and to purify the masculine body "thereby preserving it against contamination" (Herdt 1981:240).

The ideologies of both the Sambia and Gahuku-Gama that are transmitted through male initiation practices focus on the differences and proper relations between men and women and explain the basis of masculinist power and supremacy over women (Herdt 1981, 1984c; Read 1952, 1982). The cosmological aspect of this knowledge consists not only in the teachings about gender but also in the ways such knowledge is constructed to explain and describe men's meaningful social world. For the Sambia this world consists of the constellation of beliefs about semen as the embodiment of all that is vital in Sambia society. In Herdt's accounts, Sambia men view semen as the lifeblood of their society: a substance that creates and nurtures children (by causing breastmilk to flow), turns boys into men and young girls into wives, and transmits masculine spirit familiars (Herdt 1984c). Men alone claim to have the power to regenerate Sambia society through drinking the sap of patrilineally owned trees, which they believe restores their depleted semen reserves and masculine vitality (Herdt 1981, 1984c). Thus is semen constructed by Sambia men as the fount of Sambia life. Men's control over this fount places them in symbolic control of the cosmological power to regenerate their society over time and the power to shape it in the present.

Understanding the instantiation of masculine gender ideologies in these Melanesian societies is, I suggest, more accurately effected by utilizing the notion of fluid or flexible conceptual categories as it is being developed by some Melanesianists. In the cited description of the Gahuku-Gama, for example, men's cane swallowing and nosebleeding are indigenously cast as a means by which female substances are expurgated from the bodies of social actors trying to be purely culturally masculine. Meigs has suggested that tracing the meanings and paths of substances (body fluids such as blood, semen, vaginal fluids, and breastmilk, as well as foods) reveals the ways in which categories such as masculinity and femininity are constructed in numerous Melanesian societies as permeable and subject to change through contact with other substances (Meigs 1976, 1978, 1984, n.d.). Such categories as gender, then, are depicted as having far more flexible boundaries in Melanesian than in Western societies, with important implications for ideas about personhood: if substances are a key element in the formation and maintenance of social identities or social categories, then the focus on semen as constitutive of masculinity or masculine gender identity becomes part of a broader Melanesian cultural theme – the efficacy of substances for constituting persons.[18]

Gender Trouble and the Performative Work of Substances

In the Sambia flute teachings a symbolic parallel is drawn between the flutes as penises and mothers' breasts, both of which produce growth-inducing substances and both of which are (at different times in the life cycle) cast as nurturant and essential to male growth (Herdt 1982:62–3, 79). The flutes are always played in pairs, one of which is designated female and the other male (Herdt 1982:58). The spirit said to animate the flutes and bring them to life is a female spirit, which Herdt argues is a symbolic mother substitute (1982:78): it is the bachelors who are ultimately fellated who play the flutes, and thus it is symbolically as the female/mother deity that they give "milk" (another term denoting semen) to younger initiates (1982:78–9). Sambia symbolism about mother's milk attests to the salience of substances: breastmilk is a key substance of nurturance on which semen is metaphorically predicated both as materially similar to mother's milk and as functionally nurturant like mother's milk.

This subtext on nurturance, playing as it does on a complex relationship between semen and breastmilk as parallel nurturing substances, articulates with broader Melanesian themes about the efficacy of substances in constituting social identities. More specifically, it reflects a widespread complex of ideas about the relationship between semen and breastmilk. Postpartum taboos on sexual intercourse between breastfeeding women and their male sexual partners are widespread in Melanesia. They are informed by a cluster of ideas asserting, first, that there is a physiological connection between the uterus and breasts that allows semen to enter a lactating woman's breastmilk through her uterus and, second, that breastmilk will be contaminated by semen and thereby make the suckling infant sick (Counts 1985:167). This complex of ideas on the dangers of semen to breastmilk and hence to children is counterpointed by the parallels drawn in many societies between the nurturing qualities of both substances. The Kaliai, for example, have a linguistic category (*aisuru*) that designates "those liquid substances which have the capacity to create social ties: semen or male substance, breastmilk (*turuturu aisuru*), and the fluid of the green coconut (*niu aisuru*)" (Counts 1985:159). Among the Kaliai, the relationship between a mother's brother and his sister's children is constructed through the sharing of substance: the mother's brother gives his sister's children coconuts from palms the children will eventually inherit from him and from which the substance *niu aisuru* (the fluid of green coconuts) is drawn (Counts 1985:160). The Hua, another Highlands group, have a similar complex of ideas about substances, in which semen and breastmilk are constructed as partible and constitutive of social identities (Meigs 1984).

Among the Sambia there is ample evidence for a substance-based notion of gender difference. The ritual teachings in the boys' initiations represent breastmilk as semen transformed within the mother's body; this renders semen the ultimate or originary substance of nurturance. Whether semen is the archsubstance or is the more limited substance of choice for the masculinist social ideology merits further investigation. Can a substance other than semen (e.g., breastmilk or blood) inform a substance-based feminine gender ideology or, as Herdt (1984c) claims, is semen the overarching substance that constitutes both feminine and masculine identities and social relationships? Herdt encountered lively disagreement among Sambia women, for example, over whether – as Sambia men claimed – women needed semen in order to make breastmilk; the women claimed they created breastmilk on their own (Herdt 1984c). Among the Gahuku-Gama a similar theme of the power of substances to construct social identities is evidenced by the masculine purification rites in which men engage in response to close contact with women. I turn next to examine the Kaluli, among whom food is a crucial substance for constituting social identities and relationships, and among whom semen practices were used in the past to help grow boys into men.

Substances among the Kaluli

According to Edward Schieffelin, the Kaluli did not have boys' initiation (1982:194–7); the *bau a*, however, he describes as a "ritual of manhood" in which the Kaluli engaged until the early 1970s. The *bau a* was characterized by an extended period of seclusion (about 15 months) for adolescent boys and young men (aged 9–28) and focused on the quintessentially masculine activity of hunting. Two basic and interrelated themes undergirded the *bau a*: hunting for purposes of initiating, meeting, or expanding exchange relationships, and masculine gender identity. Bambi Schieffelin's recent analysis of Kaluli social life highlights food as the highly symbolized medium that constructs and mediates Kaluli social relationships and that perpetuates social relations between coresidents in the villages as well as between affines (1990:4–5). Edward Schieffelin also highlights social giving and daily exchange as fundamental in Kaluli social life (1976:26). In the *bau a*, hunting was undertaken with the goal of amassing enough meat to fulfill each participant's social exchange relationships: by giving away appropriate amounts of *mado* (a category of meat prestation), a young man proved his ability to take part in ongoing food exchanges, a key criterion for adult status for men (1982:175).

The *bau a* also instantiated masculinity. Edward Schieffelin writes that the *bau a* "expressed what men liked best about themselves, what they stood for and wanted to be" (1982:166). In addition to learning and practicing the masculine activity of hunting, masculinity was instantiated both within the context of the *bau a* and temporally and ritually outside it through anal intercourse. This semen practice was explained in terms of boys' need for a "boost" in order to become men (Schieffelin 1976:124). Semen is conceptualized by Kaluli as having a "magical quality that promotes physical growth and mental understanding" (1976:124). It is occasionally mixed with salt and ginger and orally ingested by young Kaluli in need of heightened mental understanding (1976:124), especially to assist in learning a foreign language (B. Schieffelin, personal communication, January 1992). Yet among the Kaluli this semen practice was not ritualized. Temporally outside the *bau a*, when a boy reached the age of 10 or 11 he or his father would choose an inseminator for the boy. Edward Schieffelin writes that "the two would meet privately in the forest or a garden house for intercourse over a period of months or years" (1982:162). Temporally within the *bau a*, semen practices took place between older bachelors and younger boys, with the paired or even triadic relationships designated either formally by the *bau a* leader or informally by the participants themselves (1982:177). Even at the formal designations, both the inseminators and the inseminated were self-selected, and Schieffelin notes that not all *bau a* participants involved themselves in the semen practices (1982:178).

The Kaluli masculine gender ideology that exalts hunting as a quintessentially masculine activity was connected to the mythologically empowered notion that virgins made better hunters because animals do not appear to men who have "too much to do with women" (Schieffelin 1982:178). Virginity was therefore a requirement for all participants for the duration of the *bau a*. In such a scheme, if anal intercourse is viewed as a "sexual" practice it occupies a liminal position between this sacred virginity and the profane relations with women prohibited to *bau a* participants: semen practices were both profane and allowed in the *bau a*, with the older bachelors who were inseminators being required to sleep in the children's rather than the older bachelors' end of the hunting lodge (1982:177). If not viewed as "sexual" but as a substance-based practice, the use of semen practices both within and outside the *bau a* context can be interpreted as one component in an intensive symbolic conversation about masculinity that revolves around the exchange of substances: food or meat prestations and their initiation of exchange relationships enable boys to grow into socially recognized men; similarly, semen practices help to "grow" boys into socially recognized men by giving them the socially recognized substance they require to achieve manhood.

The Kaluli data reveal another Melanesian society in which substances are highly symbolized in the processes of negotiating and constituting social identities: masculinity is performed through hunting that, by enabling exchange relationships, demonstrates a youth's eligibility for adult masculine status. The Kaluli data also demonstrate that semen practices as a cultural form need not be connected to a masculine supremacizing ideology or to a secret men's cult. The ritual teachings of the *bau a*, unlike the Gahuku-Gama and Sambia boys' initiatory teachings, are not predicated on or organized around an ideology of masculine superiority: they do not cast women as hostile or threatening to men's corporate interests. Rather, the *bau a* inculcates masculinity through the practice of hunting, that is, through the successful demonstration of a youth's ability to join ongoing food exchanges and thereby provide food not only for his kin but ultimately for his future spouse and her relatives. Finally, the Kaluli semen practices are clearly based on a belief in the efficacy of semen as a substance capable of conveying masculinity; Kaluli statements about the meanings of semen therefore again challenge the claim that semen practices are either intrinsically erotic or primarily meaningful in terms of sexuality.

Erotics and Gender Reconsidered

The core of this critique of the category "ritualized homosexuality" is that the term exports a Western model of sexuality to non-Western societies. This is revealed most clearly in Herdt's focus on erotics. In conjunction with his use of a psychodynamic framework, itself focused on erotics, Herdt's construction of "ritualized homosexuality" is predicated on a Western concept of sexuality in which "sexual identity" comprises a central feature of personhood. Foucault's analyses of Western sexuality evince the centrality of "speaking the truth" of one's sexual desires to Western individualism (1990a[1978], 1990b[1985]), identifying this as a core forum in which persons are made self-actualizing, that is, through which subjectification takes place. The salience of the confessional mode in the West, in reference to sexuality, articulates a culturally specific notion of desire as deeply individuated (authentic or unique to individuals) and internalized in relation to an exteriorized "reality." Thus is sexuality in the West, in key respects, the signature of individualism writ large. The use of this Western construction of sexuality in societies organized around very different cultural ideologies and constructs of the person is inappropriate at best and grossly distorting at worst.

Erotics and sexuality certainly merit anthropological investigation. The problem, however, is how to investigate these domains without assuming that we already know what it is we seek. The tendency in the literature on "ritualized homosexuality" has been to treat erotics and sexuality as pancultural or precultural universals. Just as gender and kinship initially appeared in anthropological writings as precultural givens, and were problematized only later, so must sexuality and erotics be problematized and investigated – not articulated through the sexual/erotic equivalent of sex differences or the genealogical grid. The interesting questions and insights will not emerge until we move beyond whatever seemingly biological elements are involved in these domains and recognize that cultural belief systems play a profound role in shaping the meanings of, and people's experiences of, erotics and sexuality.

Toward that end I have argued, contra Herdt, that to begin by characterizing ostensibly sexual practices as strictly "sexual" is not an appropriate methodology. Herdt's writings focus on semen practices and his anthologies sort, and effectively exoticize, societies on the basis of those practices – resulting in what I have argued are distorted analyses. Instead of that approach, I have tried to resituate the meanings of semen practices within the context of the common cultural concerns to which they are addressed and the common cultural themes with which they resonate. This symbolic approach could also be useful for the study of erotics. What will count as erotic must be the site of concerted critical discussion among anthropologists working on the subject; to assume that genitally organized activities between same-sexed bodies signifies eroticism is simplistic. I believe anthropology as well as lesbian and gay studies are at a point where more refined methodologies and terms of analysis are needed.

One of the more difficult aspects of dealing with the multivocal and highly ambiguous category of "erotics" lies in attending to the cultural construction of desire. In a popular article on the anthropology of homosexuality, Newton (1988) has called for detailed study of the different metaphors and images that inform thinking about desire and sexuality in different societies. Newton draws on Gregor's (1985) work on sexuality among the Mehinaku (Amazonian Indians), whose folktale about "the wandering vagina" tells of hungry vaginas that travel at night in search of satiation and whose metaphors liken sex to food preparation and eating. Newton asks how Mehinaku women and men experience desire when genitals are constructed as hungry (vaginas) and edible (penises), and also raises questions about the construction of sexual agency along gender lines. Such attention to culturally specific metaphors and images about sexuality and eroticism provide crucial insights into the variety of meanings that structure desire and sexuality cross-culturally. In conjunction with structural analyses of gender, kinship, and economic domains (such as those explored in Blackwood [1986]) such images and metaphors could provide the ethnographic detail needed to flesh out the locations and meanings of sexuality and eroticism in different societies.

Erotics could also be analyzed by situating such metaphors and images in a semiotic framework where such metaphors and images comprise a signifying system in which desire – among the Mehinaku, for example – is partially constructed through an analogy to everyday practices like cooking and eating. Myers's (1988) essay on anger among the Pintupi (a Western Desert Australian aboriginal people) lays out such a semiotic framework for the analysis of emotions. Myers' framework attempts to mediate between positivist and interpretivist approaches by advocating that anthropologists treat emotion meaning "like any other semiotic practice, as a product of signification" (1988:591). For Myers the "existential situation of human subjects in a socio-moral order" (1988:591) addresses the striking continuity of the same range of emotions evidenced across cultures, while attending to how emotions "acquire concrete meaning in contexts of action" (1988:592) provides a tool for seeing the cultural specificities of emotions. In problematizing erotics for the "ritualized homosexuality" practices I have discussed, one could use Myers' semiotic framework to direct attention to the role of desire in semen practices as well as to the role of fear as experienced by the initiates. Instead of essentializing "erotics," one might develop an analysis of how desire, pleasure, and fear may be co-constructed and enacted in boys' initiations, with perhaps some interesting insights into how it is that Sambia youths – over the course of boys' initiation and through daily engagement in semen practices – reconcile or complicate their fear of semen practices into the possible enjoyment or eroticization of semen practices and how this may or may not be connected to the symbolics of semen and the meanings of heterosexual intercourse in their later marriages to women.

The attention directed to the study of homosexualities cross-culturally by way of the "ritualized homosexuality" writings of the past decade has certainly been an improvement over the prior anthropological reluctance to discuss homosexualities, in the West or elsewhere. As I have argued throughout this article, however, the form that this exploration of homosexualities has taken has been fundamentally problematic. Semen practices have been interpreted as "erotic" on the basis of their resemblance to the Western domain of the "sexual." In addition to standing as a lesson in erotic ethnocentrism, this points to the need to look beyond specific practices to the cosmological, sociostructural, symbolic, and productive relations with which semen practices articulate, and to see the parallels between those relations and non-semen-focused practices in other Melanesian societies. The ethnographic data from societies with semen practices indicate that erotics and sexuality are not central – and probably not even relevant – to the meanings of these practices. Rather, as I have argued, the emphasis in Melanesian societies with semen practices (like the Sambia), as well as those without semen practices (like the Gahuku-Gama), turns on several Melanesian themes: the need for men's cultural assistance in the project of growing boys into men; the efficacy of substances for constituting social, including gender, identities; and the salience of hierarchy in engraving the meanings of masculinity and gerontocracy onto boys' bodies in a form modeled on gender hierarchies. This article is a call to remove semen practices from the "ritualized homosexuality" discourse in which they have been both focal point and organizing motif, and to resituate these practices in a more symbolic theoretical framework where these Melanesian themes can come to the analytic foreground.

In addition, this article has more fundamental implications for the cross-cultural study of sexualities. I have argued that in diverting attention away from the meaning systems that animate semen practices, analyses of "ritualized homosexuality" have enabled and advocated sequestering ostensibly homosexual practices into a categorical homosexual "type" of society, sorting societies on the basis of the presence of semen practices and treating these societies as if they belonged to their "own place and time" (Herdt 1981:318). I want to suggest that this analytical sequestration, at one level, stands as a logical outcome of homophobia in the academy – one that cross-culturally useful theories of sexualities clearly must overcome.[19] To erect boundaries around "deviant" and ostensibly "sexual" practices in this way avoids more fundamental questions about the cultural construction of sexuality. At base such boundaries reinstate and preserve the delineation of heterosexual practices as the norm in relation to which "ritualized homosexuality" is comprehensible primarily as an isolated domain of "perversion."[20] On the other hand, to treat semen practices as continuous with other cultural practices must entail challenging the "naturalness" of heterosexual practice itself.[21] The parallels I have described between the Sambia and Gahuku-Gama societies evidence the extent to which the ideologies informing semen practices in the boys' initiations of the former are eminently and fruitfully comparable with those informing purging and purification rites of the latter, and of numerous other Melanesian societies as well. By way of detailing the ideological continuities between the Sambia, Gahuku-Gama, and Kaluli, I have tried to demonstrate that more appropriate axes of comparison exist beyond the narrow and conservative confines of a "ritualized homosexuality" "type" of society, and indeed that these confines must be challenged if we are to develop adequate analytical tools with which to theorize sexualities cross-culturally.

NOTES

1 The typology to which I allude, and that Herdt endorses (1993:ix), defines the possible social organizations of homosexuality cross-culturally as falling into one of four ideal types: age-structured, gender-structured, role- or profession-structured, and egalitarian/ "gay" (Adam 1986; Greenberg 1988; Murray 1992). Generated from exclusively androcentric data, this typology has been described and deployed as if analytically capable of encompassing all homosexualities, and it remains the most prominent anthropological paradigm for analyzing homosexualities cross-culturally despite its many shortcomings. For example, it cannot account for many female homosexualities, in part because it holds no theoretical place for the centrality of culturally specific gender ideologies and practices for shaping the social organization of homosexualities (see Blackwood 1986; Elliston 1993).

2 I use the terms *masculine* and *feminine* throughout this article to designate the gendered dimensions of social identities. While *feminine* may have misleading connotations, it is a more useful term than, for example, *women* or *female*, both of which align sex/gender with bodies and with sexuality in ways that can elide the culturally specific meanings of both gender and sexuality (see Butler 1990; de Lauretis 1987; Yanagisako and Collier 1987). My use of the terms *masculine* and *feminine*, then, is meant to focus on gender as a cultural construct.

3 I use the terms *Western* and *Euro-American* interchangeably in this article, and with reservations. Both terms gloss complex and multiple histories and contemporary situations and are, therefore, fundamentally troubling. My use of such shorthand labels is meant to draw attention to patterns of behavior and belief systems that are, minimally, familiar to social actors within the geopolitical boundaries of Euro-American societies, with the recognition that many individuals – such as, for example, members of different identity groups (cultural, ethnic, religious, and sexual, among others) and marginalized to varying degrees – may not wholly participate in or wholly subscribe to the dominant patterns of behaviors and belief systems.

4 Herdt has joined this tradition in writing of the need to "distinguish between outward sexual behavior and internal identity" in his works on "ritualized homosexuality" (1984a:x; 1993:ix; see also Herdt 1991a, 1991b).

5 Feminist philosopher Marilyn Frye (1990) has questioned whether lesbians in the United States even "have sex," arguing that American cultural and historical understandings of "sex" are not only heterosexual but contingent on male orgasm.

6 In his recent "Introduction to the Paperback Edition" of *Ritualized Homosexuality in Melanesia*, Herdt renames the subject boy-man semen practices "boy-inseminating rites" (1993:ix), a term he identifies as instrumentally based and designed to avoid some of the problems he now recognizes as endemic to his use of the term "homosexuality." His reconsideration of the difficulties of the category "homosexuality" is, however, for the most part confined to this level: it does not lead him to a reconfiguration of the domain of "the sexual" that, I argue, remains fundamentally problematic in the writings on "ritualized homosexuality."

7 Knauft (1990) has challenged Herdt's account of the geographical distribution of semen practices, arguing that only societies west of the Trans-Fly area actually included semen practices in their boys' initiations (see also Knauft 1993).

8 See Blackwood 1986 for a discussion of biological explanations.

9 In a recent book Knauft (1993) analyzes the distribution and meanings of "ritualized homosexuality" in Melanesia as part of his larger project of problematizing the analytical construction of culture areas. As with the present analysis, Knauft is critical of the ways "ritualized homosexuality" has been used to sort societies and create culture areas and he calls for more fine-grained analyses of the meanings of the different homosexualities, heterosexualities, and bisexualities found in South New Guinea societies. In contrast to what I have argued here, however, Knauft is not interested in "devolving to a disagreement about categories, definitions or Western tropes" used for the analysis of "ritualized homosexuality" and sees such disagreements as the "expected outcome of changing the scale of comparative analysis" (1993:58). In the present article it is precisely the "categories, definitions and Western tropes" that are at issue and that I treat as having fundamental epistemological and methodological significance for the anthropological study of sexualities.

10 In response to scholarly writings appearing in the decade since *Ritualized Homosexuality in Melanesia* was first published, Herdt allows, in his recent "Introduction to the Paperback Edition" of that book, that "ritualized homosexuality" may not be as widespread or as geographically systemic as he had originally claimed (Herdt 1993; see also Herdt 1984b). Even as he makes this acknowledgment, however, Herdt reiterates his claim that semen practices are "prehistoric, perhaps 10,000 or more years old" (1993:xv) and moves to dismiss challenges to his theory that semen practices constitute an ancient ritual complex by writing that "[t]hough the numbers of groups are open to dispute, their importance for theory and the understanding of Melanesian area-wide cultural structure and ontology clearly is not" (1993:xvii).

11 Knauft, for example, in a review that engages some of the psychodynamic issues raised in Herdt's *Ritualized Homosexuality in Melanesia* collection, concludes that "an explanation of Melanesian homosexuality [*sic*] based on psychodynamic factors and one based on social or cultural determinants are each partial and incomplete"; he calls for "a perspective that can link" these approaches (1987:177). While Knauft's suggestion would probably improve the study of most cultural phenomena, he is also only too exemplary in identifying semen practices as in particular need of explanation. My point is that to isolate these practices as requiring explanation – as most writers on the subject have done – is intrinsically problematic, more problematic is that the explanations proffered generally reflect Western biases and ideologies.

12 Whitehead (1986a, 1986b) has also attempted to reanalyze boys' initiations in Papua New Guinea in a broader context, treating initiations involving semen practices alongside other kinds of initiatory techniques through a focus on what she more generally labels Melanesian "fertility cults." Her concern in the subject essays is with the forms of political community that fertility cults help to instantiate and regulate, with manhood and clanhood being primary contrasts. While her essays are not focused on "ritualized

homosexuality," they utilize and develop some of the concerns prominent in the present article, most significantly the meanings of gender and of substances, demonstrating the relevance and importance of retheorizing both in order to better understand Melanesian societies.

13 See the discussions and examples in Weston 1991 and Blackwood 1986.

14 See Stoltenberg 1989 for an interesting analysis of the variation in what counts as the "facts" of male sexual arousal.

15 Whether, for example, there is something qualitatively different about the act of orgasm that would make the exchange of orgasmic fluids more meaningful, more highly charged, or more significant than the exchange of any other substance should, I suggest, be treated as an open, empirical question.

16 For elaboration on some important differences between Western and Melanesian gender categories, see Strathern 1988:98–132 and Meigs 1990. This article does not attempt an analysis of Western epistemology or of what many philosophers and historians have identified as a Western intolerance of ambiguity at the level of conceptual categories (see Foucault 1990a[1978]; Jay 1981; Lloyd 1984). For an interesting example of what may be at stake in Western gender and sexuality boundary transgression see Foucault's introduction to the journals of Herculine Barbin, and the journals themselves (Foucault, ed. 1980); see also Butler 1990:93–106 on Foucault's analysis.

17 See Meigs 1984 and Counts 1985 on the exchange of foods and body substances; Weiner 1976, 1992 on exchange in the Massim; and Strathern 1971 and Strathern 1988 on the exchange of pigs.

18 Adopting a perspective that analyzes substances as media of exchange suggests alternative ways of theorizing the references to women's "debilitating" and "contaminating" influences so common in the literature on boys' initiations. In particular it suggests a need to study more thoroughly local constructs of how femininity is culturally produced, with particular attention to the role of substances identified as feminine. The ways in which the notion of "female pollution" has been deployed in Melanesian ethnography, especially in the writings on "ritualized homosexuality," frequently obstructs analysis of the meanings of feminine substances by failing to distinguish the notion that feminine substances threaten masculinity from the notion that such substances symbolize femininity – where, in a cultural context in which substances signify and produce gender differences, men's contact with feminine substances would undermine the symbolic bases, and thus the cultural construction, of masculinity itself.

19 I thank the anonymous *American Ethnologist* reviewer who highlighted this implication and suggested I pursue it.

20 It is from such a perspective, for example, that questions about how Sambia men "switch" from homosexual to heterosexual motivation gain the appearance of relevance or appropriateness (see Herdt 1981).

21 This in turn should propel the much-needed anthropological investigations into how heterosexual desires and practices are made culturally normative, meaningful, or appropriate, and should also generate critical examination of the organizing axes of homosexuality and heterosexuality themselves.

REFERENCES

Adam, Barry D.
1986 Age, Structure and Sexuality. Journal of Homosexuality 11:19–33.

Allen, Michael R.
1984 Homosexuality, Male Power, and Political Organization in North Vanuatu: A Comparative Analysis. *In* Ritualized Homosexuality in Melanesia. Gilbert H. Herdt, ed. Pp. 83–126. Berkeley: University of California Press.
Blackwood, Evelyn
1986 Breaking the Mirror: The Construction of Lesbianism and the Anthropological Discourse on Homosexuality. *In* The Many Faces of Homosexuality: Anthropological Approaches to Homosexual Behavior. Evelyn Blackwood, ed. Pp. 1–17. New York: Harrington Park Press.
Blackwood, Evelyn, ed.
1986 The Many Faces of Homosexuality: Anthropological Approaches to Homosexual Behavior. New York: Harrington Park Press.
Butler, Judith
1990 Gender Trouble: Feminism and the Subversion of Identity. New York: Routledge.
1993 Bodies That Matter. New York: Routledge.
Counts, Dorothy A.
1985 Infant Care and Feeding in Kaliai, West New Britain, Papua New Guinea. *In* Infant Care and Feeding in the South Pacific. Leslie B. Marshall, ed. Pp. 155–69. New York: Gordon and Breach.
Creed, Gerald W.
1984 Sexual Subordination: Institutionalized Homosexuality and Social Control in Melanesia. Ethnology 23(3):157–76.
Davis, D. L., and R. G. Whitten
1987 The Cross-Cultural Study of Human Sexuality. Annual Review of Anthropology 16:69–98.
de Lauretis, Teresa
1987 Technologies of Gender: Essays on Theory, Film, and Fiction. Bloomington: University of Indiana Press.
Elliston, Deborah A.
1993 *Review of* Oceanic Homosexualities. Journal of the History of Sexuality 4:319–21.
Foucault, Michel
1990a[1978] The History of Sexuality, Volume 1: An Introduction. New York: Vintage Books.
1990b[1985] The Use of Pleasure: The History of Sexuality, Volume 2. New York: Vintage Books.
Foucault, Michel, ed.
1980 Herculine Barbin, Being the Recently Discovered Memoirs of a Nineteenth-Century Hermaphrodite. Richard McDougall, trans. New York: Colophon.
Frye, Marilyn
1990 Lesbian "Sex." *In* Lesbian Philosophies and Cultures. Jeffner Allen, ed. Pp. 305–16. Albany: State University of New York Press.
Greenberg, David F.
1988 The Construction of Homosexuality. Chicago: University of Chicago Press.
Gregor, Thomas.
1985 Anxious Pleasures. Chicago: University of Chicago Press.
Hage, Per
1981 On Male Initiation and Dual Organisation in New Guinea. Man (n.s.) 16:268–75.
Herdt, Gilbert H.
1981 Guardians of the Flutes: Idioms of Masculinity. New York: McGraw-Hill.
1982 Fetish and Fantasy in Sambia Initiation. *In* Rituals of Manhood. Gilbert H. Herdt, ed. Pp. 44–98. Berkeley: University of California Press.

1984a Editor's Preface. *In* Ritualized Homosexuality in Melanesia. Gilbert H. Herdt, ed. Pp. vii–xvii. Berkeley: University of California Press.
1984b Ritualized Homosexual Behavior in the Male Cults of Melanesia, 1862–1983: An Introduction. *In* Ritualized Homosexuality in Melanesia. Gilbert H. Herdt, ed. Pp. 1–82. Berkeley: University of California Press.
1984c Semen Transactions in Sambia Culture. *In* Ritualized Homosexuality in Melanesia. Gilbert H. Herdt, ed. Pp. 167–210. Berkeley: University of California Press.
1987 The Accountability of Sambia Initiates. *In* Anthropology in the High Valleys: Essays on the New Guinea Highlands in Honor of Kenneth E. Read. L. L. Langness and Terence E. Hays, eds. Pp. 237–81. Novato, CA: Chandler & Sharp Publishers.
1991a Representations of Homosexuality in Traditional Societies: An Essay on Cultural Ontology and Historical Comparison, Part 1. Journal of the History of Sexuality 1:481–504.
1991b Representations of Homosexuality in Traditional Societies: An Essay on Cultural Ontology and Historical Comparison, Part 2. Journal of the History of Sexuality 2:603–32.
1993 Introduction to the Paperback Edition. *In* Ritualized Homosexuality in Melanesia. Gilbert H. Herdt, ed. Pp. vii–xliv. Paperback ed. Berkeley: University of California Press.

Herdt, Gilbert, ed.
1982 Rituals of Manhood: Male Initiation in Papua New Guinea. Berkeley: University of California Press.
1984 Ritualized Homosexuality in Melanesia. Berkeley: University of California Press.
1993 Ritualized Homosexuality in Melanesia. Paperback ed. Berkeley: University of California Press.

Herdt, Gilbert, and Robert J. Stoller
1990 Intimate Communications: Erotics and the Study of Culture. New York: Columbia University Press.

Jay, Nancy
1981 Gender and Dichotomy. Feminist Studies 7(1):38–56.

Katz, Jonathan Ned
1990 The Invention of Heterosexuality. Socialist Review 90(1):7–34.

Keesing, Roger M.
1982 Introduction. *In* Rituals of Manhood. Gilbert H. Herdt, ed. Pp. 1–43. Berkeley: University of California Press.

Knauft, Bruce M.
1987 Review Essay: Homosexuality in Melanesia. The Journal of Psychoanalytic Anthropology 10(2):155–91.
1990 The Question of Ritualized Homosexuality among the Kiwai of South New Guinea. The Journal of Pacific History 25:188–210.
1993 South Coast New Guinea Cultures: History, Comparison, Dialectic. Cambridge: Cambridge University Press.

Lederman, Rena
1990 Contested Order: Gender and Society in the Southern New Guinea Highlands. *In* Beyond the Second Sex: New Directions in the Anthropology of Gender. Peggy Reeves Sanday and Ruth Gallagher Goodenough, eds. Pp. 45–73. Philadelphia: University of Pennsylvania Press.

Lindenbaum, Shirley
1984 Variations on a Sociosexual Theme in Melanesia. *In* Ritualized Homosexuality in Melanesia. Gilbert H. Herdt, ed. Pp. 337–61. Berkeley: University of California Press.

1987 The Mystification of Female Labors. *In* Gender and Kinship: Essays Toward a Unified Analysis. Jane Fishburne Collier and Sylvia Junko Yanagisako, eds. Pp. 221–43. Stanford, CA: Stanford University Press.

Lloyd, Genevieve

1984 The Man of Reason: "Male" and "Female" in Western Philosophy. Minneapolis: University of Minnesota Press.

Meigs, Anna S.

1976 Male Pregnancy and the Reduction of Sexual Opposition in a New Guinea Highlands Society. Ethnology 15(4):393–407.

1978 A Papuan Perspective on Pollution. Man (n.s.) 13:304–18.

1984 Food, Sex, and Pollution: A New Guinea Religion. New Brunswick, NJ: Rutgers University Press.

1990 Multiple Gender Ideologies and Statuses. *In* Beyond the Second Sex: New Directions in the Anthropology of Gender. Peggy Reeves Sanday and Ruth Gallagher Goodenough, eds. Pp. 101–12. Philadelphia: University of Pennsylvania Press.

n.d. Kinship and Gender: A Fluid Model. Unpublished MS.

Murray, Stephen O.

1992 Oceanic Homosexualities. New York: Garland Publishing.

Myers, Fred R.

1988 The Logic and Meaning of Anger among Pintupi Aborigines. Man (n.s.) 23:589–610.

Newton, Esther

1988 Of Yams, Grinders & Gays: The Anthropology of Homosexuality. Out/Look (Spring) 1(1):28–37.

Read, Kenneth E.

1952 Nama Cult of the Central Highlands, New Guinea. Oceania 23(1):1–25.

1965 The High Valley. New York: Charles Scribner's Sons.

1982 Male-Female Relationships among the Gahuku-Gama: 1950 and 1981. *In* Sexual Antagonism, Gender, and Social Change in Papua New Guinea (special issue of Social Analysis). Fitz John P. Poole and Gilbert H. Herdt, eds. Pp. 66–78. Adelaide, South Australia.

1984 The *Nama* Cult Recalled. *In* Ritualized Homosexuality in Melanesia. Gilbert H. Herdt, ed. Pp. 211–47. Berkeley: University of California Press.

Schieffelin, Bambi B.

1990 The Give and Take of Everyday Life. Cambridge: Cambridge University Press.

Schieffelin, Edward L.

1976 The Sorrow of the Lonely and the Burning of the Dancers. New York: St. Martin's Press.

1982 The *Bau a* Ceremonial Hunting Lodge: An Alternative to Initiation. *In* Rituals of Manhood. Gilbert H. Herdt, ed. Pp. 155–200. Berkeley: University of California Press.

Schwimmer, Eric

1984 Male Couples in New Guinea. *In* Ritualized Homosexuality in Melanesia. Gilbert H. Herdt, ed. Pp. 248–91. Berkeley: University of California Press.

Stoltenberg, John

1989 Refusing to Be a Man: Essays on Sex and Justice. Portland, OR: Breitenbush Books.

Strathern, Andrew J.

1971 The Rope of Moka: Big Men and Ceremonial Exchange in Mount Hagen. Cambridge: Cambridge University Press.

Strathern, Marilyn

1987 Introduction. *In* Dealing with Inequality: Analysing Gender Relations in Melanesia and Beyond, Marilyn Strathern, ed. Pp. 1–32. Cambridge: Cambridge University Press.

1988 The Gender of the Gift: Problems with Women and Problems with Society in Melanesia. Berkeley: University of California Press.
Van Baal, J.
1984 The Dialectics of Sex in Marind-anim Culture. *In* Ritualized Homosexuality in Melanesia. Gilbert H. Herdt, ed. Pp. 128–66. Berkeley: University of California Press.
Weiner, Annette B.
1976 Women of Value, Men of Renown: New Perspectives in Trobriand Exchange. Austin: University of Texas Press.
1992 Inalienable Possessions: The Paradox of Keeping-While-Giving. Berkeley: University of California Press.
Weston, Kath
1991 Families We Choose: Lesbians, Gays, Kinship. New York: Columbia University Press.
1993 Lesbian/Gay Studies in the House of Anthropology. Annual Review of Anthropology 22:339–67.
Whitehead, Harriet B.
1986a The Varieties of Fertility Cultism in New Guinea: Part I. American Ethnologist 13:80–99.
1986b The Varieties of Fertility Cultism in New Guinea: Part II. American Ethnologist 13:271–89.
Yanagisako, Sylvia Junko, and Jane Fishburne Collier
1987 Toward a Unified Analysis of Gender and Kinship. *In* Gender and Kinship: Essays toward a Unified Analysis. Jane Fishburne Collier and Sylvia Junko Yanagisako, eds. Pp. 14–50. Stanford, CA: Stanford University Press.

7

Gender, Genetics, and Generation: Reformulating Biology in Lesbian Kinship

Corinne P. Hayden

The complicated historical relationship between ideas about homosexuality and concepts of "the family" in American culture makes the idea of gay and lesbian families – "chosen" or "created" – a provocative one in the study of American kinship. Insofar as lesbians and gay men have been ideologically excluded from the realm of kinship in American culture (Weston 1991: 4–6), it is perhaps not surprising that claims to the legitimacy of gay and lesbian family configurations are often articulated *and* contested in terms of their perceived difference from (or similarity to) normative ideologies of "the American family." In her pivotal work, *Families We Choose* (1991), Kath Weston argues for the *distinctiveness* of a certain configuration of gay and lesbian kinship in which biological ties are decentered and choice, or love, becomes the defining feature of kin relationships. For Weston, gay and lesbian chosen families are neither derivative of, nor substititutes for, "straight," biological families; rather, they are distinctive in their own right (1991:210). Ellen Lewin takes a markedly different approach to the value of distinctiveness in her recent book, *Lesbian Mothers* (1993). By her own account exceeding the goal of her earlier work on maternal custody strategies – showing that lesbian mothers are "just as good" as heterosexual mothers – Lewin finds that "motherhood" in American culture constitutes a defining feature of womanhood that indeed supersedes the "difference" of lesbian identity (1993:3). In this reading, there is nothing particularly unique about the ways in which lesbian mothers negotiate relatedness and relationships.

Though they are not explicitly foregrounded in such terms, I would argue that these two pivotal ethnographies together suggest that "biology," broadly conceived, is a crucial axis around which claims to the "distinctiveness" of gay and lesbian kinship revolve. Thus the relative centrality of biology in gay and lesbian families might be seen to signal a corollary assimilation into, or departure from, "traditional" forms of American kinship. In this logic, the argument would read as follows: when biological ties are displaced (as in Weston's work), claims to distinctiveness can be made; where biological ties are central (especially in the case of motherhood), claims to difference lose their relevance or legitimacy.

I want to disrupt the flow of this argument on several levels. To that end, this article is an exploration of the ways in which many lesbian mothers employ notions of biology, in the context of donor insemination, to articulate their own sense of uniquely lesbian kinship. I offer, then, an ethnographic reading of specific kinds of claims I have encountered in recent lesbian-feminist writings, newspaper articles, court cases, and informal conversations. I must stress that these particular articulations of lesbian familial desire in no way offer a "representative" stance on parenting within lesbian and gay communities.[1] On the one hand, the question of whether or not to become a parent has a long and complicated history for many gay men and lesbians; for lesbians in particular, the centrality of motherhood to American cultural narratives of womanhood has long made mothering a particularly potent site of contestation. Current articulations of the radical potential of lesbian families must be placed within the context of continuing debates over reproductive "choice" – and the choice *not* to mother – within various lesbian and feminist communities.[2]

On the other hand, for lesbians and gay men who are parents, the two-parent "intentional" family (Lewin 1993) is obviously not the only model. Lesbians and gay men have children through previous heterosexual relationships; they adopt children; they are single parents or raise children with several co-parents. Moreover, gay and lesbian parenting families have long existed, and certainly predate the current interest in "alternative" families. I focus specifically on lesbians who create families through donor insemination not because they are a defining model for lesbian kinship (if there could be such a thing) but rather because of the particular ways in which biology is made both explicit and mutable in these visions of a "distinct" family configuration.[3] Moreover, these claims to a uniquely lesbian kinship often challenge the (heterosexual) gender configuration that is foundational to American cultural notions of kinship. These articulations of lesbian families thus provide a context in which to continue important theoretical discussions of the relationship among gender, sexuality, and kinship (see Collier and Yanagisako 1987; Rubin 1975; Weston 1991).

I want to follow Marilyn Strathern in resisting the temptation to argue for wholly novel conceptual developments in ideas about kinship, though I do hope to retain space for imagining how "images pressed into new service acquire new meanings" (Strathern 1992b: 15). Such an approach assumes from the outset that there is nothing "truly new" under the sun; at the same time, the continual back and forth between "new" and "old" ideas allows for the possibility of reformulating existing symbols in creative and meaningful ways.

Taking on "American Kinship"

The claim to a distinctive gay and lesbian kinship elicits questions about the elasticity of American kinship as a symbolic system and implies the possibility of transforming the dominant model of American kinship. Such moves call for a clarification of exactly what *kind(s)* of kinship one has in mind and how one chooses to define dominant, transformative, or derivative versions of American kinship. Though it has been challenged on many fronts, the foundational model of American kinship laid out by David Schneider (1980[1968]) more than 25 years ago remains an enduring one. Discussions of gay and lesbian kinship, and arguments about its sameness (and therefore derivative nature) or difference (implying the potential for transformation), continue to resonate with the terms that Schneider set forth in 1968. American kinship, he argued, is a symbolic system resting on the two contrasting but mutually dependent elements of blood (shared biogenetic substance) and love (a code for conduct both legitimating the creation of blood ties and governing the behavior of those who are related by blood). Characterizing Americans' (and American anthropologists') understanding of kinship as a "folk theory of biological reproduction," Schneider declared the *symbol* of (hetero)sexual intercourse – mediating and mediated by blood and marriage – as central to American kinship (1980[1968]:37–8).

Not surprisingly, this premise has been made problematic by lesbians and gay men, who have been symbolically excluded from the realm of kinship. The supposed exclusion from, and threat to, family that marks gay men and lesbians has amounted to a virtual denial of their cultural citizenship, as Weston has noted (1991:4–6). Indeed, one has only to glance at the most basic manifestations of homophobia in the United States to grasp their foundation on the inter-dependent web of kinship, sexuality, gender, and procreation. Exemplified by the pseudo-evolutionary theory that homosexuals must *recruit* progeny because they cannot reproduce themselves, this particular version of the "threat to family" argument highlights the ways in which heterosexuality, gender, and kinship are mutually constituted.[4]

The perceived centrality of procreative sexuality to the stability of "the family" underlies such familiar statements as, "I have a problem with homosexuals who flaunt what they're doing... before the public in an effort to destroy and break down family life.... The family creates. Homosexuals only cause trouble. They can't create anything" (Glasgow quoted in Green 1991:1–2). It is likewise this notion of creativity that figures so strongly in claims to the legitimacy of gay and lesbian families, with or without children. At stake in such contests over creativity is the meaning of sexual intercourse in American kinship and, subsequently, the ways in which blood and love are privileged as defining features of families. Weston notes the ways in which chosen families complicate "traditional" notions of blood and love: "Familial ties between persons of the same sex that may be erotic *but are not grounded in biology or procreation* do not fit any tidy division of kinship into relations of blood and marriage" (1991:3, emphasis added). Weston's work focuses on families of friends and lovers – "chosen families" that challenge the sanctity of blood and marriage as the sole determinants of legitimate kin ties.

Although these chosen families bring up crucial questions about kinship *without* biological connections (or without the *expectation* of creating biological kin through procreation),[5] quite differrent questions arise in the creation of lesbian and gay parenting families in which biology, via procreation, reenters the picture. Using Weston's work as a foundation for exploring lesbian and gay critiques of the central premises of American kinship, I will focus below on the complicated intersections of biological procreation and lesbian kinship. I am interested not simply in the assertion that biology *is* mobilized in articulations of "uniquely" lesbian family configurations; my concern lies more in the ways in which the symbol of biology is unpacked, dispersed, and distributed within these configurations.[6] In this way, certain articulations of lesbian kinship provide important ground on which to theorize biology as a symbol that is continually refigured within the contested symbolic field(s) of American kinship.

Love Makes a Family[7]

Weston implicates chosen families in an explicit challenge to the dominant model of American kinship and its foundation in procreation and biological ties. In *Families We Choose*, she writes,

> The very notion of gay families asserts that people who claim nonprocreative sexual identities . . . can lay claim to family ties of their own. . . . Theirs has not been a proposal to number gay families among variations in "American kinship," but a more comprehensive attack on the privilege accorded to a biogenetically grounded mode of determining what relationships will *count* as kinship. [1991:35, emphasis in original]

The families to which Weston refers are families forged out of ties to friends and lovers. United by choice and love, not by biological ties or the expectation of creating such, these families clearly set themselves apart from the dominant model of American kinship and its maxim that "blood is thicker than water." Without denying that blood ties "work" (Strathern 1992b), chosen families nonetheless level a profound critique at the *centrality* in American kinship of heterosexual, procreative relationships and the biogenetic ties that arise from these relationships.

Weston clearly believes that chosen families are neither imitative nor derivative of the dominant model of American kinship. Rather, she argues that they constitute a distinctive form of kinship, contrastive rather than analogous to straight kinship (Weston 1991:211).[8] Still, she maintains that choice cannot be read as license to create a family structure unfettered by conventional notions of kinship. Situating chosen families within the bounded symbolic universe of American kinship, Weston's analysis posits a continuum in which gay, chosen families have emerged in explicit opposition to, but coexisting with, straight, biological families. Thus the very idea of chosen families becomes meaningful only in the context of the cultural belief in the power of blood ties (Weston 1991:211).

There is another dimension to chosen families' position within the dominant symbolic matrix of American kinship. In her review of *Families We Choose*, Strathern writes that perhaps *the* fundamental critique enacted through chosen families is that they "make explicit the fact that there was always a choice as to whether or not biology is made the foundation of relationships" (1992b:3). This, indeed, is one of Schneider's central points throughout *American Kinship*: though American believe that blood determines family, there is and always has been a necessary element of choice in the degree to which blood ties become "relationships" in any given family (not to mention the ways in which blood ties are conceived in the first place) (Schneider 1980[1968]:62–3; see also Strathern 1981).

Schneider's and Strathern's reminders of the centrality of choice in heterosexual kinship dislodge biology from its privileged place in that model; they assert unequivocally that there is much more at work in the creation of kinship in American culture than a fervent belief in the self-evidence of blood ties might allow. In the context of lesbian and gay kinship, this displacement of biology as *the* central and defining feature of family connotes a challenge to the direct, exclusive correlation that is assumed between heterosexual procreation and the production of kin ties.

In Strathern's analysis, chosen families challenge the privilege enjoyed by straight kinship by shifting the emphasis from blood to choice *on two levels* — explicitly, through their own chosen families, and implicitly, by suggesting that despite its supposed basis in the "facts of nature," straight, blood-based kinship is itself a construction. As the focus of this article now turns to lesbian motherhood, Strathern's point bears elaboration. The creation of lesbian and gay families with children cannot be discussed in exactly the same terms as chosen families, since each indexes somewhat different notions of biology. Where chosen families may *decentralize* biology, lesbian families' explicit mobilization of biological ties challenges the notion of biology as a *singular* category through which kin ties are reckoned. Far from depleting its symbolic capital, the dispersal of the biological tie seems here to highlight its elasticity within the symbolic matrix of American kinship.

Gender and Kinship

While the chosen families of lesbians and gay men may forge new ground in kinship divorced from procreation, lesbian co-parenting families engender a slightly different set of symbolic renegotiations, since the presence of procreation refigues the blood/choice dichotomy. Does biological reproduction ground kinship "back" in biology, thereby negating the "progress" achieved by chosen families? Does lesbian sex itself create kinship different from that mediated by heterosexual sex? Does a child with two mothers come from a different kind of kinship arrangement than a child with one mother and/or one father? As these questions suggest, sex and gender, in the context of a procreative family, become central elements of contestation in efforts to define the place of lesbian families in American kinship.

Many feminist anthropologists, in critique of Schneider, contend that "the American Kinship System" does not exist apart from its constituent elements of gender, age, ethnicity, race, or class, among other things (Collier and Yanagisako 1987; Delaney and Yanagisako, 1995; McKinnon 1992; Strathern 1992a). For Schneider, these mediating factors do not inhabit the realm of "pure culture." Collier and Yanagisako (1987) have argued that the split between the "cultural" realm of kinship and the "mediating factor" of gender is illusory, at least in American culture. Kinship and gender are mutually constituted, they write, because both categories are based on the same ideas of biological difference. Gender assumptions about the facts of sexual reproduction pervade kinship theory, just as sexual reproduction is central to the definition of gender (Collier and Yanagisako 1987:23–34). Thus even a separation of the two on a "purely analytical" level, as Schneider enjoins, becomes problematic.[9]

Further, categories such as gender, age, class, and so on, produce structural distinctions that mediate relationships within families; to talk about any of them, therefore, means to talk about power. Schneider's insistence on separating gender from kinship has, by extension, opened him up to criticisms that his model ignores issues of power and inequality (Delaney and Yanagisako 1995; McKinnon 1992). Delancy and Yanagisako write, "Schneider did not address the question of how inequality is embedded in cultural systems, in part because he did not follow out the logic of the specificity of symbols and instead made abstractions of them" (1995:3). Standing firm in the position that symbolic analysis of kinship – kept separate from gender, age, power, and so on – goes only so far as blood and love, Schneider ensures the stability of his model of kinship. For, in these fairly abstract terms, a "transformation" in kinship would necessitate a complete departure from the blood-love (or blood-choice) symbolic matrix. Thus, for example, chosen families as described by Weston cannot claim distinctiveness because they remain enmeshed within the tension between blood and love. A more contextualized, power-conscious analysis such as that enjoined by Delaney, Yanagisako, McKinnon, and Strathern allows for the stability of Schneider's symbolic *universe* while leaving room for reconfigurations of the meanings of these symbols.

Power and Parenthood

The centrality of power and gender to American kinship is particularly illuminated by lesbian families in which both parents are explicitly considered mothers. These families potentially unsettle the "dominant" vision of American kinship in several ways, perhaps most significantly in their challenge to ideas about gendered hierarchy and parenthood. For women with a clear and gendered agenda for lesbian motherhood, its promise is deeply bound to the existence of a second female parent, who is neither downplayed nor de-gendered. She is not a father substitute, nor is she a gender-neutral parent; she is clearly another mother. Resonating with a legacy of feminist and lesbian-feminist writings on "compulsory heterosexuality" (most notably, of course, Adrienne Rich's [1984] article by that name), such understandings of the radical potential of lesbian motherhood are offered in criticism of – and as an alternative to – the institutionalized gender inequities seen to inhere in heterosexuality.

There is a dual implication to this oppositional construction of parental roles. First, embracing rather than contesting the image of motherhood as a distinctly female, nurturant enterprise, the benefits of the family are construed in terms of a doubling of maternal love and support. In the feminist volume *Politics of the Heart: A Lesbian Parenting Anthology*, one contributor writes, "I'm not opposed to fathers, but I do believe every baby should have at least two mothers" (Washburne 1987: 144–5). Another notes that "when straight mothers find out my son has two moms, they are actually envious on some level; there are two people doing the job they often do alone" (Hill 1987: 118).

Second, more than the "convenience" of double motherhood, claims to the distinctiveness of lesbian co-parenting rest heavily on a critique of the power relationships that many of these women associate with heterosexual families. Such understandings of lesbian parenting allege, on the one hand, that heterosexuality contains built-in power inequities; by contrast, lesbian mothers claim to offer gender equality and therefore parental equality. Counteracting the accusations that same-sex relationships are, by definition, pathological (and therefore detrimental to children's development), many mental health professionals and theorists contend that the gender configurations of gay and lesbian relationships are indeed as healthy as, if not healthier than, those of their straight counterparts.[10] Contributing to this compensatory project is psychologist Margaret Nichols, who writes,

> In my experience, far too many heterosexual relationships become bogged down in the mire of sex-role conflicts and never transcend these conflicts to a point where both partners see each other as full human beings. I do not mean to imply that lesbian and gay relationships are without conflict, simply that the conflicts... are certainly much less likely to exhibit the vast power differentials that can be found in many heterosexual relationships. [1987:102]

If the absence of gender *difference* is portrayed as a positive attribute, then the gendering of both partners as *female* is seen to multiply the benefits exponentially. Suzanne Cusick writes that a lesbian relationship is

> a relationship based on non-power – that is, a relationship in which a porous boundary exists at all moments between she who seems to have the power and she who doesn't, allowing for a flow of power in both directions. *No one in the relationship is formed to be the power figure, though all can play at it.* [1991:10, emphasis added]

De-eroticizing this last point for a moment, the thesis of equal or fluid power – given the premise of non-power – forms the basis of a politicized view of the potential for difference in certain lesbian co-parenting families. Thus, bearing and raising a child in a lesbian household is understood as a tool for "radical motherhood" to combat "heteromothering" (Cooper 1987:223); a "unique opportunity in history to raise children in a home with two parents with potentially equal power" (Polikoff 1987:329); or, on the other side of the coin, perhaps creates a perverse environment in which men and women do not "adhere to their roles" (Polikoff 1990:560).

Further, as Cusick's erotic gender equation amply suggests, gender roles within kinship are inextricably linked to the act and symbol of sex itself. Schneider contends that sexual intercourse is a central symbol in American kinship because it is through sex (or the symbol thereof) that blood ties are created and family relationships mediated:

> Sexual intercourse (the act of procreation) is the symbol which provides the distinctive features in terms of which both the members of the family as relatives and the family as a cultural unit are defined and differentiated. [1990(1968):31]

He continues, "Father is the genitor, mother the genetrix of the child which is their offspring.... Husband and wife are lovers and the child is the product of their love as well as the object of their love" (1980[1968]:43). In these terms, lesbian parents do not fit easily into American kinship. Genetrix and genitor are not interchangeable; to replace one with the other is dramatically to change the character of the union between parents. The union between man and woman (as husband and wife) is one imbued with deep symbolic meaning in American culture, not the least of which is, as Schneider says, the means through which family relationships are created and differentiated.

Strathern notes that this symbolic union is also deeply imbued with gendered relations of power:

> In... Euro-American formulations, male and female parents are differently placed with respect to parenthood: *an equal union is also an asymmetric pairing*.... The relationship of the sexual act to conception is not, therefore, simply a technical one. It serves to reproduce parenthood as the perceived outcome of a union in which the parties are distinguished by gender. Apart from anything else, it thus plays a *conceptually* significant part in procreation. [1992a:4, emphasis added]

In an analysis conscious of gender and power relations, a family mediated by lesbian sex arguably makes kinship look different than a family "unified" through the sexual relationship between mother and father. Strathern clearly implicates sexual intercourse in the symbolic reproduction of structural gender relations. For those invested in a feminist reworking of parental roles, the unity symbolized by lesbian lovers as mothers reproduces a different gender and power configuration through which the lesbian family is organized. To follow the logic of Collier and Yanagisako's argument that gender and kinship are mutually constituted, this particular understanding of lesbian kinship carves out its own place along the spectrum of American kinships *precisely because* it refigures the alignment of gender and power roles which have traditionally marked the American family.

All Lesbian Mothers Do Not Create Equally

As might be expected, this somewhat utopian, egalitarian vision of lesbian kinship runs into trouble in the face of a legal structure that retains its historic commitment to the equation of blood ties with family. The promise that some women see in lesbian families – the opportunity to raise children in an environment of gender equality – is often thrown into disarray when one partner bears a child. Having children through donor insemination automatically introduces its own asymmetry into the relationship among lesbian parents and child. The "birth mother" has a validated and immediately recognizable relationship with her child, while her partner (as neither a biological parent nor a legally recognized spouse) is doubly excluded from the realm of kinship. Her marginality is expressed in the dearth of established, much less positive, terms for the role of the "co-mother." Often represented as the proverbial "lack," she is the "nonbiological mother," the "nonbirth mother," the "other mother" (Riley 1988:89).

This structural inequality is perceived to have profound repercussions for the dynamics of lesbian families. Psychologist Sally Crawford writes.

> When the relationship between parents is unrecognized... then no matter how defined the system may be internally, ex-lovers, ex-husbands, and members of the couple's

> family of origin can often walk in and walk out at will, as though the family unit does not exist. [1987:203]

One mother notes, "If the family structure is not reflected legally, then our families are distorted, they're not supported, and we're not able to function fully as the families we are" (Keen 1991:8).

While both mothers may talk of the ways their family is distorted by the lack of legal recognition, co-mother and birth mother often express significantly different concerns. Toni Tortorilla writes,

> There is no readily definable slot [for nonbiological parents in a lesbian or gay relationship]. The parameters of society's vision are stretched by our very existence.... And yet, though standing outside the protection and sanction of the system, many adults still choose to enter into a parental role with the children of their lovers. They commit time and energy to loving, nurturing, and supporting these children while risking the changes which could lead to separation from those whose lives they nourished and formed. It is a risk the biological parent often minimizes or fails to recognize in her own need for support with childrearing. [1987:174]

Another woman writes of feeling like a fraud "if I act like he's my baby. I'm afraid someone will ask me about labor or my husband or something. I have to keep telling myself he *is* my baby and he will be perceived that way because it's the truth" (Gray 1987:136, emphasis in original).

Though not articulated as frequently, there is a flip side to this imbalance, which one woman terms "The Comother's Choice." She writes,

> Kathleen is angry that I have [a choice].... My doubts – "I don't know if I can do my writing and be in This Situation" – all point to the imbalance between us. She can't choose anymore.... Andrew is the new life. That's not the choice I made. That's the choice of the biological mother. I chose parenting without complete sacrifice. [Gray 1987:137]

The dilemmas engendered by the absence of a biological tie between a child and co-mother illuminate the centrality of blood ties to the dispensation of familial rights and obligations in American kinship. The element of choice in these families simultaneously heightens the sense of "risk," "creativity," and freedom from "complete sacrifice" for the nonbiological partner. The myriad ways in which lesbian mothers attempt to legitimize their family structures by rectifying this asymmetry, symbolically and legally, demonstrate the complexity with which the symbol of the blood tie retains its salience even in the midst of an explicit challenge to certain "traditional" notions of American kinship.

Blood and Other Fluid Symbols

In contrast to the attempts by chosen families to decentralize biology in kinship, many gay and lesbian co-parenting families often attempt to create equality between parents precisely by establishing a figurative or literal sharing of blood between the nonbiological mother and her child. Whether calling up the metaphor of shared blood ties or creating a more direct genetic link between comother and child, these families employ biology as an important symbol that can be articulated and embodied in a number of ways.

In the recent case *Alison D. v. Virginia M.* (552 N.Y.S.2d 321), in which the comother petitioned for a hearing for visitation rights after she and her partner separated, one *Amici Curiae* brief (Gay and Lesbian Parents Coalition et al. 1990) delineated explicit actions generally taken by co-parents to indicate their intention to enter into a fully functioning parental role with their children. The brief cites actions that imply a desire to maintain an equal relationship between parents vis-à-vis the child. These actions include combining or hyphenating the co-parents' names to form the child's surname, "a practice which identifies the child with both co-parents," and having the child call both parents names that reflect equal parental obligations, as in "Daddy Wayne and Daddy Sol," or "Momma G and Momma D" (Gay and Lesbian Parents Coalition et al. 1990: 29–31). Further, they often "manifest their equal roles as parents by having the parents and siblings – *on both sides* – participate as aunts, uncles, and grandparents" (Gay and Lesbian Parents Coalition et al. 1990:31, emphasis added). Kinship terms thus become one medium through which gay and lesbian co-parenting families declare equal claims, for both parents, to a legitimate relationship with their children. These relationships and their assertion of familial love clearly infer blood ties (and the rights and obligations that accompany blood relations) among children, parents, and extended family.

The mobilization of kinship terms is part of an overall display of "deliberateness," a symbolic flag that signals partners' commitment to forming a "real" family. As the *Amici* brief states, "The acts and declarations of co-parents leave little doubt that they intend to assume all the obligations of parenthood, including financial support, on a permanent basis" (Gay and Lesbian Parents Coalition et al. 1990:29). Part of the determination of intent to form a family is, arguably, co-parents' extensive deliberation over the decision to have a child: "These couples take the act of parenting very seriously" (Gay and Lesbian Parents Coalition et al. 1990:29).

This strategy leads to an intriguing attempt to locate the metaphor of biological, *generative* power in the co-parent. Claiming that co-parents engage in a *joint* decision to raise a child, the *Amici* brief argues that lesbians and gay men claim an active role, both figuratively and literally, in the creation of the child:

> It is because *both* co-parents wish to act as parents that a child is brought into their home. The non-biological co-parent is thus partly responsible for the child's presence in the home, *or even for the child's very existence*.... The non-biological co-[mother] typically participates in every step of the ... pregnancy to the fullest extent possible. [Gay and Lesbian Parents Coalition et al. 1990:32, emphasis added]

By asserting the co-parent's responsibility for the existence of the child, gay and lesbian parents make clear their investment in the central relationship between procreation and unity within the family. On one level, such a declaration of procreative agency is equally significant for both gay men and lesbians, given the context of a cultural logic in which gay and lesbian relationships are deemed illegitimate because of their figurative impotence/sterility.

Further, the appropriation of generative power specifically by a lesbian co-parent places her squarely in the realm of (male) authorship. She grounds her claim to chosen motherhood in the image of agency and biological creativity – an image that has defined American cultural conceptions of the male contribution to procreation. As Carol Delaney (1986) has argued, the cultural narrative of paternity as authorship positions the male contribution as central and irreplaceable to the identity of the product of conception. Thus paternity "has meant the primary and creative role" (Delaney 1986:502). Despite a general sense that men and women contribute equally to the genetic makeup of their progeny, this symbolic asymmetry persists (Delaney 1986; Rothman 1989). Thus the woman is not a co-creator but a provider of a nurturant environment; "female receptivity" is glorified at the expense of "female creativity" (Delaney 1986:495).[11]

Lesbian co-mothers who take on a generative role in the conception of their children claim space for female creativity. In so doing, the co-mother does not attempt to become male; rather, she carves out a distinctive but recognizable place in the birth of her child.[12] Nancy Zook and Rachel Hallenback write of their experience performing donor insemination at home:

> The jar [of semen] was handed over, hugs exchanged, and he was on his way. With Nancy's hips on pillows at a forty-five degree-angle, Rachel, taking a quick breath, inserted the semen into Nancy's vagina with a sterile syringe.... Rachel's participation in conception was crucial to us, as this was to be her child as well. [1987:90]

By impregnating Nancy, Rachel becomes intimately connected with the act of conception in a way that challenges the dichotomy between (female) gestation/receptivity and (male) authorship/agency.

Central to this transformed reading of generative power is the "uncertainty" of the physical bond of paternity. Generation becomes less a genetic concept than a kinetic one; it is less an issue of the *ownership* of biogenetic substance than one of placing this substance in motion, of being responsible for starting off the "unseen process unfolding in Nancy's body" (Zook and Hallen-back 1987:90). Rachel's claim to generative power and the sharing of her identity with the child's thus constitutes a powerful reworking of the idea of genetic authorship. The act of begetting is separated from authorship; shared parenthood can be demonstrated through active participation in the process, without necessarily laying claim to a genetic relationship as well.[13]

Where such claims to female creativity can remove the sperm donor's genetic contribution from the picture, other strategies unreservedly embrace the underlying American cultural understanding of genetics as a defining feature of personhood, an indicator of health and personality, a blueprint for appearance and disposition. Thus some lesbian co-mothers use donor insemination in ways that more directly establish biogenetic ties *within* the family. In cases where each woman bears a child, the same donor is sometimes used so that the children will be related (Gay and Lesbian Parents Coalition et al. 1990:30–1). This tactic is often utilized not only by women who want a consistent "male presence" for their children but also by those who desire an anonymous donor while retaining genetic connections within the family (Hill 1987:112). One couple interviewed in *Politics of the Heart* (1987) alternated donors to make the identity of the father unclear, only to decide later that they wanted to identify him in response to their daughter's fascination with a friend's father. The mothers imply that the father, if known, will become the donor for the next child, though they do not envision that he will have a relationship with the children (Hill 1987:111).[14] In such instances, the donor gains significance within the family, not through his direct involvement as a person who is a "relative" (Schneider 1980 [1968]), but rather through his ability to provide the substance that will ensure biogenetic continuity between offspring. Biogenetic substance itself becomes the object of importance, separate from the identity of the donor.

Biology here is abstracted and dispersed in a way that challenges the cultural assumption of the primacy of the male seed (Delaney 1986). Though lesbians may take great care in choosing a donor, the act of insemination, by eliminating direct physical contact, is often seen to minimize the man's role *as a gendered individual* in conception. The focus is then not on the person of the donor, but rather on semen, "making the procreative pair (if any) woman plus sperm, gendered person plus gender signifier" (Weston 1991:171).

Weston suggest that lesbians are somewhat unique in creating a distinction between male personhood, on the one hand, and the male's physical contribution to conception, on the other; such a distinction does not seem to be an inevitable consequence of the technology itself (1991:171). She cites a 1989 study indicating that married heterosexual women associated insemination with adultery and extramarital sex, and believed that insemination would allow an unwanted third party into their marriage relationship. The lesbians surveyed by Weston (1991:171), in contrast, did not view insemination as a substitution for something that would otherwise have come from their sexual partners; their link to the donor was patently nonsexual. This disjuncture allows the nonbiological mother to take on a parenting role without the danger of displacing another (male) individual who is also a parent; she *is* the other parent. Though genetic continuity is powerful as an abstracted, disembodied signifier of family, it is also employed as a literal signifier for kinship and love in a more "connected" or "owned" sense (Laqueur 1990:212). A couple may choose a donor whose physical characteristics in some way resemble those of the co-mother, suggesting again the sharing of substance and the reproduction of her image. Or, the brother of the nonbiological parent-to-be may be the donor, giving both women a biogenetic link to the child. Thus, when the donor possesses desirable traits (i.e., a genetic relationship with, or physical resemblance to, the co-mother), lesbian mothers may choose to incorporate those traits into their notions of family. Genetic continuity, whether literal or implied, becomes an integral resource in such attempts to bring a certain unity to lesbian parenting families.

Finally, in the most old-fashioned sense of biogenetic relatedness, the donor might be incorporated into the family, whether as a gendered individual (the proverbial "male presence") or as a co-parent. Of course, such relationships are not always simple matters of unilateral choice. On the one hand, they can be complicated by donors' contestatory attempts to secure paternity and parental rights; on the other hand, not uncommonly, lesbian mothers may rethink their initial decision on the matter and attempt to create a more (or less) involved relationship with the donor than they had originally planned.

As the myriad examples above suggest, lesbian mothers' strategies to gain symbolic legitimation for their families (in the context of donor insemination) effectively disperse the "biological connection" as it has been conceived in American kinship. Insemination is perceived to give lesbian parents space to negotiate the degree to which a donor's sperm is imbued with (or disabused of) distinctive features of identity. In many cases, the mobility of disembodied sperm allows the deployment of genetic ties in the service of unifying lesbian families. Thus genetic substance *itself* can become the referent for relatedness (as when the same anonymous donor is used so that the children will be related); a donor may be chosen on the basis of features that he shares with the "nonbiological" mother, thereby implying a biogenetic connection between her and the child; or the donor, by virtue of his biogenetic connection to the child, can be incorporated into the family configuration. On the one hand, these moves reify the importance of genetic continuity in the construction of kin relations; however, insofar as they allow for varying gradations of the separation of genetic substance from its "owner," they disrupt the cultural narrative of paternity as authorship. But, again, just as genetic ties retain their appeal (in dispersed form), so too does this notion of authorship persist though it is reinscribed here with a different kind of gender/genetic symbolism. Within the logistics of insemination, the *act* of begetting can be separated from the ownership of genetic substance. Here, a kinetic reading of generation, of bringing into being, supersedes genetic connection as the privileged signifier of relatedness.

The notion of biological relatedness in this context takes on an excess of meanings. One effect of this excess is that biogenetic connection explicitly becomes a contingent, rather than immutable, feature of relatedness. Yet, as is apparent above, its contingency does not signal trivialization. Instead, the creative lengths to which many lesbian mothers go to inscribe their families with genetic continuity speak eloquently to the tremendous, continued salience of biological relatedness.

Reformulating the "Single" Mother

The enterprising mobilization of genetic/kinetic relatedness in these visions of lesbian kinship often calls up an arguably "old-fashioned" notion of motherhood as the quintessential fulfillment of womanhood (see Lewin 1993). Indeed, as I noted earlier, the very distinctiveness of lesbian families is often predicated on the fact that they offer a multiplication of femaleness; it is perhaps not entirely surprising that the cultural narrative of motherhood as the ultimate expression of female identity often finds its way into these claims. This, arguably, is the central paradox that arises in casting lesbian motherhood as "unique"; just as the gender configuration of lesbian co-parenting families promises an ostensibly different model of parenthood, the supposed naturalness, and therefore universality, of motherhood both highlights and undermines that uniqueness. Thus the virtues of lesbian families are articulated in terms of the virtue of having not just two parents, but two *mothers;* at the same time, motherhood can eclipse the difference encoded in a lesbian identity. Thus, as one woman notes, "even when someone knows I am a lesbian my motherhood makes me seem normal" (Polikoff 1987:53).

Lewin's work (1993) is particularly instructive regarding the ways in which motherhood can become the core of identity for heterosexual and lesbian mothers alike. Quite apart from my focus here, her concern is with single mothers. Arguably, the challenges of single parenthood magnify the centrality of motherhood to the identities of the women Lewin describes. Lesbians who enter into motherhood with one or more co-parents confront slightly different demands, including negotiating the place of the so-called nonbiological mother within the family configuration. It is here, in the space occupied by this "other mother," that the radical potential of lesbian co-parenting is often envisioned.[15]

How then does the "naturalness" of motherhood intersect with negotiations of nonbiological motherhood in lesbian family configurations? Quite in line with conventional American cultural constructions of maternity and paternity, it is the perceived singularity or unitariness of biological motherhood that might be seen, in the first place, to impel the mobilization of genetic continuity (associated with paternity) in creating a biogenetic connection for the "nonbiological" mother. For, unlike paternity, which is understood in terms of alienable relationships and mobile biogenetic substance, maternity is understood to be less easily dispersed (see Barnes 1973). If it is "inconceivable to Euro-Americans that a child could be born motherless" (Strathern 1992a:12), it has been equally inconceivable that a child could have two biological mothers – thus the troubling legal and symbolic asymmetry between the biological mother and her partner. Of course, current possibilities for "assisted reproduction" – especially in-vitro fertilization and surrogate motherhood – are fragmenting, in popular and legal views, the supposedly self-evident idea of real, biological motherhood.[16] In the context of these reproductive technologies, maternity has become thinkable in tripartite form, divvied up among genetic mother, birth mother, and social mother. Awareness of such possibilities informs what is sometimes imagined as the obvious and "perfect" option for lesbian families: one woman could contribute the genetic material, and her partner could become the gestational/birth mother. The implied self-evidence of this techno-fantasy of distributed maternity suggests the degree to which biology is operative, in the imaginings of some women, even as it is dispersed. More commonly practiced on this front is a kind of dual motherhood, in which each mother gives birth. If the same donor is used, the children will be related to each other. To complete this particular circle of biological and legal unification, it is becoming increasingly common for courts to grant lesbian partners the right to adopt each other's (biological) children.[17]

In one sense, this move does little to unsettle the supposed unitariness of maternity. Yet there is an important slippage implied here between "maternity" and "motherhood." Maternity, I suggest, signals the epitome of embodied relationality – that is, gestation and birth – whereas motherhood connotes both this physical relationship *and* a gendered, naturalized code for conduct. This biologized desire to mother is expressed quite nicely in the euphemism of the maternal instinct. I would argue that the so-called naturalness of motherhood – not only as a biological relationship but also as a supposedly nurturing, explicitly feminine propensity – in some ways makes intelligible the notion of the two-mother family. Implied here is a latent split between the "natural" and the "biological"; if biological motherhood can re-naturalized a lesbian's womanhood, so too, I would suggest, does the mothering performed by a so-called nonbirth mother become intelligible as natural in the name of women's propensity "to mother."[18] While I do not want to make too much of this (rather speculative) point, I consider it an important element within the amalgamation of ideas that both makes sense of and asserts dissonances in the notion of a family composed of mothers – who are lovers – and their children.

Conclusion

Underlying this entire discussion, as I noted at the beginning of this article, is a persistent cultural narrative denying the naturalness of lesbian and gay sexuality quite explicitly because it is perceived to be inherently nonprocreative. As a key context from which these lesbian procreative families emerge, this narrative lends a complex oppositionality to many lesbians' mobilization of the "naturalness" of motherhood, as well as to their desire to endow co-parenting families with biogenetic continuity. When put into service in the name of creating a uniquely lesbian kinship configuration, these "old" ideas of what constitutes relatedness are both made explicit and reformulated.

The so-called core symbols of American kinship, blood and love, are mediated here by very different unifying symbols (and gender/power configurations) than the central emblem of (hetero) sexual intercourse described by Schneider. On the one hand, lesbian sex provides a different model for love partly, to build on Strathern's (1992a:4) argument, by reproducing a gender configuration that is seen to promise gender equality rather than asymmetry. At the same time, the symbol of blood, also inscribed as biogenetic substance or biological relatedness, is deployed to give unity to families that are marked both by proscribed gender relations *and* the particular asymmetries of biological and nonbiological motherhood.

In the process, these lesbian mothers simultaneously affirm the importance of blood as a symbol and challenge the American cultural assumption that biology is a self-evident, singular fact and *the* natural baseline on which kinship is built. Biology is not understood here to stand on its own as a defining feature of kin, nor does biogenetic connection retain any single, transparent meaning. The dominant idea of American kinship as Schneider describes it posits a belief in the genetic tie as a baseline, elaborated into a relationship through certain kinds of behavior. In the negotiations of lesbian motherhood discussed above, the creation of blood ties – varying in kind and degree – instead becomes an indicator (if not enhancement) of parent-like behavior. The baseline then becomes the co-mothers' generative agency, broadly conceived. Central to this subtle reformulation of the blood/love symbolic hierarchy is a disruption of the once taken-for-granted matrix of paternity, authorship, generation, and genetic substance. As the perceived meanings of these notions of blood and code, authorship and agency, are made contingent rather than self-evident, these lesbian mothers set forth quite complex notions of what constitutes both distinctiveness and unity in the creation of their kin ties.

As the symbol of the blood tie is both embraced and dispersed within certain lesbian families, so too does the dichotomy between straight biological families and gay and lesbian chosen families become muddied. Rather than trying to determine which understanding of gay and lesbian kinship promises a more radical critique of American kinship, I have been concerned here with drawing out some of the ways in which the so-called core symbols of kinship – the ideas that define what constitutes relatedness – are reworked and recontextualized. As reproductive and genetic technologies continue to proliferate, blood and love will surely continue to be (re)inscribed in notions of relatedness, in often predictable but perhaps also surprising ways. The ways in which lesbians and gay men negotiate such reinscriptions make explicit not only the contingency of these symbols but also – equally important in theorizing kinship – the dynamic, mutual construction of gender, generation, kinship, and sexuality.

NOTES

1 I thank Ellen Lewin for her helpful comments on this subject. The question of representativeness is here, as ever, not a simple one. First, my intention is to examine certain articulations of distinctiveness; I do not claim to represent a "critical mass" of lesbian families. I recognize also that access to reproductive technologies (though donor insemination is one of the most low-tech practices on the menu) is a key foundation for the visions of lesbian motherhood discussed in this paper. Access inevitably raises questions of class, as well as race; the creation of lesbian families through insemination is, arguably, an option most available to a largely white, middle-class clientele. Though insemination can certainly take place without the intervention of sperm banks or health care providers (as attested to by the legendary turkey-baster joke), laws protecting women from donors' paternity suits encourage the institutionalization of such arrangements. Thus a California statute on insemination protects married couples from "any claim of paternity by any outsider," regardless of physician involvement, while "unmarried" women are provided such protection only if they broker their insemination through a physician (*Jhordan C. v. Mary K.* 1986). The implication is that although access to sperm banks is not necessary to the creation of these families, it is certainly made desirable in terms of maintaining their legal integrity. And insofar as many lesbians choose gay male friends as donors, the specter of HIV transmission also contributes to increasing medical intervention in the insemination process.

2 For a rich contextualization of the recent "lesbian baby boom" vis-à-vis ongoing lesbian and feminist debates on motherhood, see Pollack and Vaughn's anthology, *Politics of the Heart* (1987). Jan Clausen, for example, writes,

> Most interesting and most painful is a totally irrational feeling of betrayal: I thought other lesbians were with me in the decision not to give birth, in that defiance of our expected womanly role – and now here these new lesbian mothers go, showing me up, *proving* that the fact that I'm a dyke is no excuse for my failure to have a baby. [1987:338]

See also Lewin (1993:14) for a discussion of the heightened salience, for lesbians, of the narrative of motherhood as an "achievement." Paralleling shifts in American cultural notions of gender and reproduction, the notion of achieved motherhood indexes the complexities with which women's assertions of autonomy and individualism circulate within existing narratives of conventional femininity (see Ginsburg 1990 and Ginsburg and Tsing 1990:7).

3 See Marilyn Strathern, *Reproducing the Future* (1992), for a discussion of the ways in which new reproductive technologies provide a context for making the "natural" mutable.

4 Several pivotal feminist works speak to this argument for the mutually instituted categories of heterosexuality, gender, and kinship, including Collier and Yanagisako's *Gender and Kinship: Toward a Unified Analysis* (1987), Rich's "Compulsory Heterosexuality" (1984), and Rubin's "The Traffic in Women" (1975).

5 I use the phrase "expectation of creating biological kin" in anticipation of the question of how same-sex couples (which are only one facet of chosen families) differ from heterosexual couples without children in terms of their relation to blood and choice. Expectation here is a simplified reference to the complicated cultural belief in the interdependence of heterosexual marriage, biological procreation, and social reproduction. Legal scholar Hannah Schwarzschild quotes a 1971 Minnesota decision denying same-sex couples the right to marry:

> The state's refusal to grant a [marriage] license . . . is based upon the state's recognition that our society as a whole views marriage as the appropriate and desirable forum for procreation and the rearing of children. . . . [I]t is apparent that no same-sex couple offers the possibility of the birth of children by their union. Thus the refusal of the state to authorize same-sex marriage results from such impossibility of reproduction. [Schwarzschild 1988:116]

In this logic, all heterosexual couples conceptually have the potential to beget and raise offspring; whether or not they can or choose to is irrelevant to the defenders of the primacy of heterosexual marriage. Chosen families, whether composed of friends or lovers, or both, take on this assigned nonprocreative identity and challenge its implications for their place in kinship. Thus the contestation emerges in their claim that kinship can exist beyond blood and marriage, both of which assume procreative relations as their central referent.

6 See Biddick 1993, Spillers 1987, and Strathern 1991 for perspectives on dispersed kinship and distributed maternity.

7 A popular bumper sticker sold in many lesbian and gay bookstores.

8 This point is highlighted in Strathern's review of *Families We Choose* (1993:196).

9 Personal communication with David Schneider, August 13, 1992.

10 See, for example, psychologist Charlotte Patterson's landmark review article, "Children of Lesbian and Gay Parents" (1992).

11 Among those who make sperm their business, the assumption that the male role in conception is *the* creative one remains strong. Beautifully articulating the 19th-century vision of sperm as the "purest extract of blood" and the "sum and representation of its bearer" (Barker-Benfield 1972:49), the director of a California sperm bank distributed T-shirts with a picture of swimming sperm, captioned "Future People" (Rothman 1989:35).

12 The association of a nonbiological parent with the creative, generative aspect of conception also appeared in a 1985 custody case in slightly macabre form. In *Karin T. v. Michael T.* (1985), the two parties had been married, had given birth to two children through donor insemination, and Michael T. had signed the birth certificate as Karin T.'s husband. Upon their separation, Michael T. claimed to be exempt from child support. The grounds? Michael T. was actually a woman who presented herself to the world as a man. She argued that she should not have to pay child support because she was "a woman who was not biologically or legally related to the children." Given the usual legal response to such situations, Michael T. could reasonably expect to get away with such an allegation. But judicial interpretation is full of surprises: the court rejected her argument. "Defining parent as 'one who procreates, begets, or brings forth off-spring,' the Court determined that Michael T.'s actions 'certainly brought forth these offspring *as if done biologically*'"

(1985:784, emphasis added). This remarkable opinion is not the watershed lesbian and gay parents might hope for; the court clearly aims *not* to establish lesbian and gay co-parents' claim to children but rather to punish Michael T. for gender fraud. The court's assertion that she had an active part in bringing forth the children is apparently predicated on her appropriation of the male role, since she played "husband" by seeking out "men's work." In the interest of punishment, the court becomes curiously complicit in this game of gender-switching.

13 This idea of generativity is in no way limited to articulations of lesbian and gay kinship. See, for example, Helena Ragone's (1994) work on surrogacy, where the intent to conceive signals an act of generation. I am also reminded of international patent laws regarding biotechnological manipulation of DNA; legal ownership of genetic substance is not determined in terms of its original "source" but rather in terms of the party responsible for manipulating and replicating the DNA. Here, and in concert with other developments in the enterprising management of life itself, the act of replication or manipulation itself becomes the moment of authorship. Such developments suggest intriguing intersections among notions of reproduction, ownership, and (kinetic?) intervention. For discussions of replication, authorship, and ownership, see Lury 1993; see also Sarah Franklin's notions of auto-paternity in "Romancing the Helix" (1995).

14 Alternating donors is similar to the practice, used by some heterosexual couples, of having sexual intercourse immediately after the woman is inseminated. The scientific uncertainty of the paternal bond enables the couple to entertain the possibility that, if the woman does become pregnant, her (thought-to-be-sterile) husband is the father. Uncertainty here is used to fictionalize the identity of one specific father, whereas for lesbians, uncertainty can help perpetuate anonymity.

15 This is not to argue that couples are more radical than single mothers but merely to point out that the challenges facing co-parents are different than those facing single mothers; the implication is that the particular challenges of co-parenting also open up space for creating uniquely "lesbian" families. Of course, the location of radical potential in the second parent effects a somewhat ironic inversion of the argument that the valuation of the "mating pair" is a decisively conservative move (see Ettelbrick 1992). I am indebted to Anna Tsing for this insight.

16 For a discussion of negotiations of "natural" parenthood within surrogacy arrangements, see Ragone 1994. For a discussion of anxieties surrounding the relationships engendered via surrogate motherhood and other technologies of reproduction, see Gallagher 1993 and Franklin 1993.

17 See, for example, Keen 1991, Sullivan 1992, *The New York Times* 1993. Of course, the legitimation of lesbian parental relationships conferred by these joint adoptions is by no means a new legal standard; Sharon Bottoms and April Wade, a lesbian couple in Virginia, recently had their child taken from them on the basis of their "immoral" relationship. Without assuming too much coherence in the rationale informing these particular decisions, it is impossible to dismiss the significance of class here. Of the three successful cases cited above, one couple consists of two physicians, another of a physician and a PhD. In contrast, Sharon Bottoms and April Wade are characterized in court and in the press as working class. Their unfitness as parents – as charged by Sharon Bottoms' mother, Kay – rests not only on their lesbianism but also on the "instability" of their working-class home (see Kelly 1993).

18 Arguably, women's appropriation of generativity is also made intelligible in terms of the naturalness of maternal desire. Again, see Ragone 1994 for a discussion of the generative potential of intent. The other side of this logic, of course, is that the decision not to mother is often used to demonize women as unnatural. In addition to the vast literature on abortion in the United States, see Tsing 1990.

REFERENCES

Barker-Benfield, Ben
1972 The Spermatic Economy: A Nineteenth-Century View of Sexuality. Feminist Studies 1(1):45–74.
Barnes, John A.
1973 Genetrix: Genitor:: Nature: Culture? *In* The Character of Kinship. Jack Goody, ed. Pp. 61–73. Cambridge: Cambridge University Press.
Biddick, Kathleen
1993 Stranded Histories: Feminist Allegories of Artificial Life. Research in Philosophy and Technology 13:165–82.
Clausen, Jan
1987 To Live outside the Law You Must Be Honest: A Flommy Looks at Lesbian Parenting. *In* Politics of the Heart: A Lesbian Parenting Anthology. Sandra Pollack and Jeanne Vaughn, eds. Pp. 333–42. Ithaca, NY: Firebrand Books.
Collier, Jane Fishburne, and Sylvia Junko Yanagisako, eds.
1987 Gender and Kinship: Essays Toward a Unified Analysis. Stanford, CA: Stanford University Press.
Cooper, Baba
1987 The Radical Potential in Lesbian Mothering of Daughters. *In* Politics of the Heart: A Lesbian Parenting Anthology. Sandra Pollack and Jeanne Vaughn, eds. Pp. 233–40. Ithaca, NY: Firebrand Books.
Crawford, Sally
1987 Lesbian Families: Psychosocial Stress and the Family-Building Process. *In* Lesbian Psychologies. Boston Lesbian Psychologies Collective, ed. Pp. 195–214. Urbana and Chicago: University of Illinois Press.
Cusick, Suzanne
1991 On a Lesbian Relationship to Music: A Serious Effort Not to Think Straight. Paper presented at the Feminist Theory and Music Conference, Minneapolis, MN.
Delaney, Carol
1986 The Meaning of Paternity and the Virgin Birth Debate. Man (n.s.) 21:494–513.
Delaney, Carol, and Sylvia Junko Yanagisako, eds.
1995 Naturalizing Power: Essays in Feminist Cultural Analysis. New York: Routledge.
Ettelbrick, Paula
1992 Since When Is Marriage a Path to Liberation? *In* Lesbian and Gay Marriage: Private Commitments, Public Ceremonies. Suzanne Sherman, ed. Pp. 20–6. Philadelphia: Temple University Press.
Franklin, Sarah
1993 Making Representations: The Parliamentary Debate on the Human Fertilization and Embyrology Act. *In* Technologies of Procreation: Kinship in the Context of the New Reproductive Technologies. Jeanette Edwards, Sarah Franklin, Eric Hirsch, Frances Price, and Marilyn Strathern, eds. Pp. 96–131. Manchester: Manchester University Press.
1995 Romancing the Helix. *In* Romance Revisited. Jackie Stacey and Lynne Pearce, eds. London: Falmer Press.
Gallagher, Janet
1993 Eggs, Embryos and Fetuses: Anxiety and the Law. Paper presented at Conceiving Pregnancy/Creating Mothers: Perspectives on Maternal/Fetal Relations Conference, March 26–27, University of Virginia, Charlottesville.

Gay and Lesbian Parents Coalition et al.
1990 Brief *Amici Curiae*. New York Court of Appeals, *In the Matter of the Application of Alison D.* Submitted by Janet E. Schomer and Susan R. Keith.
Ginsburg, Faye
1990 The Word-Made Flesh: The Disembodiment of Gender in the Abortion Debate. *In* Uncertain Terms: Negotiating Gender in American Culture. Faye Ginsburg and Anna Lowenhaupt Tsing, eds. Pp. 59–75. Boston: Beacon Press.
Ginsburg, Faye, and Anna Lowenhaupt Tsing
1990 Introduction. *In* Uncertain Terms: Negotiating Gender in American Culture. Faye Ginsburg and Anna Lowenhaupt Tsing, eds. Pp. 1–16. Boston: Beacon Press.
Gray, Pamela
1987 The Other Mother: Lesbian Co-Mother's Journal. *In* Politics of the Heart: A Lesbian Parenting Anthology. Sandra Pollack and Jeanne Vaughn, eds. Pp. 133–9. Ithaca, NY: Firebrand Books.
Green, Leonard
1991 Anti-Gay ABC Laws Challenged. Our Own Community Press October: 1–2.
Hill, Kate
1987 Mothers by Insemination. *In* Politics of the Heart: A Lesbian Parenting Anthology. Sandra Pollack and Jeanne Vaughn, eds. Pp. 111–19. Ithaca, NY: Firebrand Books.
Jhordan C. v. Mary K.
1986 224 Cal. Rptp. 530 (Cal. App. 1 Dist. 1986).
Karin T. v. Michael T.
1985 484 N. Y. S. 2d 780 (Fam. Ct. 1985).
Keen, Lisa
1991 D.C. Lesbians Become the First to Adopt Each Other's Children. The Washington Blade, September 13:1, 8.
Kelly, Deborah
1993 Mother Said Unfit in Appeal of Custody: Grandmother Cites More Than Lesbianism. Richmond Times-Dispatch, December 9:B1.
Laqueur, Thomas
1990 The Facts of Fatherhood. *In* Conflicts in Feminism. Marianne Hirsch and Evelyn Fox Keller, eds. Pp. 205–21. New York: Routledge.
Lewin, Ellen
1993 Lesbian Mothers: Accounts of Gender in American Culture. Ithaca, NY: Cornell University Press.
Lury, Celia
1993 Cultural Rights: Technology, Legality and Personality. London and New York: Routledge.
McKinnon, Susan
1992 American Kinship/American Incest. Paper presented at the 91 st Annual Meeting of the American Anthropological Association, San Francisco.
The New York Times
1993 Court Grants Parental Right to Lesbian Mother and Lover. September 12:42.
Nichols, Margaret
1987 Lesbian Sexuality: Issues and Developing Theory. *In* Lesbian Psychologies. Boston Lesbian Psychologies Collective, ed. Pp. 97–125. Urbana and Chicago: University of Illinois Press.
Patterson, Charlotte
1992 Children of Lesbian and Gay Parents. Child Development 63(5):1025–42.

Polikoff, Nancy D.
1987 Lesbians Choosing Children: The Personal is Political. *In* Politics of the Heart: A Lesbian Parenting Anthology. Sandra Pollack and Jeanne Vaughn, eds. Pp. 48–54. Ithaca, NY: Firebrand Books.
1990 This Child Does Have Two Mothers: Redefining Parenthood to Meet the Needs of Children in Lesbian-Mother and Other Nontraditional Families. Georgetown Law Journal 78(3):459–575.
Pollack, Sandra, and Jeanne Vaughn, eds.
1987 Politics of the Heart: A Lesbian Parenting Anthology. Ithaca, NY: Firebrand Books.
Ragone, Helena
1994 Surrogate Motherhood: Conception in the Heart. Boulder: Westview Press.
Rich, Adrienne
1984 Compulsory Heterosexuality and Lesbian Existence. *In* Powers of Desire: The Politics of Sexuality. Ann Snitow, Christine Stansell, and Sharon Thompson, eds. Pp. 177–205. New York: Monthly Review Press.
Riley, Claire
1988 American Kinship: A Lesbian Account. Feminist Issues 8(2): 74–94.
Rothman, Barbara Katz
1989 Recreating Motherhood: Ideology and Technology in a Patriarchal Society. New York: W. W. Norton.
Rubin, Gayle
1975 The Traffic in Women: Notes on the "Political Economy" of Sex. *In* Toward an Anthropology of Women. Rayna Reiter, ed. Pp. 157–210. New York: Monthly Review Press.
Schneider, David M.
1980[1968] American Kinship: A Cultural Account. 2nd ed. Chicago: University of Chicago Press.
Schwarzschild, Hannah
1988 Same-Sex Marriage and Constitutional Privacy: Moral Threat and Legal Anomaly. Berkeley Women's Law Journal 4:94–127.
Spillers, Hortense
1987 Mama's Baby, Papa's Maybe: An American Grammar Book. Diacritics 17(2):65–81.
Strathern, Marilyn
1981 Kinship at the Core: An Anthropology of Elmdon, a Village in North-West Essex in the Nineteen-Sixties. Cambridge: Cambridge University Press.
1991 Displacing Knowledge: Technology and the Consequences for Kinship. Paper presented at Fulbright Colloquium, The Social Consequences of Life and Death Under High Technology Medicine, London.
1992a Gender: A Question of Comparison. Lecture, University of Vienna, May 23.
1992b Reproducing the Future. Anthropology, Kinship, and the New Reproductive Technologies. New York: Routledge.
1993 Families We Choose: Lesbians, Gays, Kinship. Man (n.s.) 28(1):195–6.
Sullivan, Ronald
1992 Judge Allows for Adoption by Lesbian. The New York Times, January 31:B1, B3.
Tortorilla, Toni
1987 On a Creative Edge. *In* Politics of the Heart: A Lesbian Parenting Anthology. Sandra Pollack and Jeanne Vaughn, eds. Pp. 168–74. Ithaca, NY: Firebrand Books.
Tsing, Anna Lowenhaput
1990 Monster Stories: Women Charged with Perinatal Endangerment. *In* Uncertain Terms: Negotiating Gender in American Culture. Faye Ginsburg and Anna Tsing, eds. Pp. 282–99. Boston: Beacon Press.

Washburne, Carolyn Knott
1987 Happy Birthday from Your Other Mom. *In* Politics of the Heart: A Lesbian Parenting Anthology. Sandra Pollack and Jeanne Vaughn, eds. Pp. 142–5. Ithaca, NY: Firebrand Books.
Weston, Kath
1991 Families We Choose. New York: Columbia University Press.
Zook, Nancy, and Rachel Hallenback
1987 Lesbian Coparenting: Creating Connections. *In* Politics of the Heart: A Lesbian Parenting Anthology. Sandra Pollack and Jeanne Vaughn, eds. Pp. 89–99. Ithaca, NY: Firebrand Books.

8

Transsexualism: Reflections on the Persistence of Gender and the Mutability of Sex

Judith Shapiro

There is a story about two small children in a museum standing in front of a painting of Adam and Eve. One child asks the other, "Which is the man and which is the lady?" The other child answers, "I can't tell – they don't have any clothes on." A story to delight those favoring the social constructionist view of gender. An even better story would be one in which the body itself becomes a set of clothes that can be put on.

All societies differentiate among their members on the basis of what we can identify as "gender." All gender systems rely, albeit in differing ways, on bodily sex differences between females and males. How can we understand the grounding of gender in sex as at once a necessity and an illusion?

Powerful cultural mechanisms operate to ensure that boys will be boys and girls will be girls. Such mechanisms appear to include turning some of the girls into boys and some of the boys into girls.

The purpose of this paper is to take transsexualism as a point of departure for examining the paradoxical relationship between sex and gender. In its suspension of the usual anatomical recruitment rule to gender category membership, transsexualism raises questions about what it means to consider sex as the "basis" for systems of gender difference. At the same time, the ability of traditional gender systems to absorb, or even require, such forms of gender-crossing as transsexualism leads us to a more sophisticated appreciation of the power of gender as a principle of social and cultural order. While transsexualism reveals that a society's gender system is a trick done with mirrors, those mirrors are the walls of our species' very real and only home.

Defining Transsexualism

The term "transsexual," as understood in its Euro-American context, is used in the following related senses: most broadly, to designate those who feel that their true gender is at variance with their biological sex; more specifically, to designate those who are attempting to "pass" as members of the opposite sex; and, most specifically, to designate those who have either had sex change surgery or are undergoing medical treatment with a view toward changing their sex anatomically.[1]

Male to female transformation appears to be far more frequent than the reverse.[2] There is also a general tendency in the literature for male to female transsexualism to function as an unmarked form, that is, for it to stand for the phenomenon in general.[3] Studies of transsexualism are overwhelmingly focused on men who have become women – an interesting twist on androcentric bias in research.

Transsexualism first captured the popular imagination both nationally and internationally with Christine Jorgensen's much publicized "sex-change operation" in Denmark in 1952. Her subsequent career can be seen as a prototype of the transsexual as celebrity, subsequent examples being Jan Morris (formerly James Morris, correspondent to the London *Times* and journalist who covered the first expedition to Mount Everest in 1953), and Renée Richards (tennis star and successful ophthalmologist, born Richard Raskind, the son of two Jewish doctors from New York). All three have written widely-read autobiographies (Jorgensen 1967, Morris 1974, Richards & Ames 1983), which are valuable sources of ethnographic information on the place of gender in the construction of personal identity.

In the course of the 1960s, transsexualism became a focus of medical/psychiatric attention and the contested ground of competing therapies, from the psychoanalytic to the behaviorist to the surgical. Up until the mid-60s, the American medical establishment had taken a generally negative view of sex change surgery; with a few exceptions, those seeking operations generally had to go abroad to obtain it – the Mecca being Casablanca and the clinic of Dr. Georges Burou.[4] Through the efforts of a small number of physician advocates like the endocrinologist Harry Benjamin,[5] who is credited with propagating the use of "transsexualism" as a diagnostic category and who urged greater understanding and tolerance of the transsexual condition, gender clinics were established at some major American hospitals and sex change surgery became one of the forms of available therapy.

The turn to sex change surgery followed upon the apparent ineffectiveness of all forms of psychological therapy in dealing with transsexualism.[6] As two sociologists writing about transsexualism in 1978 noted, "[g]enitals have turned out to be easier to change than gender identity... [w]hat we have witnessed in the last 10 years is the triumph of the surgeons over the psychotherapists in the race to restore gender to an unambiguous reality" (Kessler and McKenna 1978: 120).

Prominent early contributors to the biomedical and psychological literature on transsexualism include, along with Benjamin, John Money, Robert Stoller, and Richard Green.[7] These researchers and clinicians, who accomplished a transfer in the frame of reference for transsexualism from the moral to the medical, generally viewed themselves as part of a movement to foster more enlightened, liberal and scientific attitudes toward sexuality. At the same time, their work reflects a highly traditional attitude toward gender, an issue that will be explored more fully below.

In the medical literature, the transsexual condition has commonly been designated by the term "gender dysphoria syndrome."[8] In fact, transsexuals usually claim to have a quite definite sense of their gender; it is their physical sex that is experienced as the problem.[9] The term "sexual dysphoria" was thus at one point suggested as being more appropriate (Prince 1973). And yet, the concept of biological "sex" is not without its own problems; the more we learn about it, the more complicated things become, since we might be talking about chromosomal (or genetic) sex, anatomical (or morphological) sex, genital (or gonadal) sex, germinal sex, and hormonal sex.[10] Perhaps the most satisfactory formulation is that transsexuals are people who experience a conflict between their gender assignment, made at birth on the basis of anatomical appearance, and their sense of gender identity.[11]

This, however, opens up the question of what is meant by "gender identity." According to the literature of developmental psychology, a core gender identity is something that is established early and is relatively impervious to change. It designates the experience of belonging clearly and unambiguously to one – and only one – of the two categories, male and female.[12] Given such a notion of gender identity, transsexualism can be diagnosed as a form of crossed wiring. Whatever the reason for it, even if we cannot ultimately specify what causes it,[13] individuals can simply be recategorized, which has the considerable advantage of leaving the two-category system intact. The problem with this approach, as we shall see below, is that one cannot take at face value transsexuals' own accounts of a fixed and unchanging (albeit sex-crossed) gender identity, given the immense pressure on them to produce the kinds of life histories that will get them what they want from the medico-psychiatric establishment. To take the problem one step further, the project of autobiographical reconstruction in which transsexuals are engaged, although more focused and motivated from the one that all of us pursue, is not entirely different in kind. We must all repress information that creates problems for culturally canonical narratives of identity and the self, and consistency in gender attribution is very much a part of this.

Transsexualism as a diagnostic category is defined in relation to such other categories as transvestism and homosexuality. Transsexualism is generally distinguished from transvestism understood as cross-dressing that does not call into question a person's basic sense of gender identity. In cases in which cross-dressing becomes increasingly central to a person's life and comes to reflect a desire to assume the opposite gender role, transvestism and transsexualism can be seen as developmental stages in a gender-crossing career.[14] In recent years, the term "transgenderist" has come to be used to designate a career of gender-crossing, which may or may not be directed toward an ultimate physical sex change.

The way in which transsexualism is seen as being related, or not related, to homosexuality is a particularly interesting question, since it leads into general issues concerning the relationship between gender and sexual orientation, and how each enters into the construction of personal and social identity. The literature indicates that most transsexuals consider themselves to be heterosexual. A male to female transsexual who feels herself to be a woman wants to be able to have sex with a man as a woman, not as a male homosexual.[15] There are also homosexual transsexuals –

for example, male to female lesbian feminist transsexuals, who caused a great deal of havoc in the separatist wing of the women's movement in the late 70s.

When I have shared my work and thoughts on transsexualism with colleagues, either at seminars or in informal conversations, I have frequently encountered the argument that transsexualism is a form of disguised homosexuality. Psychiatrists and psychologists are particularly apt to make the argument that men who believe themselves to be women are seeking an appropriate way to have other men as objects of desire while avoiding the stigma of homosexuality. It is hard to know whether such arguments reflect the homophobia of the person presenting them or a response to the level of homophobia found in society. In either event, they seem to indicate a certain obliviousness to the difficulties of life as a transsexual.

Some gays and lesbians view transsexuals as homosexuals who have found a particularly desperate and insidious way of staying in the closet. Transsexuals, for their part, often express negative attitudes toward homosexuals.[16] While it might be argued that transsexuals' hostility toward homosexuality is a form of denial, the same argument can be made (and often is made) about nontranssexual heterosexuals. Although denial of homosexuality may play a role in the transsexualism of particular individuals, the general argument that transsexualism is an epiphenomenon of homosexuality is neither convincing nor logically parsimonious. In the context of the analysis of transsexualism developed here, it can be understood as reflecting a fundamentalist approach to the relationship between sex and gender, that is, an inability to see an anatomical male as anything other than a man and an anatomical female as anything other than a woman.

Transsexualism and the Conservation of Gender

Transsexualism has attracted a considerable amount of attention from sociologists, in particular those of the ethnomethodological persuasion, who have seen it as a privileged vantage point from which to observe the social construction of reality – in this case, gender reality. Transsexuals shed a self-reflective light on what we are all engaged in as we perform our gender roles. Because transsexuals have to work at establishing their credentials as men or women in a relatively self-conscious way, whereas the rest of us are under the illusion that we are just doing what comes naturally, they bring to the surface many of the tacit understandings that guide the creation and maintenance of gender differences in ongoing social life. Sociological studies of transsexualism thus belong not only to the literature on deviance, as one might expect, but are at the core of the sociological study of gender.

One of the major findings of the sociological literature on transsexualism is the degree of conservatism in transsexuals' views about masculinity and femininity. While transsexuals may be deviants in terms of cultural norms about how one arrives at being a man or a woman, they are, for the most part, highly conformist about what to do once you get there. The following summary characterization is representative of those commonly found in the literature:

> ...many transsexuals said they viewed themselves as passive, nurturing, emotional, intuitive, and the like. Very often, many expressed a preference for female dress and

> make-up. Others saw their feminine identification in terms of feminine occupations: housework, secretarial, and stewardess work. Some expressed feminine identification in terms of marriage and motherhood – wanting to "meet the right man," "have him take care of me," "adopt kids," and "bring them up." One expressed very definite views on child-rearing that were quite ironic in this context: "I would definitely teach my kids that boys should be boys and girls should be girls". (Raymond 1979: 78)[17]

Many transsexuals are, in fact, "more royalist than the king" in matters of gender. The sociologist Thomas Kando, who worked with a group of transsexuals who had undergone sex change surgery at the University of Minnesota in 1968–1969, reported test and questionnaire results showing that transsexuals were more conservative about sex role norms than both men and women (or, to be precise, than non-transsexual men and women), women being the least conservative. Male to female transsexuals tested higher in femininity than women. Most of the transsexuals in Kando's sample held stereotypical women's jobs and seemed, on the average, to be "better adjusted" to the female role than women were. As Kando noted, "[transsexuals] are, in many of their everyday activities, attitudes, habits, and emphases what our culture expects women to be, only more so" (Kando 1973: 22–7).[18]

The gender conservatism of transsexuals is encouraged and rein-forced by the medical establishment on which they are dependent for therapy. The conservatism of the doctors is in turn reinforced by their need to feel justified in undertaking as momentous a procedure as sex change surgery. In order to be convinced that such surgery is more likely to help than to harm, they feel the need to engage in close preoperative monitoring of the candidate's behavior, attitudes, and feelings. This is particularly important, since some of those who present themselves as candidates for surgery would not be appropriately diagnosed as transsexuals.[19] The gender identity clinics operated in conjunction with programs of sex change surgery provide the context of determining whether such surgery is indeed the most appropriate form of therapy for a particular individual, and also provide therapists and surgeons with an opportunity to judge how successful an applicant for surgery is likely to be at playing the desired gender role.

Given the preponderance of male to female transsexuals, it is interesting to keep in mind that the professional community in which this transformation is effected is largely male. It has been male surgeons' and psychiatrists' expectations about femininity that have had to be satisfied if a sex change operation is to be performed. There are reports in the literature of doctors using their own responses to a patient – that is, whether or not the doctor is attracted to the patient – to gauge the suitability of sex change surgery (Kessler and McKenna 1978: 118). Physical attractiveness seems to have provided the major basis for an optimistic prognosis in male to female sex change.

But looks aren't everything. Members of the medical establishment have also felt the need to socialize male to female transsexuals into their future roles in a gender-stratified economy. In the following excerpt from an "advice" column, published in the December 1963 issue of *Sexology Magazine*, Harry Benjamin, who had been outlining all the obstacles that lie before those seeking sex change surgery, from the physical rigors of the operation and related medical procedures themselves to the difficulties of learning to behave like a woman in matters of dress, make-up, body movement, speech style, etc., moved on to the bottom line:

> Finally, but highly important, how do you know you can make a living as a woman? Have you ever worked as a woman before? I assume that so far, you have only held a man's job and have drawn a man's salary. Now you have to learn something entirely new. Could you do that? Could you get along with smaller earnings? (Benjamin 1966: 109).[20]

Thus, while transsexualism may strike most people as being far out, it is clearly at the same time fairly far in. Thomas Kando put it as follows:

> Unlike various liberated groups, transsexuals are reactionary, moving back toward the core-culture rather than away from it. They are the Uncle Toms of the sexual revolution. With these individuals, the dialectic of social change comes full circle and the position of greatest deviance becomes that of the greatest conformity. (Kando 1973: 145)

Those who have been involved in the political struggle to transform the gender system and do away with its hierarchies have been particularly distrustful of transsexuals. Dwight Billings and Thomas Urban, in their socialist critique of transsexualism, noted the way in which "the medical profession has indirectly tamed and transformed a potential wildcat strike at the gender factory" (Billings and Urban 1982: 278). Janice Raymond, the author of a radical feminist critique of transsexualism that will be discussed further below, diagnosed transsexuals as gender revolutionaries manqué, carriers of a potentially subversive message who instead serve the interests of the patriarchal establishment (Raymond 1979: 36, 124). She viewed female to male transsexuals, who in her opinion should rightly have become lesbian feminists, as "castrated women," who have cut themselves off from their authentic source of female power. She compared them to the so-called "token woman" who becomes acceptable to the male establishment by aping men (Raymond 1979: xxiv). Raymond contemplated transsexualism with all the frustration and disgust of a missionary watching prime converts backslide into paganism and witchcraft.

Passing

The efforts of transsexuals to achieve normal gender status involve them in what is generally referred to as "passing." Since the term "passing" carries the connotation of being accepted for something one is not, it is important to consider the complexities that arise when this term is applied to what transsexuals are doing.

First of all, transsexuals commonly believe that it is when they are trying to play the role of their anatomical sex, as opposed to their subjectively experienced gender, that they are trying to pass as something they are not. The way they frequently put this is to say that they feel they are "masquerading" as a man or a woman.[21]

At the same time, transsexuals must work hard at passing in their new gender status, however more authentic they may themselves believe it to be. They have, after all, come to that status in a way that is less than culturally legitimate. They may also continue to have gender-inappropriate physical attributes, as well as behavioral habits acquired from years spent in the opposite gender role. Some transsexuals are, of course, more successful at passing than others, much of this depending on secondary sexual characteristics. Physical repairs are possible in certain areas: corrective surgery to reduce the size of an "Adam's Apple," electrolysis to remove facial and body hair.[22] Voice pitch cannot be changed, but transsexuals often seek speech therapy to help them achieve habits in conformity with their new gender.

The obstacles to successful passing provide an important context for the gender conservatism of transsexuals, discussed above. The strategies transsexuals use for passing in everyday life involve outward physical appearance, the more private body (which must be revealed in some contexts, for example, doctors' offices or communal dressing rooms), general conversation in a variety of social settings, and the construction of a suitable retrospective biography.[23] One aspect of biographical revision that transsexuals engage in, both for social purposes and for reasons of personal identity, is a recategorization of kinship ties they carry with them from the period before their sex change, particularly those associated with marriage. Jan Morris, for example, recategorized herself as a sister-in-law to her wife and an aunt to the children she fathered (Morris 1974: 122). A male to female transsexual in Thomas Kando's study reported the following conversation with a daughter:

> "...as far as Paula [the daughter] is concerned, what brought it to a head is, I was praying for a way to advise her, and then she called me one time and asked me 'Are we going to get together, because remember, 15th is Father's Day.' And I said, 'Paula, of course I love you very much, but I do have to tell you that I can no longer accept Father's Day gifts. If you wish to continue relations with me I could be your special Aunt Vanessa or something like that, but please don't remind me of that situation and certainly don't bring me any male clothing under any circumstances." (Kando 1973: 71)

The way in which transsexuals go about establishing their gender in social interactions reminds us that the basis on which we are assigned a gender in the first place (that is, anatomical sex) is not what creates the reality of gender in ongoing social life. Moreover, the strategies used by transsexuals to establish their gender socially are the same when they are playing the role associated with their original anatomical sex and when they are playing the role associated with their new achieved sex (Kessler and McKenna 1978: 127). In neither case is this accomplished by flashing. Transsexuals make explicit for us the usually tacit processes of gender attribution. As Harold Garfinkel put it, the transsexual reveals the extent to which the normally sexed person is a "contingent practical accomplishment" (Garfinkel 1967: 181).[24] In other words, they make us realize that we are all passing.

While establishing your gender credentials is a more demanding and riskier project if you are a transsexual, gender is not what could be called a sinecure for any of us. Fortunately, we receive a great deal of help from those around us who order their perceptions and interpretations according to the expectation that people should fall into one of two gender categories and remain there. The literature on transsexualism gives repeated examples of how slips and infelicities pass unnoticed as people discount incongruous information (see, for example, Kessler and McKenna 1978: 137–8).[25]

In this project of passing and being helped to pass, transsexuals sustain what the ethnomethodologist Harold Garfinkel called the "natural attitude" with respect to gender, which is made up of the assumptions that there are only two genders, that one's gender is invariant and permanent, that genitals are essential signs of gender, that there are no exceptions, that gender dichotomy and gender membership are "natural" (Garfinkel 1967: 122–8). At the same time, transsexuals reveal to the more detached and skeptical observer the ways in which such a natural attitude is socially and culturally achieved.

If transsexuals are commonly successful in passing as members of their gender of choice, the question arises as to how they are viewed when their particular circumstances become known. Are transsexuals accepted by nontranssexuals as "women" and as "men"?

Available research indicates that their status is problematic. The claims transsexuals make for the authenticity of their gender status are not convincing to most nontranssexuals. Transsexuals themselves are, in fact, ambivalent about the issue, sometimes saying they are "real" men and women and sometimes not. (See, for example, Kando 1973: 28–30.) Questions about the gender authenticity of transsexuals provide an occasion for culturally revealing negotiation around the definition of gender, transsexuals and non-transsexuals each gravitating toward definitions that work best to validate, or privilege, their own membership.

One transsexual who has argued forcefully and publicly for her status as a woman is Renée Richards, whose particular motivation came from her desire to pursue her career in tennis. Appealing to biology selectively, but in accordance with cultural definitions of gender, she considered that her female genitals settled the matter beyond question. That being the case, she felt that the chromosome tests administered by the various major tennis associations were an inappropriate and unfair barrier to her acceptance for women's tournament play. In fact, she asserted that of all players in women's tennis, her sex was least in question given all the publicity about it (Richards & Ames 1983: 320–1, 343). Clearly, the domain of physical sex differences leaves room for maneuver in finding a biological charter for gender. We can probably expect an increasing tendency to think of "real" biological sex in terms of chromosomes, although chromosomes clearly do not serve as the basis for determining sex, and hence gender, in ordinary practice.[26]

A particularly interesting case of negotiating the gender status of transsexuals came out of one segment of the feminist community in the late 1970s. In a book entitled *The Transsexual Empire*, Janice Raymond presented a critique of transsexualism motivated primarily by a felt need to exclude male to female transsexuals from the category of women, and, more specifically, to address the vexing issue of male to female lesbian feminist transsexuals. Her approach was to draw a picture of these transsexuals as men in ultimate drag, intruding on a world in which women have chosen to dedicate themselves socially and sexually to one another – a scenario reminiscent of *The Invasion of the Body Snatchers*.[27]

In denying womanhood to transsexuals, Raymond insisted on the physical limits of what can be accomplished through sex change operations and emphasized that male to female transsexuals can't, after all, have babies and don't have two X chromosomes (Raymond 1979: 10, 188). In the following representative passage from her argument, we see a once-a-man-always-a-man line of reasoning that slides between a definition of womanhood based on historical/biographical experience and one defined biologically in terms of sex:

> We know that we are women who are born with female chromosomes and anatomy, and that whether or not we were socialized to be so-called normal women, patriarchy has treated us and will treat us like women. Transsexuals have not had this same history. (Raymond 1979: 114).

To this argument, which apparently relies on the notion that chromosomes are destiny, is added an etherealized essentialism in which the defining attributes of womanhood that attract the male to female transsexual transcend the physical plane:

> [T]he creative power that is associated with female biology is not envied primarily because it is able to give birth physically but because it is multidimensional, bearing culture, harmony, and true inventiveness. (Raymond 1979: 107)

If this had been intended simply as an ethnographic description of transsexual motivation, it would have captured well the desires and wishes expressed by many transsexuals. It is more accurately seen, however, as being itself ethnographic data on the feminine mystique that has characterized much feminist writing over the past couple of decades, in which there has been a somewhat unprincipled marriage of convenience between a social constructionist view of gender and an essentialist view of womanhood.

If asking what gender transsexuals "really" belong to begs a number of fundamental questions, an alternative that seems to capture their distinctive place in a particular cultural scheme of things is to think of them as "naturalized" women and men. Such a formulation can evoke multiple meanings of "naturalization": (1) a status acquired in the way foreigners acquire citizenship,[28] (2) a change in gender that entails a change in the body, which we associate with the domain of nature, and (3) a recognition of the transsexuals' own experience of sex change as validating what they believe to be their true nature.

Transsexual Embodiment

In order to achieve the sense of a unified gender that forms an essential part of the more general sense of a unified self, the transsexual must acquire an appropriate body. Jan Morris, for example, who flirted with mystic visions of transcending the body altogether,[29] expressed what was ultimately her dominant desire to be properly embodied with a particularly fierce vividness:

> ...if I were trapped in that cage again [a man's body] nothing would keep me from my goal, however fearful its prospect, however hopeless the odds. I would search the earth for surgeons, I would bribe barbers or abortionists, I would take knife and do it myself, without fear, without qualms, without a second thought. (Morris 1974: 169)

To those who might be tempted to diagnose the transsexual's focus on the genitals as obsessive or fetishistic (see, for example, Raymond 1979: 122), the response is that transsexuals are, in fact, simply conforming to their culture's criteria for gender assignment. Transsexuals' fixation on having the right genitals is clearly less pathological than if they were to insist that they were women with penises or men with vaginas (Kessler and McKenna 1978: 123).

Transsexuals can make use of the mind/body dualism when arguing for the primacy of their gender identity over their original anatomical sex, while at the same time insisting on the need to acquire the right kind of body. Consider, for example, the following arguments by a female to male transsexual:

> "Your body is just something that holds you together; it's part of you; it's an important part – but your mind is strong; it is your will; your mind is everything. I mean as far as everything you want to be. If you had the body, the hands to play baseball, and it just wasn't in your mind, and it wasn't what you enjoyed, you might go and be a doctor. When all this was going on, I thought of God: Am I doing wrong? God created me as a girl, so maybe I should be. But I couldn't be, and which is more important, your mind or your body? God created my mind too . . . " (cited in Stoller 1968: 200)

This same person considered it self-evident that her sexual organs should be changed from female to male. Similarly, Jan Morris, whose desperation for physical sex change surgery has just been seen, at the same time identified gender with the soul and insisted upon the incorporeal nature of her quest:

> To me gender is not physical at all, but is altogether insubstantial. It is the soul perhaps . . . It is the essentialness of oneself, the psyche, the fragment of unity. (Morris 1974: 25)
>
> . . . that my conundrum might simply be a matter of penis or vagina, testicle or womb, seems to me still a contradiction in terms, for it concerned not my apparatus, but my *self*. (Morris 1974: 22; italics in original)

The bodily outcome of sex change surgery is itself somewhat make-shift. As Dr. Georges Burou put it: "'I don't change men into women. I transform male genitals into genitals that have a female aspect. All the rest is in the patient's mind'" (cited in Raymond 1979: 10). In a famous case study analyzed by the sociologist Harold Garfinkel in *Studies in Ethnomethodology*, his informant, Agnes, admitted that her artificial vagina was inferior to one provided by nature. Her feeling about this reflected not only considerations of physical practicality, but also what we might call cultural metaphysics. At the same time, though, it was a vagina to which she felt legitimately and morally entitled, given that she was "really" a woman. Agnes spoke of her penis and testicles as if they were some unfortunate, pathological growth, a kind of tumor; getting rid of them was like removing a wart (Garfinkel 1967: 126–7, 181–2).

The relationship of the transsexed body to the "naturally" sexed body calls attention to notions of nature as being associated, on the one hand, with "reality" and, on the other, as something to be manipulated and controlled by science. In this sense, transsexualism is located at the intersection of bio-material fundamentalism and voluntaristic transcendence. Sex change surgery, for its part, belongs to the domain of heroic medicine,[30] destined, however, to be left behind as science marches on. The prospects of such things as recombinant DNA technology already permit us to look ahead to a time when these operations would be viewed as a crude and primitive approach to transforming our natural endowments. The futuristic possibilities of transsexualism are invoked in the following passage by a defensive male to female transsexual seeking to assert her superiority over what are here called "Gennys," or genetic females:

> Free from the chains of menstruation and child-bearing, transsexual women are obviously far superior to Gennys in many ways... Genetic women are becoming quite obsolete, which is obvious, and the future belongs to transsexual women. We know this, and perhaps some of you suspect it. All you will have left is your "ability" to bear children, and in a world which will groan to feed 6 billion by the year 2000, that's a negative asset. (cited in Raymond 1979: xvii)

If, on the other hand, we step back from the entire enterprise of physical sex change, as many critics of the transsexual phenomenon have done, we might see the most technologically sophisticated strategy imaginable as a crude and primitive approach to issues of personal and social identity. Though the analogy cannot be pushed too far, addressing gender issues through sex change surgery is a bit like turning to dermatologists to solve the race problem.

Transsexualism in Cross-cultural Perspective

It is instructive to compare Euro-American transsexualism with forms of institutionalized gender crossing found in other societies. I have selected three such examples from very different cultural settings. Their juxtaposition to one another and to Euro-American transsexualism throws into relief certain culturally distinctive characteristics of the gender systems of which each is a part; at the same time, they all illustrate the same basic paradox – or, to use Morris' term, conundrum – at the heart of the relationship between sex and gender.

The *Berdache* in North America

The best-known case of institutionalized gender crossing in the ethnographic literature is the so-called *berdache* found in a number of societies indigenous to North America. The term itself, which seems to come ultimately from Persian via Arabic, Italian, and French (Forgey 1975: 2) and not from any Native American language, has come to be used in the North Americanist literature as a general designation for individuals who take on gender roles in opposition to their anatomical sex by adopting the dress and performing the activities of members of the other group.[31] As in the case of Euro-American transsexualism, gender crossing in North American Indian societies is most commonly male to female; cases of girls or women who take on male behavior, dress, or activities are relatively rare.[32] The significance of such asymmetries in gender crossing will be discussed below.

Information on the *berdache* is uneven in quality and quite sparse in the case of some groups. It is also difficult to gauge how the colonial situation affected both the practices themselves and the quality of the information that outsiders were able to obtain about them. There seems to have been a great deal of variation in patterns of gender crossing from one society to another, and sometimes within a society as well. In some cases, the parents decided that a child of one sex would serve as a substitute for a child of the other. More commonly, children were allowed to take on attributes of the gender opposite to their anatomical sex if their general inclinations and preferred activities pointed in that direction. Some *berdache* were reported to have sexual relations with persons of the same sex; others seem not to have done so. As we can see from the discussion of transsexualism, it is not clear what it would mean to designate the *berdache*'s same-sex sexual activity as "homosexual," particularly in the absence of fuller data from each society in question.

The defining feature of the *berdache* status seems generally to have been adopting the dress and assuming the day-to-day activities of the opposite sex. In a comparative analysis of the *berdache*, the anthropologist Harriet Whitehead has argued that the institution is to be understood in the context of certain distinguishing features of North American Indian cultures, notably, an ethic of individual destiny that could make itself known in a variety of ways and was often the outcome of a visionary encounter with a supernatural being. Whitehead also argued that the institution of the *berdache* reflects a social system in which the division of labor is at the forefront of gender definition (Whitehead 1981: 99–103).

We do not know enough about North American Indian concepts of gender to understand how the gender of the *berdache* was construed in the various societies in which the institution was found. Should we be thinking about the *berdache* in terms of a basic two-gender system with the possibility of individuals transferring from one to the other? Or is it more appropriate to think of the *berdache* as constituting a distinct third gender, a special status with cultural functions and meanings of its own?[33] How might different societies have varied in this regard? Was the *berdache* in some societies believed to have actually "become" a member of the opposite gender? If so, what does this say about how such societies might differ from our own in terms of the distinctive criteria of gender? Might a change in activities and demeanor suffice for legitimate gender transformation?[34] While we may not be able to answer these questions satisfactorily, an encounter with the North American berdache at least provokes us to ask them.

The *Xanith* in Oman

In Oman, where men and women lead lives that are highly segregated from one another, there is a form of gender crossing in which men who adopt a distinctive form of dress and comportment can move in the world of women.[35] They may, for example, socialize freely with women who are not their relatives and may see unrelated women unveiled. The *xanith* engages in various forms of women's work, including cooking and paid domestic service. At the same time, *xanith* retain many jural privileges of male status. They may move about publicly in a way that women cannot. Their dress is not exactly the same as that of women, but is distinctive and can be seen as something in between male and female garb. While accepted as women for many purposes, they do not "pass."

The Omani status of *xanith* is coterminous with that of the male homosexual prostitute. The anthropologist who has provided the ethnographic information on this cultural practice, Unni Wikan, has argued that the *xanith* provides a means for Omani men to engage in premarital and extramarital sex without compromising the virtue of Omani women and the rights of the men who have responsibility over them.[36] Insofar as the *xanith*'s partner retains the active role in the sexual act, the partner's own masculine gender status is not in question. According to Wikan, the differential gender categorization of *xanith* and "men" indicates that the sex act takes priority over the sexual organs for purposes of establishing gender status.

Individuals may move in and out of the *xanith* status, and once a man has given it up by marrying and proving his sexual potency with his bride, he is fully accepted as a man. This presents a contrast with Euro-American transsexualism, in which the cultural current moves individuals toward an experience of essential and unchanging gender that is an intrinsic part of an essential and chronologically continuous self.

The two cases also offer interesting contrasts with respect to the relationship between sexual orientation and gender identity. Debate around the relationship between transsexualism and homosexuality in the Euro-American case reflects, on the one hand, their possible separability and, on the other, the way in which gender status is validated or challenged by considerations of sexual orientation; it also reflects the way in which both gender and sexual orientation are essentially defining of personhood and identity. Omani transgenderism involves a closer link between sexual orientation and gender status while at the same reflecting the possibilities for change in these aspects of social identity over the course of a person's – or, rather, a male person's – life.

Woman-Woman Marriage in Africa

In a number of societies in Africa, it has traditionally been possible for a woman to take another woman as a wife, and to acquire rights both to the domestic services of the wife and to any offspring she produces. This practice of 'woman-woman marriage,' as it has come to be called, while showing certain variations from one culture to another, at the same time reveals some basic similarities about the African societies in which it is found.[37] In general, woman-woman marriage operates within a system in which marriages are established through exchanges of wealth; in which they are relationships not so much between individuals as between kin groups; in which a major concern is the perpetuation of kin groups defined through descent; and in which paternity is achieved through payment of bridewealth rather than through sexual activity. The relationship between the female husband and her wife is not a sexual one. The wife has a lover or lovers, sometimes selected by the female husband and sometimes of the wife's own choosing.

Women who become husbands and fathers may do so by standing in for men of their lineage, for example, when there is no male to serve as an appropriate heir. In these cases, it seems that descent group membership is a sufficiently important aspect of social identity to override differences of role usually associated with gender. Insofar as marriages are established through exchanges of wealth, women can acquire wives if they have access to property over which they can exercise control. In societies in which women occupy positions of political leadership, they can take wives in order to form alliances with other kin groups in much the same way as men do. In some ethnographic reports, the role of female husband and father is said to be limited to barren women who have no children of their own through marriage to a male husband. In other cases, women combine their roles as wife and mother in one marriage with their roles as husband and father in another.

The question raised by woman-woman marriage for our present purposes is how the assumption of husbandhood and fatherhood affects a woman's gender status. When women become husbands and fathers, are they engaged in what would appropriately be termed gender crossing? The answer seems to be no in some cases and yes in others.

Among the Lovedu of South Africa, for example, the role of husband and father seems open to women as women. Lovedu women who acquire wives generally do so because they are entitled to a daughter-in-law from their brother's household and may themselves have no son, or no willing son, to serve as the husband. The woman may thus take her brother's daughter to be her own wife instead; in this case, the female husband is seen as being like a mother-in-law. Woman-woman marriage in Lovedu society is also linked to the ability of women to occupy various important political offices and to control the wealth they earn after they marry. The queen who traditionally ruled Lovedu society customarily received wives given to solicit political favors; some of these wives were, in turn, given away in marriage by the queen in her own strategies of alliance formation (Krige 1974: 15–22).

Among the Nandi of Western Kenya, on the other hand, a woman who becomes a husband and father is reclassified as a man. The Nandi female husband is commonly a woman of relatively advanced years who has failed to produce a male heir. The need for such an heir is tied to a "house property complex," in which each of a man's co-wives is endowed with a share of her husband's property, which will be passed on to her son or sons to manage (Oboler 1980: 69, 73). A Nandi woman may acquire a wife to produce the needed heir, while she herself takes on the interim management of her house's share of her husband's estate. When a Nandi woman takes a wife, she must cease engaging in sexual relations with her husband, since this would both compromise her reclassification as a man and, should she conceive by some chance, raise problems of succession and inheritance. Female husbands are supposed to give up women's work. The ethnographer who has described woman-woman marriage among the Nandi, Regina Oboler, noted that in the past they were expected to adopt male dress and adornment, although this was no longer the case during the period of her fieldwork (Oboler 1980: 74, 85).

According to Oboler, the Nandi reclassify the female husband as a man because she is assuming economic and managerial responsibilities that Nandi see as the exclusive preserve of men:

> It is an ideological assertion which masks the fact that the female husband is an anomaly: she is a woman who of necessity behaves as no woman in her culture should. Her situation forces her to assume male behavior in certain areas that are crucial to the

> cultural definition of the differences between the sexes. These areas have to do with the management and transmission of the family estate. (Oboler 1980: 83)

The role played by the Nandi female husband is not something simply open to both women and men, nor is it apparently sufficient for the Nandi to think of the female husband as a woman taking on a man's responsibilities. Instead, the Nandi prefer to say that the female husband "is" a man.

In fact, it would seem more accurate to say that the female husband is a man in some contexts, but not in others. It is when matters of property and heirship are at issue that Nandi are most insistent about the female husband being a man (Oboler 1980: 70). Although the ideology of the female-husband-as-man takes on a life of its own, leading the Nandi to assert that female husbands behave as men in all areas of social life, this is not actually the case. In many contexts, the female husband continues to behave more as a woman than as a man. Behaviors designated by Nandi as "masculine" in the case of female husbands are often not, in fact, gender-specific; others are characteristic of older women in general. It is also the case that the female husband whose own husband is still living continues in the role of wife to him, and mother to any children of the marriage. Thus, while the Nandi may generally characterize the female husband as a man, her manhood seems to be focused around the more specific project of maintaining the link between gender, control over property, and inheritance.

What all of these forms of gender crossing have in common, their considerable differences notwithstanding, is that they call into question systems of gender differentiation and at the same time support them. They pose an implicit, or in the Euro-American case explicit, challenge to the usual basis for sorting individuals into gender categories while operating to maintain culturally traditional distinctions between women and men.

We can see how this works more clearly if we consider the following two issues: 1) the significance of asymmetries in the directionality of culturally patterned forms of gender change, and 2) the paradoxical relationship between gender and sex.

Asymmetries of Gender Crossing

The cases of gender crossing presented here show various kinds of asymmetries. Two cases are unidirectional: the Omani *xanith* has no female to male counterpart; woman-woman marriage in African society has no comparable male-male form. The two others, Euro-American transsexualism and the North American *berdache*, are bidirectional, but show a skewed distribution with a greater frequency of male to female transformation. The reasons for these asymmetries are, in part, specific to the meanings and functions of gender in the respective societies at issue. However, they are also understandable in terms of gender hierarchy itself and the social dominance of men.

In order to see this, let us consider how asymmetry in Euro-American transsexualism can be understood. Among the factors cited in the literature are: the greater difficulty and cost of female to male sex change surgery, and its less satisfactory results; the greater propensity of men for the kind of experimentation, risk, and initiative involved in sex change surgery; the apparently greater propensity of males for sexual deviance in general; the dominant role of the mother in the rearing of children of both sexes; the relationship of transsexualism to other cultural institutions in which envious men are trying to appropriate the powers of women (for example, the dominance of men in the field of obstetrics and gynecology) – in this case, taking the ultimate step of becoming women themselves.[38]

Some authorities on transsexualism have remarked upon the apparently paradoxical relationship between the high ratio of male to female transsexuals and the results of survey research showing that it is more common for girls to say they want to be boys than the reverse, more common for adult women than for adult men to say they would rather have been born the opposite sex (see, for example, Benjamin 1966: 147; Pauly 1969: 60). This, taken together with society's greater permissiveness toward girls acting like boys than toward boys acting like girls, has been seen as a puzzle to be solved – often by recourse to biological or psychiatric speculation. A possible Freudian twist on all of this, given a view of women as castrated beings longing for possession of the penis, is that all women are transsexuals,[39] which either makes one wonder why more of them do not seek sex change surgery or makes one appreciate their success in finding symbolic substitutes.

The key to understanding the skewed Euro-American pattern of gender crossing would seem to lie in an understanding of the asymmetrical, hierarchical nature of our gender categories, and the extent to which masculinity is the unmarked category and femininity the marked category. That is, our notions of what a man should be like are linked to our notions of what a person, in general, should be like. This is an important factor in the differential tolerance for cross-gender behavior in women and in men. Women wanting to be like men can be seen as engaging in an understandable project of upward mobility. Insofar as becoming more like a man is becoming more like a person, the implications for gender reclassification are less radical than movement away from the unmarked, generic human standard.[40] When we encounter cases of female to male gender reclassification, as in some versions of African woman-woman marriage, these are perhaps best looked at in terms of social promotion to a superior status. In fact, the Nandi speak of it in just these terms (Oboler 1980: 74, 86).[41] By the same token, the absence of female to male gender crossing in a society like Oman reflects a lack of comparable opportunities for the upward mobility of women into the status of men.

Male to female transgenderists, for their part, would seem to be engaged in a willful act of downward mobility. When Renée Richards told a friend about her plans for a sex change operation, the friend said, "Anyone who voluntarily wants to become a forty-year-old woman, I take my hat off to" (Richards & Ames 1983: 308). Jan Morris was quite sensitive to the privileges she was losing in giving up her manhood. She remarked upon the shock of suddenly being condescended to and being assumed to be incompetent in a variety of areas: "[A]ddressed every day of my life as an inferior, involuntarily, month by month I accepted the condition" (Morris 1974: 149). At the same time, both Richards and Morris clearly felt that the compensations of womanhood more than made up for the drawbacks.

In the context of these considerations, we might see cultural discomfort with male to female transsexualism in Euro-American society as reflecting the fact that those who intentionally move down in the system are more threatening to its values than those seeking to move up. The latter may constitute a threat to the group concerned with maintaining its privileges, but the former constitute a threat to the principles on which the hierarchy itself is based. The greater cultural tolerance for male to female gender crossing in native North American societies may, in this light, be interpreted as an index of a less stratified relationship between men and women.

The Paradox of Sex and Gender

The terms "sex" and "gender" are generally used to distinguish a set of biological differences from a system of social, cultural, and psychological ones. The culturally structured system of differences we designate by the term "gender" bears some relationship to the biological difference between women and men, but is not reducible to it. In other words, the relationship between sex and gender is at once a motivated and an arbitrary one. It is motivated insofar as there must be reasons for the cross-culturally universal use of sex as a principle in systems of social differentiation; it is arbitrary, or conventional, insofar as gender differences are not directly derivative of natural, biological facts, but rather vary from one culture to another in the way in which they order experience and action. In any society, the meaning of gender is constituted in the context of a variety of domains – political, economic, etc. – that extend beyond what we think of as gender per se, and certainly beyond what we understand by the term "sex" in its various senses.[42] Gender is a classic example of what the sociologist Marcel Mauss called a "total social fact":

> In these *total* social phenomena, as we propose to call them, all kinds of institutions find simultaneous expression: religious, legal, moral, and economic. In addition, the phenomena have their aesthetic aspect... (Mauss [1925] 1954: 2)

We recognize "gender" as a cross-culturally distinct category of social difference by virtue of some relationship that it has to physical sex differences. When we inquire into what motivates the relationship between sex and gender, however, confusions may arise as to what kinds of connections we are talking about, given the multiple meanings of the term "sex." Is "sex" being used to designate general morphological differences between males and females? Is it being used to focus on reproductive capacities and roles more specifically? Is erotic activity what we have in mind? Are we using the term in a shifting sense, sometimes talking about all of the above and sometimes only some of it? The other major question is, of course, the extent to which our own culturally specific folk beliefs about biology saturate our view of gender and provide us with the illusory truths we hold to be self-evident.[43]

Just as the comparative study of gender differences shows how little of the specific content of such differences can be predicted by sex in any sense of the term, so the study of gender crossing shows us the robustness of gender systems in their transcendence of the usual rule of recruitment by sex. While sex differences may serve to "ground" a society's system of gender differences, the ground seems in some ways to be less firm than what it is supporting.[44]

Euro-American transsexualism presents us with the particular paradox of ascribed gender and achieved sex. While some may think of transsexuals as individuals exercising the right to "choose" their gender identity, freeing themselves from what is for most people a physically-determined fate, this identity is usually experienced by transsexuals themselves as something that is in no way subject to their own will. For transsexuals, gender is destiny and anatomy is achieved.[45]

This reversal of the Euro-American folk ontology of sex and gender was experienced by Jan Morris in terms she took from C. S. Lewis:

> Gender is a reality, and a more fundamental reality than sex. Sex is, in fact, merely the adaptation to organic life of a fundamental polarity which divides all created beings. Female sex is simply one of the things that have feminine gender; there are many others, and Masculine and Feminine meet us on planes of reality where male and female would be simply meaningless. (cited in Morris 1974: 25)

In sum, what we seem to see in systems of institutionalized gender-crossing is the maintenance of a society's gender system through the detachment of gender from the very principle that provides its apparent foundation.

NOTES

1 An earlier draft of this paper was written during a sabbatical semester at the Stanford Center for Advanced Study in the Behavioral Sciences, in the spring of 1989. I am using the term "sex change surgery" in this paper, although much of the current literature favors the term "sex reassignment surgery", or even "gender reassignment surgery." Each of these labels carries its own conceptual and analytical presuppositions, and none is completely satisfactory. My own choice is intended to be as neutral as possible; the theoretical orientation I am taking to transsexualism will emerge in the course of the discussion, as will my uses of the terms "sex" and "gender."

2 The population reported on in one important early study showed a ratio of 8:1 (Benjamin 1966: 147). The overall ratios presented in subsequent literature are lower, but still have tended to run 4:1 or 3:1 (Raymond 1979: 24). It should be noted that researchers frequently remark upon the difficulty of getting good statistical data on transsexualism and sex change surgery.

3 The following passage is an example: "Initially, many psychiatrists assumed that individuals seeking [sex change] surgery were psychotic, and they opposed the procedure in principle... However, as experience with patients seeking sex change accumulated, it became clear that there was a group of men characterized by extreme, lifelong feminine orientation and absence of a sense of maleness for whom sex change was followed by greatly improved emotional and social adjustment." (Newman and Stoller 1974: 437; note the elision from "individuals" to "men").

4 Dr. Burou's clinic is described by Jan Morris, who went there for her own surgery (Morris 1974: 135–144). Renée Richards also traveled there, but twice developed cold feet at the clinic door (Richards & Ames 1983: 246–7, 252). Garber's essay in Chapter 9 of this volume, which takes an "Orientalist" perspective on transsexualism, opens with observations on how Casablanca was viewed by Jan Morris. An engagingly bizarre fictionalized account of Burou's clinic can be found in a novel by the Brazilian author Moacyr Scliar in which the protagonists, born as centaurs, go to Morocco to have operations to turn themselves into "normal" human beings (Scliar 1980).

5 See Benjamin 1966, for his most comprehensive discussion of transsexualism. Jan Morris and Renée Richards both describe the hormone treatment they received from Benjamin (Morris 1974: 48–9, 105; Richards & Ames 1983: 161 ff.).
6 Renée Richards describes her two unsuccessful experiences with psychoanalysis, which together lasted over nine years (Richards & Ames 1983: 99 ff., 120 ff.) She gives a particularly uncomplimentary and bitter portrait of her second analyst, a prominent member of the New York psychoanalytic community (see, e.g., 161, 362–3).
7 Major influential works include Stoller 1968, 1975; Green and Money 1969.
8 The adoption of this term as an instance of the "politics of renaming" has been discussed by Dwight Billings and Thomas Urban as a part of their critique of transsexualism as a symptom of the alienation and commodification of sex and gender in capitalist society (Billings and Urban 1982).
9 See, for example, Jan Morris: "It became fashionable later to talk of my condition as 'gender confusion,' but I think it a philistine misnomer: I have had no doubt about my gender since that moment of self-realization [which Morris claims came at the age of three or four]" (Morris 1974: 25).
10 For one discussion of these various dimensions of sex, see Benjamin 1966, 5–9.
11 This is the formulation adopted by Suzanne Kessler and Wendy McKenna in their sociological study of transsexualism (Kessler and McKenna 1978: 13).
12 Billings and Urban (1982) discuss the way in which concepts of core gender identity and its imperviousness to change have figured in the analysis and treatment of transsexualism.
13 Attempts by psychologists, psychiatrists and other medical researchers to identify the causes of transsexualism include some that look to biological or constitutional factors and others that emphasize early socialization and the constellation of family relations, with a developing consensus that both nature and nurture are probably at issue. In other words, it is not known why some people become transsexuals and others don't. Renée Richards, herself a doctor and well aware of the various debates in the medical literature, began her autobiography by raising the question of causes, noting that even if it should ultimately be discovered that transsexualism is biochemically determined, her own family experience offered an embarrassingly stereotyped picture of how transsexualism can be explained by an abnormal and gender-confused family situation (Richards & Ames 1983: 2). For the major clinical attempt to find causes for transsexualism in family dynamics, and in the mother-son relationship most particularly, see Stoller 1968. Medico-psychiatric debate about the causes of transsexualism has obvious similarities with debate about the causes of homosexuality; the two have intersected at various points.
14 For a developmental approach to transvestism and transsexualism, see Docter 1988.
15 See, for example, Renée Richards' accounts of the encounters she had with male homosexuals while she was still a man, in which the parties were clearly at cross purposes (Richards & Ames 1983: 77, 294–6).
16 For examples of negative attitudes toward homosexuality among transsexuals, see Jan Morris' autobiography (Morris 1974: 24, 62, 169) and the case studies reported in Kando 1973. Robert Stoller devotes a chapter of *Sex and Gender* (Vol. 1) to a discussion of the transsexual's denial of homosexuality (Stoller 1968: 141–153). He also provides data from a female to male transsexual who became disgusted with a female lover she had during adolescence while she was still anatomically female; the other girl's interest in her genitals was experienced as unwelcome lesbianism (202–203).
17 Renée Richards expressed her relief that her own transsexualism did not in any way affect her son's clear masculine identity (Richards & Ames 1983: 370) It is important to keep in mind that the motivation for such sentiments is not simply gender conservatism,

but also the desire to spare one's children the kind of suffering one has experienced oneself.

18 In the years since studies such as this one were carried out, more has come to be known about diversity among transsexuals. Patterns of transsexualism have also been affected by the kinds of social changes that have affected the lives of women and men generally. Stone's paper in this volume contributes to an understanding of such change, as well as providing the kind of insider perspectives that did not make their way into most of the scientific and scholarly literature. Stone makes the argument that transsexuals should come out of the closet and cease disappearing into the two-gender system.

19 See, for example, Newman and Stoller 1974 for case studies in which sex change surgery would have been a grave mistake; these include a fetishistic cross-dresser who combined the desire to wear women's clothes with an underlying attachment to his masculinity; a male homosexual who thought he could hold on to his bisexual lover if he became a "real woman"; and a schizophrenic who came seeking sex change surgery after having had a revelation that Jesus Christ was really a woman and that he himself was a reincarnation of Mary Magdalen.

20 Of the 51 transsexuals in Benjamin's study, the only 2 who were reported as having failed to adjust to their new, postoperative situation were male to female transsexuals who experienced a dislocating downward mobility in income and occupational status (Benjamin 1966: 122–4). The major problem that Renée Richards encountered in trying to obtain sex change surgery in the United States was that the doctors she consulted, Harry Benjamin among them, were fearful of destroying Richard Raskind's medical career (Richards & Ames 1983: 165, 178–9, 210).

21 See, for example, Benjamin 1966: 202, 242; Stoller 1968: 202; Kessler and McKenna 1978: 126–7. Jan Morris described the experience of being in the 9th Queens Royal Lancers as akin to that of an anthropologist moving among an exotic tribe while being taken for a native (Morris 1974: 31–2).

22 For descriptions of the experience of undergoing both electrolysis and corrective surgery to the "Adam's Apple," see Richards & Ames 1983: 176–8 and 211–13.

23 These various dimensions of passing are discussed by Kessler and McKenna (1978: 127–35).

24 See also Kessler and McKenna 1978: 16–17, for a discussion of this point.

25 In this connection, we might think of the famous case dramatized in the play "M. Butterfly," in which a French diplomat carried on an affair for twenty years with a Chinese opera star who turned out not only to be a spy, but also to be a man, having deceived the diplomat on this point for the entire period of their relationship. Dorinne Kondo has provided an elegant analysis of the case and of the play by David Henry Hwang (Kondo 1990). She discusses how the opera star's ability to pass as a woman rested on his lover's propensity to interpret his behavior in terms of stereotypes involving both gender and race: the fact that the diplomat was never able to see the opera star unclothed, even in their most intimate moments, was interpreted as a sign of the "shame" and "modesty" appropriate to Asian women.

26 Stoller described an attempt on the part of a group of researchers in the late 1950s to arrive at a mathematical formula for determining gender by weighing the various components of somatic and psychological sex (Stoller 1968: 232).

27 An analysis of transsexualism shaped in response and opposition to Raymond's is presented in Stone's paper in this volume. There has, in fact, been division of opinion in the feminist community about male to female transsexuals, with some feminists adopting the liberal position that women, as a disadvantaged minority, should not be discriminating against transsexuals. Renée Richards appealed to such sentiments when

she made a point of noting the support she had received over the years from members of minority groups (Richards & Ames 1983: 317, 324–5).

28 When I presented an earlier version of this paper at the University of California at Santa Cruz in 1989, one feminist member of the audience responded to this formulation by suggesting that male to female transsexuals be seen as "defectors" from the male status (that is, as people seeking asylum from an oppressive regime). She opposed those, who, like Raymond, reject male to female transsexuals as "women," maintaining instead that the feminist goal should be for all men to become women – without, of course, having to go through sex change surgery.

29 Such a vision of disembodiment was expressed in the context of a mysterious encounter Morris had with a holy man in the course of one of his solitary rambles during the Everest expedition (Morris 1974: 87–8).

30 Billings and Urban call attention to the fact that doctors view sex change surgery as a technical tour de force (1982: 269).

31 Forgey 1975, Whitehead 1981, Kessler and McKenna 1978 (21–41), and Williams 1986 provide comparative overviews and theoretical discussions of the *berdache* in Native American societies. A case study of two *berdache*, one Zuni and one Navajo, is presented in Roscoe 1988. For a critique of the historical anachronism of some analyses of the *berdache*, particularly those that come from a contemporary Euro-American gay male perspective, see Gutierrez 1989. The North American *berdache* has often been compared with similar patterns of institutionalized gender crossing among Siberian tribal peoples.

32 One such case of female to male gender crossing in Native North American is that of the "manly-hearted woman" among the Piegan (Lewis 1941).

33 Will Roscoe, who has provided case studies of Zuni and Navajo *berdache*, argues that they are to be seen as occupying a special and intermediate status between women and men, which draws its power from the very combination of gender attributes (Roscoe 1988). An example of such a status in an area other than North America is the *waneng aiyem ser* ("sacred woman") among the Bimin-Kuskusman of Papua New Guinea, as described by Fitz John Porter Poole (1981). This role of ritual leadership, which is filled by a post-menopausal woman who is no longer married or sexually active, is intentionally ambiguous with respect to gender and is intended to evoke primordial, hermaphroditic ancestors (Poole 1981: 117).

34 These points are discussed in Kessler and McKenna 1978: 21–4, 38.

35 The material on the Omani *xanith* presented here comes from Wikan 1977. Wikan's essay provoked some criticism and interchange in the pages of the journal *Man* (sic), where it was published; the kinds of points that were raised there are taken into account in this presentation of Wikan's description and analysis. Garber's essay in this volume also includes a consideration of Omani gender-crossing and the debate around Wikan's work.

36 While there are in fact women prostitutes in Oman, it is interesting to note that the term for them is a modified form of the term *xanith* (Wikan 1977: 311, 319).

37 General and comparative discussions of woman-woman marriage can be found in Krige 1974 and O'Brien 1977. Krige's study is of particular value, since it combines a general discussion with case studies from several different societies and a detailed analysis of woman-woman marriage among the Lovedu, where Krige did fieldwork. Another excellent case study is Oboler's discussion of the female husband among the Nandi, in which particular attention is given to the gender status of the female husband (Oboler 1980). Krige offers information on how social change has affected the institution of woman-woman marriage. I use the notorious ethnographic present here, given the generality of the patterns I am addressing and their persistence over time. I should note, however, that

the usage is problematic and that changes have no doubt occurred in the time since the research drawn upon here was carried out.

38 For examples of these various explanations, see Raymond 1979: 26; Pauly 1969: 60; Stoller 1968: 263–4. Raymond, who sees transsexualism as the usurpation by men of women's bodies, also sees the male surgeon in a sex change operation as usurping the reproductive powers of women; she claims that "[t]ranssexualism can be viewed as one more androcentric interventionist procedure. Along with male-controlled cloning, test-tube fertilization, and sex selection technology, it tends to wrest from women those powers inherent to female biology" (Raymond 1979: 29). It is interesting to note here the distance traveled from the work of such feminists as Shulamith Firestone who were looking to medical technology to free women from servitude to their role in biological reproduction (Firestone 1970: 191–202).

39 Robert Stoller pointed out that Freud's view of femininity made all women transsexuals (Stoller 1968: 58–9).

40 We can see this kind of asymmetry in political revolutions that have sexual equality as one of their goals; the attempt to achieve such equality is generally a matter of trying to turn women into the social equivalents of men. A particularly clear example was the kibbutz movement in Israel, with its focus on "the problem of the woman." (There was never any comparable consideration of "the problem of the man.") Women had to be given the opportunity to work in agricultural production, in developing industries, and in the army. There was, however, no comparable effort to get men into the kitchens and laundries (Talmon 1972; Tiger and Shepher 1975; Shapiro 1976).

41 Female to male gender crossing as a form of upward mobility is also discussed in Castelli's article in this volume.

42 The way in which gender intersects with other axes of social inequality – including how it articulates with race and class differences, how it operates in societies with caste systems – has become a major focus of work on gender in recent years. Attention has also increasingly been given to the way in which gender oppositions structure and are structured by a variety of cultural symbolic domains, some familiar Euro-American examples being nature and culture, reason and emotion, domestic and public, individualism and social responsibility (see Shapiro 1988). Sex/gender difference provides a particularly powerful model for generating binary oppositions.

43 For a general discussion of this issue, see Yanagisako and Collier 1987. For a more ethnographically focused analysis of how the cultural preoccupations of Western anthropologists in matters of sex, procreation, and gender have skewed their understanding both of their own culture and others, see Delaney 1986. The attempt to liberate the study of gender from the thrall of our own bio-ideology has led some anthropologists to argue that the concept of gender should be unhooked from sex altogether (Yanagisako and Collier 1987). Elsewhere (Shapiro ms. 1989), I have argued that this is an impossible project; without reference to biological sex, the concept of gender dissolves altogether. Moreover, what has motivated the study of gender is an inquiry into the relationship between sex and culture, which, after all, includes an exploration of the limits of that relationship.

44 Jones and Stallybrass... also explore the illusory nature of the "grounding" of gender differences in a foundational definition of male and female.

45 Stoller has emphasized the extent to which the transsexual's sense of gender identity is beyond his or her control (Stoller 1968: 260, 268–9, 271). See Garfinkel 1967: 133–7 for a more theoretically elaborate discussion of the concepts of ascription and achievement as they apply to the transsexual experience.

REFERENCES

Benjamin, Harry. *The Transsexual Phenomenon.* New York: Julian Press, 1966.

Billings, Dwight B. and Thomas Urban. "The Socio-Medical Construction of Transsexualism: An Interpretation and Critique" *Social Problems* 29(3), 266–282, 1982.

Delaney, Carol. "The Meaning of Paternity and the Virgin Birth Debate." *Man* 21(3): 494–513, 1986.

Docter, Richard F: *Transvestites and Transsexuals: Toward a Theory of Cross-Gender Behavior.* New York: Plenum, 1988.

Firestone, Shulamith. *The Dialectic of Sex: The Case for Feminist Revolution.* New York: Bantham Books, 1970.

Forgey, Donald G. "The Institution of Berdache Among the North American Plains Indians." *The Journal of Sex Research* 11(1): 1–15, 1975.

Garfinkel, Harold. *Studies in Ethnomethodology.* Englewood Cliffs, New Jersey: Prentice-Hall, 1967.

Green, Richard and John Money (eds.). *Transsexualism and Sex Reassignment.* Baltimore: The John Hopkins University Press, 1969.

Gutierrez, Ramon. "Must We Deracinate Indians to Find Gay Roots?" *Out/Look* 1(4): 61–67, 1989.

Jorgensen, Christine. *Christine Jorgensen: A Personal Biography.* Introduction by Harry Benjamin, M. D. New York: Paul S. Eriksson, Inc., 1967.

Kando, Thomas. *Sex Change: The Achievement of Gender Identity Among Feminized Transsexuals.* Springfield, Illinois: Charles C. Thomas Publisher, 1973.

Kessler, Suzanne J., and Wendy McKenna. *Gender: An Ethnomethodological Approach.* New York: John Wiley & Sons, 1978.

Kondo, Dorinne. "M. Butterfly: Orientalism, Gender, and a Critique of Essentialized Identity," *Cultural Critique* 16, Fall 1990: 5–29.

Krige, Eileen Jensen. "Woman-Marriage, With Special Reference to the Lovedu – Its Significance for the Definition of Marriage." *Africa* 44: 11–37, 1974.

Lewis, O. "Manly-Hearted Women among the North Piegan," *American Anthropologist*, 43: 173–187, 1941.

Mauss, Marcel. *The Gift: Forms and Functions of Exchange in Archaic Societies.* Translated by Ian Cunnison. Illinois: The Free Press, [1925] 1954.

Morris, Jan. *Conundrum.* New York: Harcourt, Brace, Jovanovich, 1974.

Newman, Lawrence E., and Robert J. Stoller. "Nontranssexual Men Who Seek Sex Reassignment." *American Journal of Psychiatry* 131(4): 437–41, 1974.

Oboler, Regina Smith. "Is the Female Husband a Man? Woman/Woman Marriage Among the Nandi of Kenya." *Ethnology* 19(1): 69–88, 1980.

O'Brien, Denise. "Female Husbands in Southern Bantu Societies." In Alice Schlegel ed., *Sexual Stratification: A Cross-Cultural View*, 109–26, New York, 1977.

Pauly, Ira B. "Adult Manifestations of Female Transsexualism." In John Money, and Richard Green, eds., *Transsexualism and Sex Reassignment*, 59–87, Baltimore: John Hopkins University Press, 1969.

Poole, F. J. P. "Transforming 'Natural Woman': Female Ritual Leaders and Gender Ideology among Binin-Kuskusman." In S. B. Ortnes, and H. Whitehead, eds., *Sexual Meanings: The Cultural Construction of Gendes and Sexuality.* 116–65, Cambridge: Cambridge University Press, 1981.

Prince, V. "Sex vs. Gender." In D. Laub, and D. Gandy, eds., *Proceedings of the Second Interdisciplinary Symposium on Gender Dysphoria Syndrome*, Stanford: Stanford University Medical Center, 1973.

Raymond, Janice. G. *The Transsexual Empire: The Making of the She-Male*. Boston: Beacon Press, 1979.

Richards, Renée, and John Ames. *Second Serve: The Renée Richards Story*. New York: Stein and Day, 1983.

Roscoe, Will. "We'Wha and Klah: The American Indian Berdache as Artist and Priest." *American Indian Quarterly*, 12(2), Spring 1988: 127–50.

Scliar, Moacyr. *O Centauro no Jardim*. Rio de Janeiro: Editora Nova Fronteira, 1980.

Shapiro, Judith. "Determinants of Sex Role Differentiation: The Kibbutz Case." *Reviews in Anthropology* 3(6): 682–692, 1976.

—— "Gender Totemism." In Richard R. Randolph, David M. Schneider, and May N. Diaz, eds., *Dialectics and Gender: Anthropological Approaches*. 1–19, Boulder: Westview Press, 1988.

—— "The Concept of Gender." ms., 1989.

Stoller, Robert. *Sex and Gender*, Vol I. New York: Science House, 1968; Vol II (*The Transsexual Experiment*). London: Hogarth Press, 1975.

Talmon, Yonina. *Family and Community in the Kibbutz*. Cambridge: Harvard University Press, 1972.

Tiger, Lionel and Joseph Shepher. *Women in the Kibbutz*. New York: Harcourt, Brace, Jovanovich, 1975.

Whitehead, Harriet. "The Bow and the Burden Strap: A New Look at Institutionalized Homosexuality in Native North America." In Sherry B. Ortner and Harriet Whitehead, eds., *Sexual Meanings: The Cultural Construction of Gender and Sexuality*, 80–115. Cambridge: Cambridge University Press, 1981.

Wikan, Unni. "Man Becomes Woman: Transsexualism in Oman as a Key to Gender Roles." *Man* 12: 304–319, 1977.

Williams, W. *The Spirit and the Flesh: Sexual Diversity in American Indian Culture*. Boston: Beacon Press, 1986.

Yanagisako, Sylvia Junko, and Jane Fishburne Collier. "Toward a Unified Analysis of Gender and Kinship." In Jane Fishburne Collier, and Syliva Junko Yanagisako, eds., *Gender and Kinship*. Stanford: Stanford University Press, 1987.

9

Problems Encountered in Writing the History of Sexuality: Sources, Theory and Interpretation

Estelle B. Freedman and John D'Emilio

In the past decade, the history of sexuality has emerged as a fast growing offshoot of the new social history. In some ways, its maturation has resembled that of the new women's history a decade or so before. In the early 1970s, those who wanted to pursue the study of women's history had to contend with questions about its legitimacy, the availability of sources, and the relationship between scholarship and politics. Similarly, early students of the history of sexuality had to defend the study of a topic seemingly so elusive and private that it could not yield much historical data and, given the remnants of sexual reticence within the historical profession, one that threatened to embarrass its members.

Despite early resistance, historians have increasingly been drawn to the study of sexuality both by compelling sources and compelling historical questions. Just as doubts about the possibility of women's history evaporated in the face of abundant archival evidence, so, too, the supposition that so private a subject as sex would not leave adequate primary data has proven inaccurate (e.g., Sahli, 1984). Several research libraries house archival bonanzas, including the Schlesinger Library on women's history at Radcliffe College, the Kinsey Institute for Research in Sex, Reproduction, and Gender in Bloomington, Indiana, and the Social Welfare History Archives at the University of Minnesota. Historians have already begun to mine family papers, organizational records, and demographic data to create a social history of sexuality in America (Freedman, 1982). At the same time, the sexual politics of the 1970s and 1980s – from feminism and gay liberation to the New Right's Moral Majority – piqued historical curiosity about how sexuality came to be so important in modern American society.

These new sources and questions have now given rise to a rich historiography on subjects ranging from abortion to vice crusades, from courtship to venereal disease, from prostitution to sexual violence (Brandt, 1987; Gordon, 1976; Gordon, 1988;

Mohr, 1978; Pivar, 1973; Pleck, 1987; Rosen, 1982; Rothman, 1984). This growing literature has been reviewed and synthesized elsewhere (D'Emilio & Freedman, 1988). This article addresses the problems raised by primary sources about sexuality and the ways historians interpret them. It begins with a general overview of types of sources and then focusses on two problems: first, changing historical definitions of sexuality and sexual identity, and second, the relationship of sexuality to class.

Sources and Interpretations

Just as early studies of women's history drew heavily upon prescriptive, printed sources, so, too, did the first works on sexuality emphasize attitudes, ideology and prescription. Books like John and Robin Haller's *The Physician and Sexuality in Victorian America* (1974) relied on medical texts and popular health manuals read largely by middle-class men and women. In such studies, the ideals of female passionlessness and male continence loomed large. But in the mid-1970s, several critical works challenged the focus on prescriptive literature by exploring personal sources of sexual behavior. Carl Degler's use of the Mosher survey (1974), Carroll Smith-Rosenberg's study of women's letters and diaries (1975), and Jonathan Katz's collection of court records, letters, diaries and newspaper accounts of homosexuality (1976) paved the way for later studies, such as Ellen Rothman's history of courtship (1984) and Martin Duberman's essays on archival sources for gay history (1986). In the meantime, historical demographers such as Daniel Scott Smith (1973; Smith & Hindus 1975) and Robert Wells (1971, 1980) provided intriguing data on fertility, "illegitimacy" and "bastardy." Finally, long available records of deviance invited new interpretations, from the colonial court records first explored by Edmund Morgan (1942) to juvenile court cases (Schlossman & Wallach, 1978) and surveys of prostituion in the Progressive era (Rosen, 1982). Indeed, so many sources of sexual "deviance" have survived that historians must be careful not to write a history of the unusual.

Although historical studies of sexuality have progressed beyond prescriptive sources toward a history of sexual behavior and its regulation, scholars have only begun to tackle the problems of historical interpretation raised by these sources. Above all, no one has yet offered an adequate historical definition of the subject. In this regard, the parallels with women's history cease, for however culturally constructed gender might be, the category of woman is fairly well agreed upon. What, however, is sexuality? Given its changing meaning over time, what is one looking for in records of the past? The very term "sexuality" is a modern construct which originated in the nineteenth century. As we explained in our book, *Intimate Matters*, it is only in the twentieth century that American society became so "sexualized" that the term had clear meaning throughout the culture. In the contemporary era. Americans have come to use "sexuality" to refer to the erotic, that is, to a state of physical attraction to either sex. In the past, however, there was no language of "sexuality" per se. Rather, in pre-industrial America, what is now called sexuality was largely embedded within a reproductive language. In the nineteenth century, a language of passion and romance characterized middle-class discourse. The persistent acknowledgement of "lust" notwithstanding, to look for sources of what is now called the erotic before the modern period skews historical interpretation back to an older notion of "repressed" Puritans and Victorians, who seem to lack something that modern Americans have created. In short, one must interpret sexual history in the terms used by one's historical subjects.

A second problem of interpreting sources – one that might be summarized by the question "Whose sexuality?" – does parallel developments in women's history. In both fields, the earliest work concentrated on white, middle-class experience, and only gradually has it acknowledged the variety of sexualities, by class, race, region, and ethnicity. The nature of the sources has influenced this expanded view, but in problematic ways. The early studies that relied on prescriptive texts typically described white middle-class experience. As historians began to use sources such as police and court records or vice commission reports, more working-class, black and immigrant sexual history emerged. That so much of this evidence originated with middle-class authorities attempting to assert their superiority over other groups makes it hard to use as an accurate measure of distinctive class or racial practices.

A second interpretive problem confronted by historians of working-class sexuality concerns the direction of social change across class lines. As Kathy Peiss (1986) has explained, historians once maintained a "trickle down" model in which middle-class bohemians pioneered modern sexual behaviors, which only belatedly reached the working class. Along with Joanne Meyerowitz (1988), Elizabeth Ewen (1985) and other recent scholars, she posits an alternative pattern in which Progressive era, urban, working class and immigrant youth created a new sexual culture that gradually expanded to other classes, regions, and ages.

A further problem for understanding variation in sexual history is the question of divergence or convergence between various groups – including the sexual experience of men and women. How persistent are sexual subcultures, whether those in which women insist on linking sexuality, reproduction and passion; or those in which blacks tolerate non-marital sexual relations? Has sexuality become more homogenized in the modern period, or do pockets of unique values continue?

Finally, what theoretical constructs inform the interpretation of sources of sexual history? Probably the most common model used to understand the history of sexuality is social construction theory. Briefly, social constructionists (Brandt, 1987; D'Emilio, 1983; Katz, 1983; Plummer, 1975; Weeks, 1977, 1981) argue that sexuality is not primarily a biological category; it is not an innate, unchanging "drive" or "instinct" immune to the shifts that characterize other aspects of society. Instead, as social constructionists maintain, sexual behavior and sexual meanings are subject to the forces of culture. Human beings learn how to express themselves sexually, and the content and outcome of that learning vary widely across cultures and across time. Particular practices may have a universal existence, but how men and women interpret their behavior and desires, and the meaning that different societies affix to sexual behavior, are enormously diverse.

Social construction theory was initially and, perhaps, most successfully applied to the historical study of homosexuality. In an influential article, English sociologist Mary McIntosh (1968) proposed that those studying homosexuality abandon the notion that it was a universal, unchanging condition and instead appropriate the concept of "role" as a useful tool for recognizing differences in the social organization of homosexual expression. Later, the English historian Jeffrey Weeks (1977) and the French philosopher-historian Michel Foucault (1978) took this further by identifying a profound change in the social construction of homosexuality in the West: from discrete acts to a personal identity. Or, as Foucault described this evolution, "The sodomite had been a temporary aberration; the homosexual was now a species" (p. 43).

Homosexuality is not the only topic that a social construction perspective is able to illuminate. Among the white middle-class, the definition of births outside of formal marriage as "illegitimate" has structured the meaning and consequences of nonmarital childbearing in basic ways. Yet the same experience has held widely different meaning and consequences for African-Americans who have not stigmatized either the mother or the child (Gutman, 1976; Vincent, 1961). Prostitution can serve as another example. The common, popular understanding of a prostitute is simple and straightforward: a woman who sells her sexual services, is clearly set apart from other women, and is stigmatized accordingly. Yet studies of nineteenth and early twentieth century prostitution in both Britain and the United States suggest a much more complex and variable picture. Many young working-class women moved easily in and out of prostitution and were not necessarily segregated from the rest of the community (Rosen, 1982; Walkowitz, 1980). Shifting modes of state regulation and the changing structure of urban life and politics, not simply the fact of selling sexual services, have accounted for the phenomenon of the prostitute as a woman apart.

As useful as the social construction model has been, some aspects of the history of sexuality seem, at least on the surface, to be less socially constructed than others. For instance, female sexuality has at times been shaped by the model of "Eve, the Temptress," and at other times by notions of innate passionlessness. But looking at male sexuality across the span of US history, one confronts a phenomenon that in certain aspects seems unchanging and fundamentally biological. The definition and, often, the experience of male sexual desire seems uniformly to reflect lust, aggressiveness, insistence, and (without training), lack of control. For example, there is a remarkably similar condemnation of predatory male sexuality in the rhetoric of female moral reformers in the 1830s (Ryan, 1979; Smith-Rosenberg, 1971) and of anti-pornography activists in the 1970s and '80s (Dworkin, 1983). Why does this characterization recur? Is male sexuality more biologically based and less socially constructed than female sexuality? Or do historians read back into the past contemporary views about aggressive male sexuality? Is this view itself a modern construct? Is there evidence of non-aggressive male sexual patterns in the past? The poles of sexual freedom and sexual repression offer a second example of the limits of social constructionism. Throughout American history, purity reformers and their opponents have employed the rhetoric of repression and freedom (Pivar, 1973; Sears, 1977; Vance, 1984), in which sexuality is either contained by social control or liberated through individual expression free from external constraints. Why, if sexual meanings and behavior are social constructed, is there so much continuity of thought and language over the generations about this tension of repression and freedom?

Historians confront these general problems whenever they study sexuality. To illustrate how these problems influence historical interpretations, we now turn to specific examples from research on sexual history in the United States. Our first example comes from the nineteenth century and concerns the problem of historical definitions of sexual identity; the second concerns the problem of class in the twentieth century.

Identity in the Nineteenth Century

Carroll Smith-Rosenberg's 1975 essay, "The Female World of Love and Ritual," represented a critical shift away from a simplistic and presentist notion of sexuality to a more complex, nuanced and historicized understanding of sexual possibilities in an era before the emergence of a concept of sexual identity. She documented the ways in which physical and emotional affection had been normative, rather than deviant, among certain middle-class women in the late eighteenth and nineteenth centuries. Only at the end of this period, with the medicalization of sexuality, did romantic friendships between women become a deviant category. Smith-Rosenberg warned against reading our modern notion of homosexuality onto these loving relationships, whether they involved sexual contact or not. Many readers, however, interpreted her use of the term "homosocial" to mean non-sexual, a reading that comforted those who were loathe to acknowledge same-sex relations among women, and irritated others, who felt that she begged the question of whether these women did in fact have "sexual" relations (Cook, 1979; Faderman, 1981). Smith-Rosenberg (1975) also argued that these female relationships were unique, in large part because women lived in a sphere – a "female world" – emotionally apart from men of their class. Her evidence, however, looked only at that female sphere, and very little historical research has attempted to test her assumptions about female uniqueness.

Three documents that suggest both similarities and differences between male and female same-sex relations can serve to refine Smith-Rosenberg's hypothesis. Dating from 1800, 1826 and 1885, these documents suggest that in the early nineteenth century, physical intimacy between men may well have been normative, although the language men used to explore it was more physical than women's romantic discourse.[1] Men seemed to be much more comfortable describing their physical relations, although they did so with a self-distancing jocularity, interspersed with longings for women's bodies. Nonetheless, no "deviant" identity characterized these early descriptions of male-male physical intimacy. By the late nineteenth century, however, a romantic language of same-sex friendship appeared among men, as it had among women somewhat earlier. At the same time, however, men began to fear being labelled sexually "deviant" for expressing their same-sex love.

The first set of documents, a correspondence between two late eighteenth-century graduates of Brown University, illustrates the earlier comfort with male intimacy and its coexistence with heterosexual longing. In 1800, Virgil Blanding opened a letter to his cousin William by comparing the two young men's pursuits of the opposite sex. "How many girls have you had to do with since you have got to Rehobeth? I have not [?]ed any but what is better I have seen a pretty little girl's bare legs." On one occasion, he boasted, he met a "jolly girl" whom he "kissed and squeezed as much as I pleased." That night Virgil Blanding dreamt of marrying her, and the stranger who shared his bed "said in the morning that I hugged him all night." One night soon, Blanding confided, he hoped to lie with one of the girls he knew.

In the meantime, he wrote his cousin, he hated to sleep alone, "for I get to hugging the pillow instead of you. Sometimes I think I have got hold of your doodle when in reality I have hold of the bed posts" (Blanding, 1 January, 1800).

Such commentary on the antics of male bedfellows may simply have been an epistolary convention and may or may not document actual sexual play between male friends. In a second correspondence, for example, 22-year-old Thomas Jefferson Withers wrote to fellow South Carolinian James Henry Hammond in 1826:

> I feel some inclination to learn whether you yet sleep in your shirt-tail, and whether you yet have the extravagant delight of poking and punching a writhing Bedfellow with your long fleshen pole – the exquisite touches of which I have often had the honor of feeling? Let me say unto thee that unless though changest former habits in this particular, thou wilt be represented by every future Chum as a nuisance. (Duberman, 1986, p. 7)

A few months later, Withers teased his friend in another vein:

> I fancy, Jim, that your *elongated protruberance* [sic] – your fleshen pole – ... has complete mastery over you – and I really believe, that you are charing over the pine barrens of your locality, braying, like an ass, at every she-male you can discover. (Duberman, 1986, p. 8)

In his commentary on these documents, Martin Duberman (1986) suggests that Withers' and Hammond's behavior may have been typical for their class, race and region, and that "carefree" male-male sex may have taken place at some times. If it did, it coexisted rather comfortably within a dominant system of heterosexuality.

By the late nineteenth century, homosexual and heterosexual desire may have continued to coexist, but the former had become more problematic. The cult of romantic friendship now extended to men and, perhaps in its wake, new taboos about same-sex love made men more self-conscious about crossing sexual boundaries between male intimates. A third document, the diary of Frederick Ryman, a 27-year-old poet living in New York State in the 1880s, illustrates these themes. Ryman had an active sexual life with women he courted, and at least once in his bachelor days, he visited a brothel (D'Emilio & Freedman, 1988, pp. 109–11). His diary recorded a conversation with his friend "O.L.F.," who chastised Ryman for "being so fierce for the women." "F." had told Ryman "in so many words one day that he is a 'C – sucker' & that he loves & enjoys that d–d custom so revolting to every right minded person ..." (Duberman, 1986, p. 43). Ryman's friend had adopted a sexual identity, as a cocksucker, one that was at odds with heterosexual passion. Ryman himself, however, remained somewhat confused about the line between passion and sexuality. In his diary he recorded, for example, his admiration for the beauty of a young boy and wondered how he could be "so attracted to him," given his predilection for women. On another occasion, Ryman spent the night with his friend Rob. "I confess," he wrote,

> I like the oriental custom of men embracing & kissing each other if they are indeed dear friends. When we went to bed Rob put his arms around me & lay his head down by my right shoulder in the most loving way & then I put my arms around his neck & thus clasped in each others arms we talked for a long time till we were ready to go to sleep.

> ... This a.m. ... he came to the bed & threw his arms around my neck & we kissed each other good bye. ... (Duberman, 1986, p. 44)

More important than this record of male-male intimacy – both physical and emotional – is Ryman's reflection on the experience. First, he reassured himself that these physical pleasures were not "sexual," and he reaffirmed his heterosexual identity:

> I am certain there was no sexual sentiment on the part of either of us. We both have our mistresses whom we see with reasonable regularity & I am certain that the thought of the least demonstration of unmanly & abnormal passion would have been as revolting to him as it is & ever has been to me, ... (Duberman, 1986, p. 45)

"And yet," Ryman continued in a romantic, wistful, and somewhat self-justifying passage,

> I do love him & I loved to hug & kiss him because of the goodness & genius I find in his mind. Christ kissed & embraced those whom he loved I believe & why shall I fear to do the same? (Duberman, 1986, p. 45)

The problem Fred Ryman encountered in the 1880s still haunts historians, namely, what is sexual? Romantic love? Physical longing? Physical gratification? These three documents suggest that for men, categories of sexual identity tightened by the late nineteenth century. The Oscar Wilde scandal and trials of the 1890s may have accelerated this process (Katz, 1983). With the emergence of a deviant category, "the homosexual," physical intimacy that had once been accepted now called into question one's manliness. Fred and Rob still shared a bed, as had William and Virgil, and Tom and Jim, before them. But now men questioned the meaning of their romanticized embraces instead of joking about their purely physical play. Whether, or when, such a transition occurred outside of the white middle classes is unclear. For some men, however, new sexual identities had taken shape by the late nineteenth century.

Class in the Twentieth Century

A second example concerns issues of class, specifically the relationship between working-class life and sexuality in modern America. There is already a fairly well-developed literature on middle-class sexuality which suggests the ways that sexuality was integral to the formation, the shaping, and the self-definition of middle-class America (Gay, 1984; Rothman, 1984; Smith-Rosenberg, 1985). Scholarship about the nineteenth-century working class is much thinner. Despite the efflorescence of a rich "new labor history" in the last generation, this literature is notably reticent in its discussion of sexual issues. This is true even of the literature on working-class family life, where one might expect sexual issues to surface prominently (Hareven, 1982). Recently, at the point where women's history and labor history converge, this deficiency is being remedied. Monographs on working-class women in early nineteenth-century New York (Stansell, 1986), on prostitution (Rosen, 1982), on the culture of leisure among New York working women at the turn of the century (Peiss, 1986), and on working women in Chicago (Meyerowitz, 1988), are beginning to fill in the contours of at least a working women's history of sexuality.

However, for the twentieth century, particularly the period since the 1920s, the volume of historical literature on sexuality drops off considerably. This tends to be true in general, but it especially characterizes the topic of white working-class sexuality. The problem is not one of sources; the sources in fact are abundant, perhaps even too abundant. Much of this material requires careful reading because it often comes from outsiders peering in: private welfare agencies; police and court records; academic sociologists.

In our own work (D'Emilio & Freedman, 1988), we have relied largely upon published material, particularly the work of sociologists studying the lives of working-class Americans. Even in these readily accessible sources, the raw information is rich and intriguing. But the issue of interpretation still involves many more questions than answers.

The problem of interpretation does not stem from an absence of interpretation on the part of sociologists. Their point of view is generally quite clear, as illustrated by the following two examples: *Elmtown's Youth* (Hollingshead, 1949), and *And the Poor Get Children* (Rainwater, 1960). Each is an important sociological study and each clearly displays empathy toward their working-class subjects.

Elmtown's Youth is a study of high school students in a small midwestern town of the early 1940s. The hypothesis that Hollingshead sought to test, and which he demonstrated admirably, is that the experience of adolescence owes far more to one's social standing, or class status, than it does to biological processes of maturation. Class status structured, shaped, and divided the social experience and opportunity of Elmtown's young people.

This proved as true in sexual matters as in other aspects of life. In Elmtown, working-class youth displayed a distinctly different set of sexual mores. Sexual behavior and values served as one of the markers of class status. Because working-class males were more likely to drop out of school, they began earning wages at an earlier age. This gave a measure of independence, allowing them to own cars, travel farther away for dates and socializing, and escape parental control. At the same time, it raised their expectation of what a date meant in terms of sexual exchange. Working-class females were more likely to have reputations as "fast girls" who were sexually available. Since dating tended to occur among youth with a similar class position, the results were that many working-class young people became sexually active sooner than their middle-class counterparts. This, in turn, led to higher rates of illegitimacy and prenuptial pregnancy, an earlier age of marriage and, presumably, an earlier age of childbearing for women.

And the Poor Get Children tracks working-class youth at a later stage in their life cycle. Rainwater studied intensively the contraceptive practices of white working-class couples (Protestants rather than Catholics or Jews) in Cincinnati and Chicago. Like Hollingshead, he found a pattern of early marriage. He also drew a fairly bleak portrait of marriage for many of his couples. Initially, the men came into marriage far more sexually experienced than their wives. The women tended to be abysmally ignorant about sex, including about the basic facts of reproduction. As one woman explained, and she was by no means unusual in her response, "I knew nothing when

I got married. I didn't even know how a baby was born and how you got pregnant. My mother told me the night before I got married" (p. 65). Gender roles were sharply dichotomized, and both men and women agreed that the male was most fully sexual. Sex was fraught with anxiety for women. Husbands and wives communicated poorly about sex, contraception, and other matters. Family size tended to be larger than what the couple desired, contraceptive use was sporadic and haphazard, and the bedroom was often a battleground.

In both of these studies, even though the authors are frankly sympathetic toward their subjects and, at least obliquely, are advocates for them, a view of working-class sexuality as dysfunctional emerges quite clearly. Sex is one element in a larger framework that emphasizes lack of agency, and even victimization. Educational attainment is compromised by pregnancy and early marriage. Too many children stretch scarce economic resources which in turn exacerbates the conflicts in already stressful marriages. Although the authors by no means make this claim, one can easily come away from a reading of these books with the feeling that, if only the working class controlled its sexuality, social mobility and a better life would await its members.

This interpretation is problematic. For one, even from these and other similar studies, evidence can be culled which suggests that sexual passion was a source of deep satisfaction, a respite from daily worries, and even a form of transcendence. One woman in the Rain-water study commented, "I'll take it any time I can get it; I like it. ... Hell, everybody else is going to the moon, I might as well go to Heaven!" (p. 100). Another woman, married for several years and the mother of three children, said, "If God made anything better he kept it to himself. ... It's the most important thing in the world" (p. 97). Secondly, if the new social history has taught anything, it is that one needs to be skeptical of claims that the traditionally voiceless, or those denied access to formal power – African-Americans, other racial/ethnic groups, women, the working class – are simply victims of history. It would be foolhardy to believe that in this area, where a history has not yet been excavated, the victimization model applies.

A more recent anthropological study offers a contrasting account of African-American working-class sexuality. In *All Our Kin* (1974), Carol Stack writes compassionately and intelligently about the culture of an urban African-American community in the North. She moves beyond a family disorganization/pathology model – a model shared by both black and white sociologists – and instead offers new insights into African-American family structure. Stack sees the intergenerational kinship ties of the community not as a failure of the nuclear family, but rather as a creative adaptation to conditions of economic discrimination, deprivation, and insecurity. She also argues that this alternative kinship network helps structure and shape sexual relationships between men and women. Permanent sexual bonding was often compromised in the interests of kinship survival. In other cases, women and men felt compelled to make a painful choice between their family of birth and their conjugal partner. As one young woman commented, "You have to get along the best you know how, and forget about your people. ... If I ever get married, I'm leaving town!" The harsh reality of poverty created, in the words of Stack, "strong conflict between kin-based domestic units and lasting ties between husbands and wives" (pp. 108–15).

Although Stack's interpretation cannot be applied directly to the experience of whites, it does at least suggest the need to evaluate working-class sexuality on its own terms. Rather than judge working-class patterns as dysfunctional, scholars need to explore how sexuality weaves its way through the social experience of the working class. How does it help to shape working-class identity? In what ways does sexuality constitute a sphere of resistance and autonomy, and to what extent does it reinforce patterns of social inequality? In sum, how can the study of sexuality illuminate the history of class relations in the United States?

This article has discussed some of the problems involved in writing the history of sexuality. It has argued that at this stage in the development of the field, the main problem is not a lack of sources but rather a need to define more clearly the subject matter of sexuality and to be more sensitive to gender and class differences in historical experience. As sexual history continues to grow from a marginal specialization to a subfield with its own journal,[2] both definitions and theoretical approaches will no doubt proliferate, expanding our knowledge of history and of human sexuality.

NOTES

1 The first documents can be found in the Blanding Family Papers (Correspondence Box 1), Massachusetts Historical Society, Boston, Mass. They were brought to our attention by an archivist who knew of our interest in sexual history. The second and third appear in an anthology of Martin Duberman's research on gay history (1986). We are grateful to Martin Duberman for his discovery of these documents and for sharing unpublished research with us.

2 *The Journal of the History of Sexuality* [has been] published by the University of Chicago Press [since] 1990.

REFERENCES

Brandt, Allan. M. (1987). *No Magic Bullet: A Social History of Veneral Disease in the United States Since 1880* (2nd ed.). New York: Oxford University Press.

Cook, Blanche. (1979). "The Historical Denial of Lesbianism." *Radical History Review, 20* (Spring-Summer), 60–65.

D'Emilio, John. (1983). "Capitalism and Gay Identity," in Ann Snitow, Christine Stansell, and Sharon Thompson (Eds.), *Powers of Desire: The Politics of Sexuality.* New York: Monthly Review Press, 100–113.

D'Emilio, John, & Freedman, Estelle. (1988). *Intimate Matters: A History of Sexuality in America.* New York: Harper and Row.

Degler, Carl N. (1974). "What Ought to Be and What Was: Women's Sexuality in the Nineteenth Century." *American Historical Review, 79*(5), 1467–1490.

Duberman, Martin Bauml. (1986). *About Time: Exploring the Gay Past.* New York: Gay Presses of New York.

Dworkin, Andrea. (1983). *Right Wing Women.* New York: Coward, McCann.

Ewen, Elizabeth. (1985). *Immigrant Women in the Land of Dollars: Life and Culture on the Lower East Side, 1890–1925*. New York: Monthly Review Press.
Faderman, Lillian. (1981). *Surpassing the Love of Men: Romantic Friendship and Love Between Women from the Renaissance to the Present*. New York: William Morrow and Co.
Foucault, Michel. (1978). *The History of Sexuality*. Vol. One: An Introduction, trans. Robert Hurley. New York: Pantheon.
Freedman, Estelle. (1982). "Sexuality in Nineteenth-Century America: Behavior, Ideology, and Politics." *Reviews in American History* (Dec.), 196–215.
Gay, Peter. (1984). *The Bourgeois Experience, Victoria to Freud: Education of the Senses*. New York: Oxofrd University Press.
Gordon, Linda. (1988). *Heroes of Their Own Lives: The Politics and History of Family Violence*. New York: Viking.
Gordon, Linda. (1976). *Woman's Body, Woman's Right: A Social History of Birth Control in America*. New York: Grossman.
Gutman, Herbert G. (1976). *The Black Family in Slavery and Freedom, 1750–1925*. New York: Pantheon Books.
Haller, John S., Jr., & Haller, Robin, M. (1974). *The Physician and Sexuality in Victorian America*. Urbana: University of Illinois Press.
Hollingshead, A. B. (1949). *Elmtown's Youth*. New York: John Wiley.
Katz, Jonathan (Ed.). (1976). *Gay American History: Lesbians and Gay Men in the U.S.A* New York: Thomas Crowell.
Katz, Jonathan N. (Ed.). (1983). *Gay/Lesbian Almanac: A New Documentary*. New York: Harper & Row.
McIntosh, Mary. (1968, Fall). "The Homosexual Role." *Social Problems, 16*(2).
Meyerowitz, Joanne, J. (1988). *Women Adrift: Independent Wage Earners in Chicago, 1880–1930*. Chicago: University of Chicago Press.
Mohr, James C. (1978). *Abortion in America: The Origins and Evolution of National Policy, 1800–1900*. New York: Oxford University Press.
Morgan, Edmund S. (1942, Dec.). "The Puritans and Sex." *New England Quarterly, 25*(4), 591–607.
Peiss, Kathy. (1986). *Cheap Amusements: Working Women and Leisure in Turn-of-the-Century New York*. Philadelphia: Temple University Press.
Pivar, David J. (1973). *Purity Crusade: Sexual Morality and Social Control, 1868–1900*. Westport, CT: Greenwood Press.
Pleck, Elizabeth. (1987). *Domestic Tyranny: The Making of American Social Policy against Family Violence from Colonial Times to the Present*. New York: Oxford University Press.
Plummer, Kenneth. (1975). *Sexual Stigma: An Interactionist Account*. London: Routledge and Kegan Paul.
Rainwater, Lee. (1960). *And the Poor Get Children: Sex, Contraception and Family Planning in the Working Class*. Chicago: Quadrangle.
Rainwater, Lee, & Yancey, William. (1967). *The Moynihan Report and the Politics of Controversy*. Cambridge: MIT Press.
Rosen, Ruth. (1982). *The Lost Sisterhood: Prostitution in America, 1900–1918*. Baltimore: The Johns Hopkins University Press.
Rothman, Ellen K. (1984). *Hands and Hearts: A History of Courtship in America*. New York: Basic Books.
Ryan, Mary P. (1979). "The Power of Women's Networks: A Case Study of Female Moral Reform in Antebellum America." *Feminist Studies, 5*(1) (Spring), 66–86.
Ryan, Mary P. (1981). *Cradle of the Middle Class: The Family in Oneida County, New York, 1790–1865*. New York: Cambridge University Press.

Sahli, Nancy. (1984). *Women and Sexuality in America: A Bibliography*. Boston: G. K. Hall and Co.

Schlossman, Stephen, & Wallach, Stephanie. (1978). "The Crime of Precocious Sexuality: Female Juvenile Delinquency in the Progressive Era." *Harvard Educational Review*, *48*(1), 65–94.

Sears, Hal D. (1977). *The Sex Radicals: Free Love in High Victorian America*. Lawrence, KS: The Regents Press.

Smith, Daniel Scott. (1973). "The Dating of the American Sexual Revolution: Evidence and Interpretation." In Michael Gordon (Ed.), *The American Family in Social-Historical Perspective*. New York: St. Martins Press, 321–35.

Smith, Daniel Scott. (1973). "The Demographic History of Colonial New England." In Michael Gordon (Ed.), *The American Family in Social-Historical Perspective*. New York: St. Martins Press, 397–415.

Smith, Daniel Scott. (1974). "Family Limitation, Sexual Control, and Domestic Feminism in Victorian America." In Mary S. Hartman and Lois Banner (Eds.), *Clio's Consciousness Raised*. New York: Harper and Row, 119–36.

Smith, Daniel Scott, & Hindus, Michael. (1975). "Premarital Pregnancy in America 1640–1971: An Overview and an Interpretation." *Journal of Interdisciplinary History*, *5*(4), 537–70.

Smith-Rosenberg, Carroll. (1971). "Beauty, the Beast, and the Militant Woman: A Case Study in Sex Roles and Social Stress in Jacksonian America." *American Quarterly*, *23* (Oct.), 562–84.

Smith-Rosenberg, Carroll. (1975). "The Female World of Love and Ritual: Relations Between Women in Nineteenth-Century America." *Signs*, *1* (Autumn), 1–29.

Stack, Carol. (1974). *All Our Kin*. New York: Harper and Row.

Stansell, Christine. (1986). *City of Women: Sex and Class in New York, 1789–1860*. New York: Alfred A. Knopf.

Vance, Carol. (1984). *Pleasure and Danger: Exploring Female Sexuality*. New York: Routledge and Kegan Paul.

Vincent, Clark. (1961). *Unmarried Mothers*. New York: Free Press.

Walkowitz, Judith R. (1980). *Prostitution and Victorian Society: Women, Class, and the State*. New York: Cambridge University Press.

Weeks, Jeffrey. (1977). *Coming Out: Homosexual Politics in Britain from the Nineteenth Century to the Present*. London: Quartet Books.

Weeks, Jeffrey. (1981). *Sex, Politics and Society: The Regulation of Sexuality Since 1800*. London: Longman.

Wells, Robert V. (1971–72). "Demographic Change and the Life Cycle of American Families." *Journal of Interdisciplinary History*, 2, 273–82.

Wells, Robert V. (1971). "Family Size and Fertility Control in Eighteenth Century America: A Study of Quaker Families." *Population Studies*, *25*(1), 73–82.

Wells, Robert V. (1980). "Illegitimacy and Bridal Pregnancy in Colonial America." In Peter Laslett, Karla Oostervean and Richard M. Smith (Eds.), *Bastardy and Its Comparative History*. Cambridge: Harvard University Press, 349–61.

Wells, Robert V. (1982). *Revolutions in Americans' Lives: A Demographic Perspective on the History of Americans, their Families, and their Society*. Westport, CT: Greenwood Press. HB3505.W4.

Part III

Ethics, Erotics, and Exercises

10

Choosing the Sexual Orientation of Children

Edward Stein

In recent years research concerning the origins of human sexual orientation has garnered a great deal of scientific, legal, political and general attention. Many now believe that there is strong evidence to support the view that sexual orientation is genetically determined. In this context some lesbians, gay men, bisexuals and their allies have begun to worry (and some conservative commentators have begun to hope[1]) that prospective parents will be able to determine the future sexual orientation of a child by using an amniocentesis or some other genetic screening technique and, further, that they will abort or in some other way prevent the birth of the fetus if the resulting child would not be heterosexual. This seems a live possibility since parents worldwide sometimes chose to abort a fetus (or to kill an infant) if it is not of the sex they desire. Given the widespread hatred of, and prejudice and discrimination against, lesbians, gay men and bisexuals,[2] it seems quite likely that, if technology permits, abortions and other procedures will be used to select for the sexual orientation of children. The goal of this article is to explore ethical and legal questions surrounding such selection procedures.

Ethical concerns aside, I have serious worries about much of the scientific research that has been done on sexual orientation. In particular, I doubt that successful techniques for selecting the sexual orientation of children, which I call *orientation-selection* procedures, will be developed. Whether or not this suspicion is right, there are interesting and important ethical questions surrounding such procedures because people might make use of them even if they did not work. This is partly because it will be hard for people who are considering making use of orientation-selection procedures to determine whether such procedures work. First, since many children turn out to be heterosexual even without the use of such procedures, many parents who attempt orientation selection will believe that the procedure has worked on their child even though, because their child would have been heterosexual in any event, the procedure has done nothing. Second, many people take a long time to come to grips with their sexual orientation. Parents who made use of such a procedure might think that it had been successful, but only because their child had not yet figured out her sexual orientation. Third, because many lesbians, gay men and bisexuals hide their sexual orientation once they figure it out, many parents will think that their attempt at orientation selection has worked when in fact it has not. Fourth, if a lesbian, gay man or bisexual knows that his or her parents used an orientation-selection procedure to ensure that he or she would be a heterosexual, this would just increase the likelihood that the person would hide his or her sexual orientation from them. For these reasons, even if available orientation-selection procedures fail to work, such procedures are likely to *appear* to work. Given this, many people are still likely to avail themselves of these procedures. This shows that ethical questions about orientation-selection procedures remain even if they do not work.

There is an extensive philosophical literature concerning the morality of abortion and less extensive ones concerning ethical issues surrounding genetic engineering and techniques to select the sex of children. I do not attempt to deal with these issues in general, although I touch on them in what follows. Given the possibility of developing orientation-selection procedures that do not involve abortion, I can address the central questions of this paper without taking a stand on the morality of abortion in general. (I make this case in section III). With respect to genetic engineering, I will assume that it is morally acceptable for parents to try to control some genetic traits of their offspring. This assumption seems justified given the possibility of doing this without abortions or the direct altering of human genes. I discuss *sex*-selection procedures (that is, techniques to select the sex of children) primarily as an analogy for orientation selection.

I begin my discussion with a brief survey of scientific research on sexual orientation. I then consider arguments that say orientation selection is morally permissible and should be legal. Finally, I turn to arguments against orientation selection.

I Sexual Orientation and Science

We do not know how people develop sexual orientations. We do know that people have different sexual desires. Further, it seems that, at least in our culture, people divide into distinct groups depending on the sex (or gender[3]) of the people they are sexually attracted to (that is, heterosexual, homosexual, bisexual and, perhaps, asexual). Over the past one hundred years,[4] many scientists, doctors, psychologists and others (particularly in the United States and some Western European countries) have been interested in what causes people to develop sexual orientations – in particular they have been primarily concerned with what makes certain people homosexual. As part of this research, many have attempted to develop methods for detecting homosexuals and for making them into heterosexuals.[5] Partly as a result of the failure to change the sexual orientations of adults and teenagers, many people have come to believe that sexual orientation is determined at birth or by an early age.

Starting from this (and related) assumptions, several scientists have recently claimed to provide support for the view that sexual orientation is genetic, or at least biological. Among the most widely-touted studies are Simon LeVay's brain study[6] (he claims to have identified a specific region of the hypothalamus that, in males, varies in size depending on a person's sexual orientation), Dean Hamer and associates' gene study[7] (they claim to have identified a particular region of the X-chromosome that is associated with some forms of male homosexuality) and Michael Bailey and Richard Pillard's twin study[8] (they claim to have established a genetic determinant for sexual orientation on the basis of the relatively high frequency of homosexuality among the identical twins of homosexuals compared to its frequency among fraternal twins and siblings – biological and adopted – of homosexuals). I think there are various problems with all of these studies, some that relate to specific features of particular studies, others that involve conceptual problems these studies have in common.[9]

If sexual orientation is genetic, then the use of reproductive technologies to select for children of certain sexual orientations would be a serious possibility. Whether or not this is in fact possible is not, as argued above, required for the main questions of this paper to be live ones. What is required is that many people *believe* that homosexuality is genetic and that the particular genetic configuration or set of configurations that they believe to be responsible for homosexuality is identifiable (or at least is claimed to be) in fetuses. Given current trends in social attitudes on these questions[10] and trends in scientific research, it seems likely that many people will believe that some set of genes determines sexual orientation and that scientists will be able to determine whether a fetus has the genes that are believed to be responsible for sexual orientation. This is perfectly compatible with it being the case that the scientific studies of sexual orientation are deeply flawed in any number of ways. Gay men and lesbians have been and continue to be subject to various forms of medical and psychological interventions for which no evidence exists.[11] For example, gay men were injected with testosterone with the aim of turning them into heterosexuals despite studies showing no correlation between sexual orientation and testosterone levels.[12] The general point is that even if hesitations about the scientific research are well-founded and all current scientific studies are based on unsupported ontological assumptions, there is every reason to believe that people will believe such studies anyway. The result could well be the widespread selection against fetuses thought to be carrying genes for homosexuality (or bisexuality).

II Arguments in Favor of Orientation Selection

There are various reasons for thinking that it is morally acceptable to use orientation-selection procedures and that such procedures should be legal. People who think that homosexuality is unnatural,[13] abnormal[14] or an illness are especially likely to look favorably on orientation-selection procedures.[15] One does not, however, have to accept any of these views in order to think that orientation-selection procedures are morally permissible and/or should be legal. Further, having a negative view of homosexuality does not entail a positive view of orientation-selection procedures (although, all else being equal, people who think that homosexuality is a serious disease are likely to think that it is acceptable to use orientation-selection procedures to avoid having lesbian or gay offspring). A particular view of homosexuality is neither a necessary nor a sufficient condition for thinking that orientation-selection procedures are moral and should be legal.

The most general arguments in favor of the morality and legality of screening and selecting for a fetus of a particular sexual orientation have to do with reproductive liberty and the right of a woman to have control over her body and its procreative capacities; simply put, a woman should be able to decide whether or not to have children. The United States Supreme Court, in *Roe v. Wade*, argued that the government cannot prevent a woman from having an abortion during the first two trimesters of her pregnancy regardless of the reason she has for wanting to terminate her pregnancy.[16] Most people who favor a woman's right to choose whether or not to get pregnant, and whether or not to terminate her pregnancy, would agree that the state should not be involved in evaluating the reasons a woman has for terminating a pregnancy. If one accepts that women have a legal right to choose whether or not to terminate a pregnancy, then it seems to follow that it should be legal to terminate a pregnancy because of the sexual orientation of the fetus. Similarly, given that it is legal for a woman to use contraceptive devices, then it should be legal, for example, to use filtering devices to select for sperm with genes that code for a particular sexual orientation.[17] The legal permissibility of orientation selection seems to follow directly from the view that women have reproductive liberty.

That it should be legal to make use of orientation-selection procedures does not entail that one should make use of them. There are things that are legal that one should not do. For example, while it might be legal for a woman to terminate a first-trimester pregnancy because she believes that being pregnant will interfere with a planned trip to the beach, this might be a poor reason to terminate a pregnancy. Arguing that orientation-selection abortion is morally acceptable requires more than the argument that it should be legal for women to make use of such a procedure.

One argument for the moral acceptability of orientation-selection procedures stems from the view that reproductive liberty entails the right to insure that one's offspring will have desirable traits. Many people think that it is morally permissible for a woman to choose to terminate a pregnancy if the fetus has a serious genetic disorder because they think it is reasonable to want a healthy baby. Many of those who do not think this is permissible will probably allow that pre-implantation procedures (procedures that take place before a fertilized egg is implanted in the womb) to prevent the birth of such a baby are permissible. Behind this is the view that parents can engage in 'quality control'[18] with respect to their (potential) offspring. If it is permissible to engage in some selection procedures for the purpose of ensuring that an offspring will have certain desirable traits, then it seems to follow that it is morally acceptable to engage in some selection procedures for the purpose of insuring that an offspring has any desirable traits. This view is particularly plausible if you focus on *pre*-implantation selection procedures.

Even those who think that all or most abortions are immoral and/or should be illegal will allow that women have *some* reproductive liberty; they just think that the rights entailed by reproductive liberty are trumped by the rights of the fetus. The relevant question is whether the arguments against orientation-selection abortion are strong enough to trump reproductive liberty with respect to the 'quality control' of one's offspring. With respect to pre-implantation orientation-selection procedures, the question is whether anything about these procedures suggests women's reproductive liberties ought to be trumped. To answer these questions,

I turn now to arguments against orientation selection; first, I look at arguments against orientation-selection abortion specifically and then I look at arguments against orientation-selection procedures in general.

III Arguments against Orientation-Selection Abortion

Perhaps the most obvious arguments against orientation selection focus on orientation-selection abortion and appeal to the wrongness of abortion, either in general or in cases where the decision to abort is based on 'trivial' reasons. Arguments against orientation-selection abortion that turn on the supposed wrongness of abortion in general focus on the wrong to the fetus, namely, wrongfully killing it. These arguments do not typically count against orientation selection in general; in particular, they would not count against pre-implantation selection procedures.[19]

Few foes of abortion are, however, unequivocally opposed to the practice; many allow for abortions in the case of rape, incest, serious health risks to the mother, or severe fetal defects. Given that they are willing to allow some abortions, such foes of abortion need to distinguish between permissible and impermissible reasons for abortions. This seems to be the rationale behind the portion of a 1989 amendment to the Pennsylvania abortion law prohibiting abortion for the purpose of selecting the sex of a child that says 'no abortion which is sought solely because of the sex of the unborn child shall be deemed a necessary abortion'.[20] The Pennsylvania law thus prohibits physicians from performing sex-selection abortions (since such abortions are 'unnecessary' and the law allows physicians to perform only those abortions that are 'necessary'). The general idea behind positions that – like the one embodied in Pennsylvania law – allow for some abortions but not others is to distinguish trivial from non-trivial reasons for an abortion. Abortion for purposes such as saving a mother's life, preventing the birth of a child with a serious congenital disease, or terminating a pregnancy that is the result of rape would count as non-trivial reasons for terminating a pregnancy, while abortion to avoid disrupting one's vacation plans, to select for a child of a particular sex or, perhaps, to select for a child of a particular sexual orientation count as trivial.

Even accepting this distinction, it is difficult to determine, for example, whether an abortion is done for trivial and non-trivial reasons. Consider sex-selection abortion in a very sexist culture where some women will almost certainly face a life of extreme poverty if they give birth to daughters – poverty so extreme that these daughters and their mothers are likely to teeter on the edge of malnutrition for many years – while in contrast, if they give birth to sons, the sons' prospects, in both the short and long term, would almost surely be much brighter.[21] Under such conditions, it is not at all clear that a woman's reasons for aborting a female fetus would be trivial. A daughter born in this situation might suffer as much as a child born with a serious genetic disorder. If such a disorder provides grounds for an abortion, why is the sex of a fetus not also grounds for an abortion, at least given certain circumstances? Similarly, given the amount of suffering that might be involved in being a lesbian or gay man in a very homophobic society, might the future sexual orientation of a fetus also be grounds for an abortion? The point is that distinguishing between trivial and non-trivial reasons for orientation-selection abortion seems quite difficult.

Moving from a discussion of orientation-selection abortion to orientation selection in general, the arguments against orientation-selection procedures that relate to abortion become impotent. With orientation-selection abortion, there is the possibility that the rights of the fetus might trump the mother's reproductive liberty; in the case of pre-implantation orientation selection, there is no fetus and hence no rights that might conflict with those of the mother. A woman who uses a diaphragm-like filter to screen out sperm carrying genes for a serious genetic disorder does not seem to be violating any plausible general moral principle; a woman who uses a diaphragm-like filter to screen out sperm carrying genes that cause a certain sexual orientation does not seem to be doing anything morally different.

Someone who thinks all abortions are immoral and that all abortions should be illegal can allow that women have some reproductive liberty and that pre-implantation orientation-selection procedures may be permissible and, perhaps, should be legal. For such a person, the status of such procedures should turn on an evaluation of these procedures, not on the morality of abortion. Someone who thinks that some instances of abortion are moral and that some instances of abortion should be legal will also need to look at orientation-selection abortion in particular to determine whether it is among the permissible sorts of abortion. *Whatever one's views on abortion*, the legitimacy of orientation-selection procedures requires an examination of these procedures in particular. It is to such an examination that I now turn.

IV General Arguments against Orientation Selection

I begin my discussion of arguments against orientation selection in general by examining the source, strength and character of the preference for heterosexual versus non-heterosexual offspring as it is manifested in our culture and many others like it. With this as background, I discuss the likely impact of the availability of orientation-selection procedures in a society with a strong preference for heterosexual children.

Many people have strong feelings against lesbians, gay men and bisexuals. Take the United States of America for example: a recent poll found that fifty-five percent of American adults think that homosexual sexual relations between consenting adults are *always* morally wrong.[22] The same poll found that only one-third of American adults think that homosexuality is an acceptable lifestyle.[23] A society's attitude towards lesbians, gay men, and bisexuals can be further assessed by looking at its laws: in the United States, almost half of the states have laws that criminalize most forms of same-sex sexual activity;[24] it is legal in forty-two states to discriminate, for example, in terms of employment and housing against a person in virtue of his or her sexual orientation; and no state provides any sort of legal recognition of lesbian and gay relationships that comes close to the sort of recognition it provides heterosexual relationships.[25] Further, violence against lesbians, gay men and bisexuals is disturbingly common in the United States; more bias-related hate crimes are committed against people because of their sexual orientation than for any other reason.[26] Additionally, lesbian and gay teenagers are three times more likely to attempt to commit suicide than their heterosexual counterparts.[27] The evidence is overwhelming that we live in a society that has a deep hatred of lesbians and gay men, a society that discriminates against and oppresses them. The same is true in most cultures in the world (and the situation in many 'non-industrial' countries is even worse than it is the United States), although in a few countries, both the legal and the social situations for lesbians, gay men and bisexuals are better.[28]

Most people, even those who are sympathetic to the conditions of lesbians and gay men, have strong preferences for heterosexual children. According to a recent poll, *eighty* percent of adult Americans said that they would be 'upset' or 'very upset' if their college-aged child said he or she was gay or lesbian.[29] This suggests that parents would go to great lengths to prevent their children from becoming lesbian, gay or bisexual. Even many supportive parents of lesbians, gay men and bisexuals admit that they would have tried to insure that their children would be heterosexual. For example, Louise Coburn, program director of Parents and Friends of Lesbians and Gays, a group active in supporting parents of lesbians, gay men and bisexuals as well as working for lesbian and gay rights, suggested that, given the homophobia and heterosexism of our society, no one would want their kid to be gay. She said, 'No parent would choose to have a child born with any factor that would make life difficult for him or her.'[30] Judge Richard Posner, in a book sympathetic to some claims relating to lesbian and gay rights, confidently asserts that if there was a procedure that would ensure that a child would not be a homosexual, '. . . you can be sure that the child's parents would administer it to him, believing, probably correctly, that he would be better off'.[31] The point is that most heterosexuals (and some others) have a strong preference for having heterosexual children. One might wonder whether this preference is strong enough to bring people to make use of orientation-selection procedures. To help settle this question, consider the analogy with sex selection.

Most prospective parents throughout the world have preferences with respect to the sex of their future children, and, of these, most have preferences for sons over daughters. This preference for sons can take various forms, including preferring to have one's firstborn child be a son, preferring to have more sons than daughters, preferring to have only sons, or preferring to have only one child and for that child to be a boy. Son preference is stronger in some cultures than others (in particular, son preference is especially strong in India, China, and most nations of Africa and Latin America). Even in countries (like the United States) where the most common preference is for having two children, one of each sex, there is still a preference for sons that appears in the form of a preference for having a son first.[32]

Given that most people's preference for having a heterosexual child is stronger than their preference for having a son, and that some women are sometimes willing to have an abortion to avoid having a daughter, it seems that some would be willing to have an abortion to avoid having a non-heterosexual child. If pre-implantation orientation selection-procedures were available, it seems that even more people would opt for such a procedure to ensure that they would have heterosexual children. Further evidence for this claim is that parents of non-heterosexual children or children who they fear are likely to develop into homosexuals (in many cases because their children display 'gender-atypical' behavior, e.g., because they are 'sissies' or 'tom boys') frequently seek 'professional' help to insure that their children will eventually become heterosexuals.[33] The availability of orientation-selection procedures would, then, lead many people to take advantage of such procedures. Even assuming that some lesbians and gay men (by making use of artificial insemination techniques, surrogate mothers, group parenting arrangements, or some as yet undeveloped reproductive technologies) would decide to genetically reproduce and to make use of orientation-selection procedures to have gay or lesbian children,[34] it seems very likely that most people who decide to have children and to make use of orientation-selection procedures will choose to have heterosexual children. The crucial issue is not, however, the ethical significance of a decrease in the number of lesbians, gay men and bisexuals,[35] but rather the general impact of the availability and use of orientation-selection procedures in various societies.

Consider why there is a strong preference for heterosexual children versus homosexual and bisexual ones. Perhaps the most charitable explanation for the preference for heterosexual children is that parents, while not themselves against homosexuality, do not want their children to experience the intolerance, discrimination and violence faced by lesbians and gay men. One problem with this charitable interpretation is that, in many cases, it does not ring true. A significant number of people find homosexuality immoral, unnatural, and/or disgusting. These people are likely to make use of orientation-selection procedures (if they are available) and to do so because they dislike homosexuality, not simply to protect their children from social disapprobation. The claim that a parent is simply trying to protect a child from the wrath of society's prejudice often is a rationalization for homophobia and heterosexism; it is similar to a parent who reacts to a son or daughter who is dating (or marrying) a person of a different race by saying 'What will the neighbors think?' and 'Just imagine how much trouble this will cause you (and your children)'. The relevant point is that behind many of the preferences for heterosexual children is a negative attitude towards homosexuality. An ethical assessment of orientation selection needs to take this into consideration.

Even if parents desire heterosexual children because they do not want their children to face the manifestations of homophobia and heterosexism, what matters are the *effects* of making use of orientation-selection procedures. Whether or not orientation-selection procedures work, their availability, the acceptability of their use and the knowledge that they are used will contribute to attitudes (of both heterosexuals and non-heterosexuals alike) towards lesbians, gay men and bisexuals. The emergence of orientation-selection procedures in cultures with negative attitudes towards homosexuals will reinforce the preference for heterosexual children over homosexual ones and, further, is likely to encourage the view that homosexuals and bisexuals are diseased, not worthy of living, and the like. Until quite recently, the received view was that homosexuality is a disease. Although many people – even some doctors and psychiatrists – still see homosexuality as a mental illness, there has been a shift away from such a view (one indication of this shift was the American Psychiatric Association's 1973 decision to declassify homosexuality as a mental disorder).[36] The effects of this move away from seeing homosexuality as a disease have been significant – some of the stigma associated with homosexuality has lifted and more lesbians and gay men have become comfortable with their sexual orientation and become more open about it. The availability and use of orientation-selection procedures would no doubt tip the scales of public and professional opinion back towards seeing homosexuality as a physical disorder by indicating that screening for homosexuality is a reasonable and sanctioned medical procedure. Further, the availability and use of orientation-selection procedures would increase the pressure to hide one's homosexuality (which is part of what is called 'compulsory heterosexuality'[37]) and decrease the collective power of lesbians and gay men. By strengthening the disease view of homosexuality and increasing pressure to keep one's homosexuality secret, the use of orientation-selection procedures to select against non-heterosexuals would engender and perpetuate (1) attitudes that lesbians and gay men are undesirable and not valuable, (2) policies that discriminate against lesbians and gay men, (3) violence against lesbians and gay men, and (4) the very conditions that give rise to the preference for heterosexuals rather than non-heterosexuals.[38] These are serious effects that demand serious ethical consideration.

As an analogy, consider the impact of the availability of sex-selection procedures in India, where the conditions of women, particularly in certain regions, are quite poor.[39] The economic status of women compared to men is low and, in general, their job opportunities are severely limited. In many Indian families, the birth of a daughter is sometimes mourned, while the birth of a son is usually celebrated. Women receive worse health care, are less nourished, and have a lower life expectancy than men, and the death rate for female infants is substantially higher than for male infants. Since sex-selection procedures have become available in India, they have been widely used, and the sex ratio has decreased.[40] Some women in India admit that they might prefer to have a daughter if the conditions for women in their society were different, but, given the abuse and oppression that women experience, they prefer to have sons.

Several commentators have observed that the availability and use of sex-selection procedures, especially in places like India, is likely to increase sexism and lead to a worsening of the conditions of women.[41] Dorothy Wertz and John Fletcher argue that sex selection 'lowers the status of women in general and . . . perpetuates the situation that gave rise to it'.[42] They also note that 'many Indian feminists are aware of this and have lobbied for the new laws against sex selection'.[43] An overwhelming majority of actual cases of sex selection in India involve selection against females. This practice is based on seeing women as having much less value than men. The availability and use of sex-selection techniques both legitimizes and strengthens this profound sexism and also implicitly endorses associated gender stereotypes. More generally, given this context, sex selection is in tension with the principle of equality. Although it is difficult to establish with any precision the causes of changes in the conditions of women in India, the widespread use of such practices seems to contribute to both negative attitudes towards women and to the perpetuation of their poor conditions.

The availability of orientation-selection procedures will likely have a similar impact on the condition of lesbians, gay men and bisexuals. This is not to say that lesbians and gay men are oppressed in the same way that women are (in India or in general): although the oppression of lesbians, gay men and bisexuals in this society is *connected* to the oppression of women, the two forms of oppression are still quite different.[44] The availability of orientation-selection procedures in a society that is both overwhelmingly anti-gay and that has a strong preference for heterosexual versus non-heterosexual children poses a serious threat to lesbians, gay men and bisexuals. The stronger the oppression of lesbians and gay men, the greater the moral pressure to regulate orientation-selection procedures.[45] Given this, what should be said and done legally, morally, and otherwise about such selection procedures? I turn to these questions in the next section.

V Should Orientation-Selection Procedures Be Prohibited?

I noted above that concern for women's reproductive liberty counts against restrictions on orientation selection. In the previous section, I discussed the negative impact that orientation-selection procedures would likely have on lesbians, gay men and bisexuals given existing attitudes towards them. Given such societal conditions, there is a tension between protecting lesbians, gay men and bisexuals, on the one hand, and protecting women's reproductive liberty, on the other.[46] If the conditions of lesbians and gay men relative to heterosexuals in a society are poor and if the preference for heterosexuals is quite strong, I think that legal recourse is necessary to protect lesbians, gay men and bisexuals, although women's reproductive liberty should be respected as much as possible.

It is useful to contrast two laws that relate to the practice of *sex*-selection abortion: the portion of the Pennsylvania abortion law that prohibits abortions based solely on the sex of the fetus and the Regulation of Prenatal Diagnostic Techniques Act, a law passed in the Indian state of Maharashtra. The Maharashtra law, which was passed in the late 1980s in response to the widespread use of sex-selection procedures, bans prenatal tests to determine the sex of the fetus (although it allows for prenatal tests for genetic diseases). Although the law has many loopholes and there are various problems with its enforcement, it seems to have led to a decrease in the use of prenatal screening procedures to determine the sex of the fetus and a fostering of a negative attitude towards such procedures.[47] The Maharashtra law, unlike the Pennsylvania law, does not regulate abortions or attempt to assess the reasons a woman has for terminating a pregnancy. Given the complexity of a woman's decision to terminate a pregnancy,[48] it would be difficult to determine whether a particular decision involves a preference for a child of a particular sex. In fact, the Pennsylvania law, which prohibits abortions performed 'solely' based on the sex of the fetus, may fail to prohibit any abortions since no abortions are truly performed *solely* because of the sex of the fetus (such a decision is usually so complex that other factors are sure to play a role).

Besides being easier to enforce, one might claim that the Maharashtra law does not directly interfere with a woman's reproductive liberty in the way that the Pennsylvania law does. This difference may be only apparent. Some have argued that a woman's reproductive liberty includes access to all information relevant to whether or not she will want to continue her pregnancy;[49] if a woman is prohibited from gaining access to information concerning the sex of a fetus, her reproductive liberty is thereby curtailed. Even if this is the case, limiting access to information about the sex of a fetus, as in the Maharashtra law, is preferable to banning all prenatal tests or prohibiting abortions. Under a Maharashtra-like law, a woman may decide whether to terminate a pregnancy, but she is not allowed to know the sex of her fetus, and hence, cannot include this information as part of her decision-making process. This may be a restriction on reproductive liberty, but it is a relatively weak restriction. Perhaps, then, the best way to resolve the tension between women's reproductive liberty and the conditions of lesbians, gay men and bisexuals is to restrict access to genetic information concerning the future sexual orientation of the fetus.

One might point out that, short of legal intervention, there are things the state can do (if it is so inclined) to attempt to block the potential effects of the availability of orientation-selection procedures. It can attempt to educate people, especially potential parents, about sexuality, homophobia, and the potential impact of orientation-selection procedures. Doctors and genetic counselors are particularly well-placed to inform people of these facts.[50] Most importantly, the state could work in various ways to undercut the oppression of lesbians and gay men and, in general, to improve the conditions of lesbians, gay men and bisexuals in this society. This is not, however, a trivial or straightforward thing to do. The state can attempt to initiate social change, but deeply entrenched social attitudes typically can be changed only when the state wields its legal powers. The proposal to restrict access to information concerning the sexual orientation of a fetus does not even begin to go so far; it only attempts to provide certain limited protections for lesbians, gay men and bisexuals.

There is, however, a deeper problem for a Maharashtra-like law concerning orientation-selection procedures: such a law would not deal with pre-implantation selection procedures that could have the same effects as post-implantation procedures. It is, for example, legal under the Maharashtra law for a woman who wants to have a son to be artificially inseminated with sperm that has been processed to eliminate Y-chromosomes. If this technique were accurate and widely available, it could have results similar to those that the widespread use of sex-selection abortion has on women in India. The same sort of point holds with respect to orientation selection: if pre-implantation orientation-selection procedures become available, there would be moral pressure to institute laws that prohibit the use of such procedures. Such laws, however, would involve even greater restrictions on women's reproductive liberty than laws that simply restrict access to information.

A serious tension between reproductive liberty and protecting lesbians, gay men and bisexuals develops when pre-implantation selection procedures are considered. The availability of pre-implantation orientation-selection procedures would pose an even more dramatic threat to lesbians, gay men and bisexuals than post-implantation procedures. Protecting against such a threat, however, involves especially strong restrictions on a woman's reproductive liberty since such restrictions involve saying, for example, that a woman cannot use a diaphragm that keeps out sperm containing genes thought to code for homosexuality. Although I will not attempt to resolve the tension that would result from the development of such pre-implantation procedures, I do want to ask whether there is anything that might be done to prevent the realization of a conflict between protecting reproductive liberty and protecting lesbians, gay men and bisexuals. By discouraging or prohibiting the development of technologies that would enable genetic screening to determine sexual orientation, it may be possible to prevent the situation from getting to the point where laws that restrict reproductive liberty are needed. Such a prohibition would restrict certain sorts of technological and scientific research. This sort of restriction might be tantamount to prohibiting research to develop a recreational drug or to develop a gun that would elude metal detectors: the restriction would be justified because it would prevent especially negative effects. The problem is that the technology for orientation selection would probably be an unintended result of research into the origins of sexual orientation.

Some commentators have argued that such research is ethically problematic independent of whether it would produce tests that enable genetic screening for sexual orientation.[51] It is certainly true that, historically, the scientific study of sexual orientation has been bad news for lesbians, gay men and bisexuals.[52] While agreeing with this, some argue that it is possible to do such research without making problematic assumptions about homosexuality or perpetuating the oppression of lesbians and gay men.[53] Even if this is possible, there remains the further question of whether such research should be done. I would argue that the possible impact of such research, in particular, whether such research is likely to produce a genetic screening test that would make orientation-selection procedures possible, is relevant to deciding whether such research ought to be done. In particular, if research on the origins of sexual orientation is likely to lead to the availability of orientation-selection techniques, then this counts against doing such research. My claim here is a relatively weak one: the ethical implications of scientific research are relevant to deciding whether such research ought to be done.

So far I have argued that the likely impact of the availability of orientation-selection procedures justifies laws concerning genetic technologies relating to sexual orientation. Access to information concerning sexual orientation gained from pre-natal screening should be restricted and certain sorts of screening procedures might be prohibited. If pre-implantation orientation-selection procedures are developed, more dramatic legal measures may be needed. To prevent this situation from arising, the development of various screening and selection technologies should be discouraged, perhaps even prohibited.

VI Remaining Issues

Given the preceding discussion, it follows that individuals have the responsibility to consider the impact of using orientation-selection procedures. Insofar as a person is aware of the impact of making use of such a procedure, if she decides to make use of one, she is morally responsible for the impact of doing so. By using such a procedure to ensure that a child is heterosexual, a person perpetuates the conditions of lesbians, gay men and bisexuals in this society. This implies that making use of orientation-selection procedures is morally problematic; all else being equal, given the impact of such procedures, a person ought not to make use of them. Further, a person is also responsible for examining the source of her own preferences with respect to the sexual orientation of her children and to see if the reasons behind her preferences are justified. There is, in addition, cultural inertia: in societies where non-heterosexuals are oppressed, the structure of society maintains these conditions and thereby ensures the popularity of orientation-selection procedures.[54] In such a society, any individual who acts to preserve conditions that oppress lesbians, gay men and bisexuals when it is possible to do otherwise bears moral responsibility for his or her actions.[55]

One might wonder whether my overall argument proves too much. The worry is that an argument isomorphic to my argument concerning the legality and morality of orientation-selection procedures might also apply to the legality and morality of procedures to select against fetuses with serious genetic disorders. Such an argument would focus on the negative impact such selection practices would have on people who have these conditions. This is supposed to show that my argument proves too much because techniques to select against fetuses with these conditions are in fact morally and legally permissible. I do not have the space here to articulate fully a response to this worry, but I can sketch one. There is a disanalogy between the argument I have made against the permissibility of orientation-selection procedures and the proposed argument against the permissibility of using genetic technology to prevent the birth of babies with serious disorders. Such disorders may dramatically decrease life expectancy, cause great suffering, and intrinsically undermine a person's quality of life; further, a person with such a condition would say that she wishes that she did not have this condition. Homosexuality and bisexuality are not like this; in particular, the primary negative features of being a lesbian, gay man or bisexual have to do with societal attitudes towards these sexual orientations, not with intrinsic features of them. This is not to deny that there may be tricky questions about using selection procedures to prevent less serious genetic disorders (for example, epilepsy, asthma, and color-blindness); however, admitting this in no way undermines the fact that the social conditions of lesbians, gay men and bisexuals are oppressive and warrant ethical consideration.

Finally, it is worth pointing out that, although my argument is not a straightforward utilitarian argument – I do not, for example, argue that the amount of suffering that would be caused by the availability of orientation-selection procedures outweighs the amount of happiness that would be experienced by parents who make use of such procedures (assuming they work) and by their heterosexual children who would be less vulnerable to homophobia – my argument is otherwise neutral with respect to the moral theory that underlies it, namely my argument is compatible with either consequentialism or non-consequentialism. Consequentialists can read my talk about the impact of orientation-selection procedures in terms of the consequences of their use and availability. Non-consequentialists can read me as arguing that the use and availability of orientation-selection procedures, under current societal conditions, would entail violating moral principles; for example, the dignity and respect due to all persons would be denied to lesbians, gay men and bisexuals if such procedures were available and used.[56] The fact that my argument does not depend on either consequentialism or non-consequentialism does not, however, mean that I have no opinion on these two positions. Rather, I remain neutral on these issues because taking and defending a stand on them is beyond the scope of this article.

VII Conclusion

Some people have argued that the use of selection procedures to select for or against a particular genetic trait leads us down a slippery slope – once any sort of genetic engineering becomes common, we are irreversibly heading towards the day when parents choose children the way a consumer decides what kind of car to buy. In this paper, I have intentionally avoided this sort of argument. My concern has been whether there are special considerations that should be brought to bear on using reproductive technologies to selectively give birth to children on the basis of their sexual orientation. I have not argued that there is something *intrinsically* special about sexual orientation which entails that reproductive technologies should not be used to control it. Instead, I have argued that conditions of lesbians, gay men and bisexuals today are such that particular attention needs to be paid to attempts to screen for children on the basis of their sexual sexual orientation. Even if such attempts are not likely to work, the mere availability of procedures that enable parents to select their children's sexual orientation is likely to perpetuate unjust conditions for lesbians, gay men and bisexuals in our society. Determining precisely how to prevent these procedures from being widely used is a difficult task particularly because it is important to protect women's reproductive liberties. Although I have sketched a proposal that strikes a balance between protecting lesbians, gay men and bisexuals without infringing on women's reproductive liberties, a full discussion of the relevant public policy questions is a matter for more detailed examination than I can provide here. My conclusion is that the negative impact of the availability of orientation-selection procedures on lesbians, gay men and bisexuals carries a significant ethical and legal weight with respect to determining whether such procedures should be legally and morally permissible.

NOTES

1 See, for example, Chandler Burr, 'Why Conservatives Should Embrace the Gay Gene', *The Weekly Standard* (December 16, 1996), 22–26.
2 See Gary David Comstock, *Violence Against Lesbians and Gay Men* (New York: Columbia University Press, 1991); G. Herek and K. T. Berrill, eds., *Hate Crimes: Confronting Violence Against Lesbians and Gay Men* (Newbury Park, CA: Sage, 1992).
3 I here use gender in contrast to (biological) sex. A person's sex (male or female) is determined by his or her chromosomes, while a person's gender (man or woman) is determined by whether he or she fits stereotypes associated with members of a particular sex. A male who is treated by members of his society as a female typically is treated would, in terms of gender, be a woman. Gender, so defined, is socially constructed. (I am, for purposes of simplicity, side-stepping debates about whether homosexuals constitute a third gender or an 'intersex' as well as controversial questions about transexuality and hermaphroditism.)
4 Some historians of sexuality have argued that the concept of homosexuality (as well as sexual orientation more generally) is just over one hundred years old. People have, of course, been having sex with people of the same sex for all of recorded history, but, in the nineteenth century, the idea developed that people are constituted in such a way that the sex of the people they are attracted to is a distinct and important feature of their character. If this view is right, then no one could have been interested in why some people are homosexuals and others are heterosexuals much more than one hundred years ago. See Michel Foucault, *The History of Sexuality*, volume 1, Robert Hurley, trans. (New York: Pantheon, 1978); and David Halperin, *One Hundred Years of Homosexuality and Other*

Essays on Greek Love (New York: Routledge, 1990). For a collection of theoretical essays on this topic, see Edward Stein, ed., *Forms of Desire: Sexual Orientation and the Social Constructionist Controversy* (New York: Routledge, 1992).

5 See Jonathan Katz, *Gay American History* (New York: Thomas Crowell, 1976), part II, 'Treatment: 1884–1974', 197–316; Ronald Bayer, *Homosexuality and American Psychiatry*, second edition (Princeton: Princeton University Press, 1987); Fred Suppe, 'Curing Homosexuality', in *Philosophy and Sex*, revised edition, Robert Baker and Frederick Elliston, eds. (Buffalo: Prometheus Books, 1984), 394–420; Timothy Murphy, 'Redirecting Sexual Orientation: Techniques and Justifications', *Journal of Sex Research* 29 (1992), 501–23; and Phyllis Burke, *Gender Shock: Exploding the Myths of Male and Female* (New York: Anchor Books, 1996).

6 Simon LeVay, 'A Difference in the Hypothalamic Structure Between Heterosexual and Homosexual Men', *Science* 253 (1991), 1034–7.

7 Dean Hamer, Stella Hu, Victoria Magnuson, Nan Hu, and Angela Pattatucci, 'A Linkage Between DNA Markers on the X Chromosome and Male Sexual Orientation', *Science* 261 (1993), 321–7.

8 J. Michael Bailey and Richard Pillard, 'A Genetic Study of Male Sexual Orientation', *Archives of General Psychiatry* 48 (1991), 1089–96.

9 William Byne, 'The Biological Evidence Challenged', *Scientific American* 270 (May 1994), 50–5; Anne Fausto-Sterling, *Myths of Gender: Biological Theories of Women and Men*, second edition (New York: Basic Books, 1992); William Byne and Bruce Parsons, 'Sexual Orientation: The Biological Theories Reappraised', *Archives of General Psychiatry* 50 (1993), 228–39; Frederick Suppe, 'Explaining Homosexuality: Philosophical Issues, and Who Cares Anyhow?' *Journal of Homosexuality* 27 (1994), 223–68; Janet Halley, 'Sexual Orientation and the Politics of Biology: A Critique of the New Argument from Immutability', *Stanford Law Review* 46 (1994), 503–68; Edward Stein, 'The Relevance of Scientific Research Concerning Sexual Orientation to Lesbian and Gay Rights', *Journal of Homosexuality* 27 (1994), 269–308; the essays in John DcCecco and Michael Shively, eds., *Sex, Cells, and Same-Sex Desire: The Biology of Sexual Preference*, (New York: Haworth, 1995); and Edward Stein, *Sexual Desires: Science, Theory and Ethics* (New York: Oxford University Press, forthcoming).

10 A significant percentage of people think that sexual orientation is genetic – or, at least, not chosen – and the number of people who think this is increasing. A Gallup poll released on April 28, 1993 (George Gallup, Jr., *The Gallup Poll* [Wilmington, DE: Scholarly Resources, 1993], 83–9) found that thirty-one percent of people surveyed said that 'people are born homosexual'. The other choices given were 'homosexuality develops' (14%), 'people prefer homosexuality' (25%), and other (12%). According to Gallup, the percentage of people who think people are born with homosexuality has doubled from 1983 to 1993. A CBS News / *New York Times* poll, February 9–11, 1993, found that forty-three percent of those surveyed say that homosexuals cannot change their sexual orientation while forty-four percent say people choose to be homosexuals.

11 See the works cited in note 5.

12 See, for example, Heino Meyer-Bahlburg, 'Psychoendocrine Research on Sexual Orientation: Current Status and Future Options', *Progress in Brain Research* 71 (1984), 375–97.

13 For useful critiques of the idea that homosexuality is 'unnatural', see Richard Mohr, *Gays/Justice* (New York: Columbia University Press, 1990), 34–8; and Michael Ruse, *Homosexuality: A Philosophical Inquiry* (New York: Basil Blackwell, 1988), 188–92. Both Mohr and Ruse conclude that biology will not tell us what is 'natural' in any morally interesting sense. On the notion of natural with regard to sexual desire more

generally, see Thomas Nagel, 'Sexual Perversion', *Journal of Philosophy* 66 (1969), 5–17.

14 See Michael Levin, 'Why Homosexuality Is Abnormal', *Monist* 67 (1984), 251–83. For a critique, see Timothy Murphy, 'Homosexuality and Nature: Happiness and the Law at Stake', *Journal of Applied Philosophy* 4 (1987), 195–204.

15 Burr, 'Why Conservatives Should Embrace the Gay Gene.'

16 *Roe v. Wade*, 410 U.S. 113 (1973). According to *Roe*, the state may in various ways regulate second trimester abortions but does not say that a woman's motives for an abortion are relevant to the sorts of regulations the state may invoke.

17 Throughout this paper, I will refer to various pre-implantation methods for selecting traits in children. Two such techniques are (1) extract several eggs from a potential mother, fertilize each egg with sperm *in vitro*, examine the chromosomal composition of each fertilized egg, and implant in the woman's uterus a fertilized egg that will produce a child with the desired trait and (2) separate sperm that carry genetic material for a desirable trait from those that do not and then inseminate the egg only with sperm of the former sort. For discussion of these and other actual and hypothetical techniques, see John Robinson, *Children of Choice: Freedom and the New Reproductive Techniques* (Princeton: Princeton University Press, 1995), especially 154–6; Janice Raymond, *Women as Wombs: Reproductive Technologies and the Battle over Women's Freedom* (New York: Harper Collins, 1993), 21–2; and Gena Corea, *The Mother Machine: Reproductive Technologies from Artificial Insemination to Artificial Wombs* (New York: Harper and Row, 1985), 198–201.

18 The term is from Robinson, *Children of Choice*, 10; Robinson deploys this notion extensively in Chapters 7 and 8.

19 An exception to this is an argument that says abortion is wrong because it involves interfering with nature, 'playing god', or disturbing the natural process of reproduction, pregnancy and the like. This argument might count against pre-implantation selection procedures as well as post-implantation ones. This argument, however, proves too much, since it would also count against contraception, most forms of genetic screening, and so on. Arguments against the naturalness of various practices (including homosexuality, masturbation, 'recreational' sex, as well as contraception and abortion) run the risk of proving too much and, even worse, may be incoherent since the sort of notion of naturalness that is required cannot be consistently articulated.

20 *Pennsylvania Consolidated Statutes Annotated*, title 18, [189] 3204 (c), as amended November 17, 1989, P.L. 592, No. 68, [189] 2. When the constitutionality of the Pennsylvania abortion law was challenged in *Planned Parenthood v. Casey*, 112 S. Ct. 2791 (1992), the portion of the law dealing with sex-selection abortion was not challenged. The American Civil Liberties Union lawyer who argued the case before the Supreme Court said that this portion of the law was not challenged because they could not find a woman who would claim injury from it; see Charlotte Allen, 'Boys Only: Pennsylvania's Anti-Abortion Law', *New Republic* (March 9, 1992), 16–19.

21 This is not, unfortunately, such an unrealistic scenario considering the situation of women in certain economic and social classes in various countries, notably India. See Kusum, 'The Use of Pre-natal Diagnostic Techniques for Sex Selection: The Indian Scene', *Bioethics* 7:2/3 (1993), 149–65; Elisabeth Bumiller, *May You Be the Mother of a Hundred Sons: A Journey among the Women of India* (New York: Fawcett Columbine, 1990); and Barbara Miller, *The Endangered Sex: Neglect of Children in Rural North India* (Ithaca: Cornell University Press, 1981).

22 CBS News / *New York Times* poll, February 9–11, 1993. This result is similar to that found in more recent polls. To put this number in some cross-cultural and (recent) historical context, according to Ronald Inglchart, *Cultural Shift in Advanced Industrial*

Society (Princeton: Princeton University Press, 1990), 194, table 6–8, the United States, compared to fifteen other 'advanced industrial societies' polled in 1981–82, had the *second highest* percentage – sixty-five percent – of people aged eighteen and over who think that 'homosexuality can never be justified'.

23 CBS News / *New York Times* poll, February 9–11, 1993.

24 The Editors of the *Harvard Law Review, Sexual Orientation and the Law* (Cambridge: Harvard University Press, 1990). For a discussion of how U.S. states' laws deals with sexual behavior among women, see Ruthann Robeson, 'Crimes of Lesbian Sex', from *Lesbian (Out) Law: Survival Under the Rule of Law* (Ithaca: Firebrand, 1992), 47–59.

25 Hawaii, however, may well be the first state to recognize lesbian and gay marriages depending on how *Baehr v. Lewin* – the Hawaii Supreme Court's decision against prohibitions on same-sex marriage – influences actual legal practices there.

26 Comstock, *Violence Against Lesbians and Gay Men*; and Herek and Berrill, eds., *Hate Crimes*.

27 Paul Gibson, 'Gay and Lesbian Youth Suicide', in *U.S. Department of Health and Human Services Youth Suicide Report* (1989); the relevant portions are reprinted in William Rubenstein, ed., *Lesbians, Gay Men and the Law* (New York: New Press, 1993), 163–7.

28 For example, Inglchart, *Cultural Shift*, 194, tables 6–8 found that in the Netherlands, in 1982, only twenty-two percent of people aged eighteen and over think that 'homosexuality can never be justified' (compared to sixty-five percent in the U.S.). This number has probably dropped to somewhere between ten and fifteen percent judging from the attitudes of people aged eighteen to forty-four in 1982 and from the decrease over time of the number of Americans who have a negative attitude towards homosexuality (from sixty-five percent to fifty-five). The legal situation for lesbians, gay men, and bisexuals is also much better in the Netherlands than in the United States. See A.X. van Nacrssen, ed., *Gay Life in Dutch Society* (New York: Harrington Park Press, 1987). For a general international comparison, see International Lesbian and Gay Association, *Second IGLA Pink Book: A Global View of Lesbian and Gay Liberation and Oppression* (Utrecht: Interdisciplinary Gay and Lesbian Studies Department, Utrecht University, 1988).

29 CBS News / *New York Times* poll, February 9–11, 1993; fifty percent said they would be 'very upset' and an additional thirty percent said they would be 'upset.' It is worth noting that, in 1978, when conditions for lesbians and gay men in the United States were in many ways worse than they are now, about seventy-five percent of the lesbians and gay men surveyed said that they would not be upset or they would be only upset very little if a child of theirs were homosexual; see Alan Bell and Martin Weinberg, *Homosexualities: A Study of Diversity Among Men and Women* (New York: Simon and Schuster, 1978), 339.

30 As quoted in David Gelman, 'Born or Bred?' *Newsweek* (February 24, 1992), 46–53; reprinted in *Lesbians, Gay Men and the Law*, 15–20 (the quotation is on page 17 in the reprinted version).

31 Richard Posner, *Sex and Reason* (Cambridge: Harvard University Press, 1992), 308.

32 For discussion of preferences with respect to the sex of children, see Aliza Kolker and B. Meredith Burke, *Prenatal Testing: A Sociological Perspective* (Westport, CT: Bergson and Garvey, 1994), 142–50; Raymond, *Women as Wombs*, 21–5; Mary Anne Warren, *Gendercide: The Implications of Sex Research* (Totowa, NJ: Rowman and Allenheld, 1985), 12–19.

33 See Richard Green, *The 'Sissy Boy' Syndrome and the Development of Homosexuality* (New Haven: Yale University Press, 1987); and Phyllis Burke, *Gender Shock: Exploding the Myths of Male and Female* (New York: Anchor Books, 1996).

34 See William Eskridge and Edward Stein, 'Queer Cloning', in Martha Nussbaum and Cass Sunstein, *Clones and Clones: Facts and Fantasies about Human Cloning* (New York:

Norton, forthcoming 1998). See also Timothy Murphy, 'Reproductive Controls and Sexual Destiny', *Bioethics* 4:2 (1990), 121–42.

35 Some sociobiologists (as well as various other thinkers) have argued that having a certain percentage of lesbians and gay men provides a benefit for society. This might provide support for the view that a reduction in the number of lesbians and gay men would be harmful. For a sympathetic discussion of sociobiological accounts of homosexuality, see Ruse, *Homosexuality*, especially Chapter 6. Many non-biologists embrace this view; see, for example, Andrew Sullivan, *Virtually Normal: An Argument about Homosexuality* (New York: Knopf, 1995); and Lawrence Crocker, 'Meddling with the Sexual Orientation of Children', in Onora O'Neill and William Ruddick, eds., *Having Children: Philosophical Perspectives on Parenting* (Oxford: Oxford University Press, 1979), 145–54. I find such sociobiological stories implausible, even assuming that there is a genetic basis for sexual orientation. See Philip Kitcher, *Vaulting Ambition: Sociobiology and the Quest for Human Nature* (Cambridge: MIT Press, 1985); Douglas Futuyma and Stephen Risch, 'Sexual Orientation, Sociobiology and Evolution', *Journal of Homosexuality* 9 (1983–84), 157–68; and Paul Bloom and Edward Stein, 'Reasoning Why', *American Scholar* 60 (1990), 315–20.

36 For the history of this battle concerning the declassification of homosexuality as a mental disorder, see Bayer, *Homosexuality and American Psychiatry.*

37 Adrienne Rich, 'Compulsory Heterosexuality and Lesbian Existence', *Signs* 5 (1980), 631–60.

38 See Suppe, 'Curing Homosexuality', 404–14, for a detailed development of this line of argument in the context of attempts to 'cure' homosexuality. He argues that any such attempts that involve the labeling of homosexuality as a mental disorder or as an inferior condition increase prejudice and discrimination towards lesbians and gay men.

39 See, for example, Bumiller, *May You Be the Mother of a Hundred Sons*; and Miller, *The Endangered Sex*.

40 Kusum, 'The Use of Pre-natal Diagnostic Techniques for Sex Selection.'

41 Christine Overall, *Ethics and Human Reproduction: A Feminist Analysis* (Boston: Allen and Unwin, 1987); Helen Holmes, 'Sex Preselection: Eugenics for Everyone?' in James Humber and Robert Alemeder, eds., *Biomedical Ethics Review* (Clifton, NJ: Humana Press, 1985); Vibuti Patel, 'Sex Determination and Preselection Tests in India: Recent Techniques in Femicide', *Reproductive and Genetic Engineering* 2 (1989), 111–20; Dorothy Wertz and John Fletcher, 'Sex Selection Through Prenatal Diagnosis: A Feminist Critique', in Helen Holmes and Laura Purdy, eds., *Feminist Perspective in Medical Ethics* (Bloomington, IN: Indiana University Press, 1992), 240–53; Adrian Asch and Gail Geller, 'Feminism, Bioethics, and Genetics', in Susan Wolf, ed., *Feminism and Bioethics: Beyond Reproduction* (New York, Oxford, 1996), 318–50.

42 Wertz and Fletcher, 'Sex Selection Through Prenatal Diagnosis', 242.

43 Ibid.

44 See Cheshire Calhoun, 'Sexuality Injustice', *Notre Dame Journal of Law, Ethics and Public Policy* 9 (1995), 401–34; also see Calhoun, 'Separating Lesbian Theory from Feminist Theory', *Ethics* 104 (1994), 558–81. For related discussions, see Gayle Rubin, 'Thinking Sex', in *Pleasure and Danger*, Carole Vance, ed. (New York: Routledge, 1984), 267–319; and Eve Sedgwick, *Epistemology of the Closet* (Berkeley: University of California Press, 1990), especially 27–35.

45 Murphy, 'Reproductive Controls and Sexual Destiny', considers and rejects this line of thought. He believes that, though it is wrong to make use of orientation-selection procedures, 'it would be a greater wrong to usurp by law the choices of competent adults' (139). For reasons elaborated in section V, I argue that certain choices of compe-

tent adults may be curtailed when the strength of the oppression of lesbians and gay men is great.

46 Many feminist commentators on sex selection have recognized a parallel tension. See, for example, Warren, *Gendercide*; and Overall, *Ethics and Human Reproduction*, especially 34. I reach similar conclusions with respect to orientation selection that many feminist commentators (and legislators in some regions of India) do with respect to sex selection.

47 Patel, 'Sex Determination and Preselection Tests in India.'

48 Barbara Rothman, *The Tentative Pregnancy* (New York: Viking, 1986), 142–3, has convincingly argued that in a situation in which a woman is ambivalent about terminating a pregnancy, knowledge of fetal sex is bound to have some effect on her decision.

49 See, for example, Robinson, *Children of Choice*, 158 and passim.

50 For a discussion of current practices of genetic counselors with respect to sex-screening and sex-selection procedures, see Kolker and Burke, *Prenatal Testing*, 141–62. See also Rothman, *Tentative Pregnancy*, especially Chapter 5.

51 See, for example, Suppe, 'Explaining Homosexuality'; Sedgwick, *Epistemology of the Closet*, 43; and Gunter Schmidt, 'Allies and Persecutors: Science and Medicine in the Homosexuality Issue', *Journal of Homosexuality* 10 (1984), 127–40. For a discussion of these views, see Stein, 'Relevance of Scientific Research', 249–300; Udo Schüklenk, 'Is Research into the Cause(s) of Homosexuality Bad for Gay People?' *Christopher Street* 208 (1992), 13–15; Timothy Murphy, 'Abortion and the Ethics of Genetic Sexual Orientation Research', *Cambridge Quarterly of Healthcare Ethics* 4 (1995), 340–50; and Edward Stein, Udo Schüklenk and Jacinta Kerin, 'Scientific Research on Sexual Orientation', in Ruth Chadwick ed., *Encyclopedia of Applied Ethics* (San Diego: Academic Press, 1997).

52 See, for example, Katz, *Gay American History*, 197–316; and Siobhan Somerville, 'Scientific Racism and the Emergence of the Homosexual Body', *Journal of the History of Sexuality* 5 (1994), 243–66.

53 For example, Simon LeVay, *Queer Science: The Use and Abuse of Research on Homosexuality* (Cambridge: MIT Press, 1996).

54 Warren, *Gendercide*, 105, makes a similar point about sex-selection procedures. See Gail Weiss, 'Sex-Selective Abortion: A Relational Approach', *Hypatia* 10 (1995), 202–17, for further discussion.

55 For a discussion of moral responsibilities relating to sexual orientation, see Joyce Trebilcot, 'Taking Responsibility for Sexuality', in *Philosophy and Sex*, 421–30.

56 For arguments in support of lesbian and gay rights that focus on dignity and respect, see Mohr, *Gays/Justice*, especially 144–51 and 315–17; and Richard Mohr, *Gay Ideas* (Boston: Beacon Press, 1992), especially 94–7.

11

Yoshiya Nobuko: Out and Outspoken in Practice and Prose

Jennifer Robertson

"Many women have never heard of the Women's Patriotic Association (Aikokufujinkai), but there isn't a woman alive who hasn't heard of Yoshiya Nobuko."[1] Ikeda Hiroshi, a literary critic, made this declaration in the popular magazine *Hanashi* (Talk) in 1935, by which time Yoshiya (1896–1973) had emerged as one of the most prolific and well-known writers in Japan. She was also the best-paid writer. She earned three times more than the prime minister, although she still resented paying taxes, "especially since women do not have the right to vote."[2] The overwhelmingly favorable public reception of her novel, *Onna no yūjō* (Women's friendship), serialized in the monthly *Fujin Kurabu* (Women's Club) between 1933 and 1935, had secured her celebrity status, on which her publisher capitalized by printing a twelve-volume anthology of her fiction shortly thereafter. Yoshiya's star never dimmed during her lifetime, and her numerous publications, which include "girls' fiction," historical novels, social commentary, and autobiographical essays, continue to be reissued. Although women in general are absent from the Japanese literary canon, it is hard to fathom why Yoshiya is also absent from (especially Anglophone) anthologies of Japanese women writers published to incorporate women into the otherwise androcentric canon of "pure literature."[3]

Born the year after Japan's victory in the Sino-Japanese War (1894–95), Yoshiya grew up in a social environment shaped by a succession of wars marking the transformation of Japan from an isolated and feudal country to an aggressive imperial power. She was raised as a privileged and affluent member of the small but growing urban middle class, yet her life choices clashed with "traditional" norms – especially with respect to sex and gender roles – underlying even the political and literary avant-garde. Neither an activist nor apolitical, Yoshiya, the writer, was more of a maker of future worlds than a fixer of the real world. Doubtless, her careful negotiations of the social and political instability and confusion that characterized early-twentieth-century Japanese society enabled her both to choose her own future and, most *atypically*, to secure financial independence outside of marriage, which she eschewed.

Coming Out

Yoshiya Nobuko was born on January 12, 1896, in Niigata city, the youngest child and only girl among her four siblings. Both of her parents claimed prestigious samurai genealogies, and the affluent Yoshiya household retained the atmosphere of an earlier, feudal time. Capitalizing on Nobuko's precocious reading abilities, Yoshiya Masa kept her daughter hostage to moral and instructional texts for girls and women and taught her how to sew and cook, two skills at the core of the dominant "good wife, wise mother" gender role. Her father, Yoshiya Yūichi, was the Niigata police chief, and one might speculate that his job to enforce law and order influenced the conservative politics and disciplinary rigor of the Yoshiya household. The adult Nobuko herself was a paragon of self-discipline. She reserved mornings for writing and wasted no time – she was reputedly a "fast writer."

Yoshiya Nobuko's precocious literary talent was apparent to her teachers by her third year in elementary school (in Ibaraki prefecture, where her father had been transferred), when she wrote an essay on "Mizu" (Water). Her mother, however, was unimpressed by her daughter's skill, and their relationship grew increasingly strained. Nevertheless, Nobuko continued to write. By 1908, when she was twelve years old, her short stories were published in *Shōjokai* (Girls' Circle), *Shōjo Sekai* (Girls' World), and *Shōjo no Tomo* (Girls' Friend). Five years later, readers encountered her prose in such prestigious literary magazines as *Bunshō Sekai* (Literary World) and *Shinchō* (New Tide). She also won first place in a girls' fiction contest sponsored by *Girls' World* for her submission, "Narazu no taiko" (Soundless drum).

The trajectory of Nobuko's life began to diverge from that of her parents in 1915, when her father was transferred to Utsunomiya, where he assumed the directorship of the Red Cross, and she moved to Tokyo to live with her youngest brother, Tadaaki, who was a student of agricultural science at Tokyo Imperial University. Nobuko's eldest brother Sadakazu had opted to pursue an unillustrious career as a fine arts painter, and her middle brother, Michiaki, had also disappointed their father by displaying no aptitude for higher education. Tadaaki had always been supportive of his sister's literary aspirations. Not only did he keep Nobuko supplied with the latest publications, he often argued on her behalf when their parents sought to terminate her education, fearing that too much erudition would spoil her chances of an upwardly mobile marriage.

What actually spurred Nobuko's move to Tokyo was a letter from the celebrity artist, Takehisa Yumeji, a good friend of Sadakazu. Yumeji's hugely popular pictures of willowy, wide-eyed young women complemented Nobuko's fictional characters in ambience and affect. Recognizing their shared feminine aesthetic, Yumeji wrote to Nobuko suggesting that they meet in Tokyo and discuss ideas for collaborative projects. Despite her low opinion of his decadent and philandering behavior, Nobuko agreed to have Yumeji illustrate some of her work. During her first year in Tokyo, she also embarked on an eight-year project that propelled her into the literary limelight. This was the series of short stories, *Hanamonogatari* (Flower tales), serialized for eight years (1916–24) in the popular magazine, *Shōjo Gahō* (Girls Illustrated).[4] Today, many female authors claim that *Flower Tales* inspired them to pursue a literary career.

The celebrity of both Yumeji and Nobuko was contingent in large part upon the turn-of-the-century emergence of a new target audience and category of consumer: the *shōjo*, or girl, but literally, a "not-quite-female female." A "really real" female was a married woman with children. The so-called *shōjo* period defined the emergent space between puberty and marriage that began to grow into a life-cycle phase, unregulated by convention, as more and more young women found employment in the service sector of the new urban industrializing economy. Included in the *shōjo* category were the "new working woman" and her jaunty counterpart, the flapper-like "modern girl," or *moga* (*modan gāru*), who was cast in the popular media as the antithesis of the "good wife, wise mother." Obviously, the spectacle of women working and cruising was not a brand-new phenomenon; rather, the prefix "new" denoted middle-class forms of urban employment for girls and women, who served as clerks in department stores, ticket sellers for trains, schoolteachers, telephone operators, typists, nurses, writers and journalists, actors, and café hostesses. These women were among Yoshiya's loyal readers and fans.

Few urban employment opportunities were available for women over the age of thirty; male employers preferred young women up to twenty-four, at which age they should be getting married. Women who, like Yoshiya, could support themselves, were treated as social anomalies, irrespective of their sexual practices. Similarly, "modern" signified a Westernized woman, not in the sense of a woman fluent in a European language but one who eschewed wifehood and motherhood and acted like a man, particularly like a flaneur. Such a woman was often referred to in the critical media as a garçon (*garuson*), one of the many labels pinned on Yoshiya by her detractors.[5] As early as 1890, social critics had claimed that women were becoming more mannish as a result of Japan's Westernization. In sum, when applied pejoratively to girls and women, "new," "modern," and "Western" were euphemisms for "unfeminine," "un-Japanese," "disorderly," and "dangerous."

The treatment of the *shōjo* and the *shōjo* period by the popular media in turn-of-the-century Japan reveals a Janus-faced object and subject of scrutiny. The latter was perceived by some as a downright dangerous phase of unstructured social interaction and unconventional behavior. Since *shōjo* "girlhood" was not determined by chronological age, unmarried adult women in general were regarded as morally depraved and biologically immature. The *shōjo* was reified by critics as a barometer of decadent and unwholesome social transformations. The ambiguous figure as the "not-quite-female female" inspired countless articles on "normal" and "deviant" sexual desires, for *shōjo* was a label that, among other things, implied heterosexual inexperience and homosexual experience. In fact, the term *dōseiai* (same-sex love) was coined at this time to refer specifically to a passionate but supposedly platonic friendship between girls or women, although sexologists found it difficult to distinguish friendship from homosexuality: Where did one end and the other begin?[6] Such friendships were regarded as typical among girls and women from all walks of life, but especially among girls'-school students and graduates, educators, civil servants, and thespians. The *ai* alludes to the term's original definition. Often translated as "agape," *ai* is contrasted with *koi*, or "eros." Because female (homo)sexuality was understood as spiritual and male (homo)sexuality as carnal, the neologism *dōseiai* was preferred by some sexologists to underscore the spiritual aspect of same-sex love between women.[7]

Controlling the *shōjo* was desirable because she was fascinating, attractive, and weak, and it was necessary because she was powerful, threatening, and different. According to some pundits, *shōjo* were "no longer discreet, obedient, or domestically inclined" due to the influence of the masculinizing tendencies attributed to various modern practices and Western popular culture.[8] Statements such as these were anachronistic and misleading, since the category of *shōjo* was a newly discovered social phenomenon. Yoshiya herself and other women who did not fit the label of "good wife, wise mother" were classified as *shōjo*. However, by eschewing a conventional female and feminine life-path, Yoshiya and others effectively expanded the dimensions of the *shōjo* period so that it defined not a phase of life, but an actual lifestyle and subculture as well.

Tamura Toshiko was one of Yoshiya's friends who also spent part of her adult life with another woman. She created a sensation with her short story, "Akirame" (Resignation, 1910), an exploration of "the sensuous nature of a young woman's attraction to another woman."[9] There were also many "ordinary" females in early-twentieth-century Japan who either lived together or who wanted to live together. Not a few of them attempted suicide, often together, out of desperate frustration at rigid social protocols that denied legitimacy to their relationship.[10] In fact, by the 1930s, the preponderance of lesbian suicide attempts reported in the press led one prominent sexologist to wonder, "Why are there so many lesbian double suicides reported in the society column of the daily newspapers? One can only infer that females these days are monopolizing homosexuality."[11]

Yoshiya is credited with playing a key role in developing and defining the genre of *shōjo* fiction aimed at this entirely new female audience cum subculture of reader-consumers. Her *Flower Tales* epitomizes the nascent genre. Each of the fifty-two chapters is named after a flower. The stories are set in girls' schools – often mission schools – in Japan, and the sometimes lonely, self-sufficient maverick heroines who populate the stories are foils for coquettish girls and unhappily married women who acquiesce to convention. The boys and men who do appear in the stories tend to be distrustful or inconsequential and remain relatively undeveloped as characters.

Ideas for the various scenarios in *Flower Tales* grew out of Nobuko's own experience. A year after her move to Tokyo, Tadaaki left for North China as part of his new job to survey forests, and Nobuko found lodging in a women's dormitory in the Yotsuya district managed by American Baptist missionaries. She also began to study English at that time. However, the dorm's early curfew interfered with her penchant for spending evenings and nights at the movies in Asakusa, the lively theater district. Within a year she had moved to the more liberally managed YWCA in Kanda, a district known for its universities and used book stores. Nobuko's roommate there was Kikuchi Yukie (of Tsuda Women's College), who became the model for Akitsu, one of the two protagonists in her *Yaneura no nishojo* (Two virgins in an attic), penned in 1919. This book is recognized as her earliest effort to write explicitly about lesbianism. Akitsu is a self-sufficient and determined young woman living in a women's dormitory who guides her roommate Akiko through the process of self-discovery and a concomitant rejection of patriarchy. The story ends with the two women deciding to leave the dorm and set out together on a lifelong journey.

Whereas Akitsu is modeled after Kikuchi, Akiko's transformation into a resolutely woman-identified character charts the progress of Yoshiya's own evolution under the tutelage of her YWCA roommate. The YWCA bore the reputation of being a refuge for women eager to escape an arranged marriage or married life itself. It was also a proving ground for lesbian relationships, including the one between Kikuchi and Yoshiya. Their archived correspondence and passages in Yoshiya's diary suggest that Kikuchi was an aggressive and jealous partner. Kikuchi clearly flouted the prevailing stereotype of women, for it was taken as common sense, or the ruling definition of the "natural," that only courtesans, prostitutes, and widows experienced sexual desire.[12] Yoshiya herself wrote in her diary (on January 25, 1920) that "SEX [*sic*] is a most natural human desire. But the irritating thing about Yukie [i.e., Kikuchi] is the way she equates sex with possession and ownership, the way men do. The physical act is just a cover for a coarseness of spirit."[13]

Yoshiya wrote the "Suiren" (Water lily) chapter of *Flower Tales* around the same time as this diary entry. It is about a young woman, much like herself, trying to stand on her own two feet. Not surprisingly, Yoshiya applauded her contemporaries who publicly declared their rejection of the self-sacrificing role of "good wife, wise mother." For example, she was deeply impressed by a "divorce petition" published in a leading daily newspaper by a popular poet, Byakuren (Itō [née Yanagihara] Akiko), seeking to sever ties with her philandering husband of ten years. Byakuren's petition for a divorce in the form of a "tearful confession" of her unhappy marriage to the wealthy Itō Den'emon, a coal-mining tycoon twenty-five years her senior, was printed verbatim in the evening edition of the *Tōkyō Asahi Shinbun* on October 23, 1921. Yoshiya was so moved by the petition, excerpted below, that she copied and underlined parts of it in her diary and included a fictionalized reference to it in her short story, "Moyuru hana" (Burning flower), which was being serialized in the same newspaper.[14]

> All that comforted me during my ill-fated marriage to you was my poetry. The hurt from the pathos of a loveless marriage was so deep that at times I would resign myself to the curse of a pointless life that would end behind a dark curtain. Fortunately, however, I have fallen in love with someone [the anarchist lawyer Miyazaki Ryūsuke] whose love will help me to rejuvenate my life and turn it around. Following my conscience, I have decided that it is time for me to fundamentally restructure the unnatural daily life of my past. That is, I must now leave behind the fictions and falsehoods and adhere to the truth. You respect only the power of money and have an utter disregard for women. Therefore, with this letter I hereby announce our separation.[15]

Byakuren's courageous choice of love and politics over financial security deeply impressed Yoshiya, who, a year earlier, in 1920, had decided to end her own relationship with the possessive and petulant Kikuchi. Yoshiya became briefly involved on the rebound with an older woman she met at the YWCA. That relationship, too, deepened her disillusionment about love – until January 1923, when she was introduced to Monma Chiyo, the woman who became her life partner.

True Love

Three years younger than Yoshiya, the twenty-four-year-old Monma was a mathematics teacher at a higher girls' school in Tokyo's wealthy Kōjimachi district. Her first, and not so subtle, impression of the popular writer was of a "cute Ainu woman" on account of Yoshiya's unusual haircut.[16] Two years earlier, in 1921, Yoshiya had decided to cut her hair short and hence was one of the first Japanese women to do so despite the (rarely enacted) law against short hair on females. Whereas short hair on males signified the rationalization of everyday life, on females it was the mark of a maverick, construed as a sign of social disorder and sex-and-gender confusion. Moreover, the short, or "masculine," haircut was interpreted by conservatives writing in the early twentieth century as a symbol of lesbian sexuality to which young women were all too susceptible. Yoshiya's *kappa* (water imp) haircut was unique and wholly unlike the trendy Eton-crop and pageboy styles sported by the sexually ambiguous "modern girl." Her hairstyle, in short, was not at all fashionable; rather, as she claimed, it embodied a manifesto of liberation from state-sanctioned womanhood. Significantly enough, Yoshiya never changed her trademark coiffure.

Yoshiya and Monma were virtually inseparable from the day they met. Until they began living together under one roof as a couple in 1926, they wrote each other letters on a regular, sometimes daily, basis. In 1924, when they were separated for ten months while Monma was teaching at a girls' high school in Shimonoseki, 1,000 kilometers west of Tokyo, the two women exchanged over 150 letters, most of which averaged between five and ten pages in length. The passionate and erotic nature of their relationship was evident not just in the sheer number of letters exchanged but also in their steamy content. These and hundreds of other pieces of Yoshiya's correspondence formed the basis of a biography – the first of only several on Yoshiya – by the feminist historian Yoshitake Teruko.

As an aside, although the loanword "love letter" was introduced to the Japanese public in the early twentieth century, letters of love (*koibumi*) have a centuries-old history in Japan. Letters incorporating poems were a staple form of communication in the gender- and ritual-bound Heian Court (795–1193), where it was considered a gross breach of etiquette for a man to neglect to send his lover a morning-after letter and poem as soon as he returned to his quarters. It is significant that during their "courtship period," Yoshiya never failed to write a letter to Monma after returning home from an outing with her.

Unlike her fiction, Yoshiya's letters were not flowery but rather crisply, if passionately, penned, as in the following poemlike example:

> Beloved Chiyo
> I will love you no matter what
> I do not wish to make you lonely
> Nor do I want to be lonely
> I want you to be the source of my strength

And, if you will let me, I would like to be the source of your strength
May 23 [1923], 8:30 P.M.
Arriving home soaking wet from the rain
Nobuko[17]

Monma's letters were almost loquaciously melodramatic in comparison:

Beloved elder sister. I am unspeakably lonely when you leave. My heart becomes hollow, and all I am able to do is to sit in a chair and stare blankly at the wall. It's now nighttime, isn't it? As I wrap my unlined black kimono around my bare skin and adjust the hem, my body is aroused by feelings of longing [for you]; instead, what stretches confusingly before my eyes is dusty reality. Ah, this evening. My heart finds no consolation in this evening dream of mine or in reality. My heart sinks from a heavy sadness. If only on this night we were together in our own little house, lying quietly under the light of a lantern, then my heart would gradually warm and neither would you be so sad. I am so sad that I won't be able see you either tomorrow or the day after. Let us please meet again on Tuesday. Farewell for now; I am forever yours. Why have I written such things, I wonder? Please don't worry too much about me. Goodbye, and please take care of yourself.
May 11, [1923] midnight
Thinking of my elder sister.
Chiyoko[18]

Other letters express their passionate love somewhat more graphically. In one of her longer letters to Monma (in 1924), Yoshiya writes, "I crave your lips. Do you know how much I crave them? When I get into bed alone at night I begin to burn deeply for you.... I am staking my entire life on you, on a woman – every prayer, every desire, every happiness, even my art [I am staking on you]. I need you and you alone; I have no life without you."[19] Kisses, caresses, and warm embraces were mentioned regularly in their letters along with subjects more overtly political and polemical than Yoshiya's published pieces. Monma's tenure in Shimonoseki inspired especially ardent missives between the two women, who also used the opportunity to polish their antipatriarchal rhetoric and to strategize against the state's paternalistic family system. Monma, for example, in a letter to Yoshiya in February 1925, vented her feelings about society's double standard:

I can only think of how soon we can arrange to live together. There's nothing I need more than your warm embrace. It is unfortunate that we are not a male and female couple, for if you were a male, our union would be quickly arranged. But a female couple is not allowed. Why is it that [in our society] love is acknowledged only by its outward form and not by its depth of quality – especially since there are so many foul and undesirable aspects to heterosexual relationships?[20]

Yoshiya's response was an audacious manipulation of historically traditional practices in the direction of radical change:

Chiyo-chan. After reading your letter I resolved to build a small house for the two of us.... Once it is constructed, I will declare it to be a branch household (*bunke*), initiate a household register [listing, by law, all family members], and become a totally inde-

> pendent househead. I will then adopt you so that you can become a legal member of my household (adoption being a formality since the law will not recognize you as a wife. In the meantime, I aim to get the law reformed). We will have our own house and our own household register. That's what I've decided.... We'll celebrate your adoption with a party just like a typical marriage reception – it will be our wedding ceremony. I want it to be really grand. We will ask Miyake Yasuko-san and Shigeri-san [the couple who had introduced them] to be our go-betweens [a formal role at weddings]. I wonder what kind of wedding kimono would look best on you?... In order for us to realize this event, I would like you to retire from your teaching position.... I just can't wait any longer.[21]

Yoshiya kept her promise and built a new house in Shimoochiai, a suburb of Tokyo, to mark their partnership. She did not formally adopt Monma until February 1957 for two reasons. First, Monma's parents initially objected to their daughter's adoption; and second, and most important, Yoshiya was keen on having their relationship legally recognized as a bona fide marriage, not as a "mother-daughter" pairing. Only when it became clear to her that the postwar constitution would retain the patriarchal ideology of its predecessor did she adopt her partner, thereby ensuring that Monma would be recognized legally as her successor. From that point onward, Monma was known legally as Yoshiya Chiyo.[22] As the option of forming a branch household was noted by another famous lesbian couple in 1935, it is probably the case that this was a primary strategy for "nontraditional" couples to achieve a modicum of legitimacy as a corporate unit.[23]

Monma agreed to quit her teaching position and became Yoshiya's fulltime secretary in 1931. Their Shimoochiai house was a landmark modernist building infused with sunlight pouring through numerous sliding glass doors. Yoshiya had a passion for architecture and often claimed that had she been born a male, she would have become an architect. Sharing this extravagant home were two maids and a German shepherd. Yoshiya built eight houses in all; moreover, she was one of the first Japanese to have a car of her own, and at one time she owned six race horses! She was generous with her wealth and offered support and mentoring at her home to many women who aspired to a literary career.[24]

Sexual Politics

The families and childhood experiences of Yoshiya and Monma were very different in every respect. Yoshiya was the youngest and only daughter of five children; Monma was the eldest of seven children (three sons and four daughters). Yoshiya's father was a government official and bureaucrat; Monma's was a scholar of Japanese literature.[25] And, although both of their mothers could be characterized as "good wives and wise mothers," Yoshiya's was wholly unsupportive of her daughter's professional aspirations, while Monma's encouraged her daughter to pursue a professional career. Biographer Yoshitake Teruko avers that the "goodness" of her mother imparted in Monma an affirmation of "same-sex longing," whereas Yoshiya's mother was adamantly opposed to her daughter's literary ambitions, deeming them to be patently unfeminine. Unlike Monma, Yoshiya did not grow up with a favorable image of women. Rather, as Yoshiya commented in her diary, her mother embodied the plight of Everywoman forced into a loveless arranged marriage and relegated to a demoralizing life devoid of any semblance of agency and self-determination.[26]

Although I find it problematic to make causal links between daughters' gender identity and sexuality with the attitudes and circumstances of their mothers, I do not doubt at all that Yoshiya and Monma's mothers – and fathers – played a role in fostering a domestic environment that either supported their daughters or created challenges for them to overcome. In fact, the notion that Monma's "same-sex longing" was nurtured by the positive influence of her mother is a relatively recent departure from the enduring notion introduced in the late-nineteenth century that lesbian sexuality was caused by mean mothers and abusive stepmothers, among other negative familial and environmental factors.[27] Like Yoshiya's mother, some conservative pundits perceived higher education as one of those negative environmental factors and were especially hostile to early-twentieth-century attempts to popularize sex education and sexual hygiene.[28] Similarly, politics was deemed an unsuitable interest or profession for women. The Peace Preservation Law enacted in March 1900 forbade political activity, broadly defined, by women (along with soldiers, police, priests, and minors). The establishment in 1911, of Seitōsha, or Bluestocking Society, a literary, urban, middle-class women's organization, signaled the public presence of self-conscious women whose political ideas and behavior far exceeded the narrow cognitive range of the "good wife, wise mother" role. The society was forced to disband in 1916.

Yoshiya Nobuko herself was deeply influenced by the Bluestocking Society. She was especially inspired by the founder, Hiratsuka Raichō, who had introduced the reading public to the concept of the "new woman" (*atarashii onna*) in 1913. Like Hiratsuka, ten years her senior, Yoshiya was a strong supporter of the American Margaret Sanger's campaign to introduce birth control both as a "positive" eugenics policy and as a fundamental right of women. She also lambasted women – including her own mother – who became pregnant without any forethought.[29] Perhaps the literary efforts of the Bluestockings inspired Yoshiya to found *Kurosōbi* (Black Rose) in 1925. This was a monthly literary magazine that she intended as a forum for exploring the more unconventional dimensions of her own fiction without worrying about censors and salability. However, it proved to be too great an effort even for her workaholic self and was discontinued after the eighth issue.[30]

Although I cannot elaborate here, I suspect that Yoshiya's diary entries and letters to Monma were proving grounds for the gender-bending ideas that, rendered in tamer rhetoric, infuse her novels and commentaries alike. Similarly, what some critics dismissed as "children's stories," namely, *shōjo* fiction, constituted for Yoshiya and her readers an interstitial space where new or unconventional configurations of everyday life might achieve materiality and practical importance and where they might question received convention. In contrast to her private correspondence, Yoshiya was artfully indirect about sex in her published work. An article titled "Dannasama muyō" (A husband is unnecessary), published in the left-of-center intellectual journal *Kaizō* (Reconstruction) in January 1931, is telling. Yoshiya defends, with exasperation, her unconventional life through subtle satire and humor, as revealed in the following excerpts:

"Why don't you marry?" everyone asks politely. Is it that I'm the epitome of a wife? People greet me with that question instead of, say, a "Good morning," or a "Good evening."... They might as well ask me if I'm simply indulging in a reckless adventure fueled by a pathetic determination to be a barren woman.

"You must be lonely?" everyone asks politely.... Rest assured; I am not at all lonely! The outdated notion that an unmarried woman is lonely, bitter and angry is completely foreign to me. I write novels, which for me, is the great work of my life.

For 365 days of the year I work from morning to night, from deadline to deadline,... and in the process, I completely forget about the great defect in my life: the absence of a husband. If I hadn't been blessed with a talent for writing, I'd probably have ended up unusually lonely, barely able to endure each minute of the day as I sobbed and wailed.... I offer my thanks to the *kami* (gods); for some reason, the omniscient *kami* made me a novelist instead of a wife. Now if the *kami* had first asked me to choose between having a husband and becoming a novelist, I... most certainly would have asked to become a novelist, not because a woman like me couldn't attract a good husband, but because with some practice, I could become a good novelist.

"Don't you like men?" Many people ask me this. Please, everyone! For crying out loud, don't make such ridiculous assumptions!... Why would I dislike men?... Please, everybody, just think for a minute. There are two types of humans, males and females. Just two types. To dislike one of them is truly too sad for words.[31]

Although Yoshiya herself was quite extraordinary, she wrote from the perspective of a young woman of the urban middle class who sensed that something was missing from her life but could not quite put a finger on just what it was. Her emphasis on heroines and same-sex friendship and love was pathbreaking. Despite her polite, ornate prose, she managed to convey rather radical ideas to her middle-class readers, female and male, married and unmarried alike, who collectively outnumbered her strictly *shōjo* fans. She stretched the parameters of the status quo and, at the same time, broadened the minds of her readers. It was for her readers, in fact, that Yoshiya consciously and constantly crafted the politics of her narrative. Thus, for example, after returning in 1929 from a year of traveling with Monma throughout Europe and the United States, which was de rigueur for Japanese women writers at the time, Yoshiya, who was "impressed by the liberated women of America," vowed "never again to write about female characters who cried a lot and simply endured their miserable lot in life."[32] Yoshiya's account of her worldwide travels, titled *Bōfū no bara* (Stormy rose), was serialized in 1930 in the women's magazine, *Shufu no Tomo* (Housewife's Friend).

During their yearlong trip, Yoshiya and Monma rendezvoused in Moscow with two writers, both women, who, unlike Yoshiya, would become part of the Japanese "feminist" literary canon: Miyamoto Yuriko[33] and Yuasa Yoshiko. In September 1928 they traveled to Paris via Moscow by train from Manchuria because, as Yoshiya explained, she "wanted to set foot in the Soviet Union, where a revolution had succeeded."[34] She and Monma made the most of a twenty-four-hour layover in Moscow where, guided by an elderly Korean man who spoke fluent Japanese, they toured the Kremlin and other sites. They then continued on to Paris for an extended stay, and in the summer of 1929 met up again with Miyamoto and Yuasa before heading for the United States. Their writer friends returned to the Soviet Union.

Miyamoto had been living in Moscow since October 1927 with Yuasa, a journalist and scholar of Russian literature. There, Yoshiya first met Yuasa; the two women later became fairly close friends, meeting at coffee shops and going to movies together back in Tokyo. The once-divorced Miyamoto and Yuasa, an "out" lesbian, lived together at that time as a couple and often visited Yoshiya's Shimoochiai home until Miyamoto decided to marry again. Yoshiya kept sympathetic tabs on her activist colleague through the mass media, for the frequent arrests of Yuasa and the eventual life sentence meted out to her husband for their activities on behalf of the Japan Communist Party made splashy headlines.[35] Yoshiya's own politics were far tamer.

Canons and Cannons

Komashaku Kimi, a feminist writer and activist, subtitled her critical biography of Yoshiya, "hidden feminist." "Hidden," not because Yoshiya was silent about feminist issues – she was not – but because her feminism was expressed neither in the context of the Japanese feminist movement nor in a politicized vocabulary. Nevertheless, her ideas about female citizenship, marriage, household succession, and so forth were patently feminist and wholly radical. Yoshiya was and remains "hidden" in another sense as well. She was snubbed by her male contemporaries, particularly those who, claiming membership in the canon of "pure literature," defined themselves against "popular literature," the category in which they lumped Yoshiya's corpus. Kobayashi Hideo, eulogized today in academe as a doyen of pure literature, was among her harshest and most misogynist critics. Parroting the dominant sex-gender ideology of the time, he dismissed Yoshiya as a "child" and her work as "childish" in a 1936 review of *Women's Friendship*, of which he could "bear to read only a few pages."[36] Yoshiya had long since honed her ability to respond acerbically to such sexist condescension, and Kobayashi was not spared. Shortly after his review was published in *Bungakkai* (Literary World), she cornered him at a well-attended party hosted by the newspaper, *Tōkyō Nichinichi*, and fired a salvo of her own:

> You refer to my work as rubbish, but would major newspapers [and magazines] serialize rubbish? You assert that I write like a child, but how old must a woman be before you cease calling her a child? *Women's Friendship* was first serialized in *Fujin kurabu* (Women's Club) [a journal for adult women]. Do you regard women as children by definition? Moreover, you have no business criticizing what you do not read from beginning to end. You cannot claim to be a literary critic if all you do is pick out short segments of my work on the basis of which you then denounce it in its entirety. That is hardly proper behavior for one who claims to be a discerning and knowledgeable man![37]

According to another of her biographers, Yoshiya's awesome popularity and lesbian sexuality provoked petty jealousies and base prejudices on the part of Kobayashi and other contemporaries. It would seem that similar attitudes today continue to impede recognition of her considerable and varied literary achievements.[38] Collectively, Yoshiya's feminist (and only) biographers have sought to dismantle the defective lens through which the image of the versatile writer has been warped and to (re)position her as an outspoken critic of the patriarchal status quo whose choice of career and life-partner alike were radical acts.

Yoshiya's sexual politics impinged upon but were not contained by political theories of either the left or the right. Because she perceived all women to constitute a discrete social class on account of their oppression by men, she not only felt alienated from her socialist contemporaries who identified with the proletariat but was equally perturbed by the overt militarization of the country in the wake of the 1923 earthquake that leveled Tokyo.[39] The brutal murders by the police of the anarchist couple Ōsugi Sakae and Itō Noe shortly after the earthquake shocked Yoshiya, who had known Ōsugi since childhood and Itō through the Blue-stocking Society. Nevertheless, about fifteen years later, she joined – or rather, was impelled to join – the Pen Corps (Pen butai), the popular name for the cultural propaganda unit organized in 1938 by the powerful Cabinet Information Bureau following Nazi precedent.[40] I should note in this connection that Yoshiya was not alone in playing some type of supporting role in the military regime. Most feminists at the time were heartened by the state's emphasis on maternal health as an adjunct to a "positive" eugenics policy aimed at improving the conditions of reproduction in order to increase the size and stature of the Japanese population.[41] Likewise, twenty-two of the most renowned writers of the time, with few exceptions – Miyamoto Yuriko was one – were organized by the bureau as literary war correspondents charged with supplying the Japanese public with riveting accounts of key battles and ethnographic stories about the diverse cultures contained within the growing empire. Yoshiya was assigned to the navy's branch of the Pen Corps, headed by the writer Kikuchi Kan; the army's branch was headed by litterateur Kumei Tadao and included novelist Hayashi Fumiko, all good friends of Yoshiya. The two women were the only females included in the "official" Pen Corps – other women writers traveled there under different auspices. In stark contrast to Yoshiya's avowed timidity in the face of war, Hayashi proved to be an intrepid and indefatigable correspondent, risking her life to visit battlefronts in central China.[42]

Yoshiya was perceived ambivalently by the wartime military regime. On the one hand, some of her fiction was deemed unfit for girls and women to read due to its affirmation of free will and liberalism. This was the reason given for the withdrawal from the *Ōsaka Mainichi Shinbun* of her serialized short story, "Atarashiki hi" (A new day), in 1942, although it was snapped up by the jointly published newspapers, *Tōkyō Nichinichi* and *Ōsaka Asahi Shinbun*, which had republished her perennially popular *Flower Tales* in serial form two years earlier. On the other hand, the state sought to harness her enormous popularity and celebrity for the purposes of raising the morale of weary citizens. As a member of the Naval Pen Corps and a special correspondent for *Housewife's Friend*, Yoshiya toured and sent regular dispatches from central and north China, Manchuria, Indonesia (Java), Thailand, Vietnam (Indochina), and other areas under Japanese domination. She also wrote a play, *Mura to heitai* (Village and soldiers), staged in 1939, and published in such wartime magazines as *Sensha* (Tank) and *Sukōru* (Squall).[43]

Yoshiya's months-long tour of Indonesia at the end of 1940 followed the "diplomatic" mission headed by Kobayashi Ichizō, then minister of commerce and industry, to secure petroleum and other resources from the Dutch colonial administrators.

The mission ended in failure, and the Japanese successfully invaded the Dutch East Indies at the beginning of 1942, securing imperial hegemony over Southeast Asia and the South Pacific. Kobayashi was the founder of the famous all-female Takarazuka Revue and, like Yoshiya, built a dream world around passionate romance, although he colored it heterosexual. Not surprisingly, the revue staged parts of Yoshiya's *Flower Tales* in 1926, from which time onward she maintained a close relationship with Kobayashi until his death in 1957 and remained a loyal "Takarazuka" fan.[44]

When not reporting from colonial outposts overseas, Yoshiya focused on her new passion for haiku, studying with Takahama Kyoshi, a renowned poet and novelist. She also oversaw the construction of a new modernist home for herself and Monma in Kamakura (now a private museum devoted to her work). Apart from her penchant for architecture, perhaps she realized that the seaside resort south of Tokyo was much safer than the metropolis, which by 1944 was undergoing heavy bombing by the Allies – and, in fact, her Tokyo home was destroyed in an air raid.

Epilogue: Last Bloom

For reasons related to the "wartime amnesia" precluding (until very recently) any critical national reflection on Japanese militarism and imperialist aggression, Yoshiya's published reports and travelogues from her tours of duty with the Pen Corps have been omitted from anthologies of her work. Relatively little is known of her wartime activities or those of her contemporaries.

After the war, Yoshiya continued to publish fiction and nonfiction prolifically. She won prestigious prizes for her writing, which defied the strict division between pure and popular literature. She was awarded the Women's Literature Prize (Joryūbungakusho) in 1951 for her short story, "Onibi" (Will-o'-the-wisp), serialized in *Fujin Kōron* (Women's Review), and the Kikuchi Kan Prize for her ambitious historical novel, *Tokugawa no fujintachi* (Tokugawa women, 1966) in November 1967. Her earlier works were republished one by one – with the exception of her wartime essays, scripts, and reports. Her novel, *Ataka-ke no hitobito* (The people of the Ataka household), serialized in the *Mainichi Shinbun* from August 1951 to February 1952, was translated into six languages.

Yoshiya began to write historical novels in the late 1960s, in part to redress the inadequate and stereotyped representation of female characters in the historical novels written by her male contemporaries, and in part to restore the images and voices of girls and women to Japanese cultural history itself. One representative example of her historical work is *Toki no koe* (The voice of the times), a "docu-novel" serialized in the *Yomiuri Shinbun* between 1964 and 1965 on the antiprostitution movement in Japan orchestrated by the Salvation Army.[45] *Tokugawa Women* and *Nyonin heike* (Heike women, 1971) are her other two major historical works. Both were serialized, and the latter was also made into a television series.

Yoshiya and Monma had moved back to Tokyo in 1950 into a newly constructed house located in Kōjimachi. Noise and pollution that accompanied the rapid and unregulated postwar growth of the city forced them back to Kamakura twelve years later in 1962, when preparations for the 1964 Olympics exacerbated the problem.

Yoshiya's health took a turn for the worse a few years after the move. She had been plagued all of her life with gastrointestinal problems and in the early 1940s had suffered from gallstones. Eventually, in May 1972, she was diagnosed with metastatic colon cancer. Monma withheld the diagnosis from Yoshiya, the first time that she had ever kept anything from her partner, but the fact that Yoshiya both agreed to be hospitalized and wrote out her will suggests that she suspected the worst. The energetic maverick was finally slowed by disease. She died at home on July 11, 1973, at the age of seventy-seven, holding Monma's hand.

Only recently have several Japanese feminists resurrected Yoshiya as a prototype of the self-sufficient female ideal for late-twentieth-century Japan, and it is from their biographical studies and other primary sources that I have culled information for this essay. That a writer of Yoshiya's celebrity and prolificacy could be ignored by scholars underscores how narrowly constructed is our knowledge and understanding of Japanese cultural history, the place of girls and women in it, and their gendered and sexual practices. Yoshiya sought to write women into her nation's cultural history and to develop a new vocabulary of female agency in her fiction. It is our responsibility to write Yoshiya back into Japanese literary history and to complicate the discourse of sex, gender, and sexuality in Japan (and Japanese Studies) by rescuing her voice from the "well of loneliness."

NOTES

1 Ikeda Hiroshi, "Yoshiya Nobuko-san no seikatsu o nozoku" [Looking in on Yoshiya Nobuko's daily life], *Hanashi* 8 (1935): 212.

2 Quoted in Yoshitake Teruko, *Nyonin Yoshiya Nobuko* [The woman Yoshiya Nobuko] (Tokyo: Bungei Shunjū, 1986), 215. The postwar (1946) constitution included universal female suffrage.

3 See, for example, Yukiko Tanaka and Elizabeth Hanson, eds., *This Kind of Woman: Ten Stories by Japanese Women Writers, 1960–1976* (New York: Perigee Books, 1984); Yukiko Tanaka, ed., *To Live and To Write: Selections by Japanese Women Writers, 1913–1938* (Seattle: The Seal Press, 1987).

4 Ōtsuka Toyoko, ed., "Yoshiya Nobuko nenpu" [Yoshiya Nobuko chronology], in *Taishū bungaku taikei* [An outline of popular literature], vol. 20 (Tokyo: Kōdansha, 1972), 384–85; Yoshitake, *Nyonin Yoshiya Nobuko*, 40–81.

5 "'Watashi' wa 'boku' e" [From (feminine) "I" to (masculine) "I"], *Ōsaka Mainichi Shinbun*, February 10, 1932.

6 Yasuda Tokutarō, "Dōseiai no rekishikan" [History of homosexuality], *Chūō Kōron* 3 (1935): 151.

7 Makoto Furukawa, "The Changing Nature of Sexuality: The Three Codes Framing Homosexuality in Modern Japan," trans. Alice Lockyer, *U.S.–Japan Women's Journal* (English Supplement) 7 (1994): 115–16.

8 Sugita Naoki, "Shōjo kageki netsu no shindan" [An analysis of the feverish interest in *shōjo* revues], *Fujin Kōron* 4 (1935): 274.

9 Tanaka, ed., *To Live and To Write*, 60.

10 For details, see Jennifer Robertson, "Dying to Tell: Sexuality and Suicide in Imperial Japan," *Signs: Journal of Women in Culture and Society* 25, no. 1 (1999): 1–36.

11 Yasuda, "Dōseiai no rekishikan," 150.

12 Yoshitake, *Nyonin Yoshiya Nobuko*, 87.
13 Ibid., 122.
14 Ōzawa Hisako, "Yoshiya Nobuko no genten to natta shōjo shosetsu" [Yoshiya Nobuko's first work of girls' fiction], *Shōjoza* 1 (1985): 25; Yoshitake, *Nyonin Yoshiya Nobuko*, 19.
15 "Den'emon e Akiko saigo no tegami" [Akiko's last letter to Den'emon], *Tōkyō Asahi Shinbun*, October 23, 1912, evening edition.
16 Yoshitake, *Nyonin Yoshiya Nobuko*, 130. The Ainu are an indigenous minority people who reside primarily in the northernmost regions of Japan. The Ainu were subjected to forced assimilation (Japanization) by the imperial state from roughly the midnineteenth century onward. Only in 1997 were they given legal recognition as a "Japanese minority" group.
17 Quoted in Yoshitake, *Nyonin Yoshiya Nobuko*, 138–9.
18 Ibid., 139–40. Monma referred to Yoshiya as *onēsama* or "older sister," a popular euphemism then and now for one half of a lesbian couple. Yoshiya called Monma by her first name, which she feminized and rendered diminutive by adding either a *ko* or *chan*, a sign of affection in this context.
19 Ibid., 189.
20 Ibid., 193.
21 Ibid., 194.
22 Ibid., 286–7. Initially, Yoshiya had adopted her brother Tadaaki's second son and his wife to serve as her successors. However, that arrangement was annulled a year later, when Yoshiya realized that the only way legally to ensure that Monma would inherit her estate was to adopt her formally.
23 See Robertson, "Dying to Tell," 19, 30.
24 Ikeda, "Yoshiya Nobuko-san no seikatsu," 214; Yoshitake, *Nyonin Yoshiya Nobuko*, 239, 220.
25 Yoshitake, *Nyonin Yoshiya Nobuko*, 40, 132.
26 Ibid., 54, 64, 132–3.
27 Hirozawa Yumi, "Iseiai chōsei to iu fuashizumu" [The fascism of compulsory heterosexuality], *Shinchinchihei* 6, no. 150 (1987): 67–73; Jennifer Robertson, *Takarazuka: Sexual Politics and Popular Culture in Modern Japan* (Berkeley: University of California Press, 1998), 70.
28 See Sabine Frühstück, "Managing the Truth of Sex in Imperial Japan," *Journal of Asian Studies* 59, no. 2 (2000): 332–58.
29 Ikeda, "Yoshiya Nobuko-san no seikatsu," 217; Komashaku Kimi, *Yoshiya Nobuko – kakure fueminisuto* [Yoshiya Nobuko – hidden feminist] (Tokyo: Riburopōto, 1994), 119–26; Yoshitake, *Nyonin Yoshiya Nobuko*, 54, 63, 109. "Positive eugenics" refers to the improvement of the conditions of reproduction, including maternal health, as a way of creating a "superior" population.
30 Yoshitake, *Nyonin Yoshiya Nobuko*, 183.
31 Yoshiya Nobuko, "Dannasama muyō" [A husband is unnecessary], *Kaizō* 1 (1931): 128–9.
32 Quoted in Yoshitake, *Nyonin Yoshiya Nobuko*, 203–4.
33 At that time she was known by her family name, Chūjō; she married Miyamoto Kenji in 1932.
34 Yoshiya Nobuko, *Jidenteki joryū bundanshi* [An autobiographical history of women writers] (Tokyo: Chūō Kōronsha, 1977), 75. The constituent chapters were originally serialized in a variety of journals from 1962 to 1966.
35 Hirozawa, "Iseiai chōsei," 69.
36 Quoted in Yoshitake, *Nyonin Yoshiya Nobuko*, 252.

37 Ibid.
38 Tanabe Seiko, "Kaisetsu" [Commentary], in Yoshitake, *Nyonin Yoshiya Nobuko*, 321.
39 After the devastating Tokyo earthquake of 1923, Yoshiya and Monma decided to spend a year in Nagasaki, where they befriended an English nun from whom they took English lessons. Yoshiya also continued to attend church on Sundays, a ritual since her days at the YWCA.
40 Komashaku, *Yoshiya Nobuko – kakure fueminisuto*, 272; Sakuramoto Tomio, *Bunkajintachi no daitōa sensō – PK butai ga yuku* [The intelligentsia's Greater East Asia War – the PK Corps advances] (Tokyo: Aoki Shoten, 1993), 11–16, 33, 40.
41 See Sumiko Ostubo, "Feminist Maternal Eugenics in Wartime Japan," *U.S.–Japan Women's Journal* (English Supplement) 17 (1999): 39–76; Jennifer Robertson, "Japan's First Cyborg? Miss Nippon, Eugenics, and Wartime Technologies of Beauty, Body, and Blood," *Body & Society* 7, no. 1 (2001).
42 Yoshiya, *Fidenteki joryū bundanshi*, 55–61; Sakuramoto, *Bunkajintachi*, 21.
43 Komashaku, *Yoshiya Nobuko – Kakure fueminisuto*, 272–3; Yoshitake, *Nyonin Yoshiya Nobuko*, 255; Ōtsuka, "Yoshiya Nobuko nenpu," 836–7; Ōzasa Yoshio, *Nihon gendai engekishi, Shōwa senchūben* [History of modern Japanese theater, Shōwa wartime], vol. 2 (Tokyo: Hakusuisha, 1994), 586–7. These works include "Utsukushii nekutai" [Beautiful necktie, August 1940] and "Genchihōkoku: ran'in" [Frontline report: Dutch Indonesia, May 1941], respectively.
44. Yoshiya Nobuko, *Watashi no mita hito* [People I have observed] (Tokyo: Asahi Shinbunsha, 1963), 27–30; see Robertson, *Takarazuka*, for a history and analysis of the "Takarazuka Revue." Revue fans were also readers of *shōjo* fiction. There was and is much overlap between the two media.
45 Yoshitake, *Nyonin Yoshiya Nobuko*, 293–94, 288; Komashaku, *Yoshiya Nobuko – kakure fueminisuto*, 242.

12

Outing as Performance/ Outing as Resistance: A Queer Reading of Austrian (Homo)Sexualities

Matti Bunzl

In late July 1995, the calm of Austria's political summer erupted with a new, American catchword: "Outing." *News*, one of Austria's most widely read magazines, had published an exposé on July 13, detailing the upcoming political plans of Kurt Krickler – a leading activist in Austria's oldest lesbian and gay organization, HOSI (short for Homosexuellen-Initiative). There, Krickler announced the imminent exposure of the clandestine homosexuality of over a quarter of Austria's Catholic bishops. Specifically, Krickler promised the "Outing" of five bishops at a press conference to be held on August 1 in the hallowed halls of Vienna's Café Landtmann – the primary site of communication between Austria's elected officials and a wider public (Kräutler 1995).

In an article published a week later in the alternative city paper *Der Falter*, Krickler elaborated on the rationale for his spectacular and unprecedented *Outing-Aktion*. Under the title "Outing as a Weapon," he focused attention on the ongoing legal discrimination that continues to denigrate lesbians and gay men in Austria (Krickler 1995). Concretely, he protested the continued existence of three anti-lesbian/gay paragraphs in the country's criminal code: Paragraphs 220 and 221 respectively interdict "propaganda" for "sexual relations between persons of the same sex" and the formation of "associations" intended to "facilitate same-sex sexual relations" (StGB 1974).[1] While these two statutes effectively outlaw the creation of lesbian and gay organizations and ban the distribution of informational material pertaining to lesbian or gay concerns, their enforcement remains sporadic, rendering the infamous Paragraph 209 the main battle ground for gay activists. The latter piece of legislation prohibits same-sex sexual relations of male persons over the age of 19 with their 14- to 18-year-old counterparts (regardless of mutual consent). In the absence of equivalent statutes outlawing heterosexual and lesbian relations (both legal at 14) in these age brackets, Paragraph 209 constitutes clear discrimination against gay male sexual relations. Moreover, the law – which has been on the books since 1971, when a general interdiction of male same-sex sexual relations was abolished (Hauer 1989:61–2) – continues to be widely executed. In 1994, for example, a total of 59 legal proceedings were initiated under Paragraph 209, resulting in 23 convictions (*Jus Amandi* 1995).

Austria's anti-lesbian/gay legislation came under particular scrutiny in the wake of the country's joining of the European Union on January 1, 1995. Appealing to liberal tenets, lesbian and gay activists had for years noted that Austria maintained the most virulently homophobic criminal code in Western Europe (see, for example, Krickler 1989).[2] However, neither the unfavorable comparison of Austria in cross-European perspective, nor the recommendations issued by the parliamentary assembly of the Council of Europe (in 1981) and the Parliament of the European Union (between 1984 and 1994) supporting the decriminalization of homosexuality, produced the desired result, leaving the country's ignominious anti-lesbian/gay legislation on the books right up to the present day (Graupner 1995: vol. 2; Krickler 1995).

Along with other lesbian and gay activists, Kurt Krickler had fought Austria's injurious criminal law unsuccessfully for well over a decade, and – seeing the country's homophobic legislation in the ever sharper relief of the comparative EU perspective – he came to regard the placid summer of 1995 as the right moment for more drastic measures (Kräutler 1995; Krickler 1989). Only a week prior to Krickler's initial announcement of the pending Outing of the Catholic bishops, Austria's church-affiliated Christian-conservative People's Party (ÖVP) had thwarted the latest in a long string of parliamentary initiatives aimed at a repeal of the anti-lesbian/gay laws (Knecht and Odehnal 1995).[3] To Krickler, the Outing-Aktion would thus expose the inherent hypocrisy of individual members of the clergy who were complicit in the "oppression of lesbians and gay men" despite their own homosexual inclinations. Figuring this mode of political activism as a form of self-defense for a besieged lesbian/gay emancipation movement, Krickler vowed to continue the systematic Outing of prominent Austrians until "the paragraphs would be repealed" (Krickler 1989).[4]

Krickler's decision to resort to the tactic of Outing as a vehicle for lesbian/gay politics revealed yet another transnational layer of Austria's Outing-affair. The politics of Outing was, after all, a recent "import," originated by the now-defunct New York magazine *Outweek*, famous for its disclosure of the homosexuality of magazine tycoon Malcom Forbes in the late 1980s and early 1990s (see Gross 1993; Mohr 1992; Murphy 1994). Though Outing had also been utilized by lesbian/gay activists in Britain shortly thereafter, it was a famous case in Germany that brought Outing to the attention of Austria's lesbian/gay scene. Following filmmaker Rosa von Praunheim's televised Outings of several German celebrities in late 1991, the political efficacy and underlying ethics of such disclosures were widely criticized – a popular position reflected in a number of commentaries issued in Austria's lesbian/gay press. A nuanced exposition published in the now-defunct lesbian/gay magazine *tamtam*, for example, concluded that – in the context of a homophobic social field – Outing would not only serve the ethically dubious purpose of individual denunciation, but would also effectively instrumentalize and thereby perpetuate the conception of homosexuality as social stigma (Sulzenbacher 1992; see also Pircher 1992).

Gay Readings

While Krickler's promise of imminent disclosure came as a complete shock for Austria's wider public, many of Austria's lesbians and gay men thus already had occasion to reflect on the dynamics of Outing. In this context, the weeks of the Outing-affair saw the unprecedented media exposure of (mostly) openly gay men – disciplined and circumscribed as both "experts" and "persons affected" – commenting on the ramifications of the pending events. In these mass-mediated texts, which replicated the heated debates conducted at many lesbian and gay locales, two distinct positions vis-à-vis Krickler's Outing-Aktion were articulated. The first endorsed the practice of Outing under the condition that concrete evidence be brought forward. The second, in contrast, opposed Outings altogether, citing liberal tolerance and the right to privacy as constitutive aspects of lesbian and gay existence.

Vienna's gay press and the demand for successful outings

A number of gay activists (writing mostly in lesbian/gay publications) publicly voiced their qualified support for an Outing-Aktion that could expose the duplicity of a social system whose closeted members were protected by a silencing veil of the unspeakable, while furthering the continuous discrimination of lesbians and gay men. As such, these activists explicitly welcomed the Outing of "persons . . . who actively worked against the interests of gay men, lesbians, and bisexuals" (Toth 1995). At the same time, however, any attempt at Outing, they argued, needed to adhere to a strict regimen of truth. Operating in a realist mode – characterized by a critical awareness of the unequal distribution of authoritative voices in a homophobic system – they doubted whether any "assertion" coming "from our corner" would "convince" an "incredulous population" for whom a simple "denial" of the "blemish of homosexuality" was enough to diffuse suspicion (Vlassakakis 1995). Thus, while "Outing might be a perfect weapon in the fight against discrimination," it could "only have the desired success" if a given "Outing was based on tangible, unambiguous, and therefore irrefutable proof" (Graupner and Toth 1995). In this essentially positivistic framework, anchored in the possibility of unequivocal truth-claims about an individual's sexual orientation and preference, it was clear that the "desired success" of Outing could only lie in the effective "exposure of the unbearable hypocrisy" of those closeted homosexuals who opposed lesbian/gay rights (Graupner and Toth 1995). It was in this sense that Krickler's Outing-Aktion came to prove a rather grave disappointment for these activists.

After all, when it came time to disclose the names of Austria's homosexual bishops at the press conference in Vienna's Café Landtmann on August 1, 1995, Krickler significantly modified his initial claims. While he had originally promised to reveal the dignitaries' manifest homosexuality, the climactic moment of revelation – at which Krickler issued the names of four (rather than the originally promised five) bishops in alphabetical order – was not accompanied by any concrete evidence. Rather, Krickler now spoke somewhat vaguely of these bishops' homosexual tendencies *(Neigungen)*, which he further qualified by insisting on the presence of homosexual leanings in all human beings (Knecht and Odehnal 1995; ORF 1995).

For those favoring the Outing of closeted opponents of lesbian/gay rights, the Outing-Aktion had imploded at that very moment. In a piece titled "Outing – eine Analyse," one pro-Outing activist characterized the events of August 1 as a "pathetic display" *(Armutszeugnis)*: "Contrary to initial announcements, Krickler only spoke of the 'homosexual tendencies' of this and that bishop; future Outings are not likely to differ from this first effort. Krickler failed to deliver the most important good: proof for the truth of his assertions, and without that his entire campaign was reduced to absurdity" (Seiler 1995:14).

Epistemologies of the closet and lesbian/gay claims to privacy

If the qualified support of some gay activists for Krickler's Outing-Aktion disintegrated only when the Outings failed to produce tangible evidence for the homosexuality of the bishops under question, a putative majority of Austria's lesbians and gay men (most of whom are not politically organized or vocal in lesbian/gay politics) had opposed Krickler's Outing-Aktion from the moment of its inception. Günter Tolar – an established television personality and Austria's most famous openly gay man, following his 1992 coming out in the wake of the AIDS-related suicide of his partner of 15 years – voiced the "mainstream" position most prominently. While Tolar deemed the anti-lesbian/gay stance of the Catholic Church and the Christian-conservative People's party reprehensible, he warned that the Outing of any particular individual would hardly alleviate the situation, while possibly making matters worse for lesbians and gay men. In a much-publicized magazine interview appearing only days before the Outings were to take place, Tolar articulated a political stance dominated by the liberal principle of reciprocal tolerance. Emphasizing the position of lesbians and gay men as socially marginalized and potentially disenfranchised individuals, he warned that Krickler's shot could backfire: "As a gay man, I cannot ask for tolerance and understanding, while at the same time, using homosexuality as a weapon against others" (Tolar, in *News* 1995a).

How much this plea for mutual tolerance was articulated in a framework of liberal humanism can be gleaned from the repeated invocation of the sanctity of an individual's right to privacy – a right that Tolar portrayed as the constitutive factor of lesbian and gay life. In an interview published a few days after the Outing, Tolar not only opposed Krickler's Outing-Aktion by asserting unequivocally that "homosexuality was a private matter," he also showed empathy with the "victims," whose (real or imagined) sexual proclivities were now exposed to a disapproving public gaze: "The situation of those who were outed is horrible and most unpleasant" (Tolar, in *News* 1995b). If the formerly closeted television-show host Tolar thus insisted on the shepherding of homosexuals' inherent right to privacy, he at once exemplified and articulated the volatile position of the majority of Austria's lesbians and gay men, whose selectively enforced enactments of various "epistemologies of the closet" continue to govern their everyday lives (compare Sedgwick 1990:67–90). Read from their point of view, the Outing-affair represented a dangerous challenge to a symbolic economy that rewarded the nonconfrontational assumption of privatized homosexuality with the cavalier homophobia of benevolent neglect – that is, "tolerance."

A Queer Critique

Despite their radically different positions on the question of Outing, it is interesting that Krickler's gay detractors adhered to a seemingly self-evident conception of homosexuality as an irreducible characteristic mapped on particular bodies. Thus, underneath both the demand to produce "truthful" Outings and the admonition to protect the privacy of lesbians and gay men lay a similar propensity to maintain homosexuality as a clearly legible social marker, signifying a distinct identity coalesced around the trope of same-sex sexual desire and practice.[5] Whether the distinct "sexual species" so constituted was to be advanced through the defiant unmasking of social hypocrisy through more "successful" Outings, or protected – much like other "minority groups" – by the goodwill of civil society, the fixity of a hegemonic construction of homosexuality as difference was ultimately left intact.

My point is not to defend Kurt Krickler's political vision – a vision whose pronounced ambiguity would make such an undertaking very difficult in any event. Nevertheless, I would suggest that by adhering to the fixity of homosexual identity and its matrix of social signification, the gay critics of the Outing-Aktion may have missed the radically emancipatory dimensions of the Outing-affair – specifically, the political insights to be gained from Krickler's challenge of the pervasive hetero/homo binary and the effective exposure of the social mechanisms through which a homophobic society at once reproduces and disciplines its sexual "deviants." In the following, I therefore propose to undertake a reading of the Outing-Aktion informed by the critical insights, analytic approaches, and political strategies generated by queer theory. For my purposes, the most important of these include the following: the insistence on the historical and cultural construction of sexual subjectivities; the questioning of naturalized and essentialized sexualities; the understanding of sexuality as a field of power; the emphasis on the inherently political constitution of the sociosexual field; the recognition of the relevance of the hetero/homo binary as an organizing principle for a wide range of institutions and social ideologies; the demand to treat sexuality as a primary category for social analysis; the need to focus on lesbian/gay struggles as a main site of conflict in the modern world; the proposition to regard fields of normalization – along with forms of intolerance – as sites of violence; the development of subversive strategies vis-à-vis oppressive sexual regimes; the undermining of heterosexual privilege through the active disruption of the injurious (re)production of the hetero/homo binary; the deconstructive exposure of the performative constitution of normative gender; the playful rearticulation and resistive resignification of hegemonic sociosexual structures; and the immanent critique of an "ethnicized" conception of lesbian and gay male identity linked in turn to a programmatic awareness of the inherent difficulty involved in defining the population whose interests would be at stake in "queer" politics (see Butler 1990:128–49; 1991; 1993:1–23; de Lauretis 1991; Halperin 1995:15–125; Sedgwick 1990:1–63; 1993:1–20; Warner 1993:x–xxviii).

With these analytic tools, I propose to read the Outing-affair as a politically veiled performative act that exposed the unequal structuration of the sociosexual field in at least three ways. First, in Austria's homophobic social field, the threat of the dissolution of the heteronormative grid[6] provoked a violent reassertion of heterosexist hegemony, which exposed the mechanisms underlying the unequal constitution and valuation of various sexual identities. Second, the ostensibly well-meaning response of liberal commentators and the liberal press revealed a deep-seated paternalism that disciplined and circumscribed lesbian and gay lives through the persistent deployment of homophobic stereotypes of sexual pathology. And third, the repeated invocation of the right to privacy not only demonstrated the unequal stratification of privacy in a hetero/homo regime, but also exposed the construction of the very concept of privacy as the bearer of the traces of sexual difference.

From such a reading of the Austrian Outing-affair it does not follow, however, that Krickler's political actions were themselves steered by an explicitly queer agenda. Quite on the contrary, while Krickler's insistence on the universal presence of homosexual tendencies accorded with queer contestations of the hetero/homo binary, the Outing-Aktion ultimately continued a long-standing "minority rights" effort, concerned less with the deconstructive critique of heterosexist hegemony than with the social and political advancement of a clearly demarcated lesbian and gay constituency (Krickler 1995).[7] Nevertheless, when analyzed from a queer theoretical perspective, the Outing-affair not only emerges as a genuinely queer moment, but can serve as a vital lesson for future lesbian/gay activism. In this sense, this article ultimately seeks to articulate a critical ethnographic stance vis-à-vis the violently heteronormative reaction to Krickler's Outing-Aktion, so as to ground a queer political project that could successfully undermine the injurious reproduction of the hetero/homo binary.

Straight Texts

In order to arrive at this queer interpretation of the Austrian events of July and August 1995, it is necessary to shift the analytic focus from the lesbian/gay partisans of the Outing-debate to those "straight voices" who produced the publicized horror of the Outing-affair – a mass-mediated narrative that readily came to double as the event's authoritative discourse of truth and reason.[8] Viewed from this perspective, Krickler's Outing-Aktion presented a concrete challenge to a sociosexual system that required for its normative and unmarked reproduction the persistence of a clearly intelligible, sharply bounded entity functioning as its abjectly constitutive Other. Put differently, Krickler's eventual assertion of universal "homosexual tendencies" threatened to undermine and destabilize society's heteronormative grid. In this vein, the complexly layered "public" reaction against the Outing-Aktion should ultimately be understood as the violent response leveled against the possible disruption of the sociosexual field. It was in this sense that the performative defense of the reigning sociosexual system effectively doubled as its reproduction, even as its heterosexist slippages made such queer interventions as the present one possible.[9]

Outing and the reassertion of the heteronormative grid

In terms of the assertion and preservation of society's heteronormative grid, the direct response of Krickler's "victims" to the Outing-Aktion was by far the most immediate and discursively violent reaction. In this regard, the clergy's principled celibacy – a sexual state that in theory is above and beyond the hetero/homo binary – needs to be taken into account. From that perspective, Krickler's initial announcement of the pending disclosure of the bishops' manifest homosexuality not only threatened to implicate the upper echelons of the clergy in the ignominious practices of an abject sexuality, but effectively undermined the cultural authority the Catholic Church derives, in part, from its representatives' sexual status of abstinence. In the context of previous allegations of sexual misconduct among prominent members of Austria's clergy,[10] Krickler's actions promised to further weaken the church's credibility, in turn provoking Austria's council of bishops to take defensive actions through recourse to the strategic deployment of homophobic rhetoric. Thus, only a few days after Krickler's initial announcement of the imminent Outings, the country's prominent clergy generated a unified front, categorically dismissing the impending disclosures as unruly accusations and self-evident lies. As Kurt Krenn – the powerful bishop of St. Pölten – explicated in an interview published almost two weeks prior to the scheduled Outing, the clergy regarded Krickler's Outing-Aktion as nothing but a "mean-spirited and disgusting scandal" *(eine ganz böse Sauerei)*. At the same time, Krenn felt confident in the public's uncompromising ability to judge not only "who lies and who tells the truth," but "who was respectable and who was not" (Krenn, in Wachter 1995). The readily intelligible chain of significations put into discursive play thus advanced a patently homophobic logic in which Krickler's Outing-Aktion could stand as an encompassing sign, conflating untruth and the lack of respectability with homosexuality. By the same token, Krenn had effectively averted the stigma of homosexuality by positioning the clergy (as symbols of respectability and truthfulness) in constitutive opposition to a self-evident (homosexual) Other.

While the bishop's reaction may have been intended to assuage doubts regarding the celibacy of Austria's clergy, the strategic recourse to the trope of the homosexual as abject Other ultimately demonstrated the church's investment in the preservation of an unequally structured hetero/homo dichotomy (and in positioning itself as hetero within it). This became even more evident when, almost a week before Krickler's scheduled press conference, Austria's council of bishops revealed the legal strategies conceived in light of the anticipated Outings. To restore the (non)-sexual reputation of any member of the clergy named there, the council promised lawsuits under the rubrics of slander *(Verleumdung)*, defamation of character *(üble Nachrede)*, and damage of personal credibility *(Kreditschädigung)* (Worm 1995). By circumscribing homosexuality under such abject legal categories, the church's response to Krickler's proposed Outings participated in a larger social technology that safeguards and perpetuates a stratified and differently valued regime of sexual subjectivities.

When Kricker finally disclosed the names of the four bishops, the church's heteronormative sociosexual identification was further cemented by their culturally resonant retorts. While Krickler's proclamation of the presence of universal homosexual tendencies neither questioned the bishops' celibacy nor commented on their "actual" sexual practices, the Outed dignitaries responded to the potential destabilization of the heteronormative grid through a reactive assertion of heterosexist normalcy. Rather than invoking celibacy as a sexual status above and beyond the hetero/homo binary, Bishop Christoph Schönborn of Vienna denounced Krickler's statement as "public misrepresentation," a response echoed by Vorarlberg's Bishop Klaus Küng, who called the disclosure an "infamous reproach" (Küng, in *Standard* 1995; Schönborn, in ORF 1995). If Schönborn and Küng sought to assert their normative sexuality through such disavowals of homosexual tendencies, it was Salzburg's Bishop Andreas Laun who deployed the violent social technology of heterosexism most prominently. In informing a presumptively understanding public that "I have only one sexual inclination, and it is normal," he not only invoked his heterosexual credentials, but affirmed and reproduced the hetero/homo binary and its violently normalizing hierarchy (Laun, in *Kurier* 1995).

By exposing the reproduction of the heteronormative sociosexual field through such socially scripted and generative acts of performative heterosexuality (with its inherently dubious claims to normalcy, truth, and respectability), the Outing-Aktion thus allowed a revealing glimpse into the socially sanctioned mechanisms of heterosexism. As the case of Austria's (Outed) bishops demonstrated, in a social order where power and respectability are at once tied to and derived (at least in part) from the intrinsically heterosexist presumption of normalcy, the aggressive preservation of an unequally stratified dichotomous sexual system represents a constitutive political act. In this sense, Krickler's challenge brought forth and exposed – in the microcosm of a summer's debate – how the abject naming, delineating, fixing, and devaluation of a homosexual Other not only constitutes and preserves the "homosexual" as a distinct species, but serves as an ongoing means for the politically interested formation of an unmarked normative Self (even if nominally celibate).

Liberal paternalism and the pathology of the gay voice

While Austria's bishops solidified the hetero/homo binary as part of a political project that derives authority from its constitutive abjection of a homosexual Other, the response by Austria's liberal media to the Outing-Aktion was somewhat more ambiguous. On the one hand, the country's liberal press was unanimous in its condemnation of Krickler's Outings. On the other hand, a number of sexually unmarked (that is, presumptively "heterosexual") commentators took the occasion of the Outing-affair to display compassion for the plight of Austria's homosexuals, especially in light of the country's anti-lesbian/gay legislation. What remains to be explored, however, is the sociodiscursive cost by which this liberal support for lesbian/gay politics was purchased.

Even a cursory glance at the liberal commentaries written in the wake of the Outing-affair reveals a perhaps surprising degree of support for the political/legal demands underlying Krickler's Outing-Aktion (see, for example, Geyer 1995; Maier 1995; Rauscher 1995). But while many editorialists were quick to concede the obvious injustice of Austria's anti-lesbian/gay statutes, few showed any tangible concern for the quality of life among the country's lesbians and gay men. Rather than exploring the adverse effects of continuous legal and social discrimination, what struck most commentators as noteworthy about the situation at hand was Austria's lackluster legislative record – especially when compared to other European countries: as the left-liberal magazine *profil* bemoaned in a rather typical flight of comparative neocolonial fancy, "in regard to criminal law, Austria has no equals in the civilized parts of Europe" (Buchacher and Seiler 1995:28).[11] But if *profil* and other liberal voices viewed the country's anti-homosexual legislative record as a liability for Austria's rightful place in Europe's progressively "civilizing" mission, such abstractly formulated sympathy for lesbian/gay causes failed to translate into active political support.

Quite on the contrary, the Outing-affair ultimately allowed a "liberal establishment" – sustained as an imagined community through strategic appeals to reason, individual rights, the regiments of civil society, and the decorum of proper political culture – to define the parameters of public debate and political action through the marginalization of an explicitly lesbian/gay-coded voice. In sociodiscursive practice, this exclusionary stratagem occurred through the conflation and coconstitution of the signifier "Kurt Krickler" with an "enlightened" trope of homosexuality as pathology. In this sense, a reading of *profil*'s much-celebrated cover story – published only a day before the Outings and advertised through a highly controversial cover picture – can serve as a vehicle for the critical analysis of this "liberal" construction of the homosexual (voice) as Other. Under the banner of pluralistic tolerance, the authors of "Confess that you are gay" ostensibly took a stance against the "continued discrimination of homosexuals" (Buchacher and Seiler 1995:28). But if this avowed position gestured to *profil*'s progressive political agenda, the tolerance it evoked was not extended to such "real-life homosexuals" as Krickler, who quickly emerged as the article's genuine object of scrutiny. Operating in a liberal framework of truth-finding, *profil* ultimately found Krickler's illiberal and unreasonable actions – rather than the predicament they were protesting – in need of explication and explanation. In this situation, *profil* avoided linking the Outing-Aktion to the social ills of homophobia, fixing its critical faculties instead on an investigation of Krickler's personal psychopathologies. With easy recourse to the always already operative "enlightened" discourses that construct homosexuality as disease, a diagnosis was readily available. As *profil* concluded, Krickler's "radicalism" and the resulting "deed of desperation" had their origin in his personal plight: "For ten years," Krickler "knows that he is HIV-positive . . . three years ago, his long-term companion died of the disease" (Buchacher and Seiler 1995:26).

The operationalization of the powerful chain of signification, "homosexuality – disease – AIDS – death – despair – unreason," ultimately served a simple purpose. In the hands of *profil*, Krickler became a pitiful gay stereotype, whose Outing-Aktion could be readily dismissed as the act of a disgruntled, desperate, and pathological activist-loner. This view of Krickler was elaborated through remarks about both his early and painful knowledge of his (deviant) sexuality and his adult experience of constant "pressure" and "fear" as well as the "suicides of numerous friends" (Buchacher and Seiler 1995:29). This reductive treatment of Krickler's actions allowed the authors of the piece to articulate an ostensibly liberal position on the Outing-affair while refusing any real engagement with Krickler's critique of and protest against prevalent power relations. In this sense, the piece itself ultimately functioned as an example of the sociodiscursive strategies by which "dangerous homosexuals" can be marginalized in "enlightened" civil society through recourse to a codified arsenal of social pathologies, which readily construct "the homosexual" (as individual or group) as an unreasoned and diseased social entity. In the final analysis, it is through such mechanisms of the social surveillance of sexual difference that the lesbian/gay speaking voice can be silenced and disciplined into accommodationist submission at the very moment of its socially intelligible constitution.

If the *profil* article thus suggested that the intrinsically "unreasoned voice of homosexuality" needed to be closely circumscribed, the general outpouring of liberal paternalism accompanying the Outing-affair represented a specific instantiation of the way a heterosexualized position can pronounce "truths" about homosexuality through recourse to a seemingly objective, quasi-neutral (that is, "liberal") stance. An editorial piece in the newspaper *Die Presse* – Austria's flagship bourgeois publication – may serve as illustration for the dynamic under question. In this case too, it was a professed concern for an "end of discrimination" that signified (or better, perhaps, "performed") the piece's liberal credentials (Rohrer 1995). But the title "Counter-productive" suggested otherwise; and indeed, the short editorial moved swiftly from a wholesale condemnation of Krickler's "counter-productive behavior" and the overtly patronizing approbation of "those homosexuals who do not condone it" to a (not-so-) veiled threat culminating in the insinuation that Krickler's actions would not only hurt the "very cause" of the "minority" he "represents," but would also lead to a "hardening of the fronts" (Rohrer 1995). The editorial's sociodiscursive strategy was thus twofold. On the one hand, it constructed "homosexuals" (exemplified by Krickler) as a homogeneous group unified by a self-regenerating minority status circumscribed by ostensibly impermeable "fronts." On the other hand, the editorial also effectively denied the group so constituted a voice of its own, prescribing instead the passive rhetoric of accommodationist silence that the editorial endorsed through its textual performance of lesbian/gay dissent to the Outing-Aktion. It was in this sense that – despite its abstract support of lesbian/gay demands – the "liberal" reaction to the Outing-affair not only reproduced the unequal stratification of the sociosexual field, but sustained a truth-regime in which lesbian and gay voices are devalued as a consequence of their location within an adversely situated and intrinsically self-interested minority group – a sociodiscursive position that allows neither the articulation of "objective" and "disinterested" "truths" nor the contestation of the "enlightened" order that constitutes that position.

Compulsory privacy and the homosexual other

Despite their disagreement over the validity of the political demands underlying the Outing-Aktion, the one aspect both liberal and conservative commentators of the Outing-affair agreed on was their denouncement of Krickler's violation of the "victims" private sphere. Thus, when an editorialist for the left-liberal *Standard* spoke of Krickler's actions as a "violation of human dignity" (Sperl 1995) due to their "invasion of the private sphere," the sentiment was echoed not only by Austria's state-run broadcasting company (which called the Outing an "attack on the personal rights of a human being" [ÖRF 1995]) but also by members of the clergy, one of whom referred to Krickler's Outing-Aktion as a "cruel destruction of a person's basic rights" (in *Die Presse* 1995).[12]

This common horror of the violation of the sanctity of privacy signified a consensus in Austria's mass-mediated sociosexual field that (re)constituted homosexuality as the social practice and sexual subjectivity that dare not speak its name in public.

To cull only one of many prominent statements whose diagnostic analyses doubled as constitutive political acts, I want to discuss an editorial published in the center-right daily *Kurier.* There, Austria's embattled bishops were given empathetic advice on how to deal with the unpleasant situation most effectively: "The most reasonable reaction of those affected would be the calm insistence on their right for the respect of their intimate lives... establishing beyond question, that homosexuality is a private matter, quite naturally among bishops as well" (Rabl 1995).

Even though the editorial went on to assert that homosexuality (personal matter that it is) should not reflect negatively on an individual's public reputation, its insistence on the private nature of same-sex sexuality remained absolute. While this oft-taken position bore obvious traces of the operative liberal principle of assigning sexuality to an exclusively "private" sphere, it was characterized by the performative focus on the sheer impossibility of public or publicized homosexuality. It was only by implication that heterosexuality functioned in the editorial's analytic framework, and its absence had clear political resonances. While homosexuality was to be diagnosed, circumscribed, and constituted as part of an inherently private domain, heterosexuality needed no boundary-setting intervention. It would have been nonsensical to Out Austria's bishops as "straight": one does not "come out" as straight – it is the presumptive state, even, or perhaps especially, among the performatively celibate. Similarly, it was unnecessary to carve a niche for heterosexuality along a public/private binary, where it always already functions as the publicly articulated operative assumption. It was in this sense that the editorial's insistence on the inherently private nature of homosexuality contributed to a general mechanism that instrumentalizes the punitive surveillance of same-sex sexuality in the construction and preservation of an always already heterosexualized, yet ostensibly unmarked, public sphere. In this manner, the *Kurier* editorial was part and parcel of the sociodiscursive technology of abjectly privatized homosexuality that has its practical counterpart in the socially and culturally sanctioned performances of public heterosexuality – ranging as they do from such legal constructs as marriage to the politics of "proper" family life. In sustaining homosexuality as the social state whose very nature signifies its status as "not public," the *Kurier* editorial – along with countless other commentaries – thus allowed a glimpse into the sociodiscursive reproduction of an ideological framework that supports the preservation of the unequally valued hetero/homo dichotomy through its practical alignment with an operative public/private distinction.

Strategic Conclusions

Ideally, the present article can function in the dual mode it was conceived: as both sociocultural analysis and political intervention. In regard to the former, I have sought to contextualize Austria's Outing-affair in the social realities of the unequal legal codes, national political fronts, and transnational developments that conditioned it. At a moment when a global cultural economy rendered the widespread deployment of such radical political tactics as Outing a topic of debate in Austria's lesbian/gay scene, Kurt Krickler's Outing-Aktion thus emerged as the theatrical capstone of years of political activism directed at the repeal of the country's anti-lesbian/gay legislation – a legislation that had come under intensified scrutiny in the wake of Austria's joining of the European Union.

In regard to the latter, I have anchored my analysis in a reading of the lesbian/gay reactions to the Outing-Aktion. As I have shown, the (overwhelmingly negative) responses were divided between two positions: one group of lesbian/gay commentators professed their principled support for the Outing of publicly homophobic persons, but found grave fault with Krickler for his failure to produce "hard" evidence of the bishops' homosexuality. Another (by and large) publicly silent group opposed the political practice altogether, insisting on the inherently private nature of homosexuality, whose unwanted publication would represent a severe violation of the sanctity of the private sphere.

As I argued, these oppositional camps may have failed to appreciate some of the emancipatory components of the Outing-Aktion. Especially when viewed from an analytic perspective informed by queer theory, Krickler's eventual insistence on the universal presence of homosexual tendencies challenged and temporarily disrupted the heteronormative grid. While Krickler's lesbian and gay critics adhered to a reified conception of homosexuality, which treated homosexuality as the always already socially intelligible. Other of an unmarked and normative heterosexuality, Krickler's Outing-Aktion (perhaps unwittingly) exposed and thereby opened for critique (some of) the violent sociodiscursive mechanisms that constitute and stabilize homosexuality qua sexual deviance in the first place.

In this sense, my queer analysis of the "straight texts" produced in the wake of the Outing-Aktion treated the Outing-affair and its concomitant textual production as a microcosm for the (re)production of an unequally stratified sociosexual field – an analytic move intended as both an inroad into the critical interrogation of the social mechanisms of homophobia and heterosexism, and a pathway to a critically informed political strategy that is inherently skeptical of the unreflected enactment of ready-made sexual categories. Within the textual economy of the present article, my use of "straight" readings thus ultimately functioned as part of an internal critique of the lesbian/gay responses to the Outing-affair. Against the uncritical adoption in these responses of the hetero/homo binary (and the lesbian/gay position within it), I initially posited the bishops' reactions to Krickler's "allegations" as a model for the socially scripted reconstitution and unequal valuation of sexual subject positions. In this sense, the bishops' professions of "innocence" and "normalcy" revealed the strategic instrumentalization of the heterosexist fictions required to sustain a heteronormative grid always already threatened by its dissolution. It is ultimately through such inherently homophobic acts of performative heterosexuality that homosexuality is cemented as its constitutive Other – a situation that suggests the need for the ongoing critical interrogation of a lesbian/gay subject position and the foundational traces of its normative devaluation.

Similarly – and in response to the qualified pro-Outing faction among Austria's lesbians and gay men – the ability to articulate truth-claims should never be taken for granted when operating from a lesbian/gay subject position. As I showed in my analysis of the reaction of Austria's liberal media to the Outing-Aktion, the reconstitution and surveillance of a marked lesbian/gay voice could readily serve a homophobic project through its selective pathologization and concomitant silencing of "dangerous gay voices." It is in this sense that the question of the "hard evidence" for an individual's homosexuality can become mute in the face of a sociodiscursive regime that articulates and reinforces a heteronormative logic through strategic recourse to a seemingly disinterested quasi-objectivity.

Finally, the frequently articulated insistence on the private nature of homosexuality prompted me to analyze the mechanisms by which homosexuality is so constituted in the first place. As I argued, the reaction to the Outing-affair documented the constitutive relegation of same-sex sexuality to an exclusively private realm – an ongoing political act sustained through recourse to an unequal social economy that readily figures the "homosexual" as that which is by definition "not public." It is by way of an always already operative default that heterosexuality signifies and performs itself as a public event, thereby legitimizing the hetero/homo binary in terms of the dichotomy of public/private. In this situation, the lesbian/gay assertion of the inherently private nature of homosexuality not only echoed the sociodiscursive technology of a homophobic regime, but actually reified its ideological stronghold in practice – not least by permitting Krickler's heteronormative detractors the strategic presentation of "acceptable" (that is, privatized and often anonymous) gay voices.

In its various dimensions, Austria's Outing-affair clearly demonstrated the perilous contingencies of lesbian/gay political work. After all, the present analysis intimates that Krickler's resistive effort – while temporarily suspending the injurious hetero/homo binary – ultimately engendered a violent reassertion of heterosexist hegemony at multiple domains of the social order. I would nevertheless propose that when viewed from a queer analytic perspective, the Outing-Aktion generated crucial insights for lesbian/gay activism. In the first place, the Outing-affair forcefully suggested that the practice of Outing may itself be an inappropriate tool for queer struggle. Setting aside the ethical conundrum of revealing an individual's homosexuality to a homophobic society, Outings – from the public disclosure of "rumors" to the "successful" exposure of overtly homophobic persons – can hardly escape the conceptual trap of enacting and reifying a heteronormative grid, which sustains itself through the ongoing figuration of "the homosexual" as distinct and abject Other. Thus, while the Outing of a homophobe's manifest homosexuality may protest a social reality of unbearable hypocrisy, it ultimately reconstitutes that reality by allowing heterosexuality to pose as the presumptive state vis-à-vis a subordinated homosexuality that is signified by a performative declaration of Otherness. In the final analysis, even Krickler's "queer" Outing strategy (marked by the eventual refusal of the hetero/homo binary) reinscribed this violent regime by rendering homosexuality as the principal site of epistemological scrutiny, while preserving heterosexuality's unchallenged status as the "normative measure of the real" (Butler 1991:21).

But if this queer critique of Outing questions the efficacy of maintaining "homosexuality" as the privileged site of lesbian/gay work, I firmly believe in the possibility of a coherent social and political position – a position, however, that aligns demands for lesbian/gay emancipation with a relentless and ongoing interrogation of the social mechanisms of homophobia and heterosexism. In this sense, lesbian/gay politics should be wary of grounding itself in the reified "reality" of "lesbian and gay experience," but should investigate the very constitution of its experiential tropes (compare Scott 1991). Only such a politically immanent critique can render queer theory's vital skepticism of the naturalized fixity of sexual categories and its concomitant focus on the reproduction of unequally stratified sociosexual fields, the building blocks of political action on behalf of lesbian and gay persons.

In view of the Austrian Outing-affair, such action should then include the systematic resistance to regimes of truth that accord discursive authority according to the injurious logic of the hetero/homo binary. In a similar vein, the public/private distinction merits continuous conceptual scrutiny, ranging from the disruptive insistence on the politically mediated nature of sexuality to the creative design of insubordinate acts that refigure homosexuality as a public spectacle. More generally, the struggle for lesbian/gay equality (such as the demand to repeal Austria's anti-lesbian/gay criminal codes) needs to be extended beyond a liberal-pluralist framework of "minority rights" to include a more widely cast analysis of homophobia and heterosexism as social ills. In this manner, an often injurious (liberal) practice of tolerance for a clearly demarcated group of lesbians and gay men could be superseded by queer alliances, enacting various forms of resistance against the "normal" and its societally sanctioned vehicles above and beyond a matrix of sexual identity categories.

Ironically, it was one of the "Outed" Austrian bishops – Egon Kapellari of Carinthia – who, by way of negative invocation, suggested such a queer strategy for political action most clearly. Regarding Krickler's Outing-Aktion as an attack on society at large rather than on any of its individual members, Kapellari warned that "the attempt to compromise the bishops was a violation of society's fundamental values" (Kapellari, in *Kurier* 1995). In thus suggesting a potential course for Austrian queer politics, I can only agree with the bishop's assessment and call for further acts that critically undermine and subversively rearticulate "society's fundamental values."

NOTES

1 The starkly pejorative connotation of the original German *gleichgeschlechtliche Unzucht* (literally, lechery between people of the same sex) is not fully conveyed by its more value-neutral translation as "same-sex sexual relations." Throughout this essay, I use "lesbian/gay" rather than "lesbian and gay" when I am discussing a situation in which lesbians and gay men struggle together politically and socially. I would use a single term to denote this, but "homosexual politics," "homosexual activists," and "homosexual scene" forbid themselves in the context of my overarching argument and political stance regarding reified "homosexuality." At the same time, "queer politics," "queer activists," "queer scene," and "queer press" would offer themselves were it not for the distinction I want to draw between the ethnic identity-based "lesbian/gay politics" and a transidentity "queer politics."

2 Among EU members, only Finland, the United Kingdom, and Ireland differentiate between heterosexual and homosexual acts in regard to codifications of the age of consent. In none of these countries, however, does the "gap" between the legal age for same-sex and opposite-sex sexual activity differ by more than two years, leaving Austria (along with Liechtenstein) the only liberal democracy to effectively enact a four-year difference between the legal commencement of straight (and lesbian) relations on the one hand (at 14), and gay male sexual relations on the other hand (at 18). Moreover, Austria's Paragraph

209 is executed more frequently and threatens much harsher penalties (a mandatory sentence of six months to five years in the case of a conviction) than comparable Western European statutes, amplifying the country's injurious criminal code in the realities of legal practice (Graupner 1995: vol. 2; in press).

3 The struggle over Austria's anti-lesbian/gay legislation continues to split the country's political field rather neatly along a "liberal"/"conservative" divide. On the liberal side, Austria's Social-Democratic Party (SPÖ), the socially progressive Green Party (*Die Grünen*), and the socially libertarian Liberal Forum (LIF) support the revocation of Paragraphs 209, 220, and 221. On the conservative side, the Austrian People's Party (ÖVP) and the ultra-right-wing Freedom Party (FPÖ) advocate the maintenance of the status quo (or, as in the case of the ÖVP, even consider the institution of tighter legal restrictions aimed against lesbians and gay men). While the conservative side has been holding a slim majority in parliament for over five years (thereby rendering the abolition of the anti-lesbian/gay statutes difficult in the first place), efforts at repealing the homophobic legislation have mainly failed because the SPÖ has continuously shied away from overtly challenging the ÖVP on the issue (the two parties have been governing the country in a coalition under the leadership of the SPÖ for the last ten years). Historically, the SPÖ has been at the forefront of the legislative decriminalization of homosexuality, engineering the revocation of the general ban on male same-sex sexual relations in 1971 over the explicit objection of the ÖVP and the Catholic Church, which were in turn mollified by the creation of Paragraphs 209, 220, and 221 (as well as Paragraph 210, which interdicted gay male prostitution until its repeal in 1989) (Hauer 1989:50–67). The fact that the analysis presented in this article critiques a "liberal" position as often concealing violent acts of normalization under the guise of ostensible tolerance should by no means be mistaken for an endorsement of the "conservative" side of the political debate. For in the framework of Austrian realpolitik, this article is squarely situated on the "liberal" side, whose understanding of progressive politics on behalf of lesbian and gay persons it seeks to refigure through critical intervention.

4 In his initial statements, Krickler vowed to continue the Outing-Aktion indefinitely, promising to follow the exposure of Austria's bishops with periodic Outings of prominent members of the political parties he considered responsible for the ongoing legal discrimination against lesbians and gay men. In this sense, Krickler not only targeted the ÖVP and FPÖ for future Outings, but also the SPÖ, whose unwillingness to pressure its coalition partner ÖVP into progressive action on behalf of lesbians and gay men he deemed a form of complicity (Krickler 1989). However, in the wake of the frenzy of the initial Outing-Aktion, none of these announced Outings took place. Krickler never disclosed why he chose Austria's clergy as the first target of his Outing-Aktion. In a sense, it must have seemed like an obvious choice, since Austria's Catholic Church was already in a state of turmoil following allegations of (homo)sexual impropriety. Four months prior to the Outing-affair, widely publicized (and essentially unanswered) accusations had surfaced, suggesting that Vienna's archbishop, Hans Hermann Groër (the country's highest ranking active member of the clergy), had molested teenage boys while a supervisor at an Austrian parochial school in the 1970s. The ensuing crisis of Austria's Catholic Church (which led to Groër's eventual resignation by way of retirement) remained a prominent news item during the spring and early summer of 1995.

5 Michel Foucault's work (especially 1978) remains the cornerstone of any critique of the fictitious construction of social identity on the basis of an irreducible conception of sexuality.

6 With the term *heteronormative grid*, I denote the social technology that constitutes, preserves, and (falsely) naturalizes heterosexuality as the privileged (and unmarked) site of sociosexual identity formation through the constitutive abjection and structured

devaluation of a homosexual Other. In this sense, the term references the hetero/homo binary while emphasizing the heterosexist valence underlying its continuous reproduction and self-evident naturalization. This notion of a culturally operative heteronormative grid, then, builds on Judith Butler's formulations of the technologies of sexual subjectification. As she notes, "the process of 'assuming' a sex" occurs in the context of "the heterosexual imperative," which

> enables certain sexed identifications and forecloses and/or disavows other identifications. This exclusionary matrix by which subjects are formed thus requires the simultaneous production of a domain of abject beings, those who are not yet "subjects," but who form the constitutive outside to the domain of the subject. The abject designates here precisely those "unlivable" and "uninhabitable" zones of social life which are nevertheless densely populated by those who do not enjoy the status of the subject, but whose living under the sign of the "unlivable" is required to circumscribe the domain of the subject. This zone of uninhabitability will constitute the defining limit of the subject's domain; it will constitute that site of dreaded identification against which – and by virtue of which – the domain of the subject will circumscribe its own claim to autonomy and to life. In this sense, then, the subject is constituted through the force of exclusion and abjection, one which produces a constitutive outside to the subject, an abjected outside, which is, after all, "inside" the subject as its own founding repudiation. [Butler 1993:3]

7 As one of the leading activists of Austria's oldest lesbian/gay organization, HOSI (*Homosexuellen-Initiative*), Krickler's political efforts had always been articulated in what could be called a liberal-pluralist framework, which demanded proper political representation and progressive social action on behalf of a marginalized minority group. Founded in 1979 with the mission of "raising emancipatory gay consciousness" (viewed in opposition to the conformist and defeatist stance of closeted homosexuals), HOSI thus always considered its primary task to be the creation of politicized lesbian and gay identities (Till 1989). The social group so constituted would in turn win official recognition and tolerant treatment through HOSI's political efforts, which consisted largely of lobbying among sympathetic circles within Austria's political left – often with an emphasis on Austria's comparatively retrograde legislative record. See Krickler 1989 and other pieces in Handl et al. 1989 which document HOSI's political stance and chronicle the organization's history. In its initial conception of disclosing the manifest homosexuality of Austria's bishops, the Outing-Aktion thus echoed (and radicalized) an older political strategy, which regarded closeted (and hence unpoliticized) homosexuality as a liability for a powerful and widely visible "ethnicized" identity politics.

8 The following analyses owe much to David Halperin's brilliant reading of the biographies of Michel Foucault, which he uses as a site from which to critique the shifting authority of the differently sexualized writing voice (Halperin 1995: 126–85).

9 This conception of the performative reassertion of a heterosexist matrix owes much to Judith Butler's seminal work on the fictive constitution of heterosexualized genders. As Butler suggests, "the naturalistic effects of heterosexualized genders are produced through imitative strategies; what they imitate is a phantasmatic ideal of heterosexual identity, one that is produced by the imitation as its effect. In this sense, the 'reality' of heterosexual identities is performatively constituted through an imitation that sets itself up as the origin and the ground of all imitations" (Butler 1991:21). As Butler emphasizes, this performative constitution of normative gender can never fully conceal its ontological vacuity, thereby allowing the disruptive resignification of hegemonic categories at the moment of their rearticulation: "It is this constitutive failure of the performative, this slippage between discursive command and its appropriated effect, which provides the linguistic

occasion and index for a consequential disobedience" (Butler 1993:122). For a more immediate resistive intervention in the Outing-affair, see Bunzl 1995b.

10 As discussed in note 4, Vienna's archbishop, Hans Hermann Groër, had been at the center of controversy a few months prior to the Outing-affair, when he failed to respond to allegations that he had pursued sexual relations with male high school students while a supervisor at a parochial school in the 1970s. The widely debated accusations leveled against Groër not only followed on the heels of years of reports and rumors concerning (mostly) heterosexual relations allegedly conducted by Austria's clergy, but hit Austria's Catholic Church during a time of deep crisis. Already weakened by massive reductions in the number of officially registered Catholics over the last two decades (from roughly 95 percent of Austria's population to roughly 75 percent), Austria's council of bishops faced severe internal criticism of the conservative political agenda it endorsed during the 1990s (in regard to such issues as the position of women in the church and contraception, for example). This resistance climaxed in 1994 in a highly successful referendum (signed by over 500,000 Austrians) demanding the radical liberalization of the country's Catholic Church.

11 To recover some of the nuances of the various "liberal" positions discussed in this article, it is instructive to reflect on the radically different deployment of comparative legal data mustered in demand of a repeal of Austria's anti-lesbian/gay legislation. In this manner, lesbian/gay activists operating in a liberal-pluralist framework (including Krickler for most of his career) tend to invoke comparative data to bolster an oppositional and politically tenuous project of gaining tolerance for lesbians and gay men in the face of overt hostility by the conservative spectrum of Austria's political field. The invocation of similar data in the context of *profil*'s Outing-story, in contrast, followed an altogether different political purpose. Rather than seeking to advance the social and political standing of lesbians and gay men, it was the standing of Austria in the concert of Western European nations that was at stake here. During the debates surrounding Austria's joining of the EU, commentators (both on the right and the left) never tired of gauging the country's *Europareife* (a state of national maturity seen as a prerequisite to a successful inclusion in a greater Europe). And it was ultimately that very Europareife (which in turn signifies a privileged and desirable position of tutelage vis-à-vis the former state socialist countries) that *profil* saw undermined by the preservation of a legislative code that seemed antiquated and unenlightened in Western European comparison.

12 It may seem surprising that in the context of such invocations of the need to preserve and protect an individual's human dignity *(Menschenwürde)*, with its implied figuration of Outing as a form of denunciation, neither Austria's Nazi past nor the fate of lesbians and gay men during the Third Reich became an object of public discussion in conjunction with the Outing-affair (these issues, in fact, were never even brought up). The reason for this situation ultimately resides in the highly problematic nature of Austrian *Vergangenheitsbewältigung* (dealing with the [Nazi] past). Put simply, Aus-tria's second republic was created through recourse to a foundational "victim myth" *(Opfermythos)*, which cast the state and its population as the target of Hitlerite aggression. The politics behind this myth were simple. By posing as victim rather than coperpetrator, Austria effectively escaped Germany's postwar ostracization, managed to evade paying reparations to victims of Nazism (until well into the 1960s, with many cases still pending), and generally avoided international scrutiny in regard to the role of its citizens in the Third Reich (until the "Waldheim affair" of 1986). For politically progressive forces in Austria (who understand themselves as actively antifascist), this situation always demanded that Austria and its citizens be effectively confronted with the actual victims of the Holocaust – Jews foremost among them. In this situation, the battle of Austrian left-liberals always

remained at a very crude level, insisting on Austrians' coresponsibility for the Nazi genocide by pointing to the Jewish victims as evidence (see Bunzl 1995a).

In consequence, there is almost no awareness of the persecution of lesbians and gay men during the Third Reich (even among progressive liberals, not to mention conservatives or neofascists). Two examples will elucidate the situation: (1) Individual lesbians and gay men who were persecuted during the Third Reich have no claims to any reparations by the Austrian government (after years of hedging and international pressures, Jewish victims do have certain claims). Nor is there any effort being made to effect a legal change that could provide reparations to the lesbian and gay victims of Nazism (lesbian/gay demands have never even generated so much as a public discussion on the issue). (2) When lesbian/gay activists staged a protest during the unveiling of a monument against war and fascism (which – in its overt iconography stylizing the various "groups" of victims of Nazism – omitted any reference to lesbian and gay victims) in 1988, the response was one of genuine surprise mixed with overt hostility against the impudent claims brought forth by the demonstrators (they had demanded restitution for lesbian and gay victims of Nazism).

All this is to suggest that in contemporary Austria, the popular historical grounding necessary to place the persecution of homosexuals in the context of debates on the Third Reich is so tenuous as to almost forbid its public articulation. For the (far) right, issues of human dignity and denunciation ultimately signify a defense of the members of the war generation, who – as soldiers of the *Wehrmacht* – are said to have only fulfilled their duty and should therefore be spared the scrutiny of "critical" historians (this position was not only Waldheim's main line of defense, but continues to be articulated frequently by Jörg Haider – the leader of the right-wing FPÖ). Among liberal circles, on the other hand, denunciation and human dignity are invariably invoked to signify Jewish suffering and the need for adequate Vergangenheitsbewältigung – a position born out of explicit opposition to Austria's victim myth. In the end, this dual mode of silencing (itself a form of sociodiscursive violence, of course) leaves very little conceptual space to articulate lesbian/gay issues in the context of Austria's Nazi past – a situation that was exemplified and prolonged in the course of the Outing-affair.

REFERENCES

Buchacher, Robert, and Christian Seiler

1995 Gestehe, dass du schwul bist. Das Zwangs-"Outing" Prominenter hat der Homosexuellen-Bewegung bisher wenig genützt – allenfalls den Boulvardmedien. profil, July 31: 26–9.

Bunzl, Matti

1995a On the Politics and Semantics of Austrian Memory: Vienna's Monument against War and Fascism. History and Memory 7(2):7–40.

1995b Unerträglich salonfähig. Das Outing der Bischöfe durch Kurt Krickler: eine Kritik an profil. profil, August 14: 70–1.

Butler, Judith

1990 Gender Trouble: Feminism and the Subversion of Identity. New York: Routledge.

1991 Imitation and Gender Insubordination. *In* inside/out: Lesbian Theories, Gay Theories. Diana Fuss, ed. Pp. 13–31. New York: Routledge.

1993 Bodies that Matter: On the Discursive Limits of "Sex." New York: Routledge.

de Lauretis, Teresa

1991 Queer Theory: Lesbian and Gay Sexualities. Differences 5:iii–xviii.
Die Presse
1995 Kirche verurteilt "Outing," aber kein Nein zu Anliegen der Homosexuellen. July 28: 3.
Foucault, Michel
1978[1976] The History of Sexuality: An Introduction. Robert Hurley, trans. New York: Vintage Books.
Geyer, Herbert
1995 Ich will's gar nicht wissen. Wochenpresse, August 3: 15.
Graupner, Helmut
1995 Sexualität, Jugendschutz, und Menschenrechte: Über das Recht von Kindern und Jugendlichen auf sexuelle Selbstbestimmung. 2 vols. Ph.D. dissertation, University of Vienna.
1997 Criminalization at the Dawn of the Third Millennium: The Austrian Situation. *In* The Socio Legal Control of Homosexuality: A Multi-Nation Comparison. Richard Green and Donald J. West, eds. New York: Plenum.
Graupner, Helmut, and Michael Toth
1995 Offener Brief des Rechtskomitees LAMBDA and die HOSI Wien. XTRA 15–16 (August 3–September 3): 12.
Gross, Larry
1993 Contested Closets: The Politics and Ethics of Outing. Minneapolis: University of Minnesota Press.
Handl, Michael, Gudrun Hauer, Kurt Krickler, Friedrich Nussbaumer, and Dieter Schmutzer, eds.
1989 Homosexualität in Österreich. Vienna: Junius.
Halperin, David
1995 Saint Foucault: Towards a Gay Hagiography. New York: Oxford University Press.
Hauer, Gudrun
1989 Lesben-und Schwulengeschichte – Diskriminierung und Widerstand. *In* Homosexualität in Österreich. Handl et al., eds. Pp. 50–67. Vienna: Junius.
Jus Amandi: Zeitschrift für gleichgeschlechtliche Liebe und Recht
1995 Letzte Meldung. Heft 1:3.
Knecht, Doris, and Bernhard Odehnal
1995 Interview: Kurt Krickler: Outing war ein Erfolg! Der Falter, August 11: 8.
Kräutler, Werner
1995 Fünf Bischöfe im Outing. Nach dem Fall Groër droht Österreichs Kirche der nächste GAU. Die Homosexuellen-Initiative droht mit dem episkopalen Outing. News, July 13: 26.
Krickler, Kurt
1989 Rechtsvergleich und Rechtsentwicklung zur Homosexualität in Europa. *In* Homosexualität in Österreich. Handl et al., eds. Pp. 68–79. Vienna: Junius.
1995 Outing als Waffe. Kommentar: Das Parlament will die homosexuellenfeindlichen Paragraphen nicht aufheben: Jetzt wird geoutet. Der Falter. July 21: 6.
Kurier
1995 Zitate. August 2: 3.
Maier, Michael
1995 Im Schatten der Nuancen. Presse, July 29: 2.
Mohr, Richard
1992 Gay Ideas: Outing and Other Controversies. Boston: Beacon Press.
Murphy, Timothy, ed.

1994 Gay Ethics: Controversies in Outing, Civil Rights, and Sexual Science. New York: Harrington Press.
News
1995a "Ich bereue nichts." Günter Tolar über sein Coming-out. July 27: 36.
1995b Tolar: Zwangs-Outing? Schuß nach hinten. August 3: 160.
ORF (Österreichischer Rundfunk)
1995 News Report. Mittagsjournal, August 1.
Pircher, Peter
1992 Outing: Steinwurf auf Schädlinge? tamtam 11:10–11.
Rabl, Peter
1995 Statistisch muß es schwule Bischöfe geben. Kurier, August 2: 2.
Rauscher, Hans
1995 Ein frustrierter Aktivist greift zur politischen Erpressung. Kurier, July 28: 2.
Rohrer, Anneliese
1995 Kontraproduktiv. Presse, July 28: 2.
Scott, Joan
1991 The Evidence of Experience. Critical Inquirv 17:773–97.
Sedgwick, Eve Kosofsky
1990 Epistemology of the Closet. Berkeley: University of California Press.
1993 Tendencies. Durham, NC: Duke University Press.
Seiler, Georg
1995 Outing – eine Analyse. XTRA 17 (August 31–September 17): 14.
Sperl, Gerfried
1995 Unter der Gürtellinie. Standard. July 28: 28.
Standard
1995 Bischöfe gehen wegen "Outings" vor Gericht. August 2: 7.
StGB (Strafgesetzbuch der Republik Österreich)
1974 Bundesgesetz vom 23. Jänner 1974 über die mit gerichtlicher Strafe bedrohten Handlungen. Wien: Österreichische Staatsdruckerei.
Sulzenbacher, Hannes
1992 Outing: Viel geliebt und viel gescholten. *tamtam* 11:14–15.
Till, Wolfgang
1989 Wechselwirkungen zwischen gesellschaftlicher Diskriminierung und subjektiver Verarbeitung, oder: Was heißt schwul zu leben? *In* Homosexualität in Österreich. Handl et al., eds. Pp. 18–25. Vienna: Junius.
Toth, Michael
1995 Das Outing geht weiter? XTRA 17 (August 31–September 17): 15
Vlassakakis, Alkis
1995 Wer, wo, was, wann, wie, und warum Outing: Die Bischöfe zittern, die Medien wüten und Menschen in der Szene werden militant: ein Rundumschlag. XTRA 15–16 (August 3–September 3): 10–12, 16.
Wachter, Hubert
1995 Krenn antwortet Weber: "Wiederspruch gegen mich kann sich disqualifizieren." News, July 20: 28–29.
Warner, Michael, ed.
1993 Introduction. *In* Fear of a Queer Planet: Queer Politics and Social Theory. Minneapolis: University of Minnesota Press.
Worm, Alfred
1995 Cui bono? Wem nützt diese Verleumdung? Die Bischofskonferenz ist auf die HOSI-Aktivitäten vom 1. August vorbereitet. News, July 27: 36.

13

Tombois in West Sumatra: Constructing Masculinity and Erotic Desire

Evelyn Blackwood

During anthropological fieldwork on gender and agricultural development in West Sumatra, Indonesia, in 1989–90, I pursued a secondary research goal of investigating the situation of "lesbians" in the area. I met a small number of "women" who seemed butch in the way that term was used in the United States at the time.[1] In West Sumatra these individuals are called *lesbi* or *tomboi* (derived from the English words *lesbian* and *tomboy*). Although there are similarities, a tomboi in West Sumatra is different from a butch in the United States, not surprisingly, for social constructionists have shown that sexual practices reflect particular historical and cultural contexts (Elliston 1995; Weston 1993). The term *tomboi* is used for a female acting in the manner of men (*gaya laki-laki*). Through my relationship with a tomboi in West Sumatra, I learned some of the ways in which my concept of "lesbian" was not the same as my partner's, even though we were both, I thought, women-loving women.

This article explores how tombois in West Sumatra both shape their identities from and resist local, national, and transnational narratives of gender and sexuality.[2] By focusing on West Sumatra, I provide an in-depth analysis of the complexities of tomboi identity for individuals from one ethnic group in Indonesia, the Minangkabau. This piece is not a general explication of tombois across Indonesia, although there may be considerable overlap (see Wieringa 1998). Much excellent work on postcolonial states explores the interplay of national and transnational narratives in the production of genders and sexualities. This article provides a cultural location for tombois oriented to Minangkabau culture as well as national and transnational discourses.

Theories concerning the intersection of genders and sexualities provide considerable insights into, and a variety of labels for, gendered practices cross-culturally (see, for example, Bullough, Bullough, and Elias 1997; Devor 1989; Epstein and Straub 1991; Herdt 1994; Jacobs, Thomas, and Lang 1997; Ramet 1996; Roscoe 1991). In opposition to biological determinism, social constructionists argue that gender is not an essence preceding social expression but an identity that is constructed and fluid.[3] The multiplication of "gender" categories in cross-cultural studies, however, suggests that gender remains a problematic concept. Part of the problem, I would argue, comes from the conflation of two distinct but interacting processes, gender as cultural category and gender as subjective experience.

Viewing gender as a cultural category foregrounds the social structural and ideological processes that make it seem bounded – all the more so in a "scientific" age replete with minute diagnostics of human experience. Studying gender as a cultural category highlights normative representations of gender and the ways they are legitimated, privileged, and hegemonic. It allows one to identify so-called traditional gender systems, or "everyday categories of gender" (Poole 1996), as ideological discourses and to establish which gender representations are dominant or acceptable, and thereby which are transgressive. By highlighting gender as a cultural category, I can delineate normative gender through an analysis of dominant ideological discourses at the local and state levels.

Viewing gender as subjective experience exposes all the processes of negotiation, resistance, manipulation, and displacement possible by human subjects. Gender in this sense constitutes a set of social identities multiply shaped from and through cultural contexts and representations (see also Bourdieu 1977; Poole 1996; Yanagisako and Collier 1987). Viewing gender as a subset of possible social identities allows one to do two things: remove gender as a fundamental aspect of sexed bodies and investigate the way culturally constituted categories shape, inflect, and infuse gender identities. Learning, piecing together, adopting, or shaping identities (such as race, class, gender, or sexuality) is an on-going social process through which individuals negotiate, produce, and stabilize a sense of who they are. These identities are shaped and redefined in relation to dominant gender ideologies that claim constancy and immutability.

Because tombois are enmeshed in several discursive domains of gender and sexual identity, I argue that they produce a complex identity not reducible to a single model. I show how the gender and kinship ideologies of the Minangkabau, the dominant ethnic group in West Sumatra, construct a system of oppositional genders ("man"-"woman") that persuades tombois to see themselves as masculine. The discourses of a modernizing Minangkabau society, the Indonesian state, and Islam reinforce this system through their representations of femininity and "female" nature. At another level, tomboi identity incorporates new models of sexuality and gender made available by the transnational flow of lesbian and gay discourse from Europe and North America.

This essay also explores the relation between gender ideology and the production of gender transgression. *Webster's College Dictionary* (1991) defines *transgression* as a violation of a law, command, or moral code; an offense or sin; or more neutrally, passing over or going beyond (a limit, boundary, et cetera). I use the term *gender transgression* to provide a new angle on a range of cultural practices not usually lumped under it. I include within it any gender identities – such as transgendered, reversed, mixed, crossed, cross-dressed, two-spirited, or liminal – that go beyond, or violate, gender-"appropriate" norms enshrined in dominant cultural ideologies. By defining gender transgression in this way, I want to highlight the way that various social structures and cultural ideologies interconnect to produce gender transgression.

Central to this analysis is the concept of hegemony as developed and used by Gramsci (1971), Williams (1977), and Ortner (1989). Hegemonic or dominant gender ideologies define what is permissible, even thinkable; they serve as the standard against which actions are measured, producing codes, regulations, and laws that perpetuate a particular ideology. Dominant ideologies generate discourses that stabilize, normalize, and naturalize gender (Yanagisako and Delaney 1995); yet within any dominant ideology there are emergent meanings, processes, and identities vying for legitimacy, authority, and recognition (Williams 1977).

Work on gender transgression has prompted some preliminary, and in most cases implicit, formulations about the conditions that produce it. The growing literature on "female-bodied" gender transgressors tends to cast the transgression as resistance to an oppressive gender ideology, usually identified as male dominance or patriarchy.[4] For instance, US gender ideology has produced at various junctures butch-femme (Kennedy and Davis 1993), camp and drag (Newton 1972, 1993), and transgendered people (Bolin 1994; Garber 1991; Stone 1991). Some scholars argue that these identities result from a hierarchical gender system of compulsory heterosexuality and oppositional genders.

Evidence from Island Southeast Asia raises questions about the relationship between oppressive gender ideology and gender transgression. In her overview of gender in Island Southeast Asia, Errington (1990) suggested that gender is less salient than other categories, such as rank and age, in determining access to status or power. According to Errington, in the central islands of Southeast Asia "male and female are viewed as complementary or even identical beings in many respects" (1990:39). The "paucity of symbolic expressions of gender difference" suggests that gender is not highly marked in those areas (Errington 1990:4).[5] Despite an apparent lack of oppositional genders, gender transgressors are well known throughout the islands (Atkinson 1990; Chabot 1960; Oetomo 1991; Peacock 1978; Van der Kroef 1954; Yengoyan 1983).

The Minangkabau tomboi poses a further challenge concerning the relationship between oppressive gender ideology and gender transgression. The Minangkabau are a hierarchical, kin-based society in which both women and men lineage elders have access to power. Because Minangkabau gender relations do not fit the usual criteria for male dominance, the presence of tombois in West Sumatra forces a deeper analysis of the conditions that produce gender transgression. Whether a dominant ideology produces gender transgressors, and in what form, depends, I argue, on a number of processes, only one of which may be an oppressive gender hierarchy. A closer reading of cultural processes circulating in West Sumatra suggests the interrelation of kinship, capitalism, religion, and the state in producing gender transgressions.

Misreading Identities

In the following I first provide a brief description of West Sumatra to set the stage for the story of my introduction to tomboi identity. This narrative of misreadings and negotiations of tomboi identity shows the moments that moved me beyond my own culture-bound interpretations and led me to realize that different identities were in operation.

West Sumatra is the home of the Minangkabau people, one of the many ethnic groups that have been incorporated into the state of Indonesia. The Minangkabau, with a population over 4 million people, are rural agriculturalists, urban merchants, traders, migrants, and wage laborers. They are also Muslim and matrilineal. Being matrilineal means that, despite the fact that they are devout Muslims, inheritance and property pass from mother to daughter. I conducted research in the province of Lima Puluh Kota near the district capital of Payakumbuh. In 1990, the province had a population of 86,000; the large majority were Minangkabau.

Far from being an isolated region, the province is well integrated into global trade networks. Rice and other agricultural products produced in the region are traded well beyond Sumatra. Many Minangkabau men and women work for years in cities outside West Sumatra, providing further connections to the national and international scene. Villages have anywhere from 15 percent to 25 percent of their residents on temporary out-migration. Despite out-migration, many villages maintain a rich cultural life based on kinship ties; most social and economic activities are centered in and organized by matrilineally related groups. Other villages are more urban oriented, particularly where migration has led to reliance on outside sources of income.

I had no trouble locating males in West Sumatra who were *bancis*, a term that is defined in Echols and Shadily's Indonesian-English dictionary (1989) as "effeminate or transvestite homosexual[s]" (see also Oetomo 1991). This definition links bancis' gender identity (effeminate or transvestite) and sexuality (homosexual). In the district capital I met several bancis or *bencong*, as they are referred to in West Sumatra. Bancis are obvious to local people, who comment on their appearance or taunt them when they walk down the street. Although bancis do not carry themselves as men do, they do not carry themselves exactly like women, either; rather, they behave in the exaggerated style of fashion models, a style that in itself is a caricature of femininity, one they have been exposed to through fashion magazines and televised beauty pageants. Their sexual partners are indistinguishable from other men and are generally thought to be bisexual, or *biseks* in local parlance, as these men might also have relationships with women.

My search for "lesbians" was more difficult. I asked some high school–aged acquaintances of mine,[6] who had friends who were bancis, whether they knew any lesbis – the term they used with me – in the area. I was told that there were several but that those women were worried about being found out. I was given the impression that such women were very coarse and tough, more like men than women. After several months in West Sumatra, one of my young friends introduced me to Day.[7] S/he, however, did not fit the stereotype.[8] In hir mid-twenties, s/he appeared to me to be boyish-looking in hir T-shirt, shorts, and short hair, but s/he did not seem masculine or tough in any way that I could perceive. I consequently felt quite certain that I had met another "lesbian." The term *lesbi* that my friends used also offered familiar footing to an outsider from the United States.

Negotiating our identities was a perplexing process in which we each tried to position the other within different cultural categories: butch-femme and *cowok-cewek*. *Butch-femme* is an American term that refers to a masculine-acting woman and her feminine partner.[9] *Cowok-cewek* are Indonesian words that mean "man" and "woman" but have the connotation of "guy" and "girl." It is the practice of female couples to refer to a tomboi and hir feminine partner as cowok and cewek. (Most Indonesians are unfamiliar with this use of the two terms.) In both the United States and West Sumatra, female couples rely on and draw from dominant cultural images of masculinity and femininity to make sense of their relationships. These similarities were enough to cause both my partner and myself to assume that we fell within each other's cultural model, an assumption I was forced to give up.

Dayan operated under the assumption that I was cewek, despite the inconsistencies of my behavior, because that fit with hir understanding of hirself in relation to hir lovers, who had all been cewek. For instance, my failure to cook for hir or organize hir birthday party were quite disappointing to Dayan. On another occasion, when I visited an American friend of mine at his hotel, s/he accused me of sleeping with him. In hir experience, ceweks are attracted to men and also like sex better with men. Yet, as the one with the cash in the relationship, I was allowed to pay for things despite it not being proper cewek behavior. In rural Minangkabau households, men are expected to give their wives their cash earnings. Expectations about the husband's responsibility to provide income are even greater for middle-class Indonesians, for men are represented as the sole breadwinners. Perhaps Dayan justified my actions on the grounds that I was an American with considerably more income than s/he. Certainly s/he was willing to entertain the possibility of my difference from hir understanding of ceweks.

One day I overheard the following exchange between Dayan and a tomboi friend. Dayan's friend asked if I was cewek, to which Dayan replied, "Of course."

"Can she cook?"

"Well, not really."

The friend exclaimed, "How can that be, a woman who can't cook? What are you going to do?"

I was surprised to find that my gender identity was so critical to this (macho) tomboi. The fact that I had a relationship with Dayan said very little to me about what kind of woman I was. I interpreted my relationship with Dayan as reflective of my sexual identity (a desire for other women).

For my part, I assumed that Dayan was a butch, more or less in congruence with the way I understood butches to be in the United States in the 1980s, that is, as masculine-acting women who desired feminine partners.[10] S/he always dressed in jeans or shorts and T- or polo shirts, a style that was not at odds with the casual wear of many lesbians in the United States. One day, however, I heard a friend call hir "co," short for cowok. I knew what *cowok* meant in that context; it meant s/he was seen as a "guy" by hir close friends, which did not fit my notion of butch. I heard another female couple use the terms *mami* (mom) and *papi* (pop) for each other, so I started calling Dayan papi in private, which made hir very pleased. But when I told Dayan s/he was pretty, s/he looked hurt. Then I realized my mistake: "pretty" (*cantik*) is what a woman is called, not a man. Dayan wanted to be called "handsome" (*gagah*), as befits a masculine self.

Dayan's personal history underscored hir feelings that s/he was a man. S/he said s/he felt extremely isolated and "deviant" when s/he was growing up and acted more like a boy. People in hir town called hir *bujang gadis*, an Indonesian term meaning boy-girl (*bujang* means bachelor or unmarried young man, and *gadis* means unmarried young woman) that used to refer to an effeminate male or a masculine female (although not much in use currently). As a teenager, s/he only had desire for girls. S/he bound hir breasts because s/he did not want them to be noticeable. They did not fit with hir self-image. As a young adult, s/he hung out with young men, smoking and drinking with them. S/he said s/he felt like a man and wanted to be one. I finally had to admit to myself that tombois were not the Indonesian version of butches. They were men.

Cowok-Cewek

I met two other tombois in West Sumatra, Agus and Bujang, who were both friends of Dayan. The first time I met Agus, s/he was wearing a big khaki shirt and jeans; even I could not mistake the masculine attitude s/he projected. S/he wore short hair that was swept back on the sides. S/he carried hirself like a "man," smoked cigarettes all the time, played cards, and made crude jokes. S/he struck me as coarse and tough like cowoks were said to be. Dayan admired Agus and thought hir the more handsome of the two.

Dayan told me that Agus, who was approximately thirty years old, had only been with women, never with a man. S/he had had several lovers, all beautiful and very feminine, according to Dayan. One former lover married and had two children, but Dayan thought Agus probably still saw her occasionally. Agus spent much of hir time with hir lover, Yul, who lived in a large house only a few minutes by bus outside of Payakumbuh. Yul, who was in her early fifties, was a widow with grown children, some of whom were still living at home. After Agus started living with her, Yul wanted her children to call Agus papi. She said she did not care if her children disapproved of her relationship. If her children did not act respectfully toward Agus, Yul would get angry with them and not give them spending money when they asked for it. But one of Yul's daughters argued that because Agus is not married to her mother, s/he should not be part of the family and be treated better than her own father had been. The frequent squabbling and lack of privacy at Yul's house was too much for Agus, who spent less and less time with Yul and finally moved back to hir sister's house nearby.

The other tomboi I met, Bujang, was at that time living at hir mother's in a rural village. Bujang seemed quiet and somber. Boyish features and oversized clothes that hid hir breasts made it impossible for me to tell if s/he was male or female. We talked very little because hir mother was there. Later Dayan told me Bujang's story. Hir mother had forced hir to marry; s/he had had a son but then left hir husband. S/he had a lover (who, Dayan said, was feminine) and moved with her to Jakarta, where they lived for some time to avoid the prying eyes of relatives. Under continued pressure from hir family, however, and lacking adequate income, Bujang finally returned home with hir son, leaving hir lover temporarily in hopes of finding a better way to support hir family. Hir cewek lover, however, eventually married a man.[11]

Partners of tombois fit within the norms of femininity and maintain a "feminine" gender identity. Their sexual relationships with tombois do not mark them as different; their gender is not in question.[12] Like an earlier generation of femmes in the United States, tombois' partners are nearly invisible (see Nestle 1992). Yul, Agus's lover, was feminine in appearance. She had shoulder-length permed hair, wore makeup and lipstick, and had long fingernails. Yul had never been with a tomboi before she met Agus. She had not even thought about sleeping with one before. Although she sometimes wore slacks and smoked, even hung out at the local coffee shop with Agus to play cards, she was called *ibu* (mother) by men and mami by Agus. No one would think she was a tomboi just because she was partners with one; she was cewek. As a cewek, she adhered to the hegemonic standards of femininity in her appearance and behavior.

Although the fact that they sleep with tombois makes them "bad" women in the eyes of local people, for premarital sex and adultery are disapproved of for women, ceweks are still women. Even tombois expect ceweks to have greater desire for men because that is seen as natural for their sex. Dayan once said, "Unfortunately, they will leave you for a man if one comes along they like. It's our fate that we love women who leave us." No one seems to consider a cewek's desire for tombois problematic; she remains a woman who desires men.

Performing Masculinity

Tombois model masculinity in their behavior, attitudes, interests, and desires. Dayan often spoke of being *berani* (brave), a trait commonly associated with men, as an important part of who s/he was. S/he attributed the ability to be a tomboi to being berani; it meant, among other things, that one could withstand family pressures to get married. S/he said the ones that are berani become cowok. In talking about Agus's situation with hir lover Yul, Dayan commented that Agus was not brave enough to sleep at Yul's house anymore. S/he thought that Agus should not let Yul's children force Hir to move out. Agus was not being as brave as Dayan thought a person should be in order to live up to the cowok identity.

Tombois pride themselves on doing things like men. They know how to play *koa*, a card game like poker, which is thought to be a men's game. They smoke as men do; rural women rarely take up smoking. They go out alone, especially at night, which is a prerogative of men. Like men, they drive motor-cycles; women ride behind (women do drive motorcycles, but in mixed couples men always drive). Dayan arrived at my house on a motorcycle one time with a man friend riding behind. Like Minangkabau husbands, they move into and out of their partners' houses. Dayan said s/he often gets taken for a man if someone only sees hir walking from behind. Sometimes in public spaces, particularly in urban areas, s/he is called *mas*, a contemporary Indonesian term of address for a man. The thought that a tomboi might marry a man or bear a child like a woman seemed unconscionable to Dayan. S/he had little sympathy for Bujang, who was forced to marry, saying, "This person is cowok! How could s/he have done that, especially having a baby. That's wrong."

The taunting and joking between Agus and Dayan reflect one way in which their masculinity is negotiated. Agus's teasing questions to Dayan about whether I was a proper cewek is one example. Another incident occurred one evening when we were hanging out with Agus at a coffee shop. S/he had been playing cards (koa) with some men for awhile and it was getting late. Dayan told Agus s/he wanted to leave. Agus said tauntingly, "You're a guy *[laki-laki]!* How come you're afraid of the night?" I knew Dayan wanted to get back to the privacy of hir own place, a 45-minute drive by motorcycle. Agus ignored that fact and implied that Dayan was acting like a woman, for women are supposed to be more timid than men and stay indoors at night.

Another time Agus heard me call Dayan by hir first name. S/he gave Dayan a disparaging look, letting Dayan know that s/he was not demanding enough respect from me as hir cewek. Minangkabau usually do not call their spouses by their first names. Women generally use the term of address for older brother *(udah)*, while *papi* is more common in urban areas or among those who live elsewhere in Indonesia.

Dayan also commented to me about a story circulating in West Sumatra concerning a female who passed as a man. This individual was rumored to have married his partner by going to another district where no one knew he was female. He (the cowok) runs a store, it was related; he wears loose clothes and straps his breasts down so they are not apparent. His wife (the cewek) is said to be very pretty. Dayan's response to this story was, "Oh, that cowok must really be a cowok," signifying that he had become the ultimate tomboi, one who passes as a man.

The sparring and comparing of masculine selves reveal one of the ways tombois create, confirm, and naturalize their identities as men. The teasing helps to reinforce and interrogate the masculine code of behavior. Their actions suggest that being cowok is an identity one can be better or worse at, more or less of; it is something that must be practiced and claimed – which is not to say that it is inauthentic, for no gender identity is more or less authentic than another, but, rather, is more or less an approximation of the hegemonic ideological domain accorded to that gender (see Butler 1991). As any man does, they are negotiating their culture's ideology of masculinity.

Tombois construct their desire for and relationships with women on the model of masculinity. The oft-repeated statement that their lovers are all feminine underscores their position as men who attract the "opposite sex." Because I was Dayan's partner, hir friend assumed that I was a particular gender, in this case the feminine woman. Their use of gendered terms of endearment, *mami* and *papi*, and the terms *cowok* and *cewek* reflect tombois' understanding of themselves as situated within the category "men" (laki-laki). Tombois' adherence to the model of masculinity and their insistence on replicating the heterosexuality of a man-woman couple point to the dominance of the normative model of gender and heterosexuality.

Gender Ideology and Gender Transgression

In constructing themselves as masculine and their relationships as heterosexual, tombois are gender transgressors who nevertheless reflect the dominant ideology. Tombois' transgressions raise the issue of the relation between gender ideology and the production of gender transgression. What social conditions produce transgression of the dominant ideology? As I noted in the introduction, some preliminary attempts have been made to identify the conditions that produce gender transgression. Several scholars argue that oppressive gender ideologies (male dominance) force gender transgression.[13] According to Kennedy and Davis, "butch-fem" identities in the United States developed in a period in which "elaborate hierarchical distinctions were made between the sexes" (1992:63).[14] Because men and women were culturally constructed as polar opposites ("the opposite sex" being a typical folk designation for the two genders in the United States), behaviors and privileges associated with men, including erotic attraction to women, were restricted to those with male genitalia. Male dominance and an ideology of oppositional genders created resistance to and subversion of the dominant paradigm by butches and femmes.

Some gender theorists argue that "women" become "men" (including female "berdache," female soldiers, and passing "women") because of sexual desire for other women (Newton 1984; Raymond 1979; Rich 1980; Rubin 1975; Trumbach 1994; Wieringa 1989). In this view, because "women" are not allowed freedom of sexual expression, they are forced to pass as men (with great caution, however) in order to be with women. Thus, the constraints on their sexual desire, which arise from an ideology of male dominance and men's control of women's sexuality, forces women to transgress. Although this interpretation may work in some cultural locations, it is problematic because it assumes the essentiality of sex. These individuals are claimed as "real" women whose desire for women forces them to take on a man's identity.[15] This explanation is implausible for tombois. As Dayan's story indicates, it was not sexual desire for women that "drove" hir to produce a masculine identity (a problematic construction anyway because being "driven" suggests a biological drive). S/he had already established a masculine identity before s/he was aware of hir sexual desires for women. Having identified hirself as masculine, s/he also laid claim to a desire for women.

Cross-cultural evidence, predominantly from societies with strict gender polarity, seems to support a strong connection between male dominance and gender transgression. On the one hand, Wikan (1977), who studied the highly sex-segregated patriarchal culture of the Omani, found that the *xanith*, a crossdressing male prostitute, moves in the women's world. By providing men with an alternative to sex with women, the xanith preserves the gender dichotomy and protects women's virtue, Wikan argued. The gender dichotomy, she claimed, is the "precondition" for a male transsexual. In my analysis of gender-stratified, patriarchal class societies, I argued that "women" in these societies were not allowed to take on a cross-gender role because such behavior was viewed as a threat to men's privilege (Blackwood 1986a). They did so, however, even at the risk of severe sanctions if they were discovered (see Crompton 1981; Cromwell 1997). On the other hand, so-called sworn virgins in the patriarchal Balkans are allowed to renounce their womanhood publicly, usually at puberty, and become social men (Dickemann 1997). Each of these cases supports the conclusion that male dominance and strict gender polarity produce individuals who reject or resist being slotted into normative gender categories. In these instances, it appears that the disadvantages of a normative feminine gender, such as the lack of access to men's privileges and the constraints against desiring women as a woman, produce gender transgressors.

Other instances of gender transgression, however, suggest that it is not always produced under oppressive conditions, nor is it always rejection of, or resistance to, normative gender. Although it goes beyond the limits or reverses cultural norms, gender transgression in some cases (in Indonesia and other cultures) is a culturally legitimated behavior believed to effect healing or give greater access to the spirit world. Examples include transformed shamans, clowns, and ritual specialists (Balzer 1996; Bogoras 1901; Jacobs, Thomas, and Lang 1997; Peacock 1978). In such cases, gender transgression is not the result of oppressive conditions but of the ritual power associated with gender. These examples suggest that transgressions can take many forms; different systems produce different types of transgressions.[16]

Another reason to ask what conditions produce gender transgressions has to do with essentialist claims about human "nature." Many scholars resort to essentialist explanations for gender transgression. For instance, a discredited theory of "berdache" gender argued that males became "berdache" because they were naturally effeminate and could not live up to the warrior role for males. Their refusal to become warriors was taken as an indication of the connection between physical nature and social identity; they were born that way. Although I do not deny the possibility of biophysical influences on human behavior, I want to pursue a social analysis further.

I use for comparison an example of the transgression of ethnic identity. In Stoler's (1996) work on colonial-indigenous relations, she found that ethnic transgressions were the subject of much concern in Dutch colonies. Colonial officials who hired indigenous women to care for their children found, to their chagrin, that their young children identified with the indigenous culture rather than that of the parents. Although every effort was made to instill in the children the language, manners, and behavior of their European parents, they often chose to speak Malay and associate with local children in ways not deemed proper for people of a "superior" race (Stoler 1996). Their behavior, a transgression of European norms of behavior, was the result not of an inborn desire to be Malay but of the conflicting identities with which they were presented. That the children chose to speak the maid's language first attests to what was most comfortable for them.

Culture works by applying social categories to bodies, but when individuals or groups reject particular categories designed for their bodies, such actions should not be deemed to result from "natural" desires. Rather, rejection or violation of cultural norms may arise from contradictory social processes and subaltern desires present in or produced by the culture itself. Thus, like ethnic transgressions, gender transgression is a rejection of social definitions that one finds intolerable or undesirable because other definitions are available that provide greater rewards or fit better with one's sense of self. In the case of tombois, certain ideologies of masculinity fit better.

Rejection is often read as "resistance" because the power of the dominant ideology and the daily practice of that ideology forces on-going resistance. The actions of Dayan's mother are a good example of a daily practice to slot Dayan back into the normative category of gender. Her efforts to have Dayan marry a man meant that Dayan was forced repeatedly to confront, question, and reassert hir own violation and reconstruction of gender. *Rejection*, which implies a one-time act, is too simplistic a term to describe an on-going struggle to maintain the identity one produces. Thus, gender transgression can be both a resistance to and rejection of cultural norms.

What social conditions produce the tomboi identity? Are tombois forced into a transgendered role by an oppressive, male-dominant society? To answer this question I turn now to social processes (cultural ideologies) in West Sumatra and the Indonesian state, looking first at the interrelations of Minangkabau kinship, gender, and economics in the production of oppositional genders.

Minangkabau Ideology and Oppositional Genders

Although the Minangkabau people are considered a single ethnic group, there are many Minangkabaus – many "fantasies" of Minangkabau ethnic identity, to borrow Sears's term (1996a). Minangkabau people are urban, rural, educated, and devout; they are civil servants, migrants, and farmers. Their identities vary according to their exposure to media, state ideology, Western-oriented education, and religious fundamentalism. The multiplicity of identities attests to the complex processes at work in contemporary Indonesia as individuals and ethnic groups situate themselves within the postcolonial state.[17]

The construction of gender in West Sumatra is equally complex. There are marked gender differences attached to male and female bodies, but these differences are produced within a matrilineal system that privileges women. Minangkabau women draw from and constantly rework several models of womanhood based on the ideologies of *adat* (local customs, beliefs, and prescriptions for behavior), Islam, and the state (Blackwood 1993, 1995b). The Minangkabau gender ideology I describe here has its basis in rural, rather than urban or nonfarming, life in West Sumatra.

Through its very commonness, something as simple as the segregation of girls and boys enculturates and reinforces ideas about sex difference. As is typical of many Islamic cultures, there is lifelong physical segregation of the sexes in most public spaces and events. Girls and boys socialize in predominantly single-sex groups. Teenaged girls and women are expected to stay in at night; going out alone after dark is frowned on. In contrast, adolescent boys and men can be outside in the evenings and often hang out in predominantly male-only spaces, such as coffee shops. These gender differences reflect the Minangkabau (and Islamic) view that men and women have different natures.[18] Men are said to be more aggressive and brave than women. Boys are admonished not to cry – crying is what girls do. Women are expected to be modest, respectful, and humble (all contained in the word *malu*), especially young unmarried women.

All ritual ceremonies – such as marriage, engagement, or death – are conducted by the sexes separately. During ceremonies women have control of the house space while men cluster outside until it is time to deliver speeches. I was told that men and women each have their own part of the ceremony and neither is more important than the other. Men make speeches, but women oversee the whole process and see it to its conclusion (see also Pak 1986). Ceremonial practices reflect the different rights and obligations of women and men but not their place in a gender hierarchy.

These gendered notions encode difference and men's privilege, yet they coexist with practices and discourses that encode women's privilege and power (Blackwood 1993, n.d.). Women lineage elders are powerful figures who, if they are wealthy, control land, labor, and kin. Economically, women control the distribution of land and its produce. Men figure peripherally in their wives' houses, but they maintain important relations with both natal and affinal houses. Husbands are treated with respect and even deference by their wives (in certain matters); some elite men hold important family titles and are considered the protectors of lineage property. Elite men and women carry out kinship affairs in democratic fashion, with neither women nor men able to enforce decisions without the agreement of the other side. Although gender ideology signifies differences in rights and privileges, it does not encode men's hegemonic superiority.

Minangkabau kinship and marriage practices provide deeper insights into the construction of gender and sexuality. Individuals, whether male or female, are not considered adult until they have married heterosexually. Everyone is expected and strongly encouraged (in some cases forced) to marry, an expectation generally true throughout Indonesia and Southeast Asia as a whole. While this expectation is commonplace in most cultures, its significance goes beyond the mere requirement to reproduce. Marriage constructs an extended network of kin and affines that forms the basis of social life in the village. For Minangkabau women, the continuation of the matrilineal kinship network through marriage and children is critical to their own standing and influence both in the kin group and in the community. An unmarried or childless daughter denies the lineage any offspring through her and risks the future status of the lineage, not only in terms of heirs but in terms of rank.[19] A man's marriage does not produce lineage heirs, making men peripheral to lineage reproduction. In contrast, a woman's marriage to a lower-ranked husband can effectively decrease their lineage standing in future generations. Women lineage heads exert control over young women to avoid the risk of a bad marriage or no marriage at all. Thus, in this matrilineal system, men are not the primary ones controlling women through marriage; senior elite women control young women through their desires to maintain and strengthen their own lineage standing (Blackwood 1993).

In the context of this rural kin-based society, heterosexual marriage is a paramount feature of Minangkabau kinship ideology. Within the terms of the kinship ideology, women are producers and reproducers of the lineage. There are no acceptable fantasies of femininity or female bodies in rural villages that do not include marriage and motherhood. This ideology remains hegemonic at the same time that emerging discourses of modernity and capitalism have opened up possibilities of resistance to marriage restrictions (Blackwood 1993).

Minangkabau culture produces gender transgression, I argue, because of restrictive definitions and expectations of masculinity and femininity attached to male and female bodies. In this case, male dominance is not an adequate reason for gender transgression because the Minangkabau do not fit any standard criteria for male dominance. It is not "men" (patriarchy) or their oppressive gender hierarchy that creates transgressions but, rather, a gender and kinship ideology that privileges women and men, yet insists on oppositional genders.

How does this sex/gender system induce the tomboi to claim a masculine identity? Why is (or was) this the form that transgression took? I am assuming here the temporal precedence of gender-based identities (cowok-cewek) relative to more recent identities available through the lesbian and gay movement internationally.

To answer these questions, one needs to look at the way tombois are treated within the dominant culture. Tombois imagine themselves masculine, and as such are tolerated to a certain extent,[20] but there is a contradiction between the way tombois define themselves and the way others define them. Tombois are under great pressure to carry out family obligations, to marry a man and be reproductive. Dayan said that every time s/he saw hir mother, she asked when s/he was getting married. Hir mother worried that a woman could not support herself alone; she needs a husband. Hir mother's statement was a clear refusal of Dayan's self-definition as a man, a refusal that typifies the attitude of others within the local community.

The constant pressure to get married and the threat of forcible marriage reveal the way a person's body determines a person's gender. In this system the hegemonic, legitimate gender is based on one's sex; gender is not considered an "identity," performed or otherwise. In many ways this ideological rendering is similar to the dominant sex/gender paradigm in European and US societies: gender is believed to derive naturally from physiological sex; a "real" woman possesses female genitalia, desires men, bears children, and acts like a woman.[21] A tomboi, according to the Minangkabau sex/gender system, is a "woman" even though s/he enacts a masculine gender, hence the refusal to legitimate that enactment and the insistence on the fulfillment of hir reproductive duties. Denying the female body is impermissible. Although tombois insist on being treated as men by their partners, their masculinity lacks cultural validation. Society insists on the priority of the body in determining gender.

Dayan said s/he played too rough and enjoyed boys' activities when s/he was little, so people called hir bujang gadis, a label that meant others perceived hir as masculine. At that time s/he had no other recourse but to assume s/he was a boy. Without other options available, and seeing that hir behavior falls outside the bounds of proper femininity, the tomboi denies hir female body, binding hir breasts so that the physical evidence will not betray hir. S/he produces the only other gender recognizable in the sex/gender system, the masculine gender. That interpretation would accord with the hegemonic cultural ideology, in which masculinity is male – with a twist, a twist that s/he continually has to substantiate and rectify in hir own mind and to others. Dominant ideologies, as noted by Poole, are "enshrined in prominent, powerful and pervasive stereotypes... and deployed in centrally institutionalized or otherwise significantly marked arenas of social action" (1996:198). The hegemonic persuasiveness of such ideologies means that other forms of identity are unimaginable.[22] Consequently, some masculine females appropriate the masculine gender because it is the most persuasive model available.

The Promotion of Motherhood and Heterosexuality

Given the importance of the state and other institutions in the production and control of gender and sexuality, as attested to by a number of recent studies,[23] what messages about gender at the national level lead to the production of tomboi identity? The Indonesian state, particularly since the inception of the New Order in 1965, has avidly pursued a policy promoting nuclear families and motherhood.[24] This state ideology emphasizes the importance of women's role as mothers and consciously purveys the idea that women are primarily responsible for their children and their family's health, care, and education (Djajadiningrat-Nieuwenhuis 1987; Manderson 1980; Sullivan 1983; Suryakusuma 1996). In fact, the state argues that motherhood has been the traditional role for women in Indonesia since before the coming of the Dutch. According to Gayatri (1995), this line of argument has been used by state officials to fend off feminist efforts to change perceptions about women. All state family policies are oriented around a nuclear family defined as a husband, wife, and children in disregard of the many forms of family found within the borders of Indonesia.

Several state organizations for women perpetuate the belief that women are nurturing and selfless, if emotional, creatures who need to be married to be happy, productive citizens. The national dress code emphasizes femininity for women, with dresses, skirts, jewelry, and makeup the only acceptable attire for work. Dharma Wanita, the state organization for wives of government officials, heavily promotes cosmetics to its members and sponsors what it assumes to be important activities for women, such as knitting and cooking.

Television and magazines are replete with images of soft, pretty, domestic women. Advertisements bombard women with the most fashionable clothes, skin care, and health care products necessary to make them successful women. Avon, Revlon, and Pond's are some of the non-Indonesian companies promoting this vision of femininity. Women characters on popular television series are primarily domestic, irrational, emotional, and obedient – and incapable of solving their own problems (Aripurnami 1996). This emphasis on hyperfemininity and the importance of motherhood reinforces restrictive gender boundaries. The message for women is that it is a national and religious duty to marry heterosexually and be feminine.

Minangkabau newspapers published in West Sumatra for local readers reflect state propaganda on femininity. The women's section in *Singgalang* is devoted to health, beauty tips, and heterosexuality. One columnist advises women not to worry if they are not beautiful; there are other characteristics they can develop that will still be attractive to men. Another column claims that men and women need each other; each sex is incomplete without the other. "Although it's not impossible for a woman to find meaning without a man," advises Fadlillah, "it gives women's lives new meaning when a man is there" (1996:3, my translation). Other articles admonish women to be modest *(malu)* and warn against too modern an attitude, *modern* here referring to the "loosened" values and attitudes of those in the cities.

Other representations of motherhood come from fundamentalist Islam, which claims that motherhood is the natural role for women and their destiny because they are female. Islamic fundamentalists idealize women as mothers and wives under the supervision of husbands (Blackwood 1995b). In regard to sexual practices, many Muslims believe same-sex sexuality is immoral, and this was Dayan's understanding of hir faith. Further, Islamic leaders teach that not being "true" to one's own sex by acting like the other is a sin and an offense to Allah because it is a rejection of the way one was made (which underscores the belief that biological sex and gender are one and the same).

The emphasis on heterosexual marriage and the nuclear family suggests that compulsory heterosexuality and women's subordination are actively being produced at the national level by religion, the state, media, and multinational corporations.

This heterosexual imperative threatens to reproduce a limiting and ultimately coercive form of gender, marriage, and sexuality predicated on male control and desire. Dominant state ideology offers no options to females other than marriage and motherhood, which in this case is a male-dominant vision of gender, further substantiating the dictates of sex/gender congruence enunciated by Minangkabau gender and kinship ideology. For those who do not fit the normative model of gender, or find it limiting and oppressive, such a model persuades them of their masculinity, producing gender transgression.

Despite the dominance of the ideology of femininity and motherhood at the state level, there are cracks within it – unintended consequences that ironically open a space for imagining other gender and sexual possibilities. In its efforts to create modern nuclear families, state discourse undermines the influence of lineage elders in several ways. First, whereas rural life in many areas of Indonesia customarily centers around kin, state discourse emphasizes the priority of the nuclear (male-headed) family over the larger kin group. State support for nuclear families allows a daughter to contest her mother's authority (Blackwood n.d.). Second, the discourse of modernity, with its emphasis on individualism and consumerism, provides a model of self-earned income for the earner's use alone. Finally, the availability of nonagricultural labor for women in a global economy also models alternatives to life in a rural household. All these processes undermine extended families and their power to require a daughter's marriage and support of the lineage (Blackwood 1995b). These imaginable alternatives help to question the ideology of oppositional genders, creating the possibility of gender and sexual identities not predicated on sexed bodies. For tombois these alternatives raise the possibility that their masculinity does not have to make them men.

Cewek Resistance to Marriage and Heterosexuality

The hegemonic heterosexuality of the state and the Minangkabau kinship system produce not only the tomboi as gender transgressor but also a different form of transgression. Some women participate in compulsory heterosexuality, marrying men and bearing children, but then quietly claim the right to choose a tomboi partner.[25] For some women, the pressure to marry a man makes refusal nearly unthinkable and marriage inevitable. For other women who marry heterosexually, their action fulfills a sense of duty to their mothers, their lineage, and themselves. Whatever the reason, women who have married and borne children are in a better position to resist both state dictates and local sanctions concerning women's sexuality. As there are few private spaces where young unmarried women can can safely pursue erotic relationships, marriage allows them to establish their own households apart from their mothers'.

Initial compliance with the dictates of heterosexual reproductivity creates new possibilities for sexual relationships. Once they have fulfilled their obligations, these women can establish relationships with female partners in the interstices of an apparently heterosexual household. Some women divorce their husbands, but others make use of the tradition of frequent separation between spouses – for instance, a husband often may be away on business or living with a second wife – to maintain the facade of marriage and carry on a relationship with a tomboi. At that point neither the state nor the local community can closely control a woman's sexuality, as long as she manages her household and attends to the care of her children adequately. Family and local officials are apparently much more willing to ignore a relationship with a tomboi once a woman has fulfilled the duties accorded to her gender, as long as such relationships are hidden. At the national level, there is a good model for such benign collusion: In the patriarchal New Order, adultery is very prominent among men who are high-ranking government officials despite its official condemnation (Suryakusuma 1996).

A "normative" woman, that is, one who has the appearance of fitting gender norms, can pursue her desire for and sexual relations with a tomboi without becoming marked as a gender transgressor. This fact points to the privilege associated with the dominant gender ideology. Enacting the gender that is appropriate for one's sex fits with the heterosexual paradigm and is less problematic than enacting the "wrong" gender.[26]

Transnational Lesbian and Gay Discourse

In addition to local and state discourses, tomboi identity is situated within a transnational lesbian and gay discourse circulating in Indonesia primarily through national gay organizations and their newsletters. First organized in the early 1980s, these groups have nurtured a small but growing nationwide community of gays and lesbians (Boellstorff 1995), thereby developing a consciously new gay identity for Indonesians. *Gaya Nusantara*, a national magazine for gay men and lesbians that began publication in 1987, has been the leading edge of the movement. *Gaya Nusantara* is produced by a working group of gay men; their chief editor is Dede Oetomo, a Cornell-educated Indonesian gay man. Articles in *Gaya Nusantara* cover topics such as gay and lesbian identity, events on the international scene, and issues of local concern. *Gaya Nusantara* also carries stories about and advice on relationships and how to make them work, as well as personal ads for those seeking to get in touch with others within and beyond Indonesia. *Gaya Nusantara* articles assume a readership "out there" who, once they understand what being gay really is, will become part of the community and identify themselves as gay. Some of the contributors to the magazine urge readers to be out as much as possible while recognizing that such a position is extremely difficult for Indonesians.

Oetomo is one of the most visible members of the *Gaya Nusantara* work group. He has published several of his own articles in the newsletter as well as in national magazines and international journals. Oetomo himself uses the terms *gay* and *lesbi* "more or less as they are in the contemporary West; they refer to people who identify themselves as homosexuals, belong to delineated communities, and lead distinct subcultural lifestyles" (1996:259, n. 1). His work has been influential in constructing an Indonesian lesbian and gay identity. Although this identity is different from the lesbian and gay identity dominant in the "West" (see also Boelstorff 1995), both are constructed primarily as sexual identities and not gender identities.

Because *Gaya Nusantara* reaches primarily a gay male audience, a few politically active lesbians have made efforts to build a nationwide network of their own. These efforts were spearheaded by Gayatri, a well-travelled activist with a college education. Gayatri briefly helped publish a newsletter called "Gaya Lestari" as a section of *Gaya Nusantara*. One author writing anonymously in "Gaya Lestari" admonished lesbians to come out, bemoaning their invisibility and their preference for GTM (Gerakan Tutup Mulut, the close-mouthed movement). References to "our lesbians" and "the lesbian world" in the article suggest that the author imagines the existence of a group of women who hold a common identity (quoted in Boellstorff 1995:31, 42, his translation). This new lesbian identity she envisions demands outward resistance to the heterosexual paradigm.

The new lesbian and gay movement in Indonesia is creating an identity distinct from the gender-marked banci and tomboi identities. Much as the post-Stonewall (post-1969) American lesbian and gay movement separated itself from butches, femmes, and drag queens (Kennedy and Davis 1993), gay and lesbian activists in Indonesia distinguish themselves from both bancis and tombois. Gay and lesbian identity is associated with a "modern," educated middle class, while banci is a "lower-class construction" distinct from the gay and lesbian community, although the distinction between the two is not that neat (Oetomo 1996:263). Similarly, cowok-cewek are thought to be predominantly from the working class and not like lesbians of the middle and upper middle classes (Gayatri 1994). Gayatri (1993) specifically excluded cowok or "female-transvestites," as she called them then, from her early work on lesbians in Indonesia because she felt that their identification as men separated them from lesbians. In the emerging lesbian movement, tombois were perceived as imitating men, and hence in need of modernization and education (see also Murray 1998), although this stance has softened over time (see Gayatri 1997).

Print media in Indonesia since the early 1980s have also been a major source of information on gays and lesbians (Gayatri 1997). Media attention to an increasingly international gay and lesbian movement has brought into common use the terms *lesbi* and *tomboi*, transformations of the English terms *lesbian* and *tomboy*. These terms coexist somewhat uneasily with older terms, such as *bujang gadis* and *banci*, which are associated with a "nonconforming" gender identity (see also Oetomo 1991). Even in urban areas in Indonesia, bancis are seen as asexual, gender nonconforming (cross-dressing) males, although bancis consider themselves to be a third gender and are sexually active with men who occupy the normative category for males in Indonesian society (Oetomo 1996). The terms *tomboi* and *lesbi* are now synonymous for many people, although *tomboi* is more consistent with the older gender identity. The media perpetuates the image that lesbis are masculine women whose partners are feminine. This usage is inconsistent, however, with the term as used by activists, who define a lesbi as a woman who is sexually active with another woman.

Despite sometimes negative and sensationalizing coverage, newspapers carry stories about gay liberation and gay couples living together in Europe and the United States. They also avidly report stories about Indonesian lesbians who try to marry (Gayatri 1997). Such stories broadcast nationally a lesbi desire to live together despite resistance from "concerned" parents, for the first time portraying an alternative (if negatively construed) lifestyle for same-sex couples.

The transnational discourse on gender and sexuality is complicated by media coverage of transgendered individuals in Indonesia and other parts of the world.

Indonesians know of both American and Indonesian transgendered people who have had sex-congruence surgery (bringing their sex into congruence with their gender). In fact Dayan's sister was so worried that s/he might want surgery that she specifically warned hir against it, at the same time pleading with hir to get married. Consequently, transnational narratives produce yet another possibility, that of surgically bringing one's body into conformity with one's gender, a model that fits with older indigenous notions of the primacy of bodies in determining gender.

The infusion of transnational gay discourse into the lives of tombois and their partners presents new cultural models of sexuality. In discussing gay culture in Indonesia's urban centers, Oetomo suggests that "whoever joins the metropolitan superculture adopts the going construction there, although traces of a local construction still may color the way s/he . . . construes gender and sexual orientation" (1996:260). Movement between urban and rural areas means that local and urban identities confront each other and must be negotiated and claimed in hybrid ways. "The going construction" is brought back "home" to be remarked on with others, reworked, and then updated with each new trip to the metropolis. (Oetomo's gay subjects are most likely permanent residents of metropolises.) Tombois and their partners have heard of Western lesbian and gay couples living together. From their urban cohort they have been told of a "lesbian" identity that is an unchanging part of self and have been urged to claim that identity. These new models are being incorporated into older gender-based models (cowok-cewek) in contradictory ways.

Plural Identities

I want to pull together the various threads of my argument to reveal how one particular tomboi is situated within these narratives of gender, sexuality, and culture. Many representations of femininity circulate in Indonesia (Sears 1996a). In like manner, female subjects who are masculine, erotically attracted to women, or both are represented in many different ways. They are seen as "deviants" from the model of mother and wife so central to Indonesian state ideology, as the stereotypically masculine lesbian portrayed by the media, as women who love each other (the model favored by some activists), and as men (the identity claimed by tombois).

Dayan is positioned within all these possibilities. A product of the postcolonial Indonesian school system, s/he graduated from a technical high school with ambitions for a career. But, like many others in the working class, s/he struggles to find work. S/he is a member of hir mother's lineage but lives with hir older sister on their deceased father's land in a community that is only 15 minutes from the district capital, where some of hir brothers work. A large number of migrants in the community work in other areas. Not a vibrant adat community, this village is moving into the margins of urban life in Indonesia.

Dayan's location on the fringes of urban culture helps to explain hir rejection of Minangkabau womanhood. Raised in a family with little matrilineal money or land and thus dependent on the father's family to provide land and house, s/he, hir mother, and hir sister have lost some of the crucial connections that authorize women's power. Further, because not all daughters benefit equally or are treated favorably by their mothers, some, like Dayan, may never attain the power of a senior woman. Beyond that, the family's marginal position between rural and urban means that their desires are directed toward urban opportunities not village and matrilineal relations. The Minangkabau world Dayan knows is that of a struggling, urban-oriented family.

Like many youth growing up, Dayan has been influenced by divergent ideologies of womanhood. Educated in the "modern" school system, Minangkabau youth have received little state validation for the importance of Minangkabau women. Recent local efforts to provide more education about Minangkabau culture have only highlighted the role of men as "traditional" leaders (see Black-wood 1995b). Schoolgirls learn "proper" gender roles and are indoctrinated in the importance of becoming wives who serve their husbands' needs. They are inundated through media with representations of urban, middle-class, docile women. Yet with the increased availability of education, civil service, and other wage-labor jobs in the last 30 years, young women now have the right to choose their spouses or to pursue higher education and careers in urban areas. Many villagers believe that the potential economic benefits of higher education or urban careers may enhance lineage status, especially when successful educated daughters use their income to remodel or build new lineage houses. Many young women grow up believing that they are better off today under the patriarchal New Order because they can seek their own jobs and choose their own husbands. To these young women, the Minangkabau world of powerful elite women, wrapped up in the "esoteric" adat of ritual ceremonies and hard work in the rice fields, seems distant and old fashioned. Thus, the images of womanhood with which Dayan is familiar underscore the burden of privilege – of marriage, children, and lineage priorities – and the fear of dependence – of being a wife under the husband's control. Within this context the Minangkabau kinship ideology that requires daughters' obedience in marrying heterosexually may seem oppressive, but only in the context of postcolonial transformations that have weakened lineage priorities and promoted other images of family and happiness.

The masculinities that tombois construct reflect their different locations in the global market as well as the local community. Hegemonic masculinity is represented and enacted differently in the village, in urban areas, and on movie screens. It also is a hybrid of local, national, and transnational representations. In rural villages a young man may smoke, drink, gamble, and use coarse language, but he is also admonished to be strong, industrious, respectful of his elders, and responsible to his lineage and his wife's family. The bravado and coarseness of young urban (poor, working-class) men in Indonesia is far from the politeness and respectfulness of rural men. While Dayan's masculinity reflects more of the village, Agus's interpretation reflects a combination of the coarse masculinity and male privilege of urban areas. Dayan told me that when Agus is at Yul's house, "s/he expects to be served and won't do anything for hir wife except give her money." This interpretation of a man's role could be drawn from middle-class Indonesian images of manhood but also seems to selectively draw on older representations of high-ranking Minangkabau husbands who, as guests in their wives' houses (male duolocal residence), were served by their wives. Agus's "macho" behavior, like the banci's performance of a fashion model persona, presents an extreme style of masculinity, one that is easily read as masculine by others.

Dayan's experience of lesbian and gay discourse creates another distinction between hirself and Agus. Dayan described Agus as an old-fashioned tomboi, one who "is like a man and won't be any other way." Hir statement implies that s/he sees Agus as holding onto certain normative ideas of gender that contemporary Indonesian lesbians no longer find satisfying. S/he said further that "Agus has never been out of the *kampung* [village]," implying that had s/he been, Agus might see other models of lesbian relations and quit trying to be so much like a man.

In the past few years, Dayan has lived in Jakarta for one to two years at a time. Both at home and in Jakarta hir friends are cowok-cewek, but these friends also know about the Euro-American model of lesbian identity. At different times Dayan claimed both a masculine identity and a lesbi identity. S/he told me s/he has always been the way s/he is, meaning s/he has always been a tomboi, but s/he also calls hirself a lesbi. Hir statements imply that despite feeling like a man, the availability of other models makes it possible to interpolate the tomboi identity with a lesbian identity. Oetomo (1996) notes a similar shift occurring between the banci and gay male identities for some Indonesian men. As with the proliferation of transgendered identities in the United States (Bolin 1994; Cromwell 1999), tomboi identity is constantly being negotiated and redefined in response to local, national, and transnational processes.

Conclusion

Identity for tombois in West Sumatra at this point in time is a bricolage, a mix of local, national, and transnational identities. If their identity growing up was shaped by local cultural forces that emphasized oppositional genders, their movement between cities and rural areas means that they have been exposed to other models of sexuality and gender identity that they have used to construct a new sense of themselves. The complexities of their gender identity make it impossible to align tombois with any one category, whether "woman," "lesbian," or "transgendered person."

Tomboi identity refracts and transgresses normative gender constructs. While some theorists identify gender transgression as resistance to male-dominant hegemonic order, tombois in West Sumatra suggest a more complicated cultural production of gender transgression. They cannot be read simply as the product of male dominance. The tomboi identity in Minangkabau culture speaks to the significance of a hegemonic kinship ideology – in which each gender is rigidly distinct and based on two sexes but not male dominant – in producing particular forms of gender transgression. For the tomboi, processes of postcolonialism, capitalism, and modernity also converge to produce and reinforce gender transgression.

At the national level the tomboi can be read as resisting the constraints of state ibuism in much the same manner as European and North American lesbians, gay men, and transgendered people are said to resist dominant gender ideology. Although the Indonesian state enforces heterosexuality, wage labor and capitalism create a space for the tomboi to live as a single female. The discourse of modernity – the importance of education, careers, and middle-class status – legitimates models other than motherhood and femininity for females. Though the tomboi remains a deviant, s/he is also finding more room to negotiate a future.

At the same time, other models of sexuality and gender are becoming visible in a globalized world, multiplying, collapsing, and refracting social identities in new ways. Where sexuality was embedded in the ideology of oppositional genders (man-woman, cowok-cewek, banci–*laki asli* [real man]), sexual "identity" and the possibility of sexuality between two women or two men are emergent cultural practices. Desiring women is being rewritten for some as a product of the variability of human sexuality rather than the "natural" urge of the male body and the prerogative of "men."

NOTES

1 I put *women* in quotes to problematize the use of "woman" for individuals who are female bodied but do not identify as women. As I use it, *female* refers to physical sex characteristics, and *woman* refers to a set of social behaviors and characteristics that are culturally constructed and attributed to female bodies. I use "women" in this instance because at the time of first meeting, I assumed these individuals were women.

2 In Indonesian, the plural is formed by doubling the noun. I choose to use a hybrid form to represent the plural, attaching the English "s" to Indonesian terms. Sears (1996b) also employs this construction.

3 For relevant literature arguing and refining the social construction perspective on gender and sexuality, see Blackwood 1986a, 1986b; Caplan 1987; Carrier 1980; D'Emilio 1983; Ortner and Whitehead 1981; Padgug 1979; Plummer 1981; Ross and Rapp 1981; Vance 1989.

4 The term *female-bodied* is Cromwell's (1997) and refers to physiological sex.

5 Recent work on Javanese culture, however, argues that the dominant ideology poses greater constraints on gender than previously thought (Brenner 1995).

6 This age group seemed to be experimenting in a range of sexual practices.

7 I use fictitious names for the individuals mentioned in this article. Dayan (pronounced "Dai-yon") lived with an older married sister in a small town about an hour from where I lived. I visited Dayan mostly on weekends at the sister's house.

8 Although I have used the pronoun *she* in the past to refer to a tomboi (Blackwood 1995a), at this point in my thinking "she" and "her/him" seem inadequate to represent the complexity of the tomboi identity, particularly because of the connotations an English-speaking reader brings to them. The Indonesian language provides no guidance in this matter because its pronouns are gender neutral. The third-person pronoun for both women and men is *dia*. I have chosen to use the pronominal constructions *s/he* (for "she/he"), *hir* (for "her/his" and "her/him"), and *hirself* (for "herself/himself"). These pronouns are gaining currency within the transgender movement in the United States (see Wilchins 1997). By doing so, I am not making any claims about the "gender" of tombois. These terms should not be read as suggesting that the tomboi is a transgendered person or some combination of masculine/feminine or not-masculine/not-feminine. Rather, by using these terms I want to unsettle the reader's assumptions about gender and gender binaries.

9 Nestle describes butches more eloquently as follows: "a butch lesbian wearing men's clothes in the 1950s was not a man wearing men's clothes; she was a woman creating an original style to signal to other women what she was capable of doing – taking erotic responsibility" (1992: 141).

10 This attribution is no longer so clear cut. Jeff Dickemann (letter to the author, November 30, 1997) argues that butches, who can be found in England as early as the 1820s, are degrees of transsexuals; there is no line between butch and female-to-male transsexual. See also for comparison, Nestle 1992 and Halberstam 1994.
11 I heard this news when I was in West Sumatra in 1996, but whether she was forced to marry or not, I do not know.
12 This practice is similar to one found in some Latin American cultures in which men who take the dominant (insertor) role in sex with another man are not marked as different because of their sexual behavior. They are seen as normatively masculine (see Carrier 1995; Parker 1986). I thank Jason Cromwell for making this connection.
13 The relevant literature includes Dickemann 1997; Frye 1983; Grimm 1987; Katz 1976; Kennedy and Davis 1992, 1993; Newton 1984; Rubin 1992; Shapiro 1991; Wikan 1977.
14 They use the spelling "butch-fem" in their book because it was the way women in the community they studied spelled the term.
15 See Cromwell's (in press) critique of the way this interpretation erases transgendered females (female-to-males [FTMs]).
16 I thank Daniel Segal for making this point.
17 For relevant literature on the postcolonial state and ethnic identities, see Bentley 1987; Friedman 1992; Gupta and Ferguson 1992; Kipp 1993; Olwig and Hastrup 1997; Williams 1989, 1995.
18 Islam in West Sumatra is part of the everyday life of the Minangkabau, who generally see no conflict between adat and Islam. The two have come to be mutually constructed. For further discussion of this point, see Ellen 1983, Delaney 1991, Whalley 1993.
19 This is not an insignificant concern because prestige, status, and property are all at risk. One young married woman I knew was in turmoil over whether to have another child because her only daughter is not strong. Although she already has two children, a number that the Indonesian state says is sufficient for a family, she thinks that she should have another daughter to ensure the perpetuation of her lineage.
20 During my stay one young banci I knew in West Sumatra was forced to go to a *dukun* (shaman) by hir sister in an effort to "cure" hir of hir desire for men.
21 Building on Schneider's (1968) formative work on kinship, feminist anthropologists and others have argued forcefully for the conceptual separation between sex and gender. See Ortner 1974; Ortner and Whitehead 1981; Shapiro 1991; Yanagisako and Collier 1987.
22 I thank Deborah Elliston for suggesting the phrase "hegemonic persuasiveness" to describe the power of dominant models to reproduce themselves.
23 Some of the relevant literature on women and the state includes Alexander 1994; Alexander and Mohanty 1997; Delaney 1995; Kandiyoti 1991; Ong 1987; Ong and Peletz 1995; Parker et al. 1992; Sears 1996b; and Williams 1996.
24 The New Order refers to the postwar regime of General Suharto, who became acting head of state in 1966 and remained president until 1998.
25 The action of Chinese marriage resistors, which was not veiled but public resistance, was explicitly interpreted as resistance to a patriarchal oppressive marriage system both by the women themselves and by outside observers (Sankar 1986; Topley 1975).
26 I thank Jason Cromwell (e-mail to the author, March 1, 1998) for his comments on this point. Cromwell notes a similar pattern in the United States. The female partners of FTM transmen are not marked nor are male partners of MTFs (male-to-females) (see also Cromwell in press).

REFERENCES

Alexander, M. Jacqui
1994 Not Just (Any)body Can Be a Citizen: The Politics of Law, Sexuality and Post-Coloniality in Trinidad and Tobago and the Bahamas. Feminist Review 48:5–23.
Alexander, M. Jacqui, and Chandra Mohanty, eds.
1997 Feminist Genealogies, Colonial Legacies, Democratic Futures. New York: Routledge.
Aripurnami, Sita
1996 A Feminist Comment on the Sinetron Presentation of Indonesian Women. *In* Fantasizing the Feminine in Indonesia. Laurie Sears, ed. Pp. 249–58. Durham, NC: Duke University Press.
Atkinson, Jane M.
1990 How Gender Makes a Difference in Wana Society. *In* Power and Difference: Gender in Island Southeast Asia. Jane M. Atkinson and Shelly Errington, eds. Pp. 59–93. Stanford, CA: Stanford University Press.
Balzer, Marjorie M.
1996 Sacred Genders in Siberia: Shamans, Bear Festivals and Androgyny. *In* Gender Reversals and Gender Cultures: Anthropological and Historical Perspectives. Sabrina Ramet, ed. Pp. 164–82. London: Routledge.
Bentley, G. Carter
1987 Ethnicity and Practice. Comparative Study of Society and History 29(1):24–55.
Blackwood, Evelyn
1986a Breaking the Mirror: The Construction of Lesbianism and the Anthropological Discourse on Homosexuality. *In* The Many Faces of Homosexuality: Anthropological Approaches to Homosexual Behavior. Evelyn Blackwood, ed. Pp. 1–17. New York: Harrington Park Press.
1993 The Politics of Daily Life: Gender, Kinship and Identity in a Minangkabau Village, West Sumatra, Indonesia. Ph.D. dissertation, Stanford University.
1995a Falling in Love with An-Other Lesbian: Reflections on Identity in Fieldwork. *In* Taboo: Sex, Identity and Erotic Subjectivity in Anthropological Fieldwork. Don Kulick and Margaret Willson, eds. Pp. 51–75. London: Routledge.
1995b Senior Women, Model Mothers, and Dutiful Wives: Managing Gender Contradictions in a Minangkabau Village. *In* Bewitching Women, Pious Men: Gender and Body Politics in Southeast Asia. Aihwa Ong and Michael Peletz, eds. Pp. 124–58. Berkeley: University of California Press.
n.d. Subverting Subordination: Gender and Peasant Households in West Sumatra. Department of Sociology and Anthropology, Purdue University, unpublished MS.
Blackwood, Evelyn, ed.
1986b The Many Faces of Homosexuality: Anthropological Approaches to Homosexual Behavior. New York: Harrington Park Press.
Boellstorff, Thomas
1995 The Gay Archipelago. Department of Anthropology, Stanford University, unpublished MS (first-year graduate paper).
Bogoras, Waldemar
1901 The Chukchi of Northeastern Asia. American Anthropologist 3:80–108.
Bolin, Anne
1994 Transcending and Transgendering: Male-to-Female Transsexuals, Dichotomy and Diversity. *In* Third Sex, Third Gender: Beyond Sexual Dimorphism in Culture and History. Gilbert Herdt, ed. Pp. 447–85. New York: Zone Books.

Bourdieu, Pierre
1977 Outline of a Theory of Practice. Cambridge: Cambridge University Press.
Brenner, Suzanne A.
1995 Why Women Rule the Roost: Rethinking Javanese Ideologies of Gender and Self-Control. *In* Bewitching Women, Pious Men: Gender and Body Politics in Southeast Asia. Aihwa Ong and Michael Peletz, eds. Pp. 19–50. Berkeley: University of California Press.
Bullough, Bonnie, Vern Bullough, and John Elias, eds.
1997 Gender Blending. Amherst, NY: Prometheus.
Butler, Judith
1991 Imitation and Gender Insubordination. *In* Inside/Out: Lesbian Theories, Gay Theories. Diana Fuss, ed. Pp. 13–31. New York: Routledge.
Caplan, Pat
1987 The Cultural Construction of Sexuality. London: Tavistock.
Carrier, Joseph M.
1980 Homosexual Behavior in Cross-Cultural Perspective. *In* Homosexual Behavior: A Modern Reappraisal, Judd Marmor, ed. Pp. 100–22. New York: Basic Books.
1995 De Los Otros: Intimacy and Homosexuality among Mexican Men. New York: Columbia University Press.
Chabot, Hendrick Theodorus
1960 Kinship, Status and Sex in the South Celebes. Richard Neuse, trans. New Haven, CT: Human Relations Area File.
Crompton, Louis
1981 The Myth of Lesbian Impunity: Capital Laws from 1270 to 1791. Journal of Homosexuality 6(1/2):11–25.
Cromwell, Jason
1997 Traditions of Gender Diversity and Sexualities: A Female-to-Male Transgendered Perspective. *In* Two-Spirit People: Native American Gender Identity, Sexuality, and Spirituality. Sue-Ellen Jacobs, Wesley Thomas, and Sabine Lang, eds. Pp. 119–142. Urbana: University of Illinois Press.
1999 Transmen and FTMS: Identities, Bodies, Genders and Sexualities. Urbana: University of Illinois Press.
Delaney, Carol
1991 The Seed and the Soil: Gender and Cosmology in Turkish Village Society. Berkeley: University of California Press.
1995 Father State, Motherland, and the Birth of Modern Turkey. *In* Naturalizing Power: Essays in Feminist Cultural Analysis. Sylvia Yanagisako and Carol Delaney, eds. Pp. 177–199. New York: Routledge.
D'Emilio, John
1983 Sexual Politics, Sexual Communities: The Making of a Homosexual Minority in the United States, 1940–1970. Chicago: University of Chicago Press.
Devor, Holly
1989 Gender Blending: Confronting the Limits of Duality. Bloomington: Indiana University Press.
Dickemann, Mildred
1997 The Balkan Sworn Virgin: A Traditional European Transperson. *In* Gender Blending. Bonnie Bullough, Vern Bullough, and John Elias, eds. Pp. 248–55. Amherst, NY: Prometheus.
Djajadiningrat-Nieuwenhuis, Madelon
1987 Ibuism and Priyayization: Path to Power? *In* Indonesian Women in Focus: Past and Present Notions. Elsbeth Locher-Scholten and Anke Niehof, eds. Pp. 43–51. Dordrecht, Holland: Foris Publications.

Echols, John M., and Hassan Shadily
1989 Kamus Indonesia Inggris: An Indonesian-English Dictionary, 3rd ed. Jakarta: PT Gramedia.
Ellen, Roy F.
1983 Social Theory, Ethnography and the Understanding of Practical Islam in South-East Asia. *In* Islam in South-East Asia. M. B. Hooker, ed. Pp. 50–91. Leiden, the Netherlands: E. J. Brill.
Elliston, Deborah
1995 Erotic Anthropology: "Ritualized Homosexuality" in Melanesia and Beyond. American Ethnologist 22:848–67.
Epstein, Julia, and Kristina Straub, eds.
1991 Body/Guards: The Cultural Politics of Gender Ambiguity. New York: Routledge.
Errington, Shelly
1990 Recasting Sex, Gender, and Power: A Theoretical and Regional Overview. *In* Power and Difference: Gender in Island Southeast Asia. Jane M. Atkinson and Shelly Errington, eds. Pp. 1–58. Stanford, CA: Stanford University Press.
Fadlillah
1996 Wanita, Malin Kundang, dan Feminisme. Singgalang, June 30:3.
Friedman, Jonathan
1992 The Past in the Future: History and the Politics of Identity. American Anthropologist 94:837–59.
Frye, Marilyn
1983 The Politics of Reality: Essays in Feminist Theory. Trumansberg, NY: Crossing Press.
Garber, Marjorie
1991 The Chic of Araby: Transvestism, Transsexualism and the Erotics of Cultural Appropriation. *In* Body/Guards: The Cultural Politics of Gender Ambiguity. Julia Epstein and Kristina Straub, eds. Pp. 223–47. New York: Routledge.
Gayatri, BJD.
1993 Coming Out but Remaining Hidden: A Portrait of Lesbians in Java. Paper presented at the International Congress of Anthropological and Ethnological Sciences, Mexico City, Mexico.
1994 Sentul-Kantil, Not Just Another Term. Jakarta, unpublished MS.
1995 Indonesian Lesbians Writing Their Own Script: Issues of Feminism and Sexuality. *In* From Amazon to Zami: Towards a Global Lesbian Feminism. Monika Reinfelder, ed. Pp. 86–98. London: Cassell.
1997 [Come] Outed but Remaining Invisible: A Portrait of Lesbians in Java. Jakarta, unpublished MS.
Gramsci, Antonio
1971 Selections from the Prison Notebooks of Antonio Gramsci. Quintin Hoare and Geoffrey N. Smith, trans. New York: International Publishers.
Grimm, David E.
1987 Toward a Theory of Gender: Transsexualism, Gender, Sexuality, and Relationships. American Behavioral Scientist 31(1):66–85.
Gupta, Akhil, and James Ferguson
1992 Beyond "Culture": Space, Identity, and the Politics of Difference. Cultural Anthropology 7:6–23.
Halberstam, Judith
1994 F2M: The Making of Female Masculinity. *In* The Lesbian Postmodern. Laura Doan, ed. Pp. 210–28. New York: Columbia University Press.

Herdt, Gilbert, ed.
1994 Third Sex, Third Gender: Beyond Sexual Dimorphism in Culture and History. New York: Zone Books.
Jacobs, Sue-Ellen, Wesley Thomas, and Sabine Lang, eds.
1997 Two-Spirit People: Native American Gender Identity, Sexuality, and Spirituality. Urbana: University of Illinois Press.
Kandiyoti, Deniz, ed.
1991 Women, Islam and the State. Philadelphia: Temple University Press.
Katz, Jonathan Ned
1976 Gay American History: Lesbians and Gay Men in the U.S.A. New York: Crowell.
Kennedy, Elizabeth, and Madeline Davis
1992 "They Was No One to Mess With": The Construction of the Butch Role in the Lesbian Community of the 1940s and 1950s. *In* The Persistent Desire: A Femme-Butch Reader. Joan Nestle, ed. Pp. 62–79. Boston: Alyson Publications.
1993 Boots of Leather, Slippers of Gold: The History of a Lesbian Community. New York: Penguin Books.
Kipp, Rita Smith
1993 Dissociated Identities: Ethnicity, Religion and Class in an Indonesian Society. Ann Arbor: University of Michigan.
Manderson, Lenore
1980 Rights and Responsibilities, Power and Privilege: Women's Role in Contemporary Indonesia. *In* Kartini Centenary: Indonesian Women Then and Now. Pp. 69–92. Melbourne: Monash University.
Murray, Alison
1998 Let Them Take Ecstasy: Class and Jakarta Lesbians. *In* Female Desires: Same-Sex Relations and Transgender Practices across Cultures. Evelyn Blackwood and Saskia Wieringa, eds. New York: Columbia University.
Nestle, Joan
1992 The Femme Question. *In* The Persistent Desire: A Femme-Butch Reader. Joan Nestle, ed. Pp. 138–46. Boston: Alyson Publications.
Newton, Esther
1972 Mother Camp: Female Impersonators in America. Chicago: University of Chicago Press.
1984 The Mythic Mannish Lesbian: Radclyffe Hall and the New Woman. Signs: Journal of Women in Culture and Society 9(4): 557–75.
1993 Cherry Grove, Fire Island: Sixty Years in America's First Gay and Lesbian Town. Boston: Beacon.
Oetomo, Dede
1991 Patterns of Bisexuality in Indonesia. *In* Bisexuality and HIV/AIDS: A Global Perspective. Rob Tielman, Manuel Carballo, and Aart Hendriks, eds. Pp. 119–26. Buffalo, NY: Prometheus Books.
1996 Gender and Sexual Orientation in Indonesia. *In* Fantasizing the Feminine in Indonesia. Laurie Sears, ed. Pp. 259–69. Durham, NC: Duke University Press.
Olwig, Karen, and Kirsten Hastrup, eds.
1997 Siting Culture: The Shifting Anthropological Object. London: Routledge.
Ong, Aihwa
1987 Spirits of Resistance and Capitalist Discipline: Factory Women in Malaysia. Albany: State University of New York.
Ong, Aihwa, and Michael Peletz, eds.
1995 Bewitching Women, Pious Men: Gender and Body Politics in Southeast Asia. Berkeley: University of California Press.

Ortner, Sherry

1974 Is Female to Male as Nature Is to Culture? *In* Woman, Culture, and Society. Michelle Zimbalist Rosaldo and Louise Lamphere, eds. Pp. 67–88. Stanford, CA: Stanford University Press.

1989 Gender Hegemonies. Cultural Critique 14:35–80.

Ortner, Sherry, and Harriet Whitehead, eds.

1981 Sexual Meanings: The Cultural Construction of Gender and Sexuality. Cambridge: Cambridge University Press.

Padgug, Robert A.

1979 Sexual Matters: On Conceptualizing Sexuality in History. Radical History Review 20:3–23.

Pak, Ok-Kyung

1986 Lowering the High, Raising the Low: The Gender Alliance and Property Relations in a Minangkabau Peasant Community of West Sumatra, Indonesia. Ph.D. dissertation, Laval University.

Parker, Andrew, Mary Russo, Doris Sommer, and Patricia Yaeger, eds.

1992 Nationalisms and Sexualities. New York: Routledge.

Parker, Richard

1986 Masculinity, Femininity and Homosexuality: On the Anthropological Interpretation of Sexual Meanings in Brazil. *In* The Many Faces of Homosexuality: Anthropological Approaches to Homosexual Behavior. Evelyn Blackwood, ed. Pp. 155–63. New York: Harrington Park Press.

Peacock, James L.

1978 Symbolic Reversal and Social History: Transvestites and Clowns of Java. *In* The Reversible World: Symbolic Inversion in Art and Society. Barbara Babcock, ed. Pp. 209–24. Ithaca, NY: Cornell University Press.

Plummer, Kenneth

1981 The Making of the Modern Homosexual. Totowa, NJ: Barnes and Noble.

Poole, John Fitz Porter

1996 The Procreative and Ritual Constitution of Female, Male and Other: Androgynous Beings in the Cultural Imagination of the Bimin-Kuskusmin of Papua New Guinea. *In* Gender Reversals and Gender Cultures: Anthropological and Historical Perspectives. Sabrina Ramet, ed. Pp. 197–218. London: Routledge.

Ramet, Sabrina Petra, ed.

1996 Gender Reversals and Gender Cultures: Anthropological and Historical Perspectives. London: Routledge.

Raymond, Janice

1979 The Transsexual Empire: The Making of the She-Male. Boston: Beacon Press.

Rich, Adrienne

1980 Compulsory Heterosexuality and Lesbian Existence. Signs: Journal of Women in Culture and Society 5(4):631–60.

Roscoe, Will

1991 The Zuni Man-Woman. Albuquerque: University of New Mexico Press.

Ross, Ellen, and Rayna Rapp

1981 Sex and Society: A Research Note from Social History and Anthropology. Comparative Study of Society and History 23:51–72.

Rubin, Gayle

1975 The Traffic in Women: Notes on the "Political Economy" of Sex. *In* Towards an Anthropology of Women. Rayna R. Reiter, ed. Pp. 157–210. New York: Monthly Review Press.

1992 Of Catamites and Kings: Reflections on Butch, Gender and Boundaries. *In* The Persistent Desire: A Femme-Butch Reader. Joan Nestle, ed. Pp. 466–82. Boston: Alyson Publications.
Sankar, Andrea
1986 Sisters and Brothers, Lovers and Enemies: Marriage Resistance in Southern Kwangtung. *In* The Many Faces of Homosexuality: Anthropological Approaches to Homosexual Behavior. Evelyn Blackwood, ed. Pp. 69–81. New York: Harrington Park Press.
Schneider, David
1968 American Kinship: A Cultural Account. Englewood Cliffs, NJ: Prentice-Hall.
Sears, Laurie J.
1996a Fragile Identities: Deconstructing Women and Indonesia. *In* Fantasizing the Feminine in Indonesia. Laurie Sears, ed. Pp. 1–44. Durham, NC: Duke University Press.
Sears, Laurie J., ed.
1996b Fantasizing the Feminine in Indonesia. Durham, NC: Duke University Press.
Shapiro, Judith
1991 Transsexualism: Reflections on the Persistence of Gender and the Mutability of Sex. *In* Body/Guards: The Cultural Politics of Gender Ambiguity. Julia Epstein and Kristina Straub, eds. Pp. 248–79. New York: Routledge.
Stoler, Ann
1996 A Sentimental Education: Native Servants and the Cultivation of European Children in the Netherlands Indies. *In* Fantasizing the Feminine in Indonesia. Laurie Sears, ed. Pp. 71–91. Durham, NC: Duke University Press.
Stone, Sandy
1991 The "Empire" Strikes Back: A Posttranssexual Manifesto. *In* Body/Guards: The Cultural Politics of Gender Ambiguity. Julia Epstein and Kristina Straub, eds. Pp. 280–304. New York: Routledge.
Sullivan, Norma
1983 Indonesian Women in Development: State Theory and Urban Kampung Practice. *In* Women's Work and Women's Roles: Economics and Everyday Life in Indonesia, Malaysia and Singapore. Lenore Manderson, ed. Pp. 147–71. Canberra: Australian National University.
Suryakusuma, Julia
1996 The State and Sexuality in New Order Indonesia. *In* Fantasizing the Feminine in Indonesia. Laurie Sears, ed. Pp. 92–119. Durham, NC: Duke University Press.
Topley, Marjorie
1975 Marriage Resistance in Rural Kwangtung. *In* Women in Chinese Society. Margery Wolf and Roxane Witke, ed. Pp. 57–88. Stanford, CA: Stanford University Press.
Trumbach, Randolph
1994 London's Sapphists: From Three Sexes to Four Genders in the Making of Modern Culture. *In* Third Sex, Third Gender: Beyond Sexual Dimorphism in Culture and History. Gilbert Herdt, ed. Pp. 111–36. New York: Zone Books.
Van der Kroef, Justus M.
1954 Transvestitism and the Religious Hermaphrodite in Indonesia. Journal of East Asiatic Studies 3(3):257–65.
Vance, Carole
1989 Social Construction Theory: Problems in the History of Sexuality. *In* Homosexuality, Which Homosexuality? Pp. 13–35. London: GMP Publishers.
Weston, Kath
1993 Lesbian/Gay Studies in the House of Anthropology. Annual Review of Anthropology 22:339–67.

Whalley, Lucy
1993 Virtuous Women, Productive Citizens: Negotiating Tradition, Islam, and Modernity in Minangkabau, Indonesia. Ph.D. dissertation, University of Illinois.
Wieringa, Saskia
1989 An Anthropological Critique of Constructionism: Berdaches and Butches. *In* Homosexuality, Which Homosexuality? Pp. 215–38. London: GMP Publishers.
1998 Desiring Bodies or Defiant Cultures: Butch-Femme Lesbians in Jakarta and Lima. *In* Female Desires: Same-Sex Relations and Transgender Practices across Cultures. Evelyn Blackwood and Saskia Wieringa, eds. New York: Columbia University Press.
Wikan, Unni
1977 Man Becomes Woman: Transsexualism in Oman as a Key to Gender Roles. Man N.S. 12:304–19.
Wilchins, Riki Anne
1997 Read My Lips: Sexual Subversion and the End of Gender. Ithaca, NY: Firebrand Books.
Williams, Brackette
1989 A Class Act: Anthropology and the Race to Nation across Ethnic Terrain. Annual Review of Anthropology 18:401–44.
1995 Classification Systems Revisited: Kinship, Caste, Race, and Nationality as the Flow of Blood and the Spread of Rights. *In* Naturalizing Power: Essays in Feminist Cultural Analysis. Sylvia Yanagisako and Carol Delaney, eds. Pp. 201–36. New York: Routledge.
Williams, Brackette, ed.
1996 Women out of Place: The Gender of Agency and the Race of Nationality. New York: Routledge.
Williams, Raymond
1977 Marxism and Literature. Oxford: Oxford University Press.
Yanagisako, Sylvia, and Jane F. Collier
1987 Toward a Unified Analysis of Gender and Kinship. *In* Gender and Kinship: Toward a Unified Analysis. Jane Collier and Sylvia Yanagisako, eds. Pp. 14–50. Stanford, CA: Stanford University Press.
Yanagisako, Sylvia, and Carol Delaney
1995 Naturalizing Power. *In* Naturalizing Power: Essays in Feminist Cultural Analysis. Sylvia Yanagisako and Carol Delaney, eds. Pp. 1–22. New York: Routledge.
Yengoyan, Aram
1983 Transvestism and the Ideology of Gender: Southeast Asia and Beyond. *In* Feminist Re-visions: What Has Been and Might Be. Vivian Patraka and Louise A. Tilly, eds. Pp. 135–48. Ann Arbor: Women's Studies Program, University of Michigan.

14

Freeing South Africa: The "Modernization" of Male-Male Sexuality in Soweto

Donald L. Donham

Identity is formed at the unstable point where the "unspeakable" stories of subjectivity meet the narratives of history, of a culture.

Stuart Hall, *Minimal Selves*

Of Dress and Drag

In February 1993, a black man in his mid-thirties named Linda (an ordinary male name in Zulu) died of AIDS in Soweto, South Africa. Something of an activist, Linda was a founding member of GLOW, the Gay and Lesbian Organization of the Witwatersrand. Composed of both blacks and whites, GLOW was and is the principal gay and lesbian organization in the Johannesburg area. Because Linda had many friends in the group, GLOW organized a memorial service at a member's home in Soweto a few days before the funeral.

Linda's father, who belonged to an independent Zionist church, attended and spoke. He recalled Linda's life and what a good person he had been, how hard he had worked in the household. But then he went on, in the way that elders sometimes do, to advise the young men present: "There was just one thing about my son's life that bothered me," he said. "So let me tell you, if you're a man, wear men's clothes. If you're colored, act colored. Above all, if you're black, don't wear Indian clothes. If you do this, how will our ancestors recognize [and protect] you?" Linda had been something of a drag queen, with a particular penchant for Indian saris.

To Linda's father and to his church, dress had ritual significance. One might even say that there was an indigenous theory of "drag" among many black Zionist South Africans, albeit one different from that in North America. To assume church dress not only indicated a certain state of personhood, it in some real sense effected that state.[1] Writing on Tswana Zionists, who like the Zulu have been drawn into townships around Johannesburg, Jean Comaroff (1985) asserted, "The power of uniforms in Tshidi perception was both expressive and pragmatic, for the uniform instantiated the ritual practice it represented" (1985:220).[2]

If dress had one set of associations within Zionist symbolism, it had others for a small group of young black South African activists who saw themselves as "gay." To the members of GLOW present, most of whom were black, Linda's father's comments were insulting. Most particularly, they were seen as homophobic. As the week wore on, GLOW began to organize to make their point and to take over the funeral.

As Saturday neared – nearly all Soweto funerals are held on the weekend – tensions rose. There were rumors that there might be an open confrontation between the family and GLOW. Along with Paul, a member of GLOW from Soweto, I attended, and the following is a description of what transpired, taken from a letter that I wrote home a few days later to my American lover:

> The funeral was held in a community center that looked something like a run-down school auditorium. There was a wide stage on which all of the men of the church, dressed in suits and ties, were seated behind the podium. In front of the podium was the coffin. And facing the stage, the women of the church were seated as an audience – dressed completely in white. (Independent churches have distinctive ways of dressing especially for women, but also sometimes for men.) To the right (from the point of view of the seated women) was a choir of young girls – again all in white: white dresses and white hats of various kinds (most were the kind of berets that you have seen South African women wear). I stood at the very back of the hall, behind the seated women, along with most of the members of GLOW and various other men and women, most dressed up. This last group was apparently made up of friends and relatives who were not members of the church.
>
> I had arrived late, about 9:30 in the morning (the service had begun at about 9:00). I was surprised to see, behind the coffin, in front of the podium, a GLOW banner being held by two members. There were flowers on the coffin and around it. Throughout the service, including the sermon, the two GLOW members holding the banner changed periodically. From the back, two new people marched up through the ladies in white to take the place of the two at the banner. Then those who had been relieved came back through the congregation to the back of the church.
>
> One GLOW member videotaped the funeral from the back. About six or seven of the members who had come were white. It was hard to tell exactly, but there were probably 10 or 15 black members. Quite a few, both white and black, wore GLOW T-shirts (the back of which said, "We can speak for ourselves"). Finally, two or three of the black members wore various stages of drag. One, Jabu, was especially notable in complete, full regalia – a West African – style woman's dress in a very colorful print with a matching and elaborately tied bonnet, one edge of which read, "Java print." Wearing a heavy gold necklace, she walked up and down the aisle to hold the banner at least twice – in the most haughty, queenly walk. It was almost as if she dared anybody to say anything. She made quite a contrast with the stolid, all-in-white ladies seated in the audience (one of whom was heard to comment to a neighbor, "She's very pretty, isn't she [referring to Jabu]? But look at those legs!").
>
> When we arrived, Simon Nkoli, one of the first black gay activists in South Africa, was speaking. Simon was dressed in an immaculately white and flowing West African

(male) outfit with gold embroidery. He spoke in English, and someone translated simultaneously (into Zulu). His speech was about gay activism in South Africa and the contributions that Linda, his dead friend, had made. At points in his speech, Simon sang out the beginning lines of hymns, at which point the congregation immediately joined in, in the [style] of black South African singing, without instruments and in part-harmony.

After Simon, there were other speeches by the ministers of the church. They emphasized that Linda was a child of the church, that his sins had been forgiven, and that he was in heaven. Diffusing any trace of tension between the church and GLOW, one of the ministers rose and apologized on behalf of Linda's father for offending the group earlier in the week.

Toward the end of the service, the gay people congregated on the front steps outside the community center and began singing in English a song that began with "We are gay and straight together..." When the people came pouring out and finally the coffin was carried out, the GLOW members in their T-shirts took the handles of the casket from the men of the church and placed it in the hearse. The several hundred people present boarded two very large transport buses hired for the occasion and probably 20 private automobiles to go to the cemetery.

Because there are so many funerals in Soweto on the weekend (probably 200 at Avalon cemetery alone) and because the cemetery had only one entrance (the better to control people), the roads were clogged and it took us an hour to go a few miles. The members of GLOW got out of the bus and *toi toied*, the distinctive, punctuated jogging-dancing that South African blacks have developed in anti-apartheid demonstrations. While waiting for the caravan to move, a giant *caspir*, one of those armored tank-like vehicles that the South African police use in the townships, passed us by, and then another police car with two white policemen inside. The temperature was not so hot, but the sun was blazing. At Johannesburg's elevation, it feels like the sun is closer (it is summer here).

Suddenly, we sped up (the cortege ahead had gone past) and we almost raced to the gravesite. There was a long row of freshly dug graves and several services were going simultaneously, side by side. Luckily for me, I was able to share someone's umbrella.

There was something about the routinized way that so many people had to bury their dead and leave (others were waiting) that brought home to me, in a way that I had not anticipated, what apartheid still means in many black people's lives.... The South African police stood in the background. Continually, another and another group arrived, and as each rushed to its gravesite, red dust began to cover us all. The sun got hotter.

In the middle of the brief graveside service for Linda (I was too far away to hear more than the few hymns that were sung), another group of buses arrived with chanting students. I was told that they were burying a young boy who had been killed by the police. Suddenly, shots rang out. Someone among the students shot into the grave and then into the air. As quickly as they had come, the kids were back on the buses, some of them dancing on the top with an ANC [African National Congress] flag. As the buses lumbered down the road, the ones on the top managed not to fall off. They were "comrades" – political activists. Things get more serious when a *tsotsi*, or gangster, is buried. It's not unusual for his friends to steal a car, fire an AK-47 into the air at the cemetery, cut figure-eights with the car after the burial, and on the way out of the cemetery, leave the stolen car burning.

After the graveside service, GLOW members gathered at one of the member's houses in Soweto and proceeded to get drunk. I had had enough. Driving back to Johannesburg (it's a little over 30 minutes), I almost had an accident. Tired and with my reflexes not working for left-hand-of-the-road driving, I turned into oncoming traffic. By the end of the day, I felt overwhelmed. Another gay man dead – yet another. And his burial had brought together, for me, a mind-numbing juxtaposition of peoples and projects, desires and fears – Zionist Christians and gay activists, the first, moreover, accommodating themselves to and even apologizing to the second. Could anything comparable have happened in the United States? A gay hijacking of a funeral in a church in, say, Atlanta?

Apartheid and Male Sexuality

Although engaged in another research project, in my free time with friends like Paul, I thus stumbled onto a series of questions that began to perplex me: Who was Linda? In the letter quoted above, I had unproblematically identified Linda as "gay." But in *his* context, was he? And if so, how did he come to see himself as so? And I quickly confronted questions of gender as well. Did Linda consider himself as male? And if so, had he always done so?

As issues like these began to pose themselves, I soon realized that for black men in townships around Johannesburg, identifying as gay was both recent and tied up, in unexpectedly complex ways, with a much larger historical transformation: the end of apartheid and the creation of a modern nation; in a phrase, the "freeing" of South Africa.

This story, more than any other, constitutes for most South Africans (certainly black South Africans) what Stuart Hall, in the epigraph at the beginning of this paper, referred to as a "narrative of history." It structures identity, legitimates the present, and organizes the past. There are indeed few places on earth in which modernist narratives of progress and freedom currently appear so compelling. This undoubtedly results, at least in part, because apartheid itself was an antimodernist project that explicitly set itself against most of the rest of the "developed" world.

As Foucault (1980) has argued, current Western views on sexuality and modernity are inextricably intertwined.[3] After Foucault, it would be difficult to interpret the conjugated transitions in South Africa as merely the result of the end of a repressive regime – a denouement that opened up spaces in which black men could, at last, claim their gayness, as if being "gay" were naturally pregiven. But if such a conclusion looks implausible, Foucault's own explanation of the formation of modern notions of sexuality also does not capture the full dynamic of the black South African case.

According to Foucault, current Western notions of homosexuality – that is, the concept of the homosexual as a distinct species of person – developed during the 19th century out of the sexual sciences and the dividing practices of modern states. Foucault's method, what he first called archaeology and later genealogy, was to work "across" time – within the same spatial unit. But what happens when one proceeds across space as well as time?[4] At a minimum, a series of new dynamics come into view – ones involving the transnational flow of persons, signs, commodities, and, I shall argue, narratives that (help) create new subject positions. Of late, communications technologies have accelerated and intensified these flows to create what seem to be qualitatively new cultural phenomena.

So how did Linda become gay? I never met or interviewed Linda, but fortunately, for the purposes of this article, before he died Linda wrote an extraordinarily self-revealing article with Hugh McLean entitled "*Abangibhamayo Bathi Ngimnandi* (Those Who Fuck Me Say I'm Tasty): Gay Sexuality in Reef Townships" (McLean and Ngcobo 1994). The collaboration between Hugh and Linda – both members of GLOW – was itself a part of the transformations I seek to understand: the creation of a black gay identity, Linda's "coming out," and the "freeing" of South Africa.

To begin with, Linda did not always consider himself – to adopt the gender category appropriate at the end of his life – to be "gay." If anything, it was female gender, not sexuality as such, that fit most easily with local disciplinary regimes and that made the most sense to Linda during his teenage years. Indeed, in apartheid-era urban black culture, gender apparently overrode biological sex to such a degree that it is difficult, and perhaps inappropriate, to maintain the distinction between these two analytical concepts below.[5]

Let me quote the comments of Neil Miller, a visiting North American gay journalist who interviewed Linda:

> Township gay male culture, as Linda described it, revolved around cross-dressing and sexual role-playing and the general idea that if gay men weren't exactly women, they were some variation thereof, a third sex. No one, including gay men, seemed to be quite sure what gay meant – were gay men really women? men? or something in between?... When Linda was in high school word went out among his schoolmates that he had both male and female sex organs. Everyone wanted to have sex with him, he claimed, if only to see if the rumors were true. When he didn't turn out to be the anatomical freak they had been promised, his sexual partners were disappointed. Then, there was the male lover who wanted to marry Linda when they were teenagers. "Can you have children?" the boy's mother asked Linda. The mother went to several doctors to ask if a gay man could bear a child. The doctors said no, but the mother didn't believe them. She urged the two boys to have sex as frequently as possible so Linda could become pregnant. Linda went along with the idea. On the mother's orders, the boys would stay in bed most of the weekend. "We'd get up on a Saturday morning, she'd give us a glass of milk, and she'd send us back to bed," Linda told me. After three months of this experiment, the mother grew impatient. She went to yet another doctor who managed to convince her that it was quite impossible for a man, even a gay man, to bear a child. Linda's relationship with his friend continued for a time until finally the young man acceded to his mother's wishes and married a woman, who eventually bore the child Linda could never give him. [Miller 1993:14–15]

The description above uses the word *gay* anachronistically. In black township slang, the actual designation for the effeminate partner in a male same-sex coupling was *stabane* – literally, a hermaphrodite. Instead of sexuality in the Western sense, it was local notions of sexed bodies and gendered identities – what I shall call sex/gender in the black South African sense – that divided and categorized. But these two analytical dimensions, gender and sex, interrelated in complex ways. While she was growing up, Linda thought of herself as a girl, as did Jabu, the drag queen at Linda's funeral about whom I shall have more to say below. Even though they had male genitalia, both were raised by their parents as girls and both understood themselves in this way.[6]

If it was gender that made sense to Linda and Jabu themselves (as well as to some others close to them, such as parents and "mothers-in-law"), strangers in the township typically used sex as a classificatory grid. That is, both Linda and Jabu were taken by others as a biologically-mixed third sex. Significantly, as far as I can tell, neither ever saw themselves in such terms.

I explored these issues with the regal drag queen who had turned everyone's eyes at Linda's funeral. In English, Jabu explained,

> When I grew up, I thought I was completely...I thought I was a woman. The girls I grew up with, when they were 13 or 14, they started to get breasts. Why didn't I? And they were different sexually. What is this? I don't have that. But they have that.

If an urban black South African boy during the 1960s and 1970s showed signs of effeminacy, then there was only one possibility: she was "really" a woman, or at least some mixed form of woman. Conversely, in any sexual relationship with such a person, the other partner remained, according to most participants, simply a man (and certainly not a "homosexual").[7]

This gendered system of categories was imposed on Linda as she grew up:

> I used to wear girls' clothes at home. My mother dressed me up. In fact, I grew up wearing girls' clothes. And when I first went to school they didn't know how to register me. [quoted in McLean and Ngcobo 1994:170]

Miller recorded the following impressions:

> Linda didn't strike one as particularly effeminate. He was lanky and graceful, with the body of a dancer. The day we met he was wearing white pants and a white cotton sweater with big, clear-framed glasses and a string of red African beads around his neck. But even as an adult, he was treated like a girl at home by his parents. They expected him to do women's jobs – to be in the kitchen, do the washing and ironing and baking. "You can get me at home almost any morning," he told me. "I'll be cleaning the house." There were girls' shopping days when he, his mother, and his sister would go off to buy underclothes and nighties. Each day, he would plan his mother's and father's wardrobes. As a teenager, Linda began undergoing female-hormone treatments, on the recommendation of a doctor. When he finally decided to halt treatments, his father, a minister of the Twelfth Apostle Church, was disappointed. It seemed he would rather have a son who grew breasts and outwardly appeared to be a girl than a son who was gay. Even today, Linda sings in the choir at his father's church – in a girl's uniform.
>
> "What part do you sing?" I asked him.
>
> "Soprano, of course," he replied. "What did you think?" [1993:15]

The fact that Linda wore a girl's uniform in church into the early 1990s offers some insight into his father's remarks that caused such a stir in GLOW. His father was not, it seems, particularly concerned with "cross-dressing." Phrasing the matter this way implies, after all, a naturally given bodily sex that one dresses "across." To Linda's family, he was apparently really a female. What the father was most upset about was dressing "across" race, and the implications that had for ancestral blessings.

In sum, black townships during the apartheid era found it easier to understand gender-deviant boys as girls or as a biologically mixed third sex. By the early 1970s, a network of boys who dressed as girls existed in Soweto, many of whom came to refer to themselves in their own slang as *skesana*.[8] Jabu was a few years younger than Linda. After the funeral, he recounted to me how he had first met Linda:

> I didn't know Linda. He heard about me. Those years, I was... among blacks, people didn't know about gay people. I was young and people didn't know whether I was a boy or a girl, and those days people thought if someone is gay he is hermaphroditic, you know. I was actually so famous, I don't know. But everyone knew that there is this child called Jabu; there is this boy called Jabu and they thought that I had two sex organs and wherever I went people got excited just to see or whatever. One day, it was a Wednesday or a Thursday, I was home with my mother, and there came this Linda. "Oh my goodness, what is this?" You know you didn't really realize as well whether he was a boy or a girl. With me, I used to tell myself I am the only one. And I was very proud of being myself. Wherever I used to go, everyone used to stare at me, and I said to myself that there is this special thing that I have, you know. And then when Linda came, I said, "Oh no, I don't want to associate with him." Luckily my mom was there. She called him and they talked. After he left, my mom called me and said, "You see, you're not the only person who is like that. That guy is also like you." "What do you mean he's like me? He's a guy. I'm not a guy, I'm a girl."

Skesanas dressed as women and adopted only the receptive role in sexual intercourse. Here is Linda speaking:

> In the township they used to think I was a hermaphrodite. They think I was cursed in life to have two organs. Sometimes you can get a nice *pantsula* [tough, macho guy] and you will find him looking for two organs. You don't give him the freedom to touch you. He might discover that your dick is bigger than his. Then he might be embarrassed, or even worse, he might be attracted to your dick. This is not what a *skesana* needs or wants. So we keep up the mystery. We won't let them touch and we won't disillusion them.... I think it makes you more acceptable if you are a hermaphrodite, and they think your dick is very small. The problem is, the *skesanas* always have the biggest dicks. And I should know.... [quoted in McLean and Ngcobo 1994:168–9, emphasis in original]

It would be a mistake to view this system of sex/gender categories as *only* being imposed upon skesanas. In adopting their highly visible role, skesanas sometimes used the traditional subordinate role of the woman to play with and ultimately to mock male power. According to Linda,

> On a weekend I went to a shebeen [informal drinking establishment] with a lady friend of mine. I was in drag. I often used to do this on the weekends – many *skesanas* do it. We were inside. It seemed as if four boys wanted to rape us, they were *pantsulas* and they were very rough. One of them proposed to my friend and she accepted. The others approached me one by one. The first two I didn't like so I said no! I was attracted by the third one, so I said yes to him. As we left the shebeen, my one said to me, "If you don't have it, I'm going to cut your throat." I could see that he was serious and I knew I must have it or I'm dead. So I asked my friend to say that she was hungry and we stopped at some shops. I went inside and bought a can of pilchards [inexpensive fish]. I knew that the only thing the *pantsula* was interested in was the hole and the smell. *Pantsulas* don't explore much, they just lift up your dress and go for it. We all went to bed in the one room. There were two beds. The one *pantsula* and my friend were in one and I was in

> the other bed with this *pantsula*. ... Sardines is one of the tricks the *skesanas* use. We know that some *pantsulas* like dirty pussy, so for them you must use pilchards, but not Glenrick [a brand] because they smell too bad. Other *pantsulas* like clean pussy, so for them you can use sardines. For my *pantsula* I bought pilchards because I could see what kind he was. So before I went to bed I just smeared some pilchards around my anus and my thighs. When he smelled the smell and found the hole he was quite happy. We became lovers for some months after that. He never knew that I was a man, and he never needed the smell again because he was satisfied the first time. [quoted in McLean and Ngcobo 1994:172–3, emphasis in original]

Although the connection would have been anathema to the Puritan planners of apartheid, skesana identity was finally tied up with the structure of apartheid power – particularly with the all-male hostels that dotted Soweto. In these hostels, rural men without the right to reside permanently in Soweto and without their wives lived, supposedly temporarily, in order to provide labor to the white-dominated economy. From the 19th century onward, there is evidence that at least some black men in these all-male environments saw little wrong with taking other, younger workers as "wives." In these relationships, it was age and wealth, not sex, that organized and defined male-male sexual relationships; as boys matured and gained their own resources, they in turn would take "wives." This pattern has been described among gangs of thieves on the Rand in the early 20th century (van Onselen 1982) and among gold mine workers into the 1980s (Moodie 1989).

Certainly, in Soweto in the 1960s, hostels populated by rural men had become notorious sites for same-sex sexual relations. Township parents warned young sons not to go anywhere nearby, that they would be swept inside and smeared with Vaseline and raped (see also Mathabane 1986:68–74). To urban-raised skesanas like Linda, however, these stories apparently only aroused phantasy and desire. Linda described a "marriage ceremony" in which she took part in one of the hostels, as follows:

> At these marriage ceremonies, called *mkehlo*, all the young *skesanas* ... sit on one side and the older ones on the other. Then your mother would be chosen. My mother was MaButhelezi. These things would happen in the hostels those days. They were famous. The older gays [*sic*] would choose you a mother from one of them. Then your mother's affair [partner] would be your father. Then your father is the one who would teach you how to screw. All of them, they would teach you all the positions and how to ride him up and down and sideways. ... [quoted in McLean and Ngcobo 1994:163, emphasis in original]

Modernity and Sexuality in the "New" South Africa

By the early 1990s, a great deal had changed in South Africa and in Linda's life. Nelson Mandela had been released from prison. It was clear to everyone in South Africa that a new society was in process of being born. This clarity had come, however, only after more than a decade and a half of protracted, agonizing, and often violent struggle – a contest for power that upended routines all the way from the structures of the state down to the dynamics of black families in Soweto. As a result, the cultural definitions and social institutions that supported the sex/gender system in which Linda had been raised had been shaken to its roots.

By the 1990s, Linda and his friends no longer felt safe going to the hostels; many rural men's compounds in the Johannesburg region had become sites of violent opposition to the surrounding black townships, the conflict often being phrased in terms of the split between the Inkatha Freedom Party and the ANC. Also, as the end of apartheid neared, rural women began to join their men in the hostels, and the old days of male-male marriages were left behind. Looking back from the 1990s, Linda commented,

> This [male-male marriage] doesn't happen now. You don't have to be taught these things. Now is the free South Africa and the roles are not so strong, they are breaking down. [quoted in McLean and Ngcobo 1994:164]

I will make explicit what Linda suggested: with the birth of a "free" South Africa, the notion of sexuality was created for some black men, or more precisely, an identity based on sexuality was created. The classificatory grid in the making was different from the old one. Now, *both* partners in a same-sex relationship were potentially classified as the same (male) gender – and as "gay."

Obviously, this new way of looking at the sexual world was not taken up consistently, evenly, or completely. The simultaneous presence of different models of same-sex sexuality in present-day South Africa will be evident by the end of this article. Whatever the overlapping ambiguities, it is interesting to note who took the lead in "modernizing" male-male sexuality in black South Africa: it was precisely formerly female-identified men like Linda and Jabu.[9] But if female-identified men seem to have initiated the shift, a turning point will be reached when their male partners also uniformly identify as gay. It is perhaps altogether too easy to overstate the degree to which such a transformation has occurred in the United States itself, particularly outside urban areas and outside the white middle and upper classes.

If one sexual paradigm did not fully replace another in black townships, there were nonetheless significant changes by the early 1990s. Three events, perhaps more than others, serve to summarize these changes. First was the founding of a genuinely multiracial gay rights organization in the Johannesburg area in the late 1980s – namely, GLOW. Linda was a founding member. Second, around the same time, the ANC, still in exile, added sexuality to its policy of nondiscrimination. As I shall explain below, the ANC's peculiar international context – its dependence on foreign support in the fight against apartheid – was probably one of the factors that inclined it to support gay rights. According to Gevisser (1994),

> ANC members in exile were being exposed to what the PAC's [Pan-Africanist Congress] Alexander calls "the European Leftist position on the matter." Liberal European notions of gender rights and the political legitimacy of gay rights had immense impact on senior ANC lawyers like Albie Sachs and Kader Asmal, who have hence become gay issues' strongest lobbyists within the ANC. [1994:75]

Finally, a third event that heralded change was the first gay pride march in Johannesburg in 1990, modeled on those held in places like New York and San

Francisco that celebrated the Stonewall riots of 1969. Linda and his friends participated, along with approximately one thousand others. This annual ritual began to do much, through a set of such internationally recognized gay symbols as rainbow flags and pink triangles, to create a sense of transnational connections for gay South Africans.

How was Linda's life affected by these changes? Exactly how did sexuality replace local definitions of sex/gender in her forms of self-identification? According to Linda himself, the black youth uprising against apartheid was the beginning:

> Gays are a lot more confident now in the townships. I think this happened from about 1976. Before that everything was very quiet. 1976 gave people a lot of confidence.... I remember when the time came to go and march and they wanted all the boys and girls to join in. The gays said: We're not accepted by you, so why should we march? But then they said they didn't mind and we should go to march in drag. Even the straight boys would wear drag. You could wear what you like. [quoted in McLean and Ngcobo 1994: 180]

As black youth took up the cause of national liberation and townships became virtual war zones, traditional black generational hierarchies were shaken to the core. Black youth came to occupy a new political space, one relatively more independent of the power of parents. But as such resistance movements have developed in other times and places, gender hierarchies have sometimes been strengthened (Landes 1988; Stacey 1983). In resisting one form of domination, another is reinforced. In the black power movement in the United States during the 1960s, for example, masculinist and heterosexist ideals were sometimes celebrated.[10]

Why did this reaction, with respect to gender, *not* take place in South Africa? One respect in which the South African case differs, certainly compared to the United States in the 1960s, is the extent to which the transnational was involved in the national struggle.[11] Until Mandela was released, the ANC was legally banned in South Africa. Leaders not in prison were based *outside* the country, and there can be no doubt that the ANC could not have accomplished the political transition that it did without international support. In this context, the international left-liberal consensus on human rights – one to which gay people also appealed – probably dampened any tendency to contest local racial domination by strengthening local gender and sexuality hierarchies. Any such move would certainly have alienated antiapartheid groups from Britain to Holland to Canada to the United States.

But the significance of the transnational in the South African struggle was not only material. The imaginations of black South Africans were finally affected – particularly, in the ways in which people located themselves in the world. And it was precisely in the context of transnational antiapartheid connections that some skesanas like Linda, particularly after they were in closer contact with white gay people in Johannesburg, became aware for the first time of a global gay community – an imagined community, to adapt Benedict Anderson's phrase, imaginatively united by "deep horizontal bonds of comradeship" (1991:7).[12]

How did this occur? Perhaps the incident, more than any other, that catalyzed such associations, that served as a node for exchange, was the arrest of Simon Nkoli.[13] Nkoli, by the 1980s a gay-identified black man, was arrested for treason along with others and tried in one of the most publicized trials of the apartheid era – the so-called Delmas treason trials. After Nkoli's situation become known internationally, he became a symbol for gay people in the anti-apartheid movement across the globe. For example, in December of 1986, while he was in prison, Nkoli was startled to receive more than 150 Christmas cards from gay people and organizations around the world (Nkoli 1994:255).

According to Gevisser,

> In Nkoli, gay anti-apartheid activists found a ready-made hero. In Canada, the Simon Nkoli Anti-Apartheid Committee became a critical player in both the gay and anti-apartheid movements. Through Nkoli's imprisonment, too, progressive members of the international anti-apartheid movement were able to begin introducing the issue of gay rights to the African National Congress. The highly respectable Anti-Apartheid Movements of both Britain and Holland, for example, took up Nkoli's cause, and this was to exert a major impact on the ANC's later decision to include gay rights on its agenda. [1994:56]

These cultural connections and others eventually helped to produce changes in the most intimate details of skesanas' lives. To return to Linda, gay identity meant literally a new gender and a new way of relating to his body. In Linda's words,

> Before, all skesanas wanted to have a small cock. Now we can relax, it does not matter too much and people don't discuss cocks as much.... Before, I thought I was a woman. Now I think I'm a man, but it doesn't worry me anyway. Although it used to cause problems earlier. [quoted in McLean and Ngcobo 1994:168–9]

In addition to how he viewed his body, Linda began to dress differently:

> I wear girl's clothes now sometimes, but not so much. But I sleep in a nightie, and I wear slippers and a gown – no skirts. I like the way a nightie feels in bed. [quoted in McLean and Ngcobo 1994:170]

Consider the underneath-of-the-iceberg for the intimacies that Linda described: it is difficult to reconstruct the hundreds of micro-encounters, the thousands of messages that must have come from as far away as Amsterdam and New York. Gevisser outlines some of the social underpinnings of this reordering:

> The current township gay scene has its roots in a generalised youth rebellion that found expression first in 1976 and then in the mid-1980s. And, once a white gay organisation took root in the 1980s and a collapse of rigid racial boundaries allowed greater interaction between township and city gay people, ideas of gay community filtered into the already-existent township gay networks. A few gay men and lesbians, like Nkoli, moved into Hillbrow. As the neighborhood started deracialising, they began patronising the gay bars and thus hooking into the urban gay subculture – despite this subculture's patent racism. GLOW's kwaThema chapter was founded, for example, when a group of residents returned from the Skyline Bar with a copy of *Exit* [the local gay publication]: "When we saw the publicity about this new non-racial group," explains Manku Madux, a woman who, with Sgxabai, founded the chapter, "we decided to get in touch with them to join." [1994:69]

The ways in which an imagined gay community became real to black South Africans were, of course, various. In Jabu's case, he had already come to see himself differently after he began work in a downtown hotel in Johannesburg in the late 1970s:

> Well, I joined the hotel industry. I started at the Carlton Hotel.... There was no position actually that they could start me in. I won't say that being a porter was not a good job; it was. But they had to start me there. But I had some problems with guests. Most of them actually picked up that I'm gay. How, I don't know. Actually... how am I going to word this? People from foreign countries, they would demand my service in a different way... than being a porter.... We had Pan Am, British Airways, American Airways coming. Probably the whole world assumes that any male who works for an airline is gay. I used to make friends with them. But the management wasn't happy about that, and they transferred me to the switchboard.

The assumption of a gay identity for Jabu affected not only his view of the present but also of the past. Like virtually all forms of identification that essentialize and project themselves backward in history, uniting the past with the present (and future) in an unchanging unity, South African black gay identity does the same. According to Jabu, being gay is "natural"; gay people have always been present in South African black cultures. But in his great-grandmother's time, African traditional cultures dealt with such things differently:

> I asked my grandmother and great-grandmother (she died at the age of 102). Within the family, the moment they realized that you were gay, in order to keep outside people from knowing, they organized someone who was gay to go out with you, and they arranged with another family to whom they explained the whole situation: "Okay, fine, you've got a daughter, we have three sons, this one is gay, and then there are the other two. Your daughter is not married. What if, in public, your daughter marries our gay son, but they are not going to have sex. She will have sex with the younger brother or the elder brother, and by so doing, the family will expand, you know." And at the end of the day, even if the next person realizes that I am gay, they wouldn't say anything because I am married. That is the secret that used to be kept in the black community.[14]

Foucault in a Transnational World

> One of the distinctive features of modernity is an increasing interconnection between the two "extremes" of extensionality and intentionality: globalising influences on the one hand and personal dispositions on the other.
>
> Anthony Giddens, *Modernity and Self-Identity*

In the West so relentlessly analyzed by Foucault, sexual identity was produced by a long, internal process of disciplining and dividing. Visiting airline stewards were not part of the story. What is striking about black South Africa is the transparency with which the transnational is implicated in and imbricated with gay identity formation. When asked to date the beginning of the gay movement in Soweto, some young black men answered that it commenced when a gay character appeared on *Dynasty* on local South African television (McLean and Ngcobo 1994:180).

It goes without saying that the category of gay people that this process has produced in South Africa is hardly homogeneous, nor is it the same as in Western countries. Being black and gay and poor in South Africa is hardly the same as being black and gay and middle-class, which is again hardly the same as being white and gay and middle-class, whether in South Africa or in North America. Despite these differences, there is still in the background a wider imagined community of gay people with which all of these persons are familiar and, at least in certain contexts, with which they identify. How this imagined community becomes "available" for persons variously situated across the globe is a major analytical question.

In Paul Gilroy's (1993) analysis of the black diaspora, he writes suggestively of the role of sailors, of ships, and of recordings of black music in making a transnational black community imaginatively real. As black identity has been formed and reformed in the context of transnational connections, black families have typically played some role – complex to be sure – in reproducing black identity. Gay identity is different to the degree that it does not rely upon the family for its anchoring; indeed, if anything, it has continually to liberate itself from the effects of family socialization.[15]

This means, ipso facto, that identifying as gay is peculiarly dependent upon and bound up with modern media, with ways of communicatively linking people across space and time. In North America, how many "coming out" stories tell about trips to the public library, furtive searches through dictionaries, or secret readings of novels that explore lesbian and gay topics (Newton 1984)? A certain communicative density is probably a prerequisite for people to identify as gay at all, and it is not improbable that as media density increases, so will the number of gay people.[16]

In less-developed societies of the world today, then, transnational flows become particularly relevant in understanding the formation of sexual communities. Sustained analysis of these connections has hardly begun, but I would suggest that we start not with ships but with airplanes, not with sailors (although they undoubtedly played their role here as well, particularly in port cities) but, in the South African case, with tourists, exiled antiapartheid activists, and visiting anthropologists; and finally not with music, but with images, typically erotic images – first drawings, then photographs, and now videos, most especially of the male body.

Given the composition of the global gay community, most of these images are of the *white* male body. For black men, then, identifying as gay must carry with it a certain complexity absent for most white South Africans. Also, the fact that international gay images are overwhelmingly *male* probably also affects the way that lesbian identity is imagined and appropriated by South African women, black and white. In any case, it could be argued that these kinds of contradictory identifications are not exceptional under late capitalism; they are the stuff of most people's lives. And lately the flow of images has been greatly accelerated; South African gays with access to a modem and a computer – admittedly, a tiny minority so far – can now download material from San Francisco, New York, or Amsterdam.

Each niche in this flow has its own characteristics. For North Americans, the national struggle was separated by two centuries from the gay struggle.[17] In South Africa, these two occurred more-or-less simultaneously, at least for black people.

The resulting unevenness of the global-in-the-local disrupts ordinary notions of political "progress." In relation to economic development, Trotsky emphasized long ago that previously "backward" areas can leapfrog ahead of "advanced" ones. At present, the constitution in South Africa prohibits discrimination on the basis of sexual orientation. Who could imagine anything similar happening in the United States?

The overlapping of the national and gay questions means that gay identity in South Africa reverberates – in a way that it cannot in the United States – with a proud, new national identity. Let me quote the reaction of one of the *white* gays present at Linda's funeral:

> As I stood in Phiri Hall behind the black gay mourners behind the hymn-singing congregants, I felt a proud commonality with Linda's black friends around, despite our differences; *we were all gay, all South African.* [Gevisser 1994:17, emphasis added]

In conclusion, let me suggest that a fuller understanding of sexual identity, in South Africa and elsewhere, requires a revitalized attention to ethnography. Foucault's work remains in many ways foundational in this enterprise, but it also presents serious limitations. Even for the "West," Foucault overstressed what Sedgwick (1990:44–8) has called a unidirectional narrative of supersession. In fact, cultural change tends to be more various, more fractured, more incomplete. What I am calling the "modernization" of male-male sexuality involves, then, not so much the replacement of one cultural system by another, but the addition of a new cultural model to older ones – with a certain splintering, a certain weighting of new schemas in the lives of at least a few particularly visible actors.

The second limitation of Foucault's work on sexuality stems from his over-reliance on the texts of medical specialists to infer the categories and commitments of ordinary people. Both Chauncey (1985) and Duggan (1993) have shown that notions about homosexuality in the United States emerged in a more complex dialectic than Foucault supposed. Popular notions, sometimes spread and reinforced in press accounts of spectacular events like trials, often formed the substratum for medical notions – which, after being inflected in certain ways, eventually affected, but only partially so, particular layers of the population. How these factors play out in any context is to be determined by textured historical ethnography, not, as Foucault seems to have sometimes imagined, by abstract philosophy.

Finally, and most important for the case at hand, Foucault did not problematize the role of cultural exchange across space, of transnational connections that bring, at ever quickening speeds, "unspeakable" stories of subjectivity into relationship with narratives of history. Ethnography is required to meet this goal, an ethnography that traces the global in the local, that analyzes the interplay between globally circulating narratives that persuasively cast past sufferings and offer future liberations, on the one hand, and the local technologies of communication that help conjure up the imagined communities that will enact those liberations, on the other.

But let me give Linda the last say. Here he uses sexuality as a point of self-identification, but in a way that is not unrelated to her previous notions of gender and sexuality:

> The thing that has done most for gays in the township are the marches we have had for gay and lesbian rights. These have been very important and I hope that we will be legalised with an ANC government. Then maybe we can even get married in Regina Mundi [one of Soweto's principal churches, one particularly associated with the struggle against apartheid] and they won't be throwing in the teargas. [quoted in McLean and Ngcobo 1994:181]

NOTES

As I make clear below, this article could not have been written without Gevisser and Cameron 1994, and most particularly, without the article by McLean and Ngcobo therein. See also Krouse 1993.

1 This notion of what might be called the production of personhood – that who one is can be transformed and worked upon by dress – appears to mirror, in important ways, local concepts of sex/gender. That is, notions of sex and gender are not understood as being simply given by nature. Rather, sex/gender is created, in part, through dress, gesture, and demeanor.
2 The classic studies on Zulu Zionists are Sundkler 1961 and 1976.
3 Parts of Foucault's argument were prefigured in McIntosh 1968 and developed more-or-less independently in Weeks 1977.
4 Stoler (1995) has posed this question in a different way, one focused more precisely upon race and colonialism.
5 For an early statement of the position that the distinction between sex and gender may reflect Western culture rather than a useful analytical device, see Collier and Yanagisako 1987:14–50.
6 As Jabu points out below, he could not understand why he did not develop breasts at puberty. And Linda's boyfriend's mother could not understand why he could not bear children. What is striking from a Western point of view is how little gender categories seem to have been constrained by sex.
7 That a special label existed (at least by the 1980s, although the timing of this development is not clear) for *injonga*, men who sexually penetrated other men, indicates that at another level, matters were more complex. According to McLean and Ngcobo (1994), "The man who calls himself an *injonga* is someone who consciously adopts the role of a man who has sex with men. He is different from the 'accidental' homosexual, the *pantsula* (macho township guy) who sleeps with what he believes to be a hermaphrodite or with someone who pretends, and who he pretends, is female" (1994:166, emphasis in original). Again, according McLean and Ngcobo, "Many *injongas* were *skesanas* once" (1994:166, emphasis in original). *Skesana*, as I shall explain below, is a slang term for men who are women, men who are penetrated by other men. Such age-related progression through sexual roles recalls the arrangements of rural black South African migrant workers described in Moodie's classic article (1989).
8 According to Linda, "A *skesana* is a boy who likes to be fucked" (quoted in McLean and Ngcobo 1994:164).
9 For a moment when female-identified men took the lead in gay identity politics in the United States, consider the Stonewall rebellion in New York City during 1969. See Duberman 1993.

10 See Eldridge Cleaver's reaction to James Baldwin (1968:97–111). At the same time, it is important to remember that there were other voices in the black resistance movement. Black Panther Huey P. Newton, before the 1970 Revolutionary People's Constitutional Convention in Philadelphia, called for an alliance with the gay liberation movement. See Stein n.d.

11 Perhaps the most interesting case to which to compare South Africa would be Israel. There also, politics is peculiarly transnationalized, with many local political actors anxious to be seen as "progressive." And there also, gays and lesbians enjoy relative legal protection, for example, the opportunity to serve openly in the Israeli military. I thank Esther Newton for calling my attention to the Israeli case.

12 The link between Anderson's work and sexual identity has been made by Parker, Russo, Sommer, and Yaeger 1992.

13 Trials often seem to serve a notable role in making "public" what is ordinarily kept "private," in circulating images of same-sex sexuality. See in particular Duggan 1993.

14 Whether this characterization – what one might call families "passing" rather than individuals "passing" – accurately represents the past in southern Africa I do not know. It appears, at least, as not inconsistent with what anthropologists know of rural African social organization. However, the terms in which the argument is stated are clearly those of the present, designed to rebut claims that homosexuality is un-African.

15 Whether heterosexually-based families must necessarily inculcate homophobic norms is an interesting question. Clearly, individual families can create non-homophobic environments. But to date, I am unaware of any society that accomplishes such an ideal across the board.

16 Historians have emphasized the urban connections of gay culture for some time; see Boswell 1980 and D'Emilio 1992:3–16.

17 This does not mean that the connections between the gay movement in the United States and previous political currents of the 1960s can be neglected. The link with the women's and black civil rights movements is obviously crucial.

REFERENCES

Anderson, Benedict
1991 Imagined Communities: Reflections on the Origin and Spread of Nationalism. Revised ed. London: Verso.

Boswell, John
1980 Christianity, Social Tolerance, and Homosexuality. Chicago: University of Chicago Press.

Chauncey, George Jr.
1985 Christian Brotherhood or Sexual Perversion? Homosexual Identities and the Construction of Sexual Boundaries in the World War I Era. Journal of Social History 19:189–212.

Cleaver, Eldridge
1968 Soul on Ice. New York: McGraw-Hill.

Collier, Jane, and Sylvia Yanagisako, eds.
1987 Gender and Kinship: Essays Toward a Unified Analysis. Stanford, CA: Stanford University Press.

Comaroff, Jean
1985 Body of Power Spirit of Resistance. Chicago: University of Chicago Press.

D'Emilio, John
1992 Capitalism and Gay Identity. *In* Making Trouble: Essays on Gay History, Politics, and the University. New York: Routledge.
Duberman, Martin
1993 Stonewall. New York: Plume.
Duggan, Lisa
1993 The Trials of Alice Mitchell: Sensationalism, Sexology, and the Lesbian Subject in Turn-of-the-Century America. *Signs* 18:791–814.
Foucault, Michel
1980[1976] An Introduction, vol. 1. The History of Sexuality. Robert Hurley, trans. New York: Vintage Books.
Gevisser, Mark
1994 A Different Fight for Freedom: A History of South African Lesbian and Gay Organisation – the 1950s to the 1990s. *In* Defiant Desire: Gay and Lesbian Lives in South Africa. Mark Gevisser and Edwin Cameron, eds. Pp. 14–88. Johannesburg: Ravan Press.
Gevisser, Mark, and Edwin Cameron, eds.
1994 Defiant Desire: Gay and Lesbian Lives in South Africa. Johannesburg: Ravan Press.
Gilroy, Paul
1993 The Black Atlantic: Modernity and Double Consciousness. Cambridge, MA: Harvard University Press.
Krouse, Matthew, ed.
1993 The Invisible Ghetto: Lesbian and Gay Writing from South Africa. Johannesburg: COSAW Publishing.
Landes, Joan B.
1988 Women and the Public Sphere in the Age of the French Revolution. Ithaca, NY: Cornell University Press.
Mathabane, Mark
1986 Kaffir Boy: The True Story of a Black Youth's Coming of Age in Apartheid South Africa. New York: Macmillan.
McIntosh, Mary
1968 The Homosexual Role. Social Problems 16:182–92.
McLean, Hugh, and Linda Ngcobo
1994 Abangibhamayo Bathi Ngimnandi (Those Who Fuck Me Say I'm Tasty): Gay Sexuality in Reef Townships. *In* Defiant Desire: Gay and Lesbian Lives in South Africa. Mark Gevisser and Edwin Cameron, eds. Pp. 158–85. Johannesburg: Ravan Press.
Miller, Neil
1993 Out In The World: Gay and Lesbian Life from Buenos Aires to Bangkok. New York: Vintage Books.
Moodie, T. Dunbar, with Vivien Ndatshe and British Sibuyi
1989 Migrancy and Male Sexuality on the South African Gold Mines. *In* Hidden From History: Reclaiming the Gay and Lesbian Past. Martin Bauml Duberman, Martha Vicinus, and George Chauncey Jr., eds. Pp. 411–25. New York: New American Library.
Newton, Esther
1984 The Mythic Mannish Lesbian: Radclyffe Hall and the New Woman. Signs 4:557–75.
Nkoli, Simon
1994 Wardrobes: Coming Out as a Black Gay Activist in South Africa. *In* Defiant Desire: Gay and Lesbian Lives in South Africa. Mark Gevisser and Edwin Cameron, eds. Pp. 249–57. Johannesburg: Ravan Press.
Parker, Andrew, Mary Russo, Doris Sommer, and Patricia Yaeger, eds.

1992 Nationalisms and Sexualities. New York: Routledge.
Sedgwick, Eve
1990 The Epistemology of the Closet. Berkeley: University of California Press.
Stacey, Judith
1983 Patriarchy and Socialist Revolution in China. Berkeley: University of California Press.
Stein, Marc
n.d. "Birthplace of the Nation": Imaging Lesbian and Gay Communities in Philadelphia. Unpublished MS.
Stoler, Ann
1995 Race and The Education of Desire: Foucault's History of Sexuality and the Colonial Order of Things. Durham, NC: Duke University Press.
Sundkler, Bengt G. M.
1961 Bantu Prophets in South Africa. London: Oxford University Press.
1976 Zulu Zion and Some Swazi Zionists. Oxford, England: Oxford University Press.
van Onselen, Charles
1982 Studies in the Social and Economic History of the Witwatersrand, 1886–1914, vol. 2. The Regiment of the Hills-Umkosi Wezintaba: The Witwatersrand's Lumpenproletarian Army, 1890–1920. London: Longman.
Weeks, Jeffrey
1977 Coming Out: Homosexual Politics in Britain. New York: Quartet Books.

15

Gay Organizations, NGOs, and the Globalization of Sexual Identity: The Case of Bolivia

Timothy Wright

Scholars who study Bolivia all agree that 1985 was a year that profoundly shook the country with the dramatic implementation of neoliberal stabilization and economic adjustment measures. In that same year, another transformative event occurred, albeit quietly: The country's first AIDS case was diagnosed (Melgar 1992). The appearance of AIDS in Bolivia initiated unprecedented challenges to tradition; it forced changes in how people talk and think about sex. In many ways, AIDS broke a wall of silence. This article explores the significance of these changes by examining both the conventional silence and the recent noise about sexuality, and specifically about male homosexuality in Bolivia.

From 1993 to 1995 I worked as the regional gay men's outreach coordinator for HIV/AIDS prevention in Santa Cruz, Bolivia with the Proyecto Contra el SIDA[1] (PCS), funded by the United States Agency for International Development (USAID). During 1992, while doing research in Bolivia unrelated to HIV/AIDS, I lobbied USAID to hire me for the purpose of creating within PCS an outreach component for men-who-have-sex-with-men (MSM). I had met numerous self-identified "homosexual" men in Cochabamba that year, and two of them had confided in me that they were HIV positive. These men had traveled to Brazil specifically to get tested since they distrusted in the "confidential testing" options available in Bolivia at that time. I began to pay more attention to the services available for HIV/AIDS in Bolivia, and discovered that no prevention services existed for men-who-have-sex-with-men. I also learned that the level of concern among MSM was high. As a registered nurse with a master's degree in public health, and as a gay man with an established network of "homosexual" friends in Bolivia, I succeeded in my lobbying efforts.

The prevalence data on HIV infection in Bolivia left little doubt about the need for this component. A USAID project paper (1988) admitted that while, "the greatest reservoir of HIV infection in Bolivia is in gay and bisexual men," accessing this population is "a difficult task." By 1992, the Ministry of Health (MOH) had identified 83 (72 male/11 female) HIV/AIDS cases nationally. Of the infections attributed to sexual transmission, 66% were reported to be in bi- or homoscxuals (Melgar 1992).[2] Still, the MOH had no outreach program targeting this group, and it was not clear how the problem should be addressed. In Bolivia, initiating a gay men's outreach effort for HIV/AIDS prevention meant charting unknown territory. The decision to contract me was not reached by unanimous agreement among all the decision-makers in USAID, PCS, and the MOH. Rather, it resulted from enthusiastic promotion by some and acquiescence by others. The less-than-robust endorsement for this type of outreach work foreshadowed the controversial nature of the work upon which I was about to embark.[3]

By the 1990s, a "gay men's outreach" component in a sexual health project was standard fare for US government programs. From the Bolivian government perspective, however, it titillated and shocked. If in 1985, "Bolivia launched itself in the global age" then by 1992, for better or for worse, globalization was reaching into the quiet, personal, and taboo corners of human sexuality.

Male Homosexualities and Silence

Sex and the tradition of reserved talk

Silence can be a powerful tool for coping with the forbidden things that people do or about which they know (Alonso and Koreck 1989). In this light, it should be no surprise that in Bolivia male homosexuality and silence have been inseparable partners. This does not mean that homosexuality is never mentioned. On the contrary, within the confines of prescribed discourses it is part of the standard inventory. Tones of indignation, repulsion, anger, or pity make it a safe topic in a wide range of public and private forums, including nervous and degrading jokes and tabloid articles about immorality and crime. However, the more personal homosexuality gets, the closer to oneself, the less is heard about it. This quietness extends to one's relatives and close friends. The fact that male homosexuality has been shrouded in silence and relegated to humorous or degrading forms of discourse is not unique to Bolivia. However, it gains unique meanings as we consider the abrupt changes introduced into Bolivia by gay men's outreach.

Popular models of male homosexuality in bolivia

The practicality of silence can be more fully considered in light of the prevailing popular model of male homosexuality in Bolivia. Barry Adam (1979, 1986) has proposed a "fourfold typology of social structuring of homosexuality: (1) age-structured, (2) gender-defined, (3) profession-defined, and (4) egalitarian/'gay' relations," observing that while different structures "may coexist in a society, one of them predominates" (Adam, quoted in Murray, 1995: 5). These academic distinctions allow us to juxtapose and contrast complex realities for easy comprehension, but their use must avoid the risk of essentializing Bolivian homosexualities. My discussion of Bolivia focuses on tensions between what Adam identifies as gender-defined and egalitarian/gay structuring of homosexuality.

I argue that in both rural and urban areas of Bolivia, gender norms structure male homoerotic behavior to an exceptionally strong extent, although we must recognize that dominant heterosexual norms are interpreted and manipulated in countless quiet ways. In this gender paradigm, the culturally dominant male/female dichotomy is preserved even when two biological males have sex together. In theory, this concept is quite simple: men penetrate, women get penetrated. This model emphasizes penetration, de-emphasizes anatomy (the orifice – vagina, mouth, or anus – is not determinant), and distributes stigma unequally in sexual encounters between men (Lancaster 1988). In male-male sex, the penetrator preserves his masculinity, while he who is penetrated loses it (and acquires the stigmatized label, "homosexual," meaning a woman-like male). Popularly, the terms *activo* and *pasivo* or *hombre* and *maricón* mark these gender distinctions between two men having sex with each other.

The gender-defined structuring of male homosexuality has been described in numerous Latin American countries. Richard Parker provides an excellent overview of the study of homosexuality in Latin America and an up-to-date bibliography in *Beneath the Equator* (Parker 1999) (also see Carrier 1995; Kulick 1997 and 1998; Lancaster 1992; Lumsden 1996). However, I believe that this popular model more vigorously defines male homosexuality in Bolivia than in the region as a whole. In the late 1980s and early 1990s, Adam's "gay/egalitarian model" with its notions of shared gay identity between the participants in male-male sex was either unheard of or seen as "alien" (*estilo americano*) by most men-who-have-sex-with-men in Bolivia. Also, the political understandings of coming out of the closet in order to fight oppression and defend gay rights had not taken root. Rather, these actors took for granted the activo-pasivo model, assuming that it was natural. It is within the context of the strict application of the two-gender social structuring of male homosexuality, and the limited influence of the egalitarian/gay model, that the practicality of silence must be interpreted.

Within the setting described above, we can now clarify key terms to be used in this article. "*El ambiente*" (the environment or atmosphere) is a traditional term used throughout the Spanish speaking world by participants in male-male erotic behavior. For the purposes of this paper it is used to describe the places, social relations, and conditions under which the gender-defined model of male homosexuality is manifest. "*Hombres de ambiente*" (sometimes simply "hombres") refers here to men-who-have-sex-with-men who, operating on the idea that gender equals sexuality, believe that their careful preservation of masculinity through penetration eliminates the "homosexuality" from their role in homoerotic behavior and, indeed, from their identity. I will use the term "homosexual" (or the common vernaculars "*marica*" and "maricón") to refer to men who identify themselves as "homosexual," an identity that carries with it the implication of playing the passive (penetrated) role in man-man sex. The term "gay" is used here to refer to a homosexual identity embraced by individuals of the same biological sex and the same sexual orientation who share their bodies in erotic ways and do not acknowledge a gender distinction based on roles played. It is also charged with the political connotations of pride and human rights. "Gay" identity is associated with the United States and Europe, although it is surely found on every continent. As local and traditional understandings interact with global and (post)modern ones, language changes. It is precisely in deference to this state of flux, and the confusion it creates, that I use cautious qualifiers here.

Silence and hombres de ambiente

The role of silence would be hard to overemphasize as the hombre/maricón model is put into practice in Bolivia. Silence here refers to the avoidance of talking about homosexuality when it is used in reference to oneself, whether in the context of sexual practice or as a basis for personal identity. Silence is a valuable and malleable resource in the social and psychological management of male-male sexual practice under Bolivia's dominant gender-defined regime. Three arguments – one focusing on the hombre, one on the maricón, and one on the larger society – defend this assertion. We start by looking at the hombre de ambiente.

The role of the hombre de ambiente seems paradoxical: is it possible to be a non-homosexual man who participates in homosexual sex? Analysis of the practice of avoiding social analysis of the privileged and the "normal," in order to focus on marginalized "others," has been analyzed elsewhere. Generally speaking, the hombres described here occupy the most privileged position that el ambiente of Bolivia has to offer. This is because they are publicly marked neither as homosexuals nor as bisexuals – labels which stigmatize – but rather as "normal men" ("hombres normales"). It is unusual for such a man to describe himself as de ambiente. Many of these men also have sex with women, are married, and/or have children. This very large group of MSM is ignored by all the AIDS and sexual health projects that I know about in Bolivia.

A man who has sex with another man and yet does not lose his sense of masculinity and "normality," is an embodied expression of ambiente social rules. According to this specific, sub-cultural knowledge, anatomy is selectively ignored as the body of an hombre connects with the body of a faux-woman. In contrast, I have spoken with many Bolivian men outside the ambiente who insist that sex is determined by gross anatomy; to these man, all male-male sex is homosexuality expressed equally by both participants. Thus, hombres de ambiente walk on thin ice in the maintenance of their masculine identity. Where ambiente rules apply, they easily preserve their hombre status by following well-known rules. Beyond el ambiente's borders, it is silence that protects them and what they have at stake: masculine identities, egos, and power related to their social positions. Actors who play the hombre role in the sub-culturally accepted model of male homosexuality generally do not want a marked sexual identity attached to their homoerotic behavior, and do not want to be studied.

Silence and maricas

Although men who identify themselves as "homosexuals" (pasivos or maricas) often say they dream of a stable relationship with a loyal hombre partner, in practice the romantic fiction of the hombre/marica couple cannot withstand the light of day or the scrutiny of society. Hombres do, however, have love affairs (*aventuras amorosas*) with "homosexuals." In fact, while different in important ways, these affairs are in many ways similar to the ones described between married *mestizo* men and *cholas* in the valley of Cochabamba. A description of mestizo/chola affairs as "socially invisible relationships . . . illicit, covert, risky, notorious, unreliable, based on self-interest, and temporary" describes with precision most hombre/"homosexual" relations. On more than one occasion, I have even heard an hombre in a temporary relationship with a marica refer to "her" as "*mi cholita*." This image serves to symbolically distance the hombre from his male partner, here represented as a feminized and indianized other. Silence plays a critical role in these affairs since the general population does not accept the identity distinction that only ambiente "insiders" understand.

Cholas and maricas, at least in some cases, share the role of gratifying the sexual urges of hombres, men they meet, among other places, in the same chicherías in the environs of Quillacollo (Avenida Blanco Galindo). It is interesting to speculate to what extent maricas, like cholas, serve as "root metaphors" in local culture and to what extent, as traditional maricas become modern "gays," hombres will feel threatened, just as they are by cholas who abandon their polleras for modern dress and more liberated ways. Certainly maricas help make male identity possible by clarifying its boundaries. It is likely that the egalitarian/gay model threatens the comforting reassurance of masculinity upon which so many current participants in male-male sex depend.

Maricas find hombres (and hombres find maricas) in plazas, parks, neighborhood streets, movie theatres, dance halls, and bars. Practicality often requires that the two improvise quick sex in all sorts of semi-private locations: in stairwells, behind bars, in alleyways, or in bushes. These rendezvous can be dangerous, and "homosexuals" in Bolivia pride themselves on being *zorras* (female foxes) with lots of urban smarts; only half-jokingly, they plead for protection to *La Santa Putana* ("Saint Whore, the marica goddess"). Clearly, silence plays an important role in the social management of these quick sex experiences; silence is one of the few resources available for making these public or semi-public events at least partially private – a goal generally seen as desirable. Silence here may take the form of denial-in-the-aftermath. While a marica may brag with another marica about "her" sexual conquests, silence is a rarely broken code of conduct in conversation with any "outsider."

Silence and the accommodation of homosexuality

It is critical to keep in mind that no man-who-has-sex-with-men, no matter how important the role of sex is in his life, defines himself only in terms of his sexual identity. People have more than one identity and each one may be compartmentalized or called upon, emphasized, or tucked away, depending on the changing circumstances of everyday life. Among themselves, individuals who identify themselves as gente de ambiente form social networks to help each other solve such problems as finding employment. *Gente de ambiente* in Bolivia also form alliances with other groups of "social outcasts," broadening the circle. However, my observations strongly suggest that for most gente de ambiente, family is their most important source of affective and material support. I feel confident in arguing that during most hours of any given day, most homoerotically-oriented men in Bolivia see themselves first and foremost as sons, brothers, and cousins. And beyond their family ties, many cherish roles as neighbors, colleagues and employees.

In exchange for broader acceptance in these relationships, most choose to de-emphasize their deviant gente de ambiente identity. It is common for quiet familial accommodations, "conspiracies of silence" (Carrier 1995), to allow sex-the-act to occur easily and frequently, so long as sex-the-deviant-identity is kept hidden. Since the popular understanding of homosexuality in Bolivia equates it with extreme femininity in men, space is open to allow men who meet normative standards of masculinity to quietly have sex with other men. Indeed, while the stereotypes of homosexuality in Bolivia persecute those identified as maricas, they also facilitate strategies of concealment for men who present themselves before the world as "normal guys." The desire for familial and social acceptance is a strong force that binds homosexuality and silence.

In fact, the traditional silence surrounding the sex lives of men-who-have-sex-with-men in Bolivia is so compelling that we need to look more closely at the question: How did the globalization of gay identity and gay organizations reach Bolivia at all? Our attention now turns to this question.

Gay Men's Identity and Noise

AIDS and a changing world

AIDS began to disturb the silence around male homosexuality even before the disease officially reached the country in 1985. New forms of discussing sexuality, including male homosexuality, and particularly in relation to AIDS, arrived from afar via mass media. Between February 1993 and February 1995, I carefully collected all articles on sexuality and/or AIDS from *El Deber*, the major newspaper of Santa Cruz de la Sierra (Wright 1999). Of this collection of 483 articles, a full 246 (51%) were sold to *El Deber* by international wire services (Reuters, Associated Press, EFE, AFP, and ANSA). These articles revealed that issues related to homosexuality were now openly debated in courts, churches, schools, legislatures, medical societies, and in the street (especially in the form of parades) in many countries abroad. Lupton (1994) argues that the texts of newspaper articles "are sensitive barometers of social process and change." I have little doubt that these articles produced at least some confusion in the minds of many Bolivian readers regarding their taken-for-granted understandings of homosexuality. This is especially likely because many middle class and elite urban Bolivians eagerly look overseas for models of "modernity" and the up-to-date standard of "science."

Between 1985 and 1992, scientific considerations of sexuality most certainly increased in the Ministry of Health as the official number of HIV/AIDS cases rose from 1 to 83 (Melgar 1992). Furthermore, AIDS became a new justification for international development assistance in 1988 when USAID awarded the MOH a three-year, $500,000 assistance grant to begin HIV/AIDS surveillance work and to provide some basic training for preventative education (USAID 1988). In short, rumblings from overseas arriving via mass media, together with development dollars deposited into the MOH's account for AIDS work began the process by which the traditional silence on homosexuality unraveled.

The rise and fall of ethnography

As mentioned above, the decision to establish a gay men's outreach HIV/AIDS prevention component involved disagreements between USAID and PCS (the financier and the administrator). Since a full consensus was never reached, gay men's outreach was viewed with skepticism by some of the project's authorities from the beginning. And what about the Ministry of Health? It is important to point out that in Bolivia, health-related initiatives that reach the country through foreign aid assistance must be approved by the MOH. And once health projects are begun, they operate under the guidance and supervision of this ministry. Yet, the sharp contrast between Bolivia's poverty and the wealth of the donor countries generally makes this more true in theory than in practice. Nevertheless, a respectful execution of protocol is required. I am not privy to knowledge of the negotiations regarding the initiation of gay men's outreach. However, I suspect that the MOH and I might have been in agreement on the following point: such an endeavor should be kept as quiet as possible. In fact, gay men's outreach was to generate much sound and fury.

According to the conventional development mindset, the scientist/professional is the agent (or subject), and "the other" is the object of study and action. What happens when the agent and the object are fused in one person? As an openly "homosexual" AIDS expert, an agent/object all at once, I was viewed as a somewhat ambiguous figure by the people who hired me, especially by the PCS national director. As time passed, considerable effort was made by the project leadership to reduce this disturbing duality and re-establish the conventional order; that is, to the extent possible, to make me a scientific/professional agent with substantial distance from the objects I was to study and help.

In 1993, I was moved from Cochabamba to Santa Cruz, the department most impacted by HIV/AIDS, where PCS had a regional office. Until that time I had been working informally among gente de ambiente via a participant-observer approach. Suddenly, in Santa Cruz, I had a desk in an office, a supervisor, abundant supplies, and a support staff-an ideal stage for "health professional" performances. There was a problem, however: unlike Cochabamba where I knew many gente de ambiente, I had no such contacts in Santa Cruz. Since my job clearly required me to find "homosexuals" in a city with no "gay neighborhood," the fancy office did me little good. However much the project leadership preferred to see me in the "health agent" role, it had little choice but to allow me to carry out ethnographic research. So, once again, I found myself playing the "object" role, being a "homosexual" in that fuzzy place called "the field." This task raised a myriad of ethical questions.[4] I noticed, for example, that my PCS colleagues were embarrassed by my detailed descriptions of what I saw "out there." Subtly, I was trained to provide sanitized, desexualized portrayals of a vague "gay community." Ironically, the discouragement in the office of my ethnographic voice encouraged me to identify more with other "homosexuals," people with whom I could communicate.

I began my field research in Santa Cruz by working with one individual, and things snowballed from there. My contacts in Cochabamba suggested that I look up

Miguel (a pseudonym), an underemployed salesman of contraband Brazilian apparel who knew his way around the city and had lots of free time. Through Miguel I made other contacts, and through them, still others. After a mere two months of field research, the basically amorphous and constantly shifting borders of ambiente geography and its cultural roles, relationships, symbols, and gestures were still only partially clear to me when the pressure increased to return to the office and to the agent role.

Based on what I had learned to that date, I produced a two-part document in the form of a cursory ethnographic report (Wright 1993) and a set of policy recommendations. By that time I had learned enough to know that ambiente identities were far from monolithic, and that understanding unspoken codes of conduct guides social coping strategies, integral to the insider's approach.

In the recommendation section of my report I wrote the following:

> The world of men-who-have-sex-with-men, the gente de ambiente, is called el ambiente precisely because it is more an atmosphere than a fixed spot on a map. The ambiente is real to people who understand it and provides opportunities for HIV prevention programming. If its rules are violated, however, swift and stern rejection follows. It is difficult to overstate the extreme concern gente de ambiente in Bolivia have for privacy and discretion. It is recommended that the project imitate the model provided by the local ambiente by NOT trying to establish geographically fixed service centers for the gente de ambiente (Wright 1993).

Rather, I proposed a telephone hotline and a team of outreach workers, selected from among the many gente de ambiente peer groups I had found, and hired at modest wages on short-term contracts. The project would select individuals who expressed an interest to learn about HIV/AIDS, and they would then share their new knowledge with their *amigos de confianza*, that small group of people who talk together frankly about their sex lives. This approach would allow outreach workers to review actual practices and to seek feasible ways for these to be adjusted, if necessary, with HIV prevention in mind. Basically, the idea was to pay individuals to get trained and then return them to their networks. The AIDS literature of the time highlighted the logic of this strategy: "Discussions of targeting messages are full of references to 'risk groups' and 'communities' when, in fact, peer groups may be the social group most relevant for purposes of educating about behavior change" (Petrow 1990). Furthermore, I reasoned that such individuals, better than anyone else, understood their friends' cherished identities, and knew the specific geographies they traversed and the off-hour schedules they kept. Put simply, peers knew how to act and where to go to get outreach work accomplished.

The development agency, however, was perplexed and disturbed by my proposals. On the one hand, I was praised for the report. On the other hand, it was promptly ignored. After I presented my findings on the structure and function of el ambiente in the national PCS office in La Paz, the national director responded by saying: "very interesting, now enough of this ethnographic stuff." The position of the project leadership was clear at this point. My job was to function as the "health professional," the agent, working for the benefit of the target population; as a doctor treats a patient. Activities that could respond to quantifiable process and outcome evaluations would be given priority. A pattern emerged in the flow of approvals and disapprovals of my proposals, and also in the recommendations that came from above, backed by funding. The ethnographic phase of gay men's outreach was over. The Gay Community Center would soon open up.

Doing development and making gays

The pressures to open up a gay community center were considerable. The *Proyecto Contra el SIDA* was institutionally linked to the Centers for Disease Control and Prevention (CDC), whose "Bolivia Team" called for the establishment of a "base of operations" for providing services to "homosexual/bisexual" men. They argued that "the target population for the services needs to be clearly defined. The project will be able to focus on its goals, move ahead, and have a visible impact only after these broad issues are addressed" (Trip Report, April 15, 1993). Funds were made available to hire two full-time outreach workers, to pay the rent of a house, and to purchase a TV and VCR plus furniture for the house. "Visible" was the operational word here and, with that in mind, in early 1994, a gay community center was inaugurated.

As a North American gay man, I have benefited tremendously from identifying with the gay community, so I came to accept the opening of a center even though it seemed unwise in the Bolivian context. I also understood public health criteria and knew that we couldn't adequately address legitimate concerns about project impact if our work was kept entirely invisible and silent. Nevertheless, the value of the gay center was always limited, and its attempts to redefine gente de ambiente as gays produced scant results.

While project personnel increasingly talked about "the gay community," in fact, this was by no means a monolithic or unified group. Two axes of differentiation in particular severely restricted the formation of, and participation in, a gay organization: socio-economic class and gender identity divisions.

The gay organization proved attractive to a specific and rather small population within el ambiente, a group known as *los placeros*, gente de ambiente who socialize in the city's central plaza. This mostly lower-middle class group chose to congregate in the plaza because they lacked the resources for more private settings; the gay center resolved this problem and therefore appealed to them. By contrast, the affluent gente de ambiente had available to them a broader range of meeting locations, and by long-standing custom, avoided publicly congregating with individuals of lower socio-economic status. Their appearance in the center was rare. There are also groups of gente de ambiente who are much poorer than los placeros. On more than one occasion they tried to find acceptance in the gay center, and even organized themselves into a block during a campaign to elect leaders of an organization that formed in the gay center – bringing social class tensions to the fore. When this group lost the election they sensed injustice and, with great bitterness, split from the organization and formed an alternative, "people's" gay group in the Villa Primero de Mayo, a poor section of town.[5] In short, social class differences excluded most of the ambiente's members from participation in the gay center.

Gender identity divisions also took their toll. Men who identified with the center tended to play the "female" role in their relations. By contrast, the very large number of men who see themselves as "hombres normales" did not show up because their masculine social image and sexual roles as penetrators informed them that they were not "homosexuals." One result of the dominant one-sex/two-gender discourse was that half of the dyad of most men-with-men sexual encounters was missing from the gay organization (as it is from the common definition of homosexuality in Bolivia). Hombres define themselves as heterosexual men, so have no reason to join the outreach project or to learn about risks of their particular sexual behavior.

Although most of the men who frequented the gay center engaged in sexual relations as the pasivo or "female" partner, they did not have strongly effeminate mannerisms and did not dress as women. In fact, because they are understood to be "like women" but appear like men, they are referred to within el ambiente as *los camuflados* (the camouflaged) (Wright and Wright, 1997). By contrast, the Santa Cruz "homosexuals" who are notably effeminate men and/or transvestites found little welcome in the organization. The placeros who dominated the gay center organization complained that such participants would give the whole group a bad name. Also, these effeminate men do not necessarily find it easy to accept the gay identity; I heard more than one transvestite comment, "*yo no soy gay, yo soy mujer*" ("I'm not gay, I'm a woman").

In short, men-who-have-sex-with-men who were too rich or too poor or too masculine or too effeminate were unlikely to be attracted to the gay center or welcomed as members of the emerging "gay community." While my ethnographic research told me that the participants of the gay organization were not representative of the full gamut of the ambiente world, from the point of view of the institution, it was a success just to get some "homosexuals" to come to the center. With them PCS could "do development" on terms it recognized. Soon after the center opened, psychologists began to appear to talk with the participants about the role of self-esteem in condom negotiation, and other qualities of self-definition. While the two full-time gay outreach workers gradually essentialized their understandings of sexual identity, few participants went along with the idea. Nevertheless, the mere existence of a gay community center drew enormous attention, both from within the ambiente and beyond its borders.

Local actors step in

The gay community center drew remarkable public attention almost from the moment it opened. Discussion about who was really behind this center placed the Bolivian Ministry of Health in a real dilemma. While financed by the US government and administered by an international project, as a health initiative, it was technically within the MOH's domain. On the one hand, if the MOH were to fully disown the gay center as the product of PCS that would mean publicly acknowledging its heavy dependency on foreigners for financing, planning, and implementing major projects; clearly an embarrassing affront to national pride and sovereignty. On the other hand, the MOH was not prepared to assume the position of an entity that actively supported a progay community center. And what about this group of people who, for the first time in Bolivia, were being referred to as "los gays"? Were these long-standing Bolivian "homosexuals," suddenly discovering a collective identity? Or were they a product of foreign imaginations, being invented, as it were, in the service of obscure international agendas? The print media had a heyday with the debates that arose around los gays and their center (Wright 1999) as the Church, the municipal government, PCS, USAID, the police, civic organizations, the inter-institutional AIDS committee, and, of course, the public health sector all jockeyed to position themselves through public statements.

Among the most contested immediate questions was, "Just how many gays are there?" Many Bolivians I spoke with over the years were quite confident that the number of male "homosexuals" in their respective cities could be counted on their fingers; in some cases they claimed that they could even name them. It was commonly believed that "one can tell" by the way they look or dress. The "homosexual" was always a man (scant acknowledgement was made of female homosexuals) who was effeminate and at least partially cross-dressed. For many, the notion that a gay community center might exist in Santa Cruz with voluntary participants who were generally unremarkable in appearance, just average-looking guys, turned the world topsy-turvy.

A journalist from *El Deber* interviewed me about my work as the coordinator of gay men's outreach. Her main interest was how many "homosexuals" there were in the city. I was unsophisticated in working with the press at that time, and unsuccessful in escaping her numbers game by arguing the true complexity of her question. The day after the interview the following headline appeared (*El Deber*, 23 June 1994): *Hay cerca de 17 mil homosexuales en Santa Cruz* (there are approximately 17,000 homosexuals in Santa Cruz).

Two days later Tacuara, a local commentator, responded to that article with a piece entitled, "Gays en Santa Cruz"? (*El Deber*, 25 June 1994). In this article he seemed to equate the apparent increase in homosexuality with modernity-a negative side effect of the otherwise positive advance of development: "Development has its price," he wrote, it improves standards of living but also brings with it "delinquency, prostitution, drug addiction and homosexualism." My sense is that his stance of resignation – a paradoxical blend of disgust with a call for tolerance – expressed the views of many.

Still, the question of the total number of "homosexuals" remained unresolved. My error in speculating with the journalist fed polemics. In the months that followed the startling "announcement" that there were 17,000 homosexuals in Santa Cruz, I heard many opinions about this issue. While I told people over and over that I had never made the claim attributed to my name and that, in fact, I had no idea how many "homosexuals" there were in Santa Cruz or even what that label meant, a debate proceeded based on the journalist's "statement-of-the-facts." For some, the report illustrated the damage being done to the country by foreigners. For others, it was a battle cry and an announcement of freedom. For still others, it was a declaration of the end of the world.

Among the physicians and epidemiologists in the Proyecto Contra el SIDA, skepticism focused on the "bad science" that produced this statistic. Of course, the numbers were based on no science at all, but rather a bad experience with an obsessed journalist bent on sensationalism. Nevertheless, a significant "hard science" faction within PCS began to push for "scientific survey research" to count the homosexuals of Bolivia. Several draft survey questionnaires were eventually elaborated and even pre-tested. According to the reasoning behind this call, the denominator (i.e., the total population) had to be quantified in order to measure HIV incidence and prevalence among los gays (Hennekens, Burning and Mayrent 1987). Development and evaluation discourses also fueled the urge to count up the homosexuals. As this reasoning went, it was important to be able to distinguish the "target population" from non-target units (Rossi and Freeman 1989). Only then could resources be reasonably allocated and effective programs designed. To the "hard science" faction in PCS, project action should be guided by the objective principles of epidemiology, development science, and evaluation methodologies; in practice, their proposed means of implementing these principles boiled down to surveys based on identities of convenience. From my point of view, these proposals drained energy and wasted time in a fruitless and unethical oversimplification of el ambiente.

There was also a "soft science" faction within PCS, made up largely of psychologists. The organizational structure of PCS reflected its two factions: in the medical department were the "hard scientists," while the "soft scientists" were in the IEC (Information, Education, and Communication) department. To the "soft scientists" the emphasis should be more on human relationships, (sub)cultural sensitivity and respecting identities, and less on quantification. At times, inter-faction battles raged between these two sets of priorities.

From these battles between the medical and IEC departments a modus operandus finally emerged for the management of gay men's outreach. As the coordinator of this component in PCS I watched an uneasy consensus slowly develop. Over time, "*la comunidad gay*" was referred to more and more in the project until it became part of the PCS lexicon. It came to be understood as meaning the people who showed up at the gay center, a group that could be both counted and treated sensitively. By defining "the gay community" in this limited way, the Proyecto Contra el SIDA presented a model that solved the Ministry of Health's dilemma: they could conceptualize the management of a gay center in a purely technical, public health framework, in which medical professionals/agents could guide, care for, and control "homosexual" objects. The center would be more about pathology than liberation.

From the Ministry of Health point of view, "homosexuals" were to be treated like another risk group: prostitutes. And working with prostitutes was nothing new to the MOH. Prostitution is simultaneously legal and illegal in Bolivia; while it is a violation of the penal code (Serrano 1972), state-run health clinics for sex workers operate throughout the country. In these facilities, female sex workers are evaluated and treated for sexually transmitted diseases. Upon receiving a clean bill of health, their *carnets de salubridad* (health cards) are stamped and these "registered" prostitutes are allowed to work in "registered" brothels. Sex workers must pay two fees in these visits – one for the medical care received and another fee to the police, for unspecified services. By 1994, PCS had substantial experience attending these "registered" sex workers in a number of the state-run health clinics. In fact, the project's work with "registered" prostitutes had become quite routine; written guidelines existed for lessons on condom negotiation, communication skills, and identifying the symptoms of diseases; one-on-one counseling sessions with psychologists had become standardized, and project posters hung on the walls.

The majority of sex workers, however, labor outside of the formal, "registered" system. Some prostitutes officialize their status with the state in order to work on a full-time basis in "registered" brothels. For the rest, there is the informal economy of the street. Nationally, PCS did very little work with these "unregistered" prostitutes, referred to by the MOH as "*las clandestinas*" (the clandestines). The Ministry of Health viewed these sex workers as renegades that ought to be captured as criminals and brought into the "registered" system. From the project point of view, they were just too hard to find. But what about los gays? If the "gay community" was to be understood as the men who showed up at the gay center and these were seen by the MOH as prostitute equivalents, the question remained: What kind of prostitutes – "registered" or "unregistered"? The evidence shows that over time los gays came to be treated much like the "registered" sex workers (with some interesting twists), at least within the confines of the gay center of Santa Cruz. Both the MOH and PCS found this to be the most convenient arrangement and importantly, it facilitated harmony between them. With some modifications, it made work possible along already well-established pathways, in a fixed site, and on a Monday through Friday, nine to five schedule.

The modifications included the promotion of a sort of gay liberationlite by the two gay outreach workers. When I left the country in 1995, outreach activities by these men still aimed at working in the ambiente's natural settings. When I returned to Bolivia for a visit in 1998, I found their work almost entirely restricted to the gay center. Their true outreach activity had been reduced to convincing gente de ambiente to attend center meetings. If they went, they were told, they would be well-received by professionals who would teach classes on sexual health issues. The managerial style control of gay men's outreach had become so complete that it erased its earlier controversial nature. The gay employees now did little more than sweep floors. Just as prostitutes did not run prostitute clinics, gay men did not run the gay center. However, this is more a theoretical depiction of how it was supposed to work. In practice, attendance was low and little education was offered by PCS or MOH professionals. In fact, the gay center was little more than a site where a small number of friends met to socialize. Clearly, it could function neither like a "registered" prostitute clinic nor a center of gay liberation.

To truly promote gay identity is to stimulate political positions and/or acts that challenge authoritarian structures. Even as the PCS/MOH coalition settled on a benign treatment of los gays at the center as "registered" prostitutes, outside the center the police regularly treated them like criminals, along the lines of las *prostitutas* clandestinas. A review of newspaper articles about meetings between public health and police officials in Santa Cruz, and reports in the policial section of *El Deber*, combined with personal testimonies from gente de ambiente (especially among the poor and effeminate) revealed a clear picture. In language that conflates "risk groups" with criminals, the police periodically raid the few gay bars that exist and especially the working class drinking establishments frequented by gente de ambiente. These raids lead to detentions and bribe payments. These degrading and emotionally devastating events become headline news in the ambiente circuit for days afterwards. They also inform the gente de ambiente that the PCS/MOH language of gay liberation is not backed by political commitment in the face of human rights abuses.

On various occasions the gente de ambiente turned to PCS for support in the wake of authoritarian abuse. Other than sending psychologists to listen empathetically, the project categorically refused to take action. Some top-rank PCS officials argued that it was doing more good to keep a low profile while promoting sexual health and offering emotional support. I would argue, however, that the option of keeping a low profile was forfeited the day the project insisted on establishing a gay center. In fact, the project's promotion of gay identity – public sexual minorities – was recognized by many gente de ambiente as motivated by bureaucratic considerations which had nothing to do with liberation.

Dennis Altman (1994:24–5) argues that, "the two major variables in the establishment of AIDS organizations appear to be epidemiological and political." Regarding the latter, he suggests that all over the world AIDS projects assume the prevailing organizational patterns characteristic of the country in which they develop. This point appears to be well-illustrated in Santa Cruz, Bolivia with its gay center seen as analogous to a "registered" prostitute health clinic run by the state. Its linkage to USAID further reinforces Altman's point in this development aid dependent country. It should be observed, however, that in the case of gay men's outreach, the continuity of officialdom's organizational pattern vis-à-vis the social management of "homosexuals" took precedence over the organizational pattern of the gente de ambiente. I argue that through the choice of which patterns to follow, important opportunities to carry out significant HIV/AIDS prevention work were squandered.

Conclusion

The AIDS epidemic has fostered the sudden foundation of gay organizations in unlikely places. Bolivia is a case in point. To start with, we have seen that gay identity is contrary to the prevalent Bolivian cultural understandings of male homosexuality. Furthermore, the socio-political and economic conditions in this poor country of less than 10 million people lack criteria normally deemed necessary for establishing a powerful community identity and organizing people to challenge authority. Nevertheless, gay organizations have been promoted in Bolivia because of international public health standards. For this reason, Bolivia can be looked at as a case study of the globalization of sexual identity. We have seen, however, that this is no simple instance of hegemony from the core to the periphery. Rather, an array of local actors interact with the suggestion of a global, public health sexuality. In the case looked at here, the results are a gamut of in-progress, globally influenced yet clearly Bolivian male homosexualities.

I expect that my experiences and frustrations as a gay man and a health professional working with HIV/AIDS in Latin America resonate with those of many others, and I hope to stimulate debate in this arena. While pro-gay, I opposed the foundation of a gay organization as I watched it established by gay-indifferent or anti-gay authoritarian structures. As I witnessed the sound and fury generated by the foundation of a gay center, the endless press coverage, the urgent call to count up the "homosexuals," and the ultimate conversion of los gays into a target group parallel to that of "registered" prostitutes, I grew to understand the meaning of silence to the gente de ambiente. AIDS work still needs to be carried out in this group, but it will not be very effective until ethnographic research sensitive to subculture realities is taken into account.

NOTES

1 Formally, this project's title was, "*Programa Colaborativo de SIDA/ETS*" (The Collaborative AIDS/STD Program); a linkage between CDC and USAID is marked in this title by the word "collaborative." More often, it was known simply as "*El Proyecto Contra el SIDA*" (The AIDS Project).

2 This set of MOH data is difficult to read. The biological sex of the identified individuals with HIV/AIDS is listed in one column, their sexual orientation in another. My experience with Bolivian health officials suggests that the individuals recorded as bisexuals or homosexuals were men.

3 It was difficult for them to believe my assertion that I knew many "homosexual" men in Cochabamba and elsewhere in the country since this population was invisible to them. In a meeting in La Paz on 28 August, 1992, with USAID, CDC, and PCS officials I challenged them to have one person from the project attend my birthday party, scheduled for the following day in Cochabamba. They sent a project psychologist. She was well-received by close to 40 "homosexual" men.

4 As a North American gay man, the ethical dilemmas that came up in the process of doing field research on Latin American homosexualities were many; this topic is beyond the scope of the present paper. However, I strongly recommend Joseph Carrier's 1999 article on this theme.

5 This group was formed more in name, as a momentary protest, than in reality.

REFERENCES

Primary Sources

Center for Disease Control and Prevention/Bolivia Team
1993 Trip Report (Draft): STD/AIDS Prevention Project in Bolivia. El Deber, 15 April, 1993.
1993a "Hay Cerca de 17 Mil Homosexuales en Santa Cruz." El Deber, 23 June, 1993. Santa Cruz: El Deber.
1993b "Gays en Santa Cruz." El Deber, 25 June, 1993. Santa Cruz: El Deber.
Melgar, Maria Luisa
1992 Situacion del SIDA en Bolivia, 1985–1992. La Paz: Departamento Nacional de Salud.
Serrano, Servando
1972 Código Penal. Cochabamba: Editorial Serrano Ltda.
1988 United States Agency for International Development. Bolivia Project Paper: AIDS Prevention and Control (Project No. 511–0608). Washington, DC: USAID.
Wright, Timothy
1993 Male Homosexuality and AIDS in Santa Cruz, Bolivia: Sexual Culture and Public Health Policy. Proyecto Contra el SIDA: Unpublished report submitted to the United States Agency for International Development.
1999 AIDS and Metaphors in the Bolivian Press. Inter-disciplinary paper submitted in partial satisfaction of the requirements for the degree Master of Arts in Latin American Studies, UCLA Unpublished manuscript.

Secondary Sources

Adam, Barry

1979 Reply. Sociologists Gay Caucus Newsletter 18:8

1986 Age, Structure, and Sexuality. *Journal of Homosexuality* 11:19–33.

Alonso, A. M. and Koreck, M. T.

1989 Silences: "Hispanics," AIDS and Sexual Practices. *Differences*, 1.1:101–24.

Altman, Dennis

1994 Power and Community: Organizational and Cultural Responses to AIDS. Bristol, PA: Taylor and Francis, Inc.

Carrier, J.M.

1995 De Los Otros: Intimacy and Homosexuality among Mexican Men. New York: Columbia University Press.

1999 Reflections on ethical problems encountered in field research on Mexican male homosexuality: 1968 to present. *Culture, Health, and Sexuality.* 1:3, 207–21.

Hennekens, C. H., J. E. Burning, and S. Mayrent

1987 Epidemiology in Medicine. Boston: Little Brown and Company. Kulick, Don

1997 Brazilian Transgendered Prostitutes. *American Anthropologist* 99 (3): 574–85.

1998 Travesti, Sex, Gender and Culture among Brazilian Transgendered Prostitutes. Chicago: University of Chicago Press.

Lancaster, Roger N.

1988 Subject Honor and Object Shame: The Construction of Male Homosexuality and Stigma in Nicaragua. *Ethnology* 27:2.

1992 Life is Hard: Machismo, Danger, and the Intimacy of Power in Nicaragua. Berkeley: University of California Press.

Lumsden, Ian

1996 Machos, Maricones, and Gays: Cuba and Homosexuality. Philadelphia: Temple University Press.

Lupton, Deborah

1994 Moral Threats and Dangerous Desires: AIDS in the News Media. Bristol, PA: Taylor and Francis, Inc.

Murray, Stephen O.

1995 Latin American Male Homosexualities. Albuquerque: University of New Mexico Press.

Parker, Richard

1999 Beneath the Equator: Cultures of Desire, Male Homosexuality, and Emerging Gay Communities in Brazil, New York: Routledge.

Petrow, Steven, ed.

1990 Ending the AIDS Epidemic: Community Strategies in Disease Prevention and Health Promotion. Santa Cruz, CA.: Network Publications.

Rossi, Peter, and Howard Freeman

1989 Evaluation: Systematic Approach. Newbury Park: Sage Publications. Wright, Timothy, and Richard Wright

1997 Bolivia: Developing a Gay Community – Homosexuality and AIDS *In* Sociolegal Control of Homosexuality. A Multi-Nation Comparison. Donald J. West and Richard Green, eds. New York: Plenum Press.

Index